Praise for the Reformation Heritage Bible Commentary Se…

The *Reformation Heritage Bible Commen*… …es to be a valuable resource for laity and preac… …tary focuses on major topics, providing clear … …nsight in keeping with how the Reformers app… …pture, and emphasizing themes that were central in their teaching. Illustrative quotes from key Reformers and their heirs, including Lutheran, Calvinist, Anglican, and Wesleyan sources, provide insights in their own words, without trying to survey the range of views represented in this heritage. This focused approach gives a clear reading of the text which engages one's mind and heart.

—The Rev. Dr. Rodney A. Whitacre
Professor of Biblical Studies
Trinity School for Ministry
Ambridge, Pennsylvania

Busy pastors and teachers of the Scriptures need commentaries that are biblical, theological, and practical. Fortunately, the Reformation Heritage Bible Commentary series fulfills those requirements. The scholarship is reverent, demonstrating that the truths of the Reformation are relevant today just as they were in the 16th century. The volumes are accessible to a wide variety of readers, for it is written in a wonderfully clear way. I commend this work gladly.

—Thomas R. Schreiner, PhD
James Buchanan Harrison Professor of New Testament
The Southern Baptist Theological Seminary
Louisville, Kentucky

The Reformation Heritage series is a "Heritage of Reformation theology" now put at the fingertips of every serious Bible student, young or old.

This commentary helps anyone to dive deeply into the Scriptures, verse by verse, even word by word. I was blessed with its academic rigor in straightforward language, the sidebar articles explaining overarching Biblical themes, and the voices of the Reformers demonstrating again that this Good News of Jesus is a message for all times. If one yearns to know the unique message of the Scripture and its meaning for life, now and forever, then join me in having the Reformation Heritage Series in your library today.

—Rev. Gregory P. Seltz
Speaker, The Lutheran Hour

The *Reformation Heritage Bible Commentary* promises to be an asset to the library of serious Bible students, whether layman or clergy. This series exemplifies the reformers' commitment to sola scriptura, that the revelation of God's saving purposes is in Scripture alone, which is primarily about Christ alone. The blend of overviews and insights from our Protestant forefathers with exegesis and application from contemporary reformed theologians makes for an interesting read. Contemporary readers will also appreciate the devotional notes in these commentaries. Because the study of God's word is not just an academic endeavor, it engages the mind, heart and will of those who trust Christ for their salvation. While many modern commentaries seem to focus on the application of the Scriptures, the intent here is gospel centered interpretation, resulting in devotional application. This is a work of serious scholastic intent combined with theological scrutiny and integrity. I am grateful for such a work and confident that it will be profitable for years to come in aiding the church's effort to know Christ more fully as He is revealed in holy Scripture.

—Kenneth R. Jones
Pastor of Glendale Baptist Church, Miami, FL
Co-host of nationally syndicated talk show—*White Horse Inn*
Contributed to: "Experiencing the Truth," "Glory Road," and
"Keep Your Head Up"; all published by Crossway.
Contributed to *Table Talk* and *Modern Reformation* magazines
Frequent conference speaker

The Reformation of the church brought with it biblical insights that revitalized churches and radically changed the course of theological studies as giants like Luther, Melanchthon, Calvin, Chemnitz, and Wesley commented extensively on Holy Scripture. The new *Reformation Heritage Bible Commentary* is a one-stop resource where the observations of these and other distinguished Reformation leaders are brought together around specific books of the New Testament.

—The Rev. Dr. R. Reed Lessing
Professor of Exegetical Theology and Director of the Graduate School
Concordia Seminary, St. Louis, MO
Member of the Society of Biblical Literature,
the Catholic Biblical Association, and
the Institute of Biblical Research

MARK

Also From Concordia

Biblical Studies

The Reformation Heritage Bible Commentary Series
- *Colossians/Thessalonians*, Edward A. Engelbrecht and Paul Deterding
- *Revelation*, Mark Brighton
- *Galatians/Ephesians/Philippians*, Jerald C. Joersz
- *Luke*, Robert Sorensen (forthcoming April 2014)

The Lutheran Study Bible, Edward A. Engelbrecht, General Editor

The Apocrypha: The Lutheran Edition with Notes, Edward A. Engelbrecht, General Editor

Today's Light Devotional Bible, Jane L. Fryar, ed. (forthcoming June 2014)

LifeLight In-depth Bible Study Series
- More than 50 studies available on biblical books and topics

Concordia's Complete Bible Handbook, 2nd ed., Jane L. Fryar, Edward A. Engelbrecht, et al.

Concordia Commentary Series: A Theological Exposition of Sacred Scripture
- *Leviticus*, John W. Kleinig
- *Joshua*, Adolph L. Harstad
- *Ruth*, John R. Wilch
- *Ezra and Nehemiah*, Andrew E. Steinmann
- *Proverbs*, Andrew E. Steinmann
- *Ecclesiastes*, James Bollhagen
- *The Song of Songs*, Christopher W. Mitchell
- *Isaiah 40–55*, R. Reed Lessing
- *Ezekiel 1–20*, Horace D. Hummel
- *Ezekiel 21–48*, Horace D. Hummel
- *Daniel*, Andrew E. Steinmann
- *Amos*, R. Reed Lessing
- *Jonah*, R. Reed Lessing
- *Matthew 1:1–11:1*, Jeffrey A. Gibbs
- *Matthew 11:2–20:34*, Jeffrey A. Gibbs
- *Mark 1–8*, James Voelz (forthcoming December 2013)
- *Luke 1:1–9:50*, Arthur A. Just Jr.
- *Luke 9:51–24:53*, Arthur A. Just Jr.
- *Romans 1–8*, Michael Middendorf
- *1 Corinthians*, Gregory J. Lockwood
- *Colossians*, Paul E. Deterding
- *Philemon*, John G. Nordling
- *2 Peter and Jude*, Curtis P. Giese
- *1–3 John*, Bruce G. Schuchard
- *Revelation*, Louis A. Brighton

Historical Studies

From Abraham to Paul: A Biblical Chronology, Andrew E. Steinmann

The Church from Age to Age: A History from Galilee to Global Christianity, Edward A. Engelbrecht, General Editor

History of Theology, 4th Rev. Ed., Bengt Hägglund

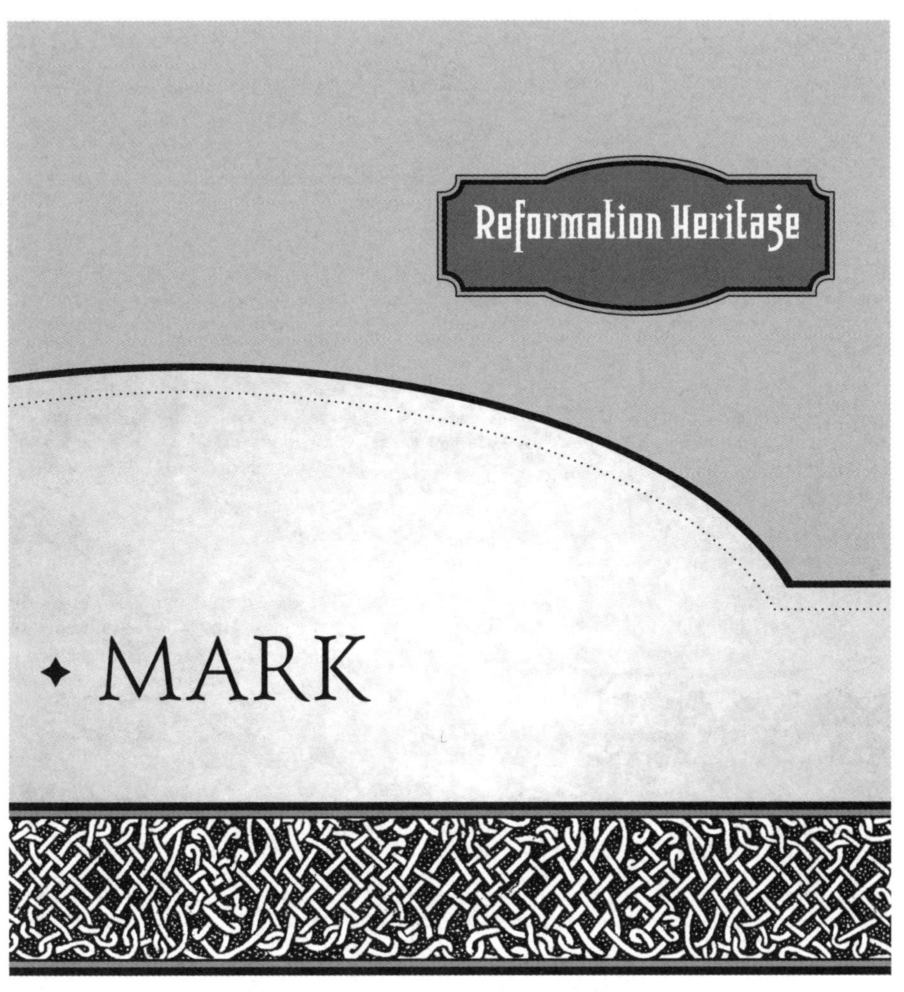

DANIEL PAAVOLA

CONCORDIA PUBLISHING HOUSE • SAINT LOUIS

3558 S. Jefferson Ave., St. Louis, MO 63118-3968
1-800-325-3040 · www.cph.org

Manufactured in the United States of America

Library of Congress Cataloging-in-Publication Data

Paavola, Daniel.
Mark / Daniel Paavola.
p. cm. — (Reformation heritage Bible commentary)
ISBN 978-0-7586-2764-3
1. Bible. N.T. Mark — Commentaries. I. Paavola, Daniel.- II. Title. III. Title: Mark.
BS2715.53.E54 2013
227'.077--dc23 2011044778

---

1 2 3 4 5 6 7 8 9 10 22 21 20 19 18 17 16 15 14 13

Contents

About This Series

The great reformers' influence upon the Bible's interpretation and application could not help but revitalize our churches. This is as true today as it was 500 years ago. This renewal happens in part because the reformers drew upon the insights of the Renaissance, which linked the medieval church back to her earlier roots in the ancient world. There the biblical texts sprang up. The reformers were among the earliest students to pursue classical studies, not only due to personal interest but especially due to the benefits such study brought to the study of the Bible. By reading the New Testament Scriptures in their ancient languages and context, the reformers dispelled many misunderstandings.

Second, the fires of controversy, which followed Luther's proclamation of justification by grace through faith on account of Christ alone, served to refine the study of Sacred Scriptures. So many ideas that medieval people took for granted or that were accepted based on human authority alone were tested and retested, leading to more careful study of God's Word.

Third, the reformers themselves taught with special insight due to their constant reading, study, translating, and preaching of the Sacred Scriptures. Their approach to the Scriptures and the insights they gained have continued to inform biblical studies even to the present day. For all of these reasons, Concordia Publishing House wished to produce a readable commentary series that would serve the current generation by sharing with them (1) insights from the reformers and (2) commentary that stemmed from their heritage.

In preparing this commentary, we drew upon the insights of the following reformers and heirs to their evangelical approach to teaching the Scriptures:

John Hus (c. 1372–1415)
Martin Luther (1483–1546)
Thomas Cranmer (1489–1556)
Philip Melanchthon (1497–1560)
John Calvin (1509–64)
John Knox (c. 1513–72)
Martin Chemnitz (1522–86)
Johann Gerhard (1582–1637)
Johann Albrecht Bengel (1687–1752)
John Wesley (1703–91)

Not every commentary in this series will include quotations from each of these reformers or heirs of the Reformation since these authors did not all comment on Books of the Scriptures with equal frequency. Other reformers may be included, as well as citations of Reformation era confessional documents such as the Augsburg Confession and Westminster Confession. Readers should not conclude that citation of an author implies complete endorsement of everything that author wrote (heaven knows, these were fallible men, as they themselves acknowledged). The works of other significant Reformation era commentators are less available in English. We have intentionally stayed away from more radical reformers such as Andreas Bodenstein von Karlstadt, Ulrich Zwingli, Thomas Münzer, etc.

The commentary is not simply a compilation of sixteenth century views but a thorough verse-by-verse commentary built from the reformers' approach of *Scripture interprets Scripture* and supplemented from their writings. Along with quotations from the reformers and their heirs, readers will also find quotations from some early and medieval Church Fathers. This is because the reformers did not wish to overthrow the earlier generations of teachers but to profit from them where they were faithful in teaching the Word.

Some readers will note that the writers listed above represent different branches in the Protestant family of churches, and they may wonder how compatible these writers will be alongside one another. It is certainly the case that the reformers held different views, especially concerning the Sacraments, biblical authority, and other matters. Some authors for the series may at times describe differences between the various reformers.

However, while it is true that these differences affect the fellowship and work of the churches of the Reformation, it is also true that the reformers shared significant agreement. For example, the great historian Philip Schaff noted, "Melanchthon mediated between Luther and Calvin" (*History of the Christian Church* vol. VII, second revised ed. [New York: Charles Scribner's Sons, 1894], 260). Early Reformation works like Melanchthon's *Commonplaces* and the Augsburg Confession served as models for the various traditions of Protestant confession and doctrine. What is more, as the writers focused on a particular biblical text for interpretation, they often reached very similar conclusions regarding that text. The text of Scripture tended to lead them toward a more unified expression of the faith. This is something I have described as "the text effect,"[1] which illustrates for

---

1 *Friends of the Law* (St. Louis: Concordia, 2011), 136.

us a way in which the Bible brings us together despite differences and always remains the most important guide for Christian teaching and practice. In view of the 500th anniversary of the Reformation in 2017, I believe it is fitting for us to draw anew upon the time honored insights of these great servants of God.

The Bible Translations

Among the translations for our commentary we have chosen, on the one hand, what many regard as the finest English translation ever produced: the King James Version. The KJV is a product of the Reformation era, and although it is now more than 400 years old, remains a most valuable tool for study. Along with the KJV we are pleased to present the English Standard Version, which has rapidly become one of the most widely used modern English translations. The success of the ESV is due in part to the translators' efforts to follow sound, classical principles of translation very like those used by the KJV translators. The result is a very readable English translation that also allows readers to grasp the biblical expressions and terms that appear repeatedly in the Bible. Due to this approach, we find the ESV an especially helpful translation for Bible study. Our notes are keyed to the ESV, but we have placed the KJV in parallel with the ESV for easy comparison. Since the ESV text is based on the broad consensus of biblical scholars who have consulted the early Greek manuscripts, it differs at points from the KJV text, which was produced when fewer manuscripts were available for study. Where significant differences between the translations appear, the notes include comment.

Our Prayer for You

The following prayer embodies the sense of study and devotion we wish to convey to all who take up these commentaries:

> Blessed Lord, You have caused all Holy Scriptures to be written for our learning. Grant that we may so hear them, read, mark, learn, and inwardly digest them that, by patience and comfort from Your holy Word, we may embrace and ever hold fast the blessed hope of everlasting life; through Jesus Christ, our Lord. Amen.

Rev. Edward A. Engelbrecht, STM
Senior Editor for Bible Resources

Preface

The shortest of the Gospels is an action-packed, urgent book. After a single verse of introduction, Mark takes us to the Jordan River where Jesus quickly comes to be baptized. Leaving the story of Jesus' birth and childhood to other evangelists, Mark launches us into the ministry of Jesus, the Son of God. This short Gospel concludes nearly as quickly as it begins. Our Lord's resurrection is proclaimed at the empty tomb. The Church is told where He will meet them, but most of the details and the story of the Church's response and growth are left for others to tell.

It is a story of action that paints a clear and compelling portrait of Jesus. Mark repeatedly tells us of things that happen "immediately" and drives us forward with urgency and anticipation for what Jesus will do and say.

We see Jesus reaching out with boldness and compassion to Jews and Gentiles, to the mighty and the lowly, in large groups and in quiet anonymity. Jesus graciously comes to people and addresses their many needs, and He is clearly revealed as the Christ.

Mark introduces his book as "the gospel of Jesus Christ, the Son of God" (1:1). That identity becomes so clear that, at the cross, a Roman centurion concludes, "Truly this man was the Son of God!" (15:39). The angel at the empty tomb proclaims that Christ, the Son of God is risen, and just as He promised, His people will see Him.

God grant us the immediacy of this Gospel, that we attend to Jesus and serve those He places in our lives through witness and acts of merciful service.

Steven P. Mueller, Ph.D.
General Editor

Abbreviations

AD	*anno Domini* (in the year of [our] Lord)
BC	before Christ
c.	circa
cf.	confer
ch.	chapter
chs.	chapters
Gk	Greek
NT	New Testament
OT	Old Testament
p.	page
pp.	pages
St.	Saint
v.	verse
vv.	verses

Canonical Scripture

Gn	Genesis
Ex	Exodus
Lv	Leviticus
Nu	Numbers
Dt	Deuteronomy
Jsh	Joshua
Jgs	Judges
Ru	Ruth
1Sm	1 Samuel
2Sm	2 Samuel
1Ki	1 Kings
2Ki	2 Kings
1Ch	1 Chronicles
2Ch	2 Chronicles
Ezr	Ezra
Ne	Nehemiah
Est	Esther
Jb	Job
Ps	Psalms
Pr	Proverbs
Ec	Ecclesiastes
Sg	Song of Solomon
Is	Isaiah
Jer	Jeremiah
Lm	Lamentations
Ezk	Ezekiel
Dn	Daniel
Hos	Hosea
Jl	Joel
Am	Amos
Ob	Obadiah
Jnh	Jonah
Mi	Micah
Na	Nahum
Hab	Habakkuk
Zep	Zephaniah
Hg	Haggai
Zec	Zechariah
Mal	Malachi

Mt	Matthew
Mk	Mark
Lk	Luke
Jn	John
Ac	Acts
Rm	Romans
1Co	1 Corinthians
2Co	2 Corinthians

Gal	Galatians	Heb	Hebrews
Eph	Ephesians	Jas	James
Php	Philippians	1Pt	1 Peter
Col	Colossians	2Pt	2 Peter
1Th	1 Thessalonians	1Jn	1 John
2Th	2 Thessalonians	2Jn	2 John
1Tm	1 Timothy	3Jn	3 John
2Tm	2 Timothy	Jude	Jude
Ti	Titus	Rv	Revelation
Phm	Philemon		

The Apocrypha

Jth	Judith	Old Grk Est	Old Greek Esther
Wis	The Wisdom of Solomon	Sus	Susanna
Tob	Tobit	Bel	Bel and the Dragon
Ecclus	Ecclesiasticus (Sirach)	Pr Az	The Prayer of Azariah
Bar	Baruch	Sg Three	The Song of the Three Holy Children
Lt Jer	The Letter of Jeremiah	Pr Man	Prayer of Manasseh
1Macc	1 Maccabees		
2Macc	2 Maccabees		

Other Books

1Esd	1 Esdras	Ps 151	Psalm 151
2Esd	2 Esdras	*1En*	*1 Enoch*
3Macc	3 Maccabees (Ptolemaika)	*2En*	*2 Enoch*
4Macc	4 Maccabees	*Jub*	*Jubilees*

Abbreviations for Commonly Cited Books and Works

AC — Augsburg Confession. From *Concordia*.

ANF — Roberts, Alexander, and James Donaldson, eds. *The Ante-Nicene Fathers: The Writings of the Fathers Down to AD 325*, 10 vols. Buffalo: The Christian Literature Publishing Company, 1885–96. Reprint, Grand Rapids, MI: Eerdmans, 2001.

Ap — Apology of the Augsburg Confession. From *Concordia*.

Bengel — Bengel, John Albert. *Gnomon of the New Testament*. 5 vols. Edinburgh: T. & T. Clark, 1877.

Chemnitz — Chemnitz, Martin. *Chemnitz's Works*. 8 vols. St. Louis: Concordia, 1971–89.

Church	Hus, John. *The Church*. David S. Schaff, trans. New York: Charles Scribner's Sons, 1915.
Concordia	McCain, Paul Timothy, ed. *Concordia: The Lutheran Confessions*. 2nd ed. St. Louis: Concordia, 2006.
CSSC	Roehrs, Walter R. (OT), and Martin H. Franzmann (NT). *Concordia Self-Study Commentary*. St. Louis: Concordia, 1971, 1979.
Definitions	Melanchthon. For volume information, see *Topics* below.
Ep	Epitome of the Formula of Concord. From *Concordia*.
ESV	English Standard Version.
FC	Formula of Concord. From *Concordia*.
Gerhard	Gerhard, Johann. *Theological Commonplaces*. Richard J. Dinda, trans. Benjamin T. G. Mayes, ed. St. Louis: Concordia, 2009–.
Harmony	Calvin, John. *Commentary on a Harmony of the Evangelists, Matthew, Mark, and Luke*. John Pringle, trans. Edinburgh: Calvin Translation Society, 1845.
H82	*The Hymnal 1982, according to the Use of The Episcopal Church*. New York: The Church Hymnal Corporation, 1985.
KJV	King James Version.
LC	Large Catechism of Martin Luther. From *Concordia*.
Life	Josephus, Flavius. *The Life of Flavius Josephus*. In *The Works of Josephus*. Translated by William Whiston. Peabody, MA: Hendrickson Publishers, 1987.
LSB	Commission on Worship of The Lutheran Church—Missouri Synod. *Lutheran Service Book*. St. Louis: Concordia, 2006.
LW	Luther, Martin. *Luther's Works*. American Edition. General editors Jaroslav Pelikan and Helmut T. Lehmann. 56 vols. St. Louis: Concordia, and Philadelphia: Muhlenberg and Fortress, 1955–1986. Vols. 56–75: Edited by Christopher Boyd Brown. St. Louis: Concordia, 2009–.
LXX	Septuagint. Koine Greek Old Testament.
*NPNF*1	Schaff, Philip, ed. *A Select Library of Nicene and Post-Nicene Fathers of the Christian Church*. Series 1, 14 vols. New York: The Christian Literature Series, 1886–89. Reprint, Grand Rapids, MI: Eerdmans, 1956.
*NPNF*2	Schaff, Philip, and Henry Wace, ed. *A Select Library of Nicene and Post-Nicene Fathers of the Christian Church*, Series 2, 14

	vols. New York: The Christian Literature Series, 1890–99. Reprint, Grand Rapids, MI: Eerdmans, 1952, 1961.
SA	Smalcald Articles. From *Concordia*.
Schaff	Schaff, Philip, ed. *The Creeds of Christendom with a History and Critical Notes*. 3 vols. 4th ed. New York: Harper, 1919.
SD	Solid Declaration of the Formula of Concord. From *Concordia*.
Topics	Melanchthon, Philip. *The Chief Theological Topics, Loci Praecipui Theologici 1559*. 2nd English ed. J. A. O. Preus, trans. St. Louis: Concordia, 2011.
TPH	*The Presbyterian Hymnal*. Louisville, KY: Westminster/John Knox Press, 1990.
TUMH	*The United Methodist Hymnal*. Nashville, TN: The United Methodist Publishing House, 1989.
Wesley	Wesley, John. *Explanatory Notes upon the New Testament*. 12th ed. New York: Carlton & Porter, 1754.

Timeline for the New Testament

Anatolia, Greece, and Rome	Egypt and Africa	Dates	Syria, Canaan, and Israel	Mesopotamia and Persia
		4 BC	Angel appears to Zechariah (c. Nov 15; Lk 1:8–22)	
		3 BC	The Annunciation (inter Apr 17–May 16; Lk 1:26–38); John the Baptist born (Aug; Lk 1:57–66)	
	Holy family in Egypt	2 BC	Jesus born (mid Jan to early Feb; Mt 1:25; Lk 2:1–7); Magi visit; flight to Egypt (mid to late in the year; Mt 2)	
		1 BC	Death of Herod the Great (after Jan 10; Mt 2:19); return to Nazareth (Mt 2:19–23)	
		AD 6	Judas the Galilean leads revolt against Rome; Judea, Samaria, and Idumaea combined to form the Roman province of Judea	
		c. 10	Rabbi Hillel dies	
		11	Jesus in temple before the elders (c. Apr 8–22; Lk 2:42)	
Tiberius, Roman emperor		14–37		
Revolt in Gaul; grain shortages cause unrest in Rome		21		
		29	Baptism of Jesus (Fall; Lk 3:1–2)	
		30	Jesus at Passover (c. Apr 8; Jn 2:20)	
		32	Jesus at Passover (c. Apr 15; Jn 6:4); Jesus arrives at Feast of Booths (c. Oct 14; Jn 7:14); Feast of Booths (Oct 17 or 18; Jn 7:37)	

Anatolia, Greece, and Rome	Egypt and Africa	Dates	Syria, Canaan, and Israel	Mesopotamia and Persia
Roman senators unable to pay debts; subsidized by Emperor Tiberius		33	Triumphal entry (Sun, Mar 29); Last Supper (Thurs eve, Apr 2); crucifixion (Fri, Apr 3); resurrection (Sun, Apr 5); ascension (May 14; Lk 24:51; Ac 1:9); Pentecost (May 24)	Jews of Parthia, Media, Elam and Mesopotamia travel to Jerusalem for Pentecost
	Ethiopian eunuch baptized, returns home (Ac 8:26–39)	c. 35		
		35–42		Revolt of Seleucia on the Tigris against Parthian rule
		36	Paul's conversion (Ac 9:1–31)	
Caligula (Gaius), Roman emperor		37–41	Josephus, Jewish historian, born	
	Philo of Alexandria leads Jewish delegation to Rome	c. 39	Caligula attempts to place statue of himself in Jerusalem temple	
		41	Martyrdom of James (late Mar; Ac 12:2); Peter in prison (Apr; Ac 12:3–4); Passover (May 4; Ac 12:4); Peter leaves Jerusalem (May; Gal 2:11)	
		41–44	Herod Agrippa I rules Judea	
Claudius, Roman emperor		41–54		
Peter on mission in Asia Minor (spr/sum; 1Pt 1:1–2); [in Corinth (fall); at Rome (mid Nov)]		42	Peter in Antioch (May 41–Apr 42; Gal 2:11)	
		44	Herod Agrippa at festival in Caesarea (Mar 5; Ac 12:19); death of Herod Agrippa (Mar 10; Ac 12:21–23)	

Anatolia, Greece, and Rome	Egypt and Africa	Dates	Syria, Canaan, and Israel	Mesopotamia and Persia
		47–48	Paul's 1st missionary journey (Ac 13:1–14:28)	
Paul goes to Macedonia; Barnabas and John Mark go to Cyprus (mid May; Ac 15:36–16:10)		49	Conference in Jerusalem (Ac 15:1–35); Peter goes to Antioch (Feb; Gal 2:11); Paul confronts Peter (Apr; Gal 2:11)	
		49–56	[Peter in Antioch (seven years)]	
Paul's 2nd missionary journey (Ac 15:39–18:22)	Philo of Alexandria leads second Jewish delegation to Rome	49–51		
Paul's 3rd missionary journey (Ac 18:23–21:17)		52–55		
Nero, Roman emperor		54–68		
		55–57	Paul imprisoned in Caesarea (Ac 23:23–26:32)	
Paul's journey to Rome (Ac 27:1–28:16)		57–58		
Paul in custody in Rome (Ac 28:17–31)		58–60		
		62	Martyrdom of James, the Lord's brother	
Paul assigns Titus at Crete (Ti 1:5)		64–65		
Paul in Ephesus, where he leaves Timothy (spr–sum; 1Tm 1:3)		65		

Anatolia, Greece, and Rome	Egypt and Africa	Dates	Syria, Canaan, and Israel	Mesopotamia and Persia
	Tiberius Julius Alexander, of Jewish descent, appointed Roman prefect of Egypt	66		
		66–70	Jewish revolt against Romans	
Peter and Paul martyred		68		
Emperor Vespasian		69–79		
		70	Titus destroys Jerusalem temple; Rabbon Yohanan ben Zakkai at Yavneh Academy	Jerusalem Jews settle in Babylonia, which becomes the new center of Judaism
		c. 73	Fall of Masada	
Emperor Titus		79–81		
Emperor Domitian		81–96		
		c. 90–115	Rabbon Gamaliel II at Yavneh Academy	
Jews revolt in Cyprus	Jews revolt in Egypt and Cyrene	115–17		Trajan captures Mesopotamia; Jews revolt
	Founding of Antinoöpolis by Emperor Hadrian	130		
		132–35	Bar Kokhba revolt; death of Rabbi Akiva, Yavneh Academy leader who hailed Bar Kokhba as the messiah	

Jesus' Ministry in the Gospels

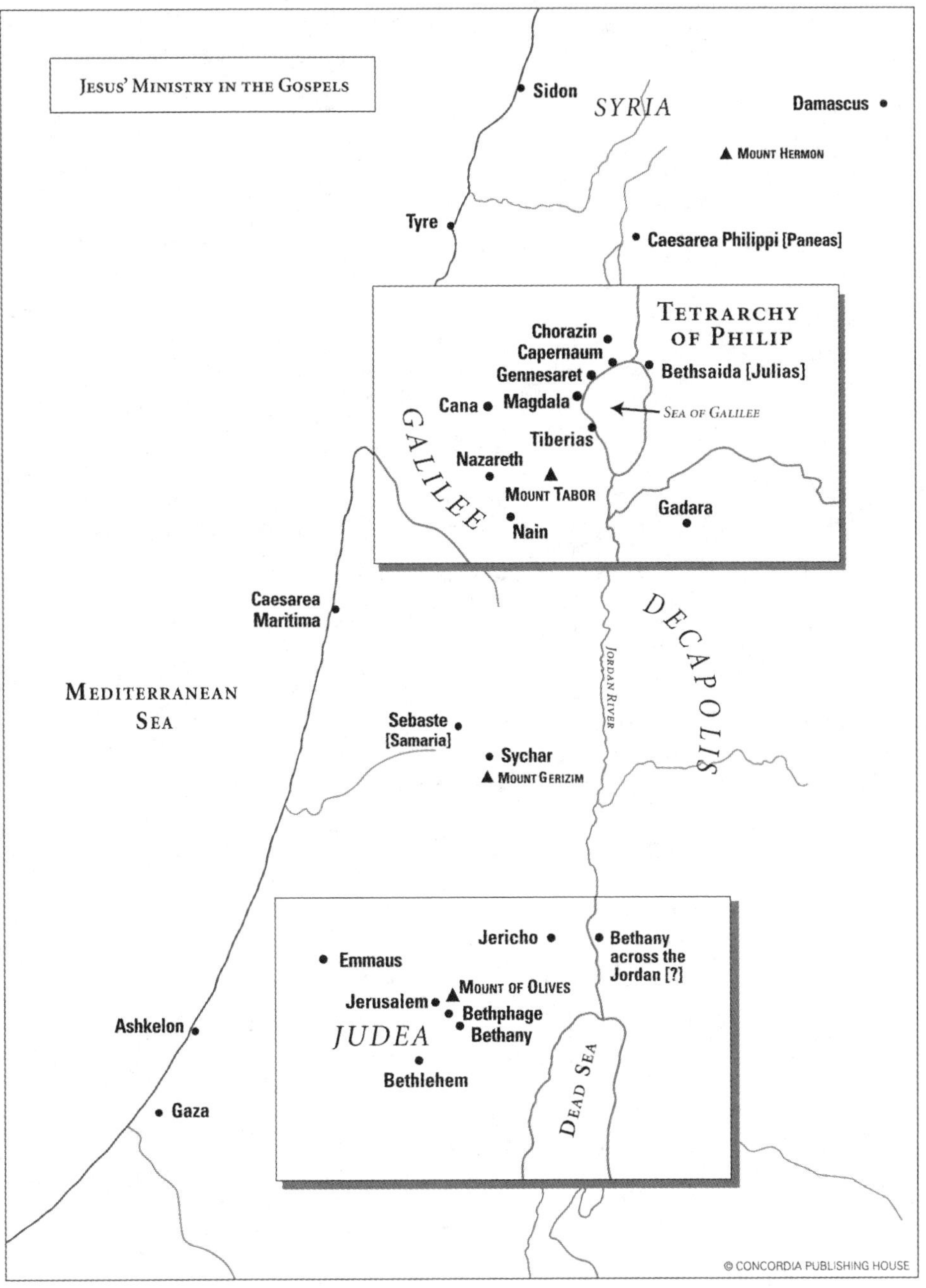

MARK

Introduction to Mark

Overview

Author

John Mark

Date

Written c. AD 50–60

Places

Galilee; Judea; Nazareth; Capernaum; Tyre; Sidon; Jerusalem; Jericho; Bethany; Jordan River; Mount of Olives; Gethsemane; see map, p. xxi

People

Jesus; John the Baptist; the 12 apostles; Jesus' family; scribes; Pharisees; Herodians; Herod Antipas; Mary the mother of Joses; Mary Magdalene; Mary the mother of James; Salome

Purpose

To proclaim Jesus the Son of God, who calls disciples to repent, to believe the Gospel, and to bear the cross

Law Themes

Repentance; political and religious opposition; uncleanness; authoritative teaching; hard-heartedness

Gospel Themes

Gospel; Baptism; compassion; mercy; cleansing; authoritative teaching; ransom; Lord's Supper

Memory Verses

Jesus' message (1:14–15); prayer for faith (9:23–24); Jesus' mission (10:42–45); a centurion's confession (15:39)

Reading Mark

The old farmer knew this corner of the field well. His plow had turned up rocks here for years. He and his brothers picked up the rocks and worked them into a retaining wall not far away. He could see there a row of sick and lame people sitting on the stones, waiting for their turn to see the Teacher. Families with small children also sat nearby, awaiting their turn. The farmer sat and scratched the soil. It felt warm and loose to the touch. Then he struck a rock. "Another rock," he said. "Still too stony—unfit for seed."

Mark describes how the disciples and the crowds immediately responded to the authority of Jesus' teaching. They flocked to receive His healing touch and blessings for their children. But beneath the surface of this excitement, their hearts remained hardened and crippled by unbelief. As you read Mark's account of Jesus' ministry and Passion, consider Jesus' patience. He plows and replows matters of repentance, faith, and the promises of God, picking out hard hearts and calling people to believe and to bear fruit.

Martin Franzmann characterizes Mark's account as follows:

> The Gospel According to Mark is a Gospel of action. As compared with Matthew, Mark emphasizes the deeds of Jesus. The deeds of Jesus are by no means isolated from His words; the word is Jesus' instrument in His deeds too; He speaks, and it is done. And Mark, besides giving two longer discourses of Jesus (4:1–34; 13:1–37), repeatedly emphasizes the centrality of the word in the ministry of Jesus and the effect of its authority on men, 1:14, 22, 38–39f; 2:2, 13; 4:1; 6:1–7; 9:7; 10:1; 11:18; cf. also 8:38. But it is chiefly by His works that Jesus is marked as the Proclaimer and the Bringer of the almighty grace of the kingdom of God, as the anointed King in whom man can trust, the Son of God in whom man can believe.
>
> Adapted from Martin H. Franzmann, *CSSC*, p. 44.

Luther on Mark

> The notion must be given up that there are four gospels and only four evangelists. . . . "Gospel" [*Euangelium*] is a Greek word and means in Greek a good message, good tidings, good news, a good report, which one sings and tells with gladness. For example, when David overcame the great Goliath, there came among the Jewish people the good report and encouraging news that their terrible enemy had been struck down and that they had been rescued and given joy and peace; and they sang and danced and were glad for it [I Sam. 18:6].
>
> Thus this gospel of God or New Testament is a good story and report, sounded forth into all the world by the apostles, telling of a true David who strove with sin, death, and the devil, and overcame them, and thereby rescued all those who were captive in sin, afflicted with death, and overpowered by the devil. Without any merit of their own he made them righteous, gave them life, and saved them, so that they were given peace and brought back to God. For this they sing, and thank and praise God, and are glad forever, if only they believe firmly and remain steadfast in faith.

> This report and encouraging tidings, or evangelical and divine news, is also called a New Testament. For it is a testament when a dying man bequeaths his property, after his death, to his legally defined heirs. And Christ, before his death, commanded and ordained that his gospel be preached after his death in all the world [Luke 24:44–47]. Thereby he gave to all who believe, as their possession, everything that he had. This included: his life, in which he swallowed up death; his righteousness, by which he blotted out sin; and his salvation, with which he overcame everlasting damnation. A poor man, dead in sin and consigned to hell, can hear nothing more comforting than this precious and tender message about Christ; from the bottom of his heart he must laugh and be glad over it, if he believes it true. (AE 35:357–59)

Calvin on Mark

Calvin did not prepare a commentary specifically on the Gospel of Mark but instead wrote a commentary on a harmony of the Evangelists, treating together Matthew, Mark, and Luke (the Synoptic Gospels). He was perhaps following the earlier example of the harmony of the four Gospels prepared by Augustine, to whom Calvin referred in his dedicatory letter (*Harmony*, p. xxxiii). The following is from Calvin's "argument" or introduction:

> Mark is generally supposed to have been the private friend and disciple of Peter. It is even believed that he wrote the Gospel, as it was dictated to him by Peter, and thus merely performed the office of an amanuensis or clerk. But on this subject we need not give ourselves much trouble, for it is of little importance to us, provided only we believe that he is a properly qualified and divinely appointed witness, who committed nothing to writing, but as the Holy Spirit directed him and guided his pen. There is no ground whatever for the statement of Jerome, that his Gospel is an abridgment of the Gospel by Matthew. He does not everywhere adhere to the order which Matthew observed, and from the very commencement handles the subjects in a different manner. Some things, too, are related by him which the other had omitted, and his narrative of the same event is sometimes more detailed. It is more probable, in my opinion—and the nature of the case warrants the conjecture—that he had not seen Matthew's book when he wrote his own; so far is he from having expressly intended to make an abridgment. (*Harmony* p. xxxviii)

Since Mark does not contain an account of Jesus' childhood, Calvin's actual comments on Mark do not begin until p. 173 of the *Harmony* in the English edition.

Gerhard on Mark

Irenaeus calls Mark "the interpreter and follower of Peter" (bk. 3, c. 1, p. 183). Nicephorus writes this about him: "Peter dictated the Gospel to him and sanctioned that it then be read in the church" (bk. 2, c. 45). Epiphanius states: "Peter ordered Mark to publish the Gospel in Rome" (*Haeres.* 51, p. 192). In *Hist.*, bk. 6, c. 11, Eusebius also cites these things from Clement of Alexandria. Jerome, *Catal. Illustr.*: "Mark was the disciples and interpreter of Peter. When the brethren at Rome asked him, he wrote in brief form the Gospel according to what he had heard Peter tell. When Peter heard it, he approved of it and stated under his authority that it should be read in the Church." . . . Others relate concerning him that he was Peter's nephew from his sister; that he was one of the seventy disciples of Christ; and that he preached the Gospel in the Egyptian city of Alexandria. . . . We gather that the last chapter of Mark was not accepted by all as canonical at the time of Jerome from his Epistle *ad Hebidiam* 150, q. 3, where he says, "Almost all the books in Greek do not have this brief chapter at the end." There appears to be a twofold reason for doubt: (1) It seems to conflict with the description of the Lord's resurrection among the rest of the evangelists. We have shown the contrary, however in our *Harmonia evangelica*, "On the Resurrection." (2) According to the statement of Jerome in *Dial. 2 adv. Pelag.*, heretics inserted in it some apocryphal sentences that have the smell of Manichaeanism: "And they were apologizing, saying, 'This is the age of iniquity and the substance of unbelief. It did not permit the true power of God to be grasped through the unclean spirits. Therefore reveal your righteousness now.' " Let the apocryphal and foreign parts be removed, however, and let the remaining canonical portions be kept. Iraenaeus (bk. 3, c. 11), Athanasius (*Synopsis*), Augustine (*De cons. Evang.*, bk. 3, c. 24), Bede (commentary [on Mark]), and others of the ancients acknowledge that this chapter is genuine. The Gospel account of Mark has sixteen chapters in which is also explained the threefold *office of Christ: prophetic, priestly, and royal.* (E 1.244)

Bengel on Mark and the Other Evangelists

> [The Evangelists] are four in number—two of them, namely John and Matthew, were themselves apostles and took part, therefore, in the things which they relate: the other two, Mark and Luke, afford, in their own persons, an example of faith, having derived the sure and accurate knowledge of the Gospel from others. Mark, however, presupposes the existence of Matthew, and, as it were, supplies his omissions; Luke does the same for both of them; John for all three. (Matthew, an apostle, wrote first, and thus established an authority for both Mark and Luke. John, also an apostle, wrote last, and confirmed to mankind, more fully, the works of Mark and Luke, already sufficiently firm in themselves. Matthew wrote especially to show the fulfillment of the Old Testament Scriptures, and to convince the Jews. Mark produced an abridgement of Matthew, adding at the same time many remarkable things which had been omitted by his predecessor, and paying particular attention to the noviciate of the apostles. Luke composed a narrative of a distinctly historical character, with especial reference to our Lord's office as Christ. John refuted the impugners of His divinity. All which is recorded by either of these Four, was actually done and said by Jesus Christ. But they severally drew from a common treasury those particulars, of which each had the fullest knowledge, which corresponded to his own spiritual character, and which were best suited to the time when he wrote, and to the persons whom he primarily addressed. (Bengel 71–72)

Bengel often comments on how a passage in one Gospel may have been derived from or expressed in one of the other Synoptic Gospels.

Wesley on Mark

Wesley did not write a distinct introduction to Mark or the other Evangelists but summarized the comments of Bengel found above since Bengel's *Gnomon* remained a leading authority throughout the eighteenth century. (See Wesley 7)

Challenges for Readers

Relationship to Other Gospels. Some critics have regarded Mark's Gospel as crudely written in comparison to the other canonical Gospels. This criticism fails to appreciate Mark's thoughtful literary construction as described below.

Jesus as the Son of God. Mark describes God's unique relationship with Jesus, who represents the heavenly Father to the world and bears His authority. This theme shows up repeatedly as Jesus is titled "the Son of God" (1:1, 11; 3:11; 5:7; 9:7; 14:61) and climaxes with the centurion's confession at the cross (15:39), which highlights the central importance of Jesus' sacrificial suffering and death (10:45). The disciples respond to Jesus' authority, the demons fear it, and all creation obeys Him. Also, Jesus foresees His crucifixion and resurrection and guides these events.

Jesus as Man. Though Mark describes Jesus' great authority, he also emphasizes Jesus' need for quiet prayer (1:35); His feelings of compassion, anger, and frustration (1:41; 3:5; 10:14, 21; 14:33); and even His need for sleep (4:38). Jesus at times seems weak or ineffectual (cf. 6:1–6; 8:22–26). However, Mark uses these times to illustrate important truths about faith.

Hard-heartedness. Of the Gospels, Mark provides the most negative description of Jesus' disciples. In 6:45–52 and 8:14–21, they fail to understand who Jesus is and what He is teaching (cf. 4:13, 35–41; 7:14–19; 8:1–10; 9:14–19, 33–37; 10:13–16, 35–45; 14:3–21, 26–31; 16:14). He repeatedly refers to hardness of heart (3:5; 6:52; 8:17; 10:5), which is how the Lord described Pharaoh in the exodus. Even the women, who faithfully mourn at Jesus' crucifixion and visit His tomb, flee in fear at the announcement of the resurrection (16:8). This emphasis prompts readers to consider the condition of their own hearts and faith.

Clean and Unclean. Mark explains and emphasizes cleanliness, an important aspect of OT Law (cf. Gn 7:2–3; 9:3–4; Lv 11–15) and rabbinic tradition (7:1–8). Jesus "made clean" a leper (1:40–44). A demon is an "unclean spirit" (e.g., 1:23). A herd of swine—unclean animals—are wiped out (5:13). These examples likely helped Mark's Gentile readers better understand the Jewish members of their early Christian congregations. But Mark also emphasized Jesus' teaching about the ultimate source of uncleanness: the sinful human heart (7:20–23).

Secrecy. Throughout the Gospel of Mark, Jesus discourages people and unclean spirits from speaking about Him and His kingdom (e.g., 1:23–25; 1:44; 3:11–12; 7:36–37; 8:26, 30; 9:9–10). Critical scholars read this feature as a device early Christians added to the story of Jesus' life. They argue that Jesus never really called Himself the

Son of God or Christ but that these beliefs about Him were added later to let people in on the secret. Such an interpretation conflicts with Mark's overall goal and account (see "Jesus as the Son of God," above). It is more likely that Jesus exercises His authority to guide the spread of His popularity, which had brought Him into conflict with political and religious authorities. E.g., outside the jurisdiction of Jesus' main opponents, He actually encourages a man to proclaim His miracles (5:19–20).

Mark's Abrupt Ending. Mark 16:9–20 does not appear in a number of early Greek manuscripts. This likely means they were not part of Mark's original composition, which may have used a "suspended" ending that left readers wanting to learn more about Jesus and His disciples. The longer ending was perhaps added later to satisfy people's interests.

Blessings for Readers

As you read Mark's account of Jesus' ministry and Passion, take special note of the emphasis on discipleship and faith. Jesus tells His followers that He will suffer and will ransom them (8:31–33; 9:30–31; 10:32–34, 45). They, too, will face suffering on account of Him and the Gospel (8:34–9:1; 10:29–30). Yet, through repentance and faith, they will inherit eternal life (cf. 10:17, 27).

When you face difficulty, cry out, "I believe; help my unbelief!" (9:24). The Son of God, who ransomed you from the bondage of sin and death (10:45; 15:22–25), will hear you in compassion and have mercy (9:22; 10:47–49).

Outline

The simplest outline of Mark has two parts: Jesus' public ministry and Jesus' Passion. The outline below provides greater detail.

- I. Prologue: "The Beginning of the Gospel of Jesus Christ, the Son of God" (1:1–13)
    - A. The Ministry of John the Baptist (1:1–8)
    - B. The Baptism and Temptation of Jesus (1:9–13)
- II. Jesus' Public Ministry of Preaching and Miracle Working (1:14–8:30)
    - A. Jesus Begins His Ministry in Galilee with Authority, but Meets Opposition (1:14–3:12)

1. Jesus proclaims the rule of God and calls disciples (1:14–20)
2. Jesus begins His ministry on a Sabbath Day in Capernaum (1:21–39)
3. Jesus continues His ministry amid growing opposition (1:40–3:6)
4. Large crowds follow Jesus (3:7–12)

B. Jesus Is Received with Both Unbelief and Faith (3:13–6:6)
   1. Jesus appoints the 12 apostles (3:13–19)
   2. Jesus confronts the unbelief facing His ministry (3:20–4:34)
      a. Jesus confronts unbelief both from the scribes and His family (3:20–35)
      b. Jesus teaches the crowds and His disciples in light of the unbelief of the religious authorities ("The Parabolic Discourse"; 4:1–34)
   3. Jesus performs miracles on and around the Sea of Galilee (4:35–5:43)
      a. Jesus calms a storm (4:35–41)
      b. Jesus heals a Gerasene demoniac (5:1–20)
      c. Jesus heals a sick woman and raises a dead girl (5:21–43)
   4. Jesus is rejected at Nazareth (6:1–6)

C. Jesus Withdraws from His Public Ministry in Galilee (6:7–8:30)
   1. Jesus sends the 12 apostles; John the Baptist dies (6:7–30)
   2. A first cycle of parallel events (6:31–7:37)
      a. Jesus feeds 5,000 in the wilderness and walks on water (6:31–56)
      b. Jesus confronts the Pharisees and scribes and teaches on the distinction between clean and unclean, but His disciples misunderstand (7:1–23)
      c. Jesus heals a Syrophoenician woman's daughter near Tyre (7:24–30)
      d. Jesus heals a deaf man in the region of the Decapolis (7:31–37)

3. A second cycle of parallel events (8:1–26)
    a. Jesus feeds 4,000 in the wilderness (8:1–10)
    b. Jesus confronts the Pharisees and warns against the yeast of the Pharisees and Herod, but His disciples misunderstand (8:11–21)
    c. Jesus heals a blind man in Bethsaida (8:22–26)
4. Peter confesses that Jesus is the Christ in Caesarea Philippi (8:27–30)

III. Jesus Prepares His Disciples for His Passion, Death, and Resurrection (8:31–16:8)

A. Jesus Reveals His Passion, Death, and Resurrection and Teaches on Discipleship (8:31–10:52)

1. The first Passion prediction and subsequent teaching and events (8:31–9:29)
    a. Jesus predicts His suffering, death, and resurrection, and rebukes Peter (8:31–33)
    b. Jesus teaches His disciples and the crowd on discipleship (8:34–9:1)
    c. Jesus is transfigured before three of His disciples (9:2–13)
    d. Jesus casts out an unclean spirit from a boy after His disciples' failure (9:14–29)
2. The second Passion prediction and subsequent teaching (9:30–10:31)
    a. Jesus predicts His suffering, death, and resurrection (9:30–32)
    b. Jesus teaches His disciples on greatness in the kingdom of God (9:33–50)
    c. Jesus teaches in the region of Judea and across the Jordan (10:1–31)
3. The third Passion prediction and subsequent teaching and events (10:32–52)
    a. Jesus predicts His suffering, death, and resurrection (10:32–34)
    b. Jesus responds to the request of James and John and teaches on greatness in the kingdom of God (10:35–45)
    c. Jesus heals blind Bartimaeus (10:46–52)

- B. Jesus Enters Jerusalem and Confronts the Religious Authorities (chs. 11–13)
  1. Jesus enters Jerusalem to the praise of the crowds (11:1–11)
  2. Jesus curses the fig tree, cleanses the temple, and teaches the disciples on faith (11:12–26)
  3. Jesus confronts the religious authorities (11:27–12:40)
     - a. Jesus responds to the question of His authority (11:27–33)
     - b. Jesus teaches the parable of the tenants (12:1–12)
     - c. Jesus responds to the question about paying taxes to Caesar (12:13–17)
     - d. Jesus responds to the Sadducees on the resurrection (12:18–27)
     - e. Jesus responds to the question on the greatest commandment (12:28–34)
     - f. Jesus questions them about the relationship of David and the Christ (12:35–37)
     - g. Jesus warns against the scribes (12:38–40)
  4. Jesus teaches His disciples through the widow's offering (12:41–44)
  5. Jesus teaches His disciples in light of His rejection by the religious authorities ("The Eschatological Discourse"; ch. 13)
     - a. Jesus predicts the temple's destruction (13:1–2)
     - b. The signs and warnings (13:3–37)
- C. Jesus' Passion, Death, and Resurrection (14:1–16:8)
  1. Jesus is anointed at Bethany amid a plot to have Him arrested and killed (14:1–11)
  2. Jesus celebrates the Passover with His disciples, predicts His betrayal, and institutes the Lord's Supper (14:12–25)
  3. Jesus predicts Peter's denial (14:26–31)
  4. Jesus prays in Gethsemane and is arrested (14:32–52)
  5. Jesus is tried before the high priest and is denied by Peter (14:53–72)

6. Jesus is tried before Pilate (15:1–15)
7. Jesus is mocked by the soldiers, crucified, and dies (15:16–41)
8. Jesus is buried (15:42–47)
9. The women find the empty tomb and hear that Jesus is risen (16:1–8)

IV. The Long Ending (16:9–20)

PART 1

PROLOGUE: "THE BEGINNING OF THE GOSPEL OF JESUS CHRIST, THE SON OF GOD" (1:1–13)

The Ministry of John the Baptist (1:1–8)

ESV

1 [1]The beginning of the gospel of
Jesus Christ, the Son of God.
[2]As it is written in Isaiah the prophet,
"Behold, I send my messenger
before your face,
who will prepare your way,
[3]the voice of one crying in the wilderness:
'Prepare the way of the Lord,
make his paths straight,' "
[4]John appeared, baptizing in the wilderness and proclaiming a baptism
of repentance for the forgiveness of
sins. [5]And all the country of Judea
and all Jerusalem were going out to
him and were being baptized by him
in the river Jordan, confessing their
sins. [6]Now John was clothed with
camel's hair and wore a leather belt
around his waist and ate locusts and
wild honey. [7]And he preached, saying,
"After me comes he who is mightier
than I, the strap of whose sandals I am
not worthy to stoop down and untie.
[8]I have baptized you with water, but
he will baptize you with the Holy
Spirit."

KJV

1 [1]The beginning of the gospel of
Jesus Christ, the Son of God;
[2]As it is written in the prophets,
Behold, I send my messenger before
thy face, which shall prepare thy way
before thee.
[3]The voice of one crying in the wilderness, Prepare ye the way of the
Lord, make his paths straight.
[4]John did baptize in the wilderness,
and preach the baptism of repentance
for the remission of sins.
[5]And there went out unto him all the
land of Judaea, and they of Jerusalem,
and were all baptized of him in the
river of Jordan, confessing their sins.
[6]And John was clothed with camel's
hair, and with a girdle of a skin about
his loins; and he did eat locusts and
wild honey;
[7]And preached, saying, There
cometh one mightier than I after me,
the latchet of whose shoes I am not
worthy to stoop down and unloose.
[8]I indeed have baptized you with
water: but he shall baptize you with
the Holy Ghost.

Introduction to 1:1–8 Mark begins the Gospel with the striking announcement that Jesus is the Son of God. This is the true beginning of the Good News for which the world has waited. With this, Mark begins a new Genesis. Now one who is true Man is also truly God. He is more than the image of God. He is God Himself and His coming is the best news that can be announced.

1:1 *beginning.* If, as many commentators believe, Mk is the first of the Gospels, then this is truly the beginning of the story of Jesus. Mark's beginning is like many biblical beginnings in that the story is already well along by the time we reach it. Much as Genesis tells only the adult lives of Noah, Abraham, and others, so Mk begins with Jesus already thirty years old. But we start with what is most important, His identity as the Son of God and John's announcement. *gospel.* This word comes from the Gk *euangelion* and means "good news." It is used here in two senses. It is a fulfillment of God's promises to Israel about forgiveness and new life through the Messiah. It is also an extended account of Jesus' teaching and healing ministry, His crucifixion, and resurrection from the dead. The Lutheran reformers note, "Sometimes [gospel] is used to mean the entire doctrine of Christ, our Lord. . . . this includes the explanation of the Law and the proclamation of the favor and grace of God His heavenly Father" (FC SD V 4). *Jesus Christ, the Son of God.* This is a major theme of Mk. He is announced the Father's Son at baptism (1:11), and again at the transfiguration (9:7). Demons recognize Him as divine (1:24; 5:7), and the centurion, following the crucifixion, declares Him to be the Son of God (15:39). Mark builds on the tension between those who clearly know Jesus as God versus His enemies and others who fail to recognize and follow Him (3:6; 10:22).

1:2–3 Two OT prophets are cited here, first Malachi and then Isaiah. The announcement of Jesus' divinity and mission has been long foretold. Luther writes,

> John the Baptist (preceding Christ) is called a preacher of repentance, but this is for the forgiveness of sins. That is, John was to accuse all and convict them of being sinners. This is so they can know what they are before God and acknowledge that they are lost. So they can be prepared for the Lord [Mark 1:3] to receive grace and to expect and accept from Him the forgiveness of sins. (SA III III 5)

Isaiah. Because he was Israel's preeminent prophet, only his name need be mentioned here. He is the only prophet quoted by name in Mark (cf. 7:6–7). Explaining how a passage from Malachi introduced a quotation from Isaiah, Bengel writes,

> Isaiah is more copious and better known, and his testimony, which has been quoted by Mark, used to be read in public on the Sabbath; and Mark here produces the testimony of Malachi in a kind of parenthetic way, equivalent to a supplement. (Bengel 498)

1:2 Malachi speaks of the messenger, John, who will announce the Lord Himself (Mal 3:1). *Messenger* in Gk is *angelos,* the same word used for angel. While Matthew and Luke begin with angels as messengers (Mt 1:20; Lk 1:11), Mark recalls John the Baptist as the bringer of the divine message.

1:3 *voice.* This recalls the creative voice of God which called all things into being, even when the world was shapeless and void (Gn 1:2). Now creation is to recognize its Creator's voice, even through a messenger, and acknowledge His step among them. This verse quotes Is 40:3 and brings that context of comfort, forgiveness and peace. S*traight* is the Gk word *euthus*, used here as an adjective meaning straight or orderly. This immediate path of Jesus will lead to Jerusalem and the cross. *Euthus* will be used frequently as an adverb meaning "immediately" or "straightaway." See 10:52 where the healed beggar Bartimaeus follows Jesus on the *way*, the same word used in 1:3, and that way leads directly to Jerusalem for Palm Sunday (11:1).

1:4 *John.* While Luke gives the vivid account of John's miraculous birth to Zechariah and Elizabeth (Lk 1:5–25, 57–66), Mark focuses on the adult John's work. *wilderness.* This is *eremos* in Gk, found also in 1:3. Prophets frequently ministered in the wilderness (e.g., Elijah; 1Ki 19:4–8). Here, wilderness probably refers to where the Jordan River empties into the Dead Sea. Jesus retreated to desolate places (*eremos*)—for prayer (1:35), and as a retreat with the disciples (6:31–32), but was also sent there by the Spirit for temptation (1:12–13). While the wilderness might have been a forbidding place for others, Jesus chose it as a place to demonstrate His power. Jesus, the perfect Son of God, doesn't begin His work in the ideal Garden of Eden, but the rugged wilderness. He starts His restoring work in a desert that recalls the curse of thorns, thistles, and a struggle to survive (Gn 3:17–19). *baptism.* Even before John the Baptist appeared, different groups within Judaism likely practiced baptism. Rabbinic literature mentions that Gentiles converting to Judaism were expected to undergo circumcision and a proselyte baptism, and to make an offering. These rites marked full acceptance into the community of God's chosen people. But John insisted that Jews needed to repent and be baptized, implying that they were no better than Gentiles. Unlike repeated ceremonial washing of people and utensils (7:3–4), this washing was done once. *repentance.* Repentance recognizes one's crooked path and turns to a new, straight direction. The prepared way of vv. 2–3 is found in each person's belief in the greater One to come and a readiness to follow His straight path. *forgiveness.* John's baptism removed the guilt of sin. Christian Baptism, which Jesus instituted after the resurrection (Mt 28:19–20), delivers this same blessing (Ac 2:38–39; 1Pt 3:21). This forgiveness allows anyone to be met by the Savior. His straight path of new life reaches each person, no matter how distant he or she appear to be. Melanchthon writes,

> We should not think improperly of [John's] Baptism or that it was merely a useless spectacle. And as for some saying that it signified only repentance, not remission [of sins], this is absurd. For the preaching of repentance without remission is heathenish and is a preaching of wrath and eternal death which is not proclaimed in the church without the preaching of remission. (Topics 264)

1:5 *all.* Mark speaks extravagantly here, catching the size and excitement of the crowds. The forbidding wilderness was no barrier for the Baptist's message. For this reason, Herod began to worry about his influence (6:17–20). The early success of John's preaching will be matched by the first reactions to Jesus in ch. 1, but then contrasted by the increased opposition from ch. 2 on. *confessing.* In Gk *exomologeo*, this is a public acknowledgment of the need for forgiveness and a belief that God provided it through this washing. This confession also looks ahead to the promise of the greater One promised by John. See the people dividing their attention from John while also scanning the crowd for a glimpse of the One who was to come.

1:6 *camel's hair . . . leather belt.* These were worn by Elijah and other prophets (2Ki 1:8). Jews of Jesus' day expected Elijah to return just before the Messiah came. Jesus later equated John's ministry with this expected return of Elijah (9:11–13; cf. 6:15). John's rugged appearance matches the wilderness setting, his serious message of repentance, and his modest standing compared to the coming Messiah. *ate locusts and wild honey.* John's diet was just as unusual as his attire. These foods functioned as "enacted prophecies" against the prevailing worldliness and excessive concern for creature comfort. Locusts are mentioned as food in the Cairo Damascus Document 12:14. They were cleansed by water or fire before being eaten. Honey recalls the eating of the scroll of the Word of God by Ezekiel (Ezk 3:3) which tasted like honey.

1:7 *preached.* In the first direct report of John's words, he turns all attention from himself to the One who is coming. John is the transparent voice (v. 3) that came more to be heard than seen. *He who is mightier.* Though John has gathered the crowds, the coming Messiah, the true Son of God, is mightier. While John comes to prepare a straight path, Jesus alone will walk a perfectly straight course without sin. Further, Jesus opens that path for all directly to the Father. Jesus later characterizes Himself as the One stronger than Satan, able to plunder Satan's holdings (3:23–27). *strap . . . untie.* Tying and untying the shoes of the master or a guest were among the lowliest tasks performed by slaves. Thus, John casts himself as a humble servant of the coming Messiah.

1:8 *water.* John's baptism with water recalls the promises of God to wash his people, "wash me thoroughly from my iniquity . . . wash me, and I shall be whiter than snow" (Ps 51:2, 7). The power of such cleansing is not within John or in the repentance of his hearers, but in the sacrificial life, death, and resurrection of Jesus. *baptize you with the Holy Spirit.* The gift of the Holy Spirit brings faith in Jesus which will be seen throughout the Gospel (Ac 11:17). Pentecost will be the clearest outpouring of the Spirit (Ac 2:33, 38). By the Word and Sacraments, the Spirit continues to work repentance and faith unto eternal life.

1:1–8 in Devotion and Prayer The Gospel begins with the best possible news from both Mark and John—the true Son of God is coming. He will follow a clear path in a barren world. Joyfully, all of us who are baptized have heard the call to repentance and have received the promised Holy Spirit, who continually forgives, restores, and focuses us on the splendor of Jesus' second coming. • Lord, remind us of the washing we received in Baptism, for through it Your Holy Spirit was poured into our hearts. Help us to continue to look for You and to You as the Greater One to come. Amen.

The Baptism and Temptation of Jesus (1:9–13)

ESV	KJV
9 In those days Jesus came from Naz- areth of Galilee and was baptized by John in the Jordan. 10 And when he came up out of the water, immedi- ately he saw the heavens being torn open and the Spirit descending on him like a dove. 11 And a voice came from heaven, "You are my beloved Son; with you I am well pleased." 12 The Spirit immediately drove him out into the wilderness. 13 And he was in the wilderness forty days, being tempted by Satan. And he was with the wild animals, and the angels were ministering to him.	9 And it came to pass in those days, that Jesus came from Nazareth of Galilee, and was baptized of John in Jordan. 10 And straightway coming up out of the water, he saw the heavens opened, and the Spirit like a dove descending upon him: 11 And there came a voice from heaven, saying, Thou art my beloved Son, in whom I am well pleased. 12 And immediately the spirit driveth him into the wilderness. 13 And he was there in the wilderness forty days, tempted of Satan; and was with the wild beasts; and the angels ministered unto him.

Introduction to 1:9–13 The identity of Jesus as the Son of God comes into clear focus here. When Jesus is found as one of the crowd being baptized, He is then set apart as the only Son. But His Baptism, which splits open the heavens, begins a difficult path. It is a straight course into the desert temptation. There He overcomes the fallen angel, Satan, while the heavenly angels minister to Him. Jesus stands as the connection between heaven and earth, man and God, the fallen and the saved.

1:9 *those days.* It is unclear how long John preached before Jesus came to him to be baptized, but it was long enough to have gathered some disciples (cf. Jn 1:35). The focus now shifts from John's ministry to that of Jesus. *Jesus came . . . baptized by John.* John predicted Jesus would be the one to baptize with fire, but He comes first here to be baptized with water. Matthew 3:13–15 records John's questioning and Jesus' insistence that this was needed to fulfill all righteousness. Mark leaves Jesus' baptism unexplained except that this is the first step of Jesus onto the prepared path of 1:2–3. When Jesus, as true man, steps forward to be baptized, He is instantly shown to be the true Son of God. Following the footsteps of others, He is baptized, but He brings the blessing of heaven to all who are baptized. Through Him, all who are baptized are accounted as having died and risen as He did (Rm 6:3–4). This moment between John and Jesus at the Jordan marks the decline of John and the rise of Jesus' power and ministry. Just as Moses' leadership ended with his death east of the Jordan (Dt 34:1–5) and Joshua began his ministry at the crossing of the Jordan (Jsh 3:1–8) John's prophetic leading comes to an end when Jesus enters the Jordan and the heavens break open.

1:10 *came up out of the water.* This suggests that Jesus was either immersed or sprinkled while standing in the river. *immediately.* In Gk this is *euthus* which occurs forty-one times in Mk but only ten additional times in the rest of the NT. It underlines both the urgency of Jesus' ministry and His march toward the cross. It is often used to begin a section, connecting the new action with what happened previously. It also shows the immediate reaction to the words of Jesus (1:18, 23; 5:29). It is used thirteen times in ch. 1 through 2:12 to show the opening power of Jesus' ministry (1:10, 12, 18, 20, 21, 23, 28, 29, 30, 42; 2:8, 12). It occurs in every chapter up to 11:3, is absent from 11:4–14:42, and then returns for four times in 14:43, 45, 72, and 15:1. There is a special correspondence between the first four and last four occurrences (see the notes on 15:1). *heavens being torn open.* The word for "torn open" in Greek is *skidzo* and is used in Mk only here and 15:38 where the Jerusalem temple curtain is torn at Jesus' death. *Spirit.* The Messiah would possess the Spirit of the Lord (Is 11:2; 42:1; 61:1). John had prophesied of Jesus baptizing with the Spirit (1:8) and it was the One on whom the Spirit descended who was to be known as the Son of God (Jn 1:32–33). Melanchthon writes,

> We should look carefully at this revelation, separate our thoughts about God and our worship of Him from pagan, Turkish, and Jewish notions, and worship only the eternal Father who has revealed Himself in sending His Son, Jesus Christ, and in showing His Holy Spirit. Let us worship the eternal Father together with the Son and the Holy Spirit as the Creator of all good things and the one who aids us. (Topics 14)

1:11 *voice.* While the Gospel begins with a prophetic voice in 1:2–3, fulfilled by John's ministry, the Father's own voice makes this the true beginning of the Gospel. The voice which created all things now points out Jesus as His own Son. In a fallen world, the Father can once again announce that there is One who is truly well pleasing. *beloved.* While Jesus is the beloved, this does not mean that He is the protected Son. Just as Abraham was to sacrifice his only son, whom he loved (Gn 22:2), so Jesus will be the beloved Son sent into a murderous world. (See the notes on 15:1–2.)

1:12 *immediately.* Straightaway, after being revealed as God's Son, Jesus is assaulted by Satan. The instantaneous beginning of the temptation contrasts with the timeless truth of Jesus being the Son of God and the lengthy forty days of testing. *drove.* The Gk word for drove out is also used for the casting out of demons (1:34, 39; 3:22). It shows the forceful entrance of Jesus into the wilderness and His willingness to take up the conflict. (See the notes on 14:72.)

1:13 *forty days.* The image of forty days spent in the wilderness recalls the forty years of Israel's exodus wandering and the forty days of Elijah's sojourn (1Ki 19:8). *tempted.* Jesus emerges from His time of testing perfectly, never falling to temptation in any way. By this, He does more than all who were tempted before Him. While on the cross, He will undergo greater temptations but will rise victorious over the grave. *with the wild animals.* Only Mk records this detail. It could be a reminder of the savage nature of the wilderness and the temptation. Or, it could forecast the messianic age when the wolf and lamb will be at peace (cf. Is 11:6–8; 65:25). Daniel's night of trial in the lion's den (Dn 6:22) is also in view. *angels.* Ministering angels contrast sharply with Satan, the fallen angel who brings temptation rather than help.

1:9–13 in Devotion and Prayer The Father declares Jesus is His Son as the Spirit descends on Jesus. Jesus' successful struggle against temptation in the wilderness prefigures His final victory at the cross over our ancient foe. From the days of Adam and Eve, we have continually fallen into Satan's traps. Jesus, after uniting Himself with fallen humans through Baptism, won a preliminary victory over the evil foe's temptations. At the cross, Jesus gained an even more wonderful victory for us. His resurrection proves that Satan cannot prevail. • Lord, when we are tempted, remind us of Your own struggles and trials. You have broken Satan's power once and for all. Amen.

The Reformers on the Gospel

From ancient times, Christians have regarded the Gospel as the one message of Christ. It is a fourfold Gospel in that the canonical Scriptures include the four books of the Gospels, from which ministers would read for the final Bible text during church services. Whether the text was taken from Matthew, Mark, Luke, or John, the reading was known as "the Gospel."

Ancient and Medieval Teaching

Before the Reformation, theologians as early as Justin Martyr (d. c. AD 165) described the Gospel as the "new law." The "old law" was the Law of Moses, which the teachings of Jesus surpassed. Unfortunately the term "new law" led to confusion so that obedience to Christ's teachings received emphasis over against the freeing and life-giving power of the Gospel described in the New Testament (e.g., Rm 1:16). This Law-based definition for the Gospel was what theologians like Luther, Calvin, and others would have learned in their early theological training. Luther commented on this issue at various points during his career.

A common theological textbook of that time was Peter Lombard's *Sentences*. In Book III, ch. XL (Migne PL, second series, 192:839–40) Peter explained that the Gospel had different promises than the Law. For contrast, he described the Law as earthly but the Gospel as heavenly. The Gospel, as the ultimate revelation, had a fullness that the Law of Moses lacked. With such points Peter accented the importance of the Gospel without overturning the notion that the Gospel was the new law.

Luther's Redefinition

Luther's study of Scripture led him to understand the Gospel differently. He based his definition on study of the Bible. In a corollary for the Lectures on Romans (1515–16), Luther described the Gospel in the following way:

> When the question is asked why the Gospel is called the Word of the Spirit, a spiritual teaching, the Word of grace and a clarification of the words of the ancient law and a knowledge that is hidden in a mystery, etc., the reply is that properly the Gospel teaches where and whence we may obtain grace and love, namely, in Jesus Christ, whom the Law promised and the Gospel reveals. The Law commands us to have love and Jesus Christ, but the Gospel offers and presents them both to us. Thus we read in Ps. 45:2: "Grace is poured abroad in Thy lips." Therefore, if we do not receive the Gospel for what it really is, then it is like the "written

> code." And properly speaking it is Gospel when it preaches Christ; but when it rebukes and reproves and gives commands, it does nothing else than to destroy those who are presumptuous concerning their own righteousness to make room for grace, that they may know that the Law is fulfilled not by their own powers but only through Christ, who pours out the Holy Spirit in our hearts.
>
> The real difference between the old and the new law is this, that the old law says to those who are proud in their own righteousness: "You must have Christ and His Spirit"; the new law says to those who humbly admit their spiritual poverty and seek Christ: "Behold, here is Christ and His Spirit." Therefore, they who interpret the term "Gospel" as something else than "the good news" do not understand the Gospel, as those people do who have turned the Gospel into a law rather than grace and have made Christ a Moses for us. (LW 25:326–27)

Notice that Luther at this early point might still use the term "new law," though he invested Gospel with important new meaning.

Melanchthon's Views

As a classicist, Melanchthon also defined the Gospel as the announcement of good news, citing Homer, Plutarch, and Cicero as historical examples. Drawing upon Luther's lectures on Romans, Melanchthon likewise defined the Gospel theologically by clearly distinguishing between the Law and the Gospel. He taught these doctrines of Scripture in that biblical order, rooted in the experience of Israel that John 1:17 described. These points did not change at all from the 1521 Loci Communes to Melanchthon's last edition (1559), where he wrote,

> The Law, as we have said above, is a teaching that requires perfect obedience toward God, does not freely remit sins, and does not pronounce people righteous, that is, acceptable before God, unless the Law be satisfied. Although it has promises, yet they have the condition that the Law must be fulfilled. On the contrary, the Gospel, even when it makes its proclamation about repentance and good works, nevertheless contains the promise of the benefits of Christ, which is the proper and primary teaching of the Gospel, and this must be separated from the Law. (Melanchthon 138–39)

Calvin's Views

Calvin tended to describe the Gospel broadly as repentance and forgiveness (Institutes 3.3.1, 19). This is an indication of how Calvin's emphasis on grace and the knowledge of God led him to see Law and Gospel not as distinct teachings but as expressions of the one covenant of grace, leading to knowledge of God. Similar to medieval theologians before him, Calvin came to see Law and Gospel as a continuum. One teaching ran into another; they were ultimately not distinguished or distinguishable since all came from God's grace.

Calvin began with Luther's order, Law then Gospel. However, he later concluded that the Gospel needed to be preached first, before the Law, since the primary purpose of the Law was to instruct the regenerate on how to behave. Faith in the Gospel as an invitation was evidence that a person was predestined to salvation, whereas rejection of the Gospel revealed that someone is predestined to damnation.

From these few examples, one can readily see how defining so basic a theological term as "Gospel" may reveal theological differences and emphases. ❧

Part 2

Jesus' Public Ministry of Preaching and Miracle Working (1:14–8:30)

Jesus Begins His Ministry in Galilee with Authority, but Meets Opposition (1:14–3:12)

Jesus proclaims the rule of God and calls disciples (1:14–20)

ESV

14 Now after John was arrested, Jesus came into Galilee, proclaiming the gospel of God, 15 and saying, "The time is fulfilled, and the kingdom of God is at hand; repent and believe in the gospel."

16 Passing alongside the Sea of Galilee, he saw Simon and Andrew the brother of Simon casting a net into the sea, for they were fishermen. 17 And Jesus said to them, "Follow me, and I will make you become fishers of men." 18 And immediately they left their nets and followed him. 19 And going on a little farther, he saw James the son of Zebedee and John his brother, who were in their boat mending the nets. 20 And immediately he called them, and they left their father Zebedee in the boat with the hired servants and followed him.

KJV

14 Now after that John was put in prison, Jesus came into Galilee, preaching the gospel of the kingdom of God,

15 And saying, The time is fulfilled, and the kingdom of God is at hand: repent ye, and believe the gospel.

16 Now as he walked by the sea of Galilee, he saw Simon and Andrew his brother casting a net into the sea: for they were fishers.

17 And Jesus said unto them, Come ye after me, and I will make you to become fishers of men.

18 And straightway they forsook their nets, and followed him.

19 And when he had gone a little farther thence, he saw James the son of Zebedee, and John his brother, who also were in the ship mending their nets.

20 And straightway he called them: and they left their father Zebedee in the ship with the hired servants, and went after him.

Introduction to 1:14–20 With John's arrest, the ministry of Jesus focuses on His own proclamation and His calling of the disciples. Jesus demonstrates His identity as the Son of God by both His own announcement of the Kingdom and His immediate calling of four disciples. Their instantaneous following demonstrates the power of Jesus' call.

1:14 *arrested.* The arrest of John is mentioned here in passing while 6:14–29 gives the full account of the prophet's imprisonment and execution. Mark's stress on Jesus demonstrates John's insistence that he, John, must decrease while Jesus increases (Jn 3:30). *Proclaiming.* This verb is used first of John's proclamation (1:4, 7), and will later describe the preaching of the disciples (6:12). With all three—John, Jesus, and the disciples—it is a message of repentance. Calvin writes,

> By the preaching of the Gospel the kingdom of God is set up and established among men, and that in no other way does God reign among men. Hence it is also evident, how wretched the condition of men is without the Gospel. (*Harmony* 1:225–26)

gospel. The blessed counterpart of repentance is the promise of God's forgiveness. Repentance is not merely turning from failed lives but is turning to the gracious promises of God fulfilled in Christ.

1:15 The Kingdom has come in the advent of Jesus. The verb "is" emphasizes completed action. He came to fulfill all of God's promises about the salvation of the world. Throughout His ministry, Jesus invites people to enjoy God's kind rule by living under His grace and righteousness. Concerning this rule, Luther writes:

> Once we have His Word, true doctrine, and true worship, we also pray that His kingdom may be in us and remain in us; that is, that He may govern us in this doctrine and life, that He may protect and preserve us against all the power of the devil and his kingdom, and that He may shatter all the kingdoms that rage against His kingdom, so that it alone may remain. (LW 21:146)

kingdom of God. Not a confined geographical territory, but wherever and whenever people are ruled by God through their faith in His Son. At Jesus' baptism, the Father spoke directly of Him as His Son. Now when Jesus first speaks, He directs people to the Kingdom and the offer of the gospel. *at hand.* With Jesus' public ministry, the Kingdom is here and now. *repent.* This echoes John's call for a public show of contrition and the start of a new way of life (1:2–4). Chemnitz writes,

> The Gospel uses the ministry of the Law, so that both repentance and remission of sins will be preached in the name of Christ. We must preserve this order [Law, then Gospel] in teaching the doctrine of justification, so that all . . . might hunger and thirst for righteousness, that is, that they might love, seek, embrace, and hold fast the grace and mercy of God which the Gospel offers and shows to us in Christ. (Chemnitz 8:1019)

Lutheran reformers also note, "In its proper sense, *Gospel* does not mean the preaching of repentance, but only the preaching of God's grace. This follows directly after the preaching of repentance" (FC SD V 6). *believe.* This is the first use of this crucial word in Mark. As a verb *pisteuo* or noun, *pistis* (faith), it will be often found in times of crisis (5:34, 36; 9:23–24; 10:52; 11:22–24). Jesus' ministry begins with the offer of faith in the Gospel. When He hangs on the cross, His opponents will scornfully offer to believe in Him if He would come down from the cross (15:32). Melanchthon writes,

> In this life, even in the saints, many sins remain which we must acknowledge and deplore with sincere repentance. Furthermore, there are others who have lapses contrary to conscience and are outside the grace of God, who, unless in this life they are converted to God, are running into eternal punishments and will forever be the enemies of God. Therefore, the chief voice of God is spoken in the church [Mark 1:15], "Repent and believe in the Gospel," that they may be delivered from eternal destruction. (Topics 285)

1:16 *Sea of Galilee.* Matthew 4:12–18 explains that after John's arrest, Jesus went north to Capernaum and the Sea of Galilee. Jesus will remain in this northern region for the first half of the Gospel until His prediction in 8:31 that He must be killed in Jerusalem. *Simon and Andrew.* While Jesus' ministry began in the broad stroke of public proclamation (1:14–15), His preaching next focuses on these two sets of brothers as examples of His work. This pattern of a broad work exemplified in a specific case occurs also with His healings. In 1:28 His fame is widespread and exemplified when He heals Peter's mother-in-law (1:30–31). Also in 1:32–34 all are healed (the cure of the lone leper is a key instance 1:40–42). *Simon.* Simon is given the name Peter (3:16) and will powerfully declare Jesus as the Christ

(8:29). Tradition explains that Mark heard the preaching of Peter in Rome and recorded that preaching as the basis for his Gospel. *net.* Circular and approximately 10–15 feet in diameter, it could be thrown either from the shore or from a boat.

1:17 Jesus' practice contrasts sharply with that of other rabbis, who were chosen by those who wanted to follow their teaching. Jesus, however, chose His followers. Like fishermen, Jesus' disciples were expected to draw others into the Kingdom. They will continue to fish, but now they will fish for the most important catch: men. Jesus promises nothing about the size of the catch, where they will work, or their profit. His call to discipleship was a personal tie to Himself. *fishers of men.* Jesus exemplifies this by going to the men Himself rather than waiting for them to come to Him. Though He has been identified as God's Son by the Father and has proclaimed the arrival of the Kingdom, He actively seeks these first disciples. Soon enough, His fame will force Him to retreat to the desert regions, 1:35, 45.

1:18 *immediately.* They respond without delay, showing their unquestioning response to Jesus' call. Given that the promises of God's kingdom were being fulfilled (v. 15), one might expect all people to respond to Jesus' invitation as Peter and Andrew did. "Immediately" will often be used in Mark to show the instantaneous power and effect of Jesus' call or healing (1:29, 42; 2:12; 5:29, 42; 7:35; 10:52). In Genesis 1, God spoke with immediate, creative power. So in Mark, when Jesus speaks, there is an immediate response. (See the notes on 14:45.)

1:19 *James . . . John.* These brothers are later called the "Sons of Thunder" by Jesus (3:17). Along with Peter, they formed an inner circle among the twelve apostles (cf. 5:37; 9:2; 14:33). *mending the nets.* This was a regular, somewhat unending task for fishermen. James and John are not fleeing the drudgery of this work, but are themselves caught by Jesus' intentional call.

1:20 *immediately.* Jesus calls without hesitation. See the notes on 14:43. *they left.* James and John's fishing business was large enough that it supported laborers from outside the family. Walking away from this business, therefore, meant leaving a successful trade and a relatively secure future. The followers of Jesus were not all desperately poor. Instead many, such as Matthew (2:14) and Zacchaeus (Lk 19:2–10), both wealthy tax collectors, and Nicodemus, a prominent Pharisee (Jn 3:1), had successful businesses and positions.

1:14–20 in Devotion and Prayer The Messiah delivers the forgiveness of sins and with it the hope of an eternal future with God. The invitation to discipleship given to the fishermen greets people today. Graciously Jesus calls, "Follow me." Thankfully, we are not left to our own devices in this regard. God's Holy Spirit, working through the Word and Sacraments, moves us to faithful discipleship and so also to eternal life. • Lord, thank You for calling us into Your kingdom, for which You declare us fit by Your grace. Keep us faithful in our calling, for Jesus' sake. Amen.

Jesus begins His ministry on a Sabbath Day in Capernaum (1:21–39)

ESV	KJV
[21]And they went into Capernaum, and immediately on the Sabbath he entered the synagogue and was teaching. [22]And they were astonished at his teaching, for he taught them as one who had authority, and not as the scribes. [23]And immediately there was in their synagogue a man with an unclean spirit. And he cried out, [24]"What have you to do with us, Jesus of Nazareth? Have you come to destroy us? I know who you are—the Holy One of God." [25]But Jesus rebuked him, saying, "Be silent, and come out of him!" [26]And the unclean spirit, convulsing him and crying out with a loud voice, came out of him. [27]And they were all amazed, so that they questioned among themselves, saying, "What is this? A new teaching with authority! He commands even the unclean spirits, and they obey him." [28]And at once his fame spread everywhere throughout all the surrounding region of Galilee. [29]And immediately he left the synagogue and entered the house of Simon and Andrew, with James and	[21]And they went into Capernaum; and straightway on the sabbath day he entered into the synagogue, and taught. [22]And they were astonished at his doctrine: for he taught them as one that had authority, and not as the scribes. [23]And there was in their synagogue a man with an unclean spirit; and he cried out, [24]Saying, Let us alone; what have we to do with thee, thou Jesus of Nazareth? art thou come to destroy us? I know thee who thou art, the Holy One of God. [25]And Jesus rebuked him, saying, Hold thy peace, and come out of him. [26]And when the unclean spirit had torn him, and cried with a loud voice, he came out of him. [27]And they were all amazed, insomuch that they questioned among themselves, saying, What thing is this? what new doctrine is this? for with authority commandeth he even the unclean spirits, and they do obey him.

John. 30Now Simon's mother-in-law
lay ill with a fever, and immediately
they told him about her. 31And he
came and took her by the hand and
lifted her up, and the fever left her,
and she began to serve them.
32That evening at sundown they
brought to him all who were sick
or oppressed by demons. 33And the
whole city was gathered together at
the door. 34And he healed many who
were sick with various diseases, and
cast out many demons. And he would
not permit the demons to speak,
because they knew him.
35And rising very early in the
morning, while it was still dark, he
departed and went out to a desolate
place, and there he prayed. 36And
Simon and those who were with him
searched for him, 37and they found
him and said to him, "Everyone is
looking for you." 38And he said to
them, "Let us go on to the next towns,
that I may preach there also, for that
is why I came out." 39And he went
throughout all Galilee, preaching
in their synagogues and casting out
demons.

28And immediately his fame spread abroad throughout all the region round about Galilee.

29And forthwith, when they were come out of the synagogue, they entered into the house of Simon and Andrew, with James and John.

30But Simon's wife's mother lay sick of a fever, and anon they tell him of her.

31And he came and took her by the hand, and lifted her up; and immediately the fever left her, and she ministered unto them.

32And at even, when the sun did set, they brought unto him all that were diseased, and them that were possessed with devils.

33And all the city was gathered together at the door.

34And he healed many that were sick of divers diseases, and cast out many devils; and suffered not the devils to speak, because they knew him.

35And in the morning, rising up a great while before day, he went out, and departed into a solitary place, and there prayed.

36And Simon and they that were with him followed after him.

37And when they had found him, they said unto him, All men seek for thee.

38And he said unto them, Let us go into the next towns, that I may preach there also: for therefore came I forth.

39And he preached in their synagogues throughout all Galilee, and cast out devils.

Introduction to 1:21–39 The pattern that we find in 1:10–20 continues here. There we find the authoritative voice of the Father (1:11), the conflict with Satan (1:12–13), and the gathering of the first disciples (1:16–20). So here Jesus begins to teach with a divine authority set apart from others (1:21–22). He is immediately confronted with a demon-possessed man. Jesus' casting out of the demon demonstrates His authority (1:23–28). And as a result of this and the healing of Peter's mother-in-law, Jesus gathers several large crowds (1:28, 32–33, 39). Yet the crowds cannot hold Him. Nor do the disciples set His course. On His own, He retreats to prayer with the Father and then moves ahead on His way.

1:21 *Capernaum.* This was an important city on the northwestern shore of the Sea of Galilee, noted for its fishing industry and trade. Jesus' miracles among the Gentiles of Capernaum become a particular offense to the people of Nazareth (Lk 4:23). *Sabbath.* In Ex 16:23, Moses initiates the Sabbath as a rest from work and travel, recalling God's rest upon the seventh day of creation. Jesus' teaching and healing ministry gave true rest to this congregation, to the demon-possessed man, and to all believers. Despite this, Jesus' teaching and healing on the Sabbath become an often-disputed point in Mark (2:24; 3:1–6; 6:2–6), resulting in His rejection by his enemies and hometown. *entered the synagogue.* Like other pious Jews, Jesus joined the community in corporate worship on the Sabbath. *synagogue.* The synagogue was a place primarily of prayer, the reading of Scripture, and teaching. *teaching.* Mark tells us more of what Jesus did than what he taught. However, the reaction of Jesus' opponents to His teaching plays a large role in Mark. In fact, Jesus' controversial teachings—most of which were accompanied by equally provocative actions—produce such outrage in His opponents (cf. 2:5–12, 16–17, 18–19, 23–28; 3:1–5) that they quickly plan to kill Him (3:6).

1:22 Jesus never used the prophetic formula "thus says the LORD." Also, in contrast to the scribes, whose authority derived from the teachings they received from their forefathers, Jesus spoke as one uniquely authorized by His Father in heaven. His authority was recognized apart from any demand by Himself or endorsement by other men. Just as He could call men to follow Him with only a few words (1:16–20), so He could impress the crowds with His distinctive teaching and power. *scribes.* Scribes were the professional interpreters of the Old Testament law, both reading the Law as it was found in the Old Testament and also interpreting how it might be kept. Their teachings were largely handed down through generations, in contrast to Jesus who pointedly separates Himself from their teaching (Mt 5:21, 27, 31, 33, 38, 42). The scribes, with one exception (Mk 12:28–34), are the chief opponents of Jesus' teaching.

1:23 *immediately*. Just as Jesus faced Satan immediately after His baptism, so also here He is met by a demon-possessed man at the beginning of His teaching ministry. Exorcisms, common in Mark (3:11; 5:13; 7:30; 9:25), reveal Jesus' identity and power. *unclean spirit*. At this crucial moment in Jesus' synagogue teaching, why should there be a demon-possessed man? We might expect a holy, secure setting for Jesus' teaching. Yet, this is the beginning of His ministry, a beginning that recalls Gn 3 and the surprising appearance of Satan in the Garden.

1:24 *us . . . us?* Either more than one demon possessed this man (as in 5:9) or Jesus' attack on one demon was a declaration of war on them all. *destroy*. After the outcome of the temptation (vv. 12–13; cf. Mt 4:10–11), the demons expect only punishment from Jesus. *Holy One of God*. This title is similar to "Son of God." In the ancient world, people believed that knowing the real name of a divine being gave one control over that deity. This demon knew Jesus' true identity and yet could not overcome Him. Though the demons often use messianic titles for Jesus, the disciples fail to do so until much later (8:29). Their slowness to recognize Jesus' messianic status is a major theme of Mark.

1:25 *Be silent*. Throughout Mark, Jesus silences demons (3:11–12; 5:13), and also commands those who have been healed to say nothing (1:44; 7:36–37). He distances Himself from the growing crowds (1:35; 4:36; 6:45–46; 8:9) and tells the disciples to say nothing of His divinity (8:30) or His transfiguration (9:9). Jesus' teaching and healing inevitably create crowds with varied motives. But He came not merely to feed the hungry each day, to do more miracles for miracle's sake, or to be insulated from His enemies by adoring crowds. He needed space and time alone to teach the disciples, and He needed finally to be rejected by the crowds in order to reach the cross.

1:26 *convulsing him and crying out*. The unclean spirit briefly shatters the relative peace and order of Jesus' teaching. But Jesus restores order to the synagogue, giving a peace that was all the greater for the conflict that had just passed.

1:27 *A new teaching with authority!* Jesus' teaching is supported by miraculous signs. Jesus needed no one to support the truth of His words. His actions spoke clearly for themselves. John (1:7–8) and God the Father (1:11) have affirmed His identity. Now even the silence following the departed demon speaks of His power. The crowd recognizes that He speaks, not as an echo of the scribes, but on His own terms. Chemnitz writes,

> The apostles therefore gathered passages that were repetitions of the most ancient statements, from the very beginning of time, to show that the doctrine of the Gospel was not something new. . . . Even the Son of God Himself, carefully sought testimonies to the doctrine of justification from almost every book of the Old Testament. (Chemnitz 8:839, 1038)

1:28 *at once.* The immediate result of Jesus' teaching and miracle is eager repeating of His words. The single voices of John and the Father are now vastly multiplied. *fame.* Jesus' incredible fame characterized the early days of His ministry (e.g., v. 45; 2:2; 3:8, 20; 4:1). The prepared way (1:2–3) could have easily been a smooth path of popularity if Jesus had so desired.

1:21–28 in Devotion and Prayer Jesus' authoritative teaching and power over the unclean spirits create an immediate stir among those watching Him in the early days of His ministry in Galilee. People continue to be amazed by Jesus' teaching, and yet many fail to depend on Him for life and salvation. By the power of His Word and Spirit, however, others are indeed brought into saving faith. • Lord Jesus, move us to an unquestioning trust and mature faith in You. By the power of Your Word and Spirit, make us steadfast in the hope of glory. Amen.

1:29 *He.* In the ESV text, "He" is used while the KJV text includes the disciples by the use of "they." It is perhaps likely that the plural "they" was the original text as it is found in a large number of manuscripts, including some very early ones. A copyist might have changed the plural pronoun to the singular in order to focus more on Jesus' actions. *house of Simon.* Rather than capitalize on His celebrity status (1:28), Jesus retreats to the relative privacy of Simon and Andrews's home, knowing also Simon's mother-in-law's need of healing. Private teaching of the disciples and the hidden healing of one was more important than the attention of the crowd. As noted in 1:25, Jesus frequently removes Himself from the spotlight to either pray alone or to be with the disciples.

1:30 *Simon's mother-in-law.* Jesus gives equal, immediate attention to her as He did to the man with the unclean spirit. She is the first of several women in Mark either healed (5:29, 41; 7:29) or noted for faith (12:42; 14:6). *fever.* Such a fever was often a symptom of a serious illness. *they.* This is at least Simon and the other three disciples called in 1:16–20, though the disciples at this point might have numbered more than these four. The complete list of Twelve comes in 3:16–19. Simon's relationship with Jesus was already close enough that he would welcome Him to his home, even despite his mother-in-law's illness. Likely Simon hoped for healing as he had just seen in the synagogue.

1:31 *lifted her up.* Unlike the exorcism of the demon in 1:25 which involved only His command, Jesus healed her with His touch. This pattern continues through the Gospel where often physical healing involved His touch (1:41; 5:27–29, 41; 6:5; 7:32–33; 8:23–25). On the other hand, exorcism of demons was done through His command only (1:25; 5:8; 7:29; 9:25). *she began to serve.* Her ready serving showed the complete and instantaneous nature of her recovery.

1:32 *sundown.* Because it was the Sabbath, the crowds waited until sunset to bring the ill, lest they break the commands against working on the Sabbath. *all who were sick or oppressed by demons.* The tide has turned. Following Jesus' healing of the demonized man, the report of His teaching and power went out to the entire region (1:28). Now this report washes back upon Jesus, bringing all who are ill. While Jesus avoids the empty praise of crowds—see the note on 1:25—He never refuses their authentic needs for either healing or food.

1:33 *whole city.* Just as in 1:5 where the whole country of Judea and all Jerusalem went to John, so, with similar hyperbole, the whole city comes to Jesus. This crowd gathering at the door will be seen again at 2:2 and similar crowds press upon Him at 3:32; 5:31; 6:34, 56; 10:46, culminating in Palm Sunday's crowd, 11:8–10.

1:34 *not permit . . . to speak.* For a brief moment, a demon might be marginally true (e.g. 1:24; 3:11; 5:7). Yet Jesus restricted the demons since their witness wouldn't be complete and couldn't be trusted. The witnesses to Jesus already stretch from the prophets through to John, the Father, and Jesus Himself. Shrieking demons have no place among them. *they knew Him.* At the end of this sentence, several manuscripts add "to be the Christ." This is clearly the point, given the knowledge of the demon in 1:24 and it would parallel Lk 4:41. However, neither the ESV nor KJV include these words as they are most likely well-intended additions to the text.

1:29–34 in Devotion and Prayer Jesus' first day of public ministry—the Sabbath—is a busy one. Given the endless series of things to which Jesus attends, we sometimes imagine that He is too busy for us and our problems. But Jesus knows and cares for each of us individually. He actually commands us to lay all our needs before Him and stands ever willing and able to help us. • Lord, teach us to turn to You in every need. Then give us grateful hearts so that, after receiving Your kindness and healing, we thank and serve You. Amen.

1:35 *very early in the morning.* This early morning setting is repeated in the calling of the disciples (Lk 6:12–13), the dawn of Good Friday (Mk 15:1), and the dawn of Easter (Mk 16:2). *desolate place . . . prayed.* Though He has been successful in Capernaum (vv. 29–34), and the city and the disciples soon search for Him, He nonetheless retreats into this forlorn place to pray. This wilderness (the same word as used in 1:3, 4, 12) is not here the place of temptation (1:12–13) but is a refuge from temptation. The Gospels repeatedly depict Jesus spending time alone in prayer (cf. 6:46; Lk 5:16; 6:12).

1:36 *searched.* The Gk word *katadioko* is used only here in the NT. It is an earnest pursuit by Simon and the others who rise early to track Him down in the dark. This is the first of many missteps by the disciples who are confused as to the nature of Jesus' ministry, His identity (4:41), His power (6:37; 8:21) and especially His determination to go to the cross (8:32; 9:32; 10:32). Jesus' patience is remarkable as He repeats His plan, explains His teaching (4:34), and endures with them to the end (15:43).

1:37 *everyone is looking for you.* Besides more teaching and miracles, this crowd likely wanted the reassurance of His presence, lest diseases and demons should return. This one region turning to Him forecasts His enemies' summary at the end of His ministry, "Look, the world has gone after Him" (Jn 12:19).

1:38–39 *preaching . . . casting out.* Jesus continued the pattern of teaching and miracles begun in 1:21. The central message is His identity as the Son by whom the kingdom of God has come. His miracles are the necessary confirmation of that message and an expression of His compassion. Jesus refused to stay within the friendly confines of Capernaum. He was committed to preaching, exorcising demons, and healing throughout Israel.

1:35–39 in Devotion and Prayer Though Jesus has much more to do among the people of Capernaum, He makes time for private devotion and then insists on moving on to visit other towns. His clear plan is the opposite of our tendency to lose focus, allow others to set our agenda, and put lesser things above what is most important. Given our weaknesses, it is reassuring that Jesus keeps things straight. His highest goal was, and is, to fulfill the Father's command that He save the lost. • Lord, preserve us from misplaced priorities. Keep us focused on Your Gospel, that we may know and do what is pleasing in Your sight. Amen.

Jesus continues His ministry amid growing opposition (1:40–3:6)

ESV	KJV
[40]And a leper came to him, imploring him, and kneeling said to him, "If you will, you can make me clean." [41]Moved with pity, he stretched out his hand and touched him and said to him, "I will; be clean." [42]And immediately the leprosy left him, and he was made clean. [43]And Jesus sternly charged him and sent him away at once, [44]and said to him, "See that you say nothing to anyone, but go, show yourself to the priest and offer for your cleansing what Moses commanded, for a proof to them." [45]But he went out and began to talk freely about it, and to spread the news, so that Jesus could no longer openly enter a town, but was out in desolate places, and people were coming to him from every quarter. 2 [1]And when he returned to Capernaum after some days, it was reported that he was at home. [2]And	[40]And there came a leper to him, beseeching him, and kneeling down to him, and saying unto him, If thou wilt, thou canst make me clean. [41]And Jesus, moved with compassion, put forth his hand, and touched him, and saith unto him, I will; be thou clean. [42]And as soon as he had spoken, immediately the leprosy departed from him, and he was cleansed. [43]And he straitly charged him, and forthwith sent him away; [44]And saith unto him, See thou say nothing to any man: but go thy way, shew thyself to the priest, and offer for thy cleansing those things which Moses commanded, for a testimony unto them. [45]But he went out, and began to publish it much, and to blaze abroad the matter, insomuch that Jesus could no more openly enter into the city,

many were gathered together, so that
there was no more room, not even at
the door. And he was preaching the
word to them. 3And they came, bringing to him a paralytic carried by four
men. 4And when they could not get
near him because of the crowd, they
removed the roof above him, and
when they had made an opening,
they let down the bed on which the
paralytic lay. 5And when Jesus saw
their faith, he said to the paralytic,
"Son, your sins are forgiven." 6Now
some of the scribes were sitting there,
questioning in their hearts, 7"Why
does this man speak like that? He is
blaspheming! Who can forgive sins
but God alone?" 8And immediately
Jesus, perceiving in his spirit that they
thus questioned within themselves,
said to them, "Why do you question
these things in your hearts? 9Which
is easier, to say to the paralytic, 'Your
sins are forgiven,' or to say, 'Rise, take
up your bed and walk'? 10But that you
may know that the Son of Man has
authority on earth to forgive sins"—
he said to the paralytic—11"I say to
you, rise, pick up your bed, and go
home." 12And he rose and immediately picked up his bed and went out
before them all, so that they were all
amazed and glorified God, saying,
"We never saw anything like this!"

13He went out again beside the sea,
and all the crowd was coming to him,
and he was teaching them. 14And as
he passed by, he saw Levi the son of
Alphaeus sitting at the tax booth, and
he said to him, "Follow me." And he
rose and followed him.

15And as he reclined at table in his
house, many tax collectors and sinners were reclining with Jesus and his

but was without in desert places: and
they came to him from every quarter.

2 1And again he entered into Capernaum after some days; and it was noised that he was in the house.

2And straightway many were gathered together, insomuch that there was no room to receive them, no, not so much as about the door: and he preached the word unto them.

3And they come unto him, bringing one sick of the palsy, which was borne of four.

4And when they could not come nigh unto him for the press, they uncovered the roof where he was: and when they had broken it up, they let down the bed wherein the sick of the palsy lay.

5When Jesus saw their faith, he said unto the sick of the palsy, Son, thy sins be forgiven thee.

6But there was certain of the scribes sitting there, and reasoning in their hearts,

7Why doth this man thus speak blasphemies? who can forgive sins but God only?

8And immediately when Jesus perceived in his spirit that they so reasoned within themselves, he said unto them, Why reason ye these things in your hearts?

9Whether is it easier to say to the sick of the palsy, Thy sins be forgiven thee; or to say, Arise, and take up thy bed, and walk?

10But that ye may know that the Son of man hath power on earth to forgive sins, (he saith to the sick of the palsy,)

11I say unto thee, Arise, and take up thy bed, and go thy way into thine house.

disciples, for there were many who
followed him. [16]And the scribes of
the Pharisees, when they saw that he
was eating with sinners and tax collectors, said to his disciples, "Why
does he eat with tax collectors and
sinners?" [17]And when Jesus heard
it, he said to them, "Those who are
well have no need of a physician, but
those who are sick. I came not to call
the righteous, but sinners."

[18]Now John's disciples and the Pharisees were fasting. And people came
and said to him, "Why do John's disciples and the disciples of the Pharisees
fast, but your disciples do not fast?"
[19]And Jesus said to them, "Can the
wedding guests fast while the bridegroom is with them? As long as they
have the bridegroom with them, they
cannot fast. [20]The days will come
when the bridegroom is taken away
from them, and then they will fast in
that day. [21]No one sews a piece of
unshrunk cloth on an old garment.
If he does, the patch tears away from
it, the new from the old, and a worse
tear is made. [22]And no one puts new
wine into old wineskins. If he does,
the wine will burst the skins—and
the wine is destroyed, and so are the
skins. But new wine is for fresh wineskins."

[23]One Sabbath he was going
through the grainfields, and as they
made their way, his disciples began
to pluck heads of grain. [24]And the
Pharisees were saying to him, "Look,
why are they doing what is not lawful on the Sabbath?" [25]And he said
to them, "Have you never read what
David did, when he was in need and
was hungry, he and those who were
with him: [26]how he entered the house

[12]And immediately he arose, took
up the bed, and went forth before
them all; insomuch that they were
all amazed, and glorified God, saying, We never saw it on this fashion.

[13]And he went forth again by the sea
side; and all the multitude resorted
unto him, and he taught them.

[14]And as he passed by, he saw Levi
the son of Alphaeus sitting at the
receipt of custom, and said unto
him, Follow me. And he arose and
followed him.

[15]And it came to pass, that, as Jesus
sat at meat in his house, many publicans and sinners sat also together
with Jesus and his disciples: for there
were many, and they followed him.

[16]And when the scribes and Pharisees saw him eat with publicans and
sinners, they said unto his disciples,
How is it that he eateth and drinketh
with publicans and sinners?

[17]When Jesus heard it, he saith unto
them, They that are whole have no
need of the physician, but they that
are sick: I came not to call the righteous, but sinners to repentance.

[18]And the disciples of John and of
the Pharisees used to fast: and they
come and say unto him, Why do the
disciples of John and of the Pharisees
fast, but thy disciples fast not?

[19]And Jesus said unto them, Can the
children of the bridechamber fast,
while the bridegroom is with them?
as long as they have the bridegroom
with them, they cannot fast.

[20]But the days will come, when the
bridegroom shall be taken away from
them, and then shall they fast in those
days.

[21]No man also seweth a piece of
new cloth on an old garment: else

of God, in the time of Abiathar the
high priest, and ate the bread of the
Presence, which it is not lawful for
any but the priests to eat, and also
gave it to those who were with him?"
27And he said to them, "The Sabbath
was made for man, not man for the
Sabbath. 28So the Son of Man is lord
even of the Sabbath."

3 1Again he entered the synagogue,
and a man was there with a withered
hand. 2And they watched Jesus, to see
whether he would heal him on the
Sabbath, so that they might accuse
him. 3And he said to the man with the
withered hand, "Come here." 4And
he said to them, "Is it lawful on the
Sabbath to do good or to do harm,
to save life or to kill?" But they were
silent. 5And he looked around at them
with anger, grieved at their hardness
of heart, and said to the man, "Stretch
out your hand." He stretched it out,
and his hand was restored. 6The Pharisees went out and immediately held
counsel with the Herodians against
him, how to destroy him.

the new piece that filled it up taketh away from the old, and the rent is made worse.

22And no man putteth new wine into old bottles: else the new wine doth burst the bottles, and the wine is spilled, and the bottles will be marred: but new wine must be put into new bottles.

23And it came to pass, that he went through the corn fields on the sabbath day; and his disciples began, as they went, to pluck the ears of corn.

24And the Pharisees said unto him, Behold, why do they on the sabbath day that which is not lawful?

25And he said unto them, Have ye never read what David did, when he had need, and was an hungred, he, and they that were with him?

26How he went into the house of God in the days of Abiathar the high priest, and did eat the shewbread, which is not lawful to eat but for the priests, and gave also to them which were with him?

27And he said unto them, The sabbath was made for man, and not man for the sabbath:

28Therefore the Son of man is Lord also of the sabbath.

3 1And he entered again into the synagogue; and there was a man there which had a withered hand.

2And they watched him, whether he would heal him on the sabbath day; that they might accuse him.

3And he saith unto the man which had the withered hand, Stand forth.

4And he saith unto them, Is it lawful to do good on the sabbath days, or to do evil? to save life, or to kill? But they held their peace.

[5]And when he had looked round about on them with anger, being grieved for the hardness of their hearts, he saith unto the man, Stretch forth thine hand. And he stretched it out: and his hand was restored whole as the other.
[6]And the Pharisees went forth, and straightway took counsel with the Herodians against him, how they might destroy him.

Introduction to 1:40–3:6 After the applauding crowds of ch. 1, Jesus encounters opposition throughout this section. He heals the leper but warns him to say nothing. Yet His fame grows and forces the Pharisees and others to confront Jesus for His healing, His Sabbath observances, and His power as the Son of God. Jesus walks a narrow path. He continues to heal and forgive, but does these things in such a way that His enemies will condemn Him (3:6). Only the Son of God has the power to forgive, heal, and command the Sabbath as Jesus does while also harnessing the plans of His enemies.

1:40 *leper.* The leper's approach broke the command that he should be far removed from others. Leviticus 13:45–46 describes the state of the leper beside the torment of the disease: torn clothes, loose, unruly hair, dwelling alone outside camp, crying "unclean" to warn others. *if you will, you can make me clean.* The leper correctly saw no barrier in his illness, his past, or his distance from others. The only limit would be Jesus' intention. The leper's bold approach is repeated often in Mark (2:4; 5:28; 7:25; 10:13, 48). Jesus' mercy was recognized by those in need, apart from any invitation from Him.

1:41 *pity.* The Gk word for "pity" (*splagchnidzomai*) refers to the center of emotion, the depth of one's feeling and pity. Only Mark includes this word here (cf. Mt 8:3; Lk 5:13). Mark records it also as the reason for Jesus' feeding of the 5,000 (6:34), feeding the 4,000 (8:2), and the casting out of a demon (9:22). *touched him.* Jesus showed His fearless compassion with this touch. The leper likely long remembered this touch and made it a central part of his retelling of the miracle. The healing touch of Jesus is repeated often in specific instances (5:28; 7:33; 8:22), and as a general method of His healing (6:56).

1:42 *immediately.* As expected, the healing was instantaneous, undoing in a moment the slow decay of years. This parallels the coming forgiveness of sins for the paralytic, God's immediate cleansing of a lifetime (2:8, 10–12).

1:43 *sternly charged.* This is the unusual Gk verb *embrimaomai.* It denotes a strong emotion, often of warning or anger, but also of deep feeling (see Jesus' feelings at the tomb of Lazarus, Jn 11:33, 38). It stands opposite the compassion of 1:41. Jesus heals the man with mercy but directs his future steps with a stern command.

1:44 Jesus sent this man to the priest so that he might be officially pronounced clean. Jesus' touch thus resulted in two restorations: first, the man was returned to physical wholeness; second, he resumed his rightful place in society. *say nothing.* While some suggest that Jesus was using some reverse psychology, actually wishing the man to speak, Jesus had no need for duplicity. Already the news of His work was spreading (1:28, 33, 37), and with that would come increased opposition. Regarding Jesus' command to remain silent, Wesley wrote, "Our blessed Lord gives no such charge to *us.* If he has made us clean from our leprosy of sin, we are not commanded to conceal it. On the contrary, it is our duty to publish it abroad" (Wesley 101). *offer . . . for a proof.* Refers to the offerings and rites by which a leper was pronounced clean and allowed to return to society. *proof to them.* Jesus wanted the priests to know He had power to heal and was abiding by OT Law.

1:45 *spread the news.* Despite Jesus' warning (v. 44), the man spoke of Him everywhere. This word, *diaphamidzo,* is used only three times in the NT (Mt 9:31; 28:15; Mk 1:45), and means to thoroughly tell or discuss. The leper told every detail to everyone he could find. He likely reveled in the chance to be among people again and to explain his healing. *Could no longer openly enter.* What a contrast between the leper and Jesus. The leper, once kept away from society, is now the center of these crowds while Jesus, the Lord of all, is driven to the wilderness. *every quarter.* Jesus' incredible popularity will soon cause conflict with the scribes and Pharisees (2:1–3:6).

1:40–45 in Devotion and Prayer When a leper seeks Jesus' help, the Lord not only heals him but also makes sure that the man is restored to his rightful place in society. People still experience alienation from family, church, and the larger community. But Jesus' healing can remedy such alienation. His grace makes peace with God, restores our broken relationships, and puts us right with one another. • Lord, thank You for Your healing power. Hear our cries for help, heal us according to Your wisdom, and then move us to tell others what You have done. Amen.

2:1 *returned.* Jesus came back from the desolate region of 1:45, but there was no rest from the crowds. The broadcasting of His work that He prohibited in 1:44 had continued with the news that He was home. We can understand the joy of the people in Capernaum, saying "He's back!" All Christians want to hear those words concerning His final return to earth. *at home.* Jesus' practice of preaching within a domestic setting, as described here, set a precedent for His followers. For the next three hundred years, Christian worship services usually took place in house churches. *Capernaum.* See notes on 1:21.

2:2 *straightaway many were gathered together* (KJV). The King James captures the tone of this gathering. The predicted straight paths of 1:2–3 were in effect here as the crowd hurried by the most direct route to His door. *preaching the word.* As with 1:21, the teaching is summarized by one verse while the miracle that follows is reported in detail. Similarly, a whole day's teaching (6:34) and three day's instruction (8:2) are compressed to one verse while the feeding of the 5,000 and 4,000 which follow are described in detail. Mark gives a relatively full account of Jesus' teaching only in ch. 4 with the parables and ch. 12–13 with His teaching during Passion Week. *not even at the door.* Mark uniquely adds this second negative, excluding even room at the door. This might be a vivid echo of Peter's preaching upon which Mark may have based his account.

2:3 *paralytic.* The man is a specific example of the many ill who were brought to Jesus in 1:32. But this man receives more than just healing and so his case needs to be told more fully. He could not move without the help of his friends. The crowd either could or would not move enough for them to enter, likely claiming that they had been there first. No one saw the paralytic as the next miracle of Jesus, or they likely would have made room for him as they must have done when he left (2:12). They lack the compassion and curiosity to make a way for him at the start, but astonishment clears a path at the end.

2:4 *removed the roof.* This would have resulted in debris and dust flying everywhere. Between the press of the crowd and the damage being done to the roof, the scene takes on elements of chaos and even danger. *bed.* This stretcher-like mat would have needed a sizable hole to let the man to be lowered full length.

2:5 *saw their faith.* What faith these men had! They trusted several characteristics of Jesus: His power to heal, His willingness to do so immediately upon having their friend before Him, and His patience in being interrupted while teaching. Few teachers would welcome the roof being torn open above their heads, but Jesus commends the men for their bold faith. When they let their friend down, we can imagine that they dropped the ropes from their hands. Their work was done. Jesus will have their friend walk out. Though Christian teaching often emphasizes—and rightly so—that people need to have personal faith, this story illustrates how one person acting in faith can benefit another. The four friends seek blessings for the paralytic because they believed Jesus could heal him. *Son.* This warm greeting implies affection and familial concern. *your sins are forgiven.* Given the widespread belief in Jesus' day that people became ill as the result of some personal sin, this word of grace is noteworthy. See the debate over whose sin caused a man to be born blind (Jn 9:1–5). As noted in Jn 9, such illness cannot be attributed to the sin of parent or child but is rather an opportunity for God's work (Jn 9:3). Jesus forgave the sin for the sake of the man's spiritual needs and to define Himself as the only God who can forgive sins.

2:6 *scribes.* See the note on 1:22 for background on the scribes. While Jesus' teaching had been compared to the scribes, this is the first of the many coming face-to-face conflicts with the scribes which will lead to the cross. *questioning in their hearts.* The word for "questioning" in Greek, *dialogidzomai,* means to reason or argue. The scribes debate His words but do so silently, each man within himself. This is the first instance of this word which will later introduce debates within the disciples (8:16–17; 9:33) and with Jesus' enemies (11:31). In each case, Jesus is fully aware of the debate which they imagine is hidden from Him.

2:7 *blaspheming!* The charge of blasphemy centers on Jesus taking the role of God. The authority of Jesus is the point of the first comparison with the scribes (1:22), and will continue repeatedly, culminating in a similar question of His authority (11:28–33). *Who* *can forgive sins but God.* The scribes' observation is correct and, unknown to them, agrees with the theme of Mk 1:1. Only God can forgive sins, and Mark has made it clear from the beginning that this is the Son of God. Here is the message of forgiveness that only He can bring. The scribes correctly note that sin is not merely between men but is an offense against God (Ps 51:4).

2:8 *immediately.* Jesus' had foreseen this conflict and knew all their thoughts without delay or any outward sign. *perceiving.* See the parallel verse that summarizes all of Jesus' familiarity with man: "[Jesus] knew all people and needed no one to bear witness about man, for He Himself knew what was in man" (Jn 2:24–25). Jesus' knowledge of His opponents' inner thoughts reveals His supernatural perception and shows His divinity. Ironically, His divine power is the very thing being called into question (v. 7). The all-knowing God, who pierces the hearts and minds of His enemies, graciously hides His eyes from the sins of this man. See Ps 51:9; 103:12 for God's hiding of our sins.

2:9 *Which is easier.* The scribes might have imagined that they would debate Jesus on some point of His teaching and His handling of the traditions they taught. But Jesus has gone far beyond these debatable points of Law. He leads them to two actions only God can do, healing and forgiving. While forgiving has the greatest significance, both are impossibly far from the power of the scribes. *easier.* The word for "easier" is used also in Mk 10:25 in comparing the ease of a camel going through a needle and the entrance of a rich man passing into heaven. In 2:9, the point is that the more difficult must be done to demonstrate the certainty of the easier. Therefore, the more difficult in its immediacy and public nature is the healing. Jesus does this to demonstrate His power, not suggesting that healing is the more vital or important. *sins are forgiven.* The conflict with the scribes focuses on Jesus' two natures. His enemies insist that He is only a man but we see that He does the work of God alone. Ambrose observes the need for both Jesus' human and divine natures to bring about forgiveness: "With His blood, then, as man, the Lord redeemed us, Who also, as God, has forgiven sins" (*NPNF*2 10:247).

2:10 *that you may know.* Jesus' coming work is both Law and Gospel. It is a warning to His enemies who should recognize that Jesus is the Son of God Himself. Yet, it is primarily the Gospel message begun in Mk 1:1. The Son of God has come to forgive sins with full, divine authority. *Son of Man.* This is the first time that Jesus uses this title in Mk. It will appear repeatedly in His predictions of His death (8:31; 9:9, 31; 10:33; 14:21, 41) and also in prophecies of His resurrection (9:12), and final return (8:38; 13:26; 14:62). It is used in regard to His authority (2:28), but, despite His glory and authority, "the Son of Man came not to be served but to serve" (Mk 10:45). The background of the phrase is Dn 7:13–14 in which the Son of Man descends with the clouds while all power is given to Him. The title "Son of Man" in Mark speaks of Jesus' divine nature, His authority over all creation, His willingness to be sacrificed and then raised again.

2:11 *I say to you, rise.* Jesus turns from the scribes to focus again on the paralyzed man. He has the man walk immediately with no delay. Ambrose says: "He charged the man to perform an action of which health was the necessary condition, even while the patient was yet praying a remedy for his disease" (*NPNF*2 10:269).

2:12 *immediately.* Jesus' immediate knowledge of His enemies' thoughts (2:8) is balanced by His immediate power of sending the man out. As the man pressed through the crowd, people likely stepped aside in awe, making a new, clear path where there had been none (2:2). The man's exit provided undeniable confirmation that Jesus fully healed him. *glorified God.* This focus on God is fitting since the miracle centered on Jesus' identity as God Himself.

2:1–12 in Devotion and Prayer In the presence of many who doubt Jesus' ability, He forgives and heals a paralyzed man simply by speaking the Word. Today, there are still some who doubt the power of Jesus' Word. But the authority of Jesus to forgive sins is forever His as the Son of God. He proves that power by raising more than just this paralytic—by raising Himself from the dead. • Lord, You can do all things. Give us such a bold confidence in You that even those around us, many of whom are paralyzed by sin and doubt, may be blessed through our steadfastness. Amen.

2:13 *teaching.* Jesus resumes the pattern of teaching to the crowd, summarized in a single verse (1:21, 39; 2:2). As before, the focus will shift quickly to an individual as a demonstration of His power and message.

2:14 *Levi.* Also named Matthew (Mt 9:9), Levi is the example of Jesus' teaching and mercy. While most manuscripts have the name "Levi," a few have "James," likely as an echo of 3:18 where the disciple James is also known as the son of Alphaeus. Since they were both sons of Alphaeus, it is possible that the two disciples, Matthew/Levi and James, were brothers. However, since no mention is made of this relationship, they were likely unrelated, sons of two different fathers. *tax booth.* Levi had long collected taxes in Capernaum. Such collaboration with the occupying Romans was considered traitorous by most Jews. *follow me.* Jesus gave Levi the same short command as given to Simon and Andrew (1:17), with the same immediate response.

2:15 *reclined at table.* Jesus' brief passing of Levi's table is contrasted by His willingness to remain and become identified with Levi's home. Just as Simon Peter's home became an early site of Jesus' work (1:29), so Levi's home becomes the soon-crowded center of His outreach. While James and John, upon being called to follow Jesus, left their father and servants (1:20), Levi, when called, gathers his associates to meet Jesus. *tax collectors and sinners.* The combination of tax collectors and sinners recalls Mt 5:46 where tax collectors are an example of the most selfish. This is the first public gathering of Jesus with tax collectors and sinners, but such meals will characterize His ministry (cf. Lk 15:1–2).

2:16 *scribes of the Pharisees.* This unusual phrase is likely correct, though many later manuscripts have the more common phrase "scribes and Pharisees." The enemies of Jesus will continue to increase throughout chs. 2 and 3, including the scribes, Pharisees (2:24), and Herodians (3:6). Notice that they ask Jesus' disciples about His actions rather than asking Jesus Himself. Perhaps they wished to emphasize their separation from the tax collectors by not approaching Jesus while He was with them. Jesus' previous healing and authoritative teaching may have made the disciples easier targets. *eating.* Pious Jews, especially Pharisees, would not associate with Gentiles, tax collectors, or openly wicked Jews. Sharing a table with sinners was regarded as a defiling act (Lk 15:1–2; Ac 11:3). In contrast, Jesus had touched the leper when healing him (1:41), and will teach that a person is made unclean by what is within himself, not by what he or she touches (7:18–20). Jesus' pure divinity was not tainted by temptation by Satan in the wilderness (1:12–13). Furthermore, He has just shown His cleansing power of forgiveness (2:9–12).

2:17 *not . . . the righteous but sinners.* Just as physicians must have contact with the diseased, so also Jesus' ministry obliged Him to associate with sinners and social outcasts. He was known by the company He kept, except that He came not to keep them as sinners, but to redeem and cleanse them.

2:13–17 in Devotion and Prayer Jesus outrages His critics by calling Levi the tax collector to follow Him, then eats with a houseful of equally "defiled" people. This story invites us to reflect: am I more like the manifest sinners of this story or like those who criticize Jesus' openness with the unworthy? Either way, we stand in need of forgiveness. Thankfully, Jesus brings healing and forgiveness to all, even manifest sinners and smug hypocrites. • Lord, preserve us from both our crass and hidden sins. Grant us a rich measure of Your grace, that others may see Your mercy and be drawn to your healing and fellowship. Amen.

2:18 *Pharisees.* Originally, the name of this party meant "the separate ones." What separated the Pharisees from other Jews was their rigorous interpretations and strict observance of the Jewish Law. Jesus pointed out the vain hypocrisy of their outward acts. He called them whitewashed tombs: beautiful outside but dead within (Mt 23:27–28). *fasting.* Pharisees fasted twice weekly on the second and fifth days of the week, according to the *Didache* (*ANF* 1:174). This went far beyond the required annual fast (affliction) on the Day of Atonement (Lv 23:26–32; Ac 27:9) and the few mentioned in Zec 8:19. Fasting, therefore, was an important aspect of the Pharisees' ritual observance. It appears that some of John's disciples, upon returning to Galilee, also followed this practice. While the two events are separate, Matthew's meal with Jesus (2:15–17) might have been on one of those days, thereby prompting this question. His opponents, grasping for any fault, oppose Him first for eating with the wrong people and now for eating on the wrong day.

2:19 *wedding guests.* John the Baptist described himself as a friend of the bridegroom (Jn 3:29) while in Hos 2:16 God says that He will be Israel's husband. Jesus uses similar language. Fasting is a time for sorrow or penitence, whereas feasting is associated with joy. Jesus emphasizes that feasting is proper because the Messiah (the Bridegroom) is now present among God's people. The exuberant joy of the first days of Jesus' ministry was completely appropriate and pleasing to Him.

2:20 *taken away.* Jesus hastens to add that He will someday be taken away from them (after His death, resurrection, and ascension), and then God's people will have occasions to fast. While this comparison seems clear, it is likely that these words were a mystery to His hearers. In a similar way, Jesus' clear prediction of His death and resurrection and His journey towards the cross will be a mystery to the disciples (8:32; 9:32; 10:32).

2:21 To further illustrate the theme that someone and something new has come, Jesus tells these two parables of the patch and the wineskin. The patch was new cloth and yet unshrunken through wear and washing. When it became wet, it would then shrink away from the original cloth. It was useless to put a new patch on old cloth, to attach a new teaching onto the old tradition of the Pharisees and scribes. They cannot move with the new teaching and will be lost.

2:22 *new wine into old wineskins.* Returning closer to the opening theme of feasts and fasts, Jesus reminds His listeners that new wine, still fermenting and expanding, cannot be held by brittle wineskins. Sadly, both wine and wineskins will be lost. So in Passion week, Jesus will go to His death while the scribes and Pharisees will continue to teach in a Jerusalem that is about to be lost (12:9; 13:2). Thankfully, when all seems completely lost, Easter brings His resurrection which saves the world. The immediacy of these two brief parables suggests that Jesus could have gone on to find innumerable examples to illustrate this or any point. All of creation held parables waiting for His explanation.

2:18–22 in Devotion and Prayer Jesus stresses that the time of fulfillment has arrived, and thus totally new ways of thinking and acting are in order. The same dynamic is at work in us. It will not suffice to patch some little bit of the Gospel onto our existing lifestyle and expect it all to hold together. Thankfully, the Lord offers such surpassingly great promises that the old is made obsolete. That is what Paul meant when he said, "If anyone is in Christ, he is a new creation" (2Co 5:17). • Lord, so fill us with the surpassingly great promises of Your Gospel that we count all else as loss for the greater hope of attaining eternity with You. Amen.

2:23 *Sabbath.* This is the second conflict that comes on a Sabbath with one more soon to follow (1:21; 3:1). While the first and the third involve healing of men, this second conflict is outside the synagogue and deals with eating, as did the previous discussions (2:15–17, 18–20). *pluck heads of grain.* Deuteronomy 23:25 allowed a traveler to eat from a grain field, as the disciples were doing, but prohibited someone from gathering more than he could hold and eat immediately. Also, he couldn't bring a sickle into someone's field and load up his bag. Exodus 34:21 said that no work, even harvesting, was to be done on the Sabbath. The Pharisees equated this momentary gleaning of a handful of grain with the day-long harvesting prohibited in Ex 34.

2:24 *they.* While previous conflicts had centered on Jesus' actions, here the Pharisees attack the disciples. Either Jesus was not gleaning Himself, or the disciples appeared to be easier targets. *not lawful.* The Gk word for lawful is *eksestin*, and is used for the first time here. It will introduce a number of conflicts between Jesus and His opponents (3:4; 10:2; 12:14). It will also bring up the conflict that caused John the Baptist's death (6:18). Overall *lawful* might be the theme of the entire body of conflicts in 2:1–3:6. His opponents complain repeatedly, "You can't do that!" But their definition of what is lawful and Jesus' true definition are widely different. Calvin writes,

> This shows clearly the malicious and implacable nature of superstition, and particularly the proud and cruel dispositions of hypocrites, when ambition is joined to hatred of the person. It was not the mere affectation of pretended holiness . . . that made the Pharisees so stern and rigorous; but as they expressly wished to carp at everything that Christ said or did, they could not do otherwise than put a wrong meaning in cases where there was nothing to blame, as usually happens with prejudiced interpreters. (*Harmony* 2:47–48)

2:25 *Have you never read.* Jesus begins with a direct attack on the Pharisees since they are proud of their ability to read and hold that knowledge over others. Jesus' question reduces them to illiterate novices.

2:26 *ate the bread of the Presence.* Loaves were put out each week and, when replaced at the end of the week, were eaten by the priests (Ex 25:30; 1Sm 21:6). This was the restricted bread which David gave to his men. The question was not whether the bread could be eaten, but rather who could eat it. Jesus' example shows that the bread, and all other parts of the Sabbath and Temple, were for the well-being of all in need.

2:27 *Sabbath was made for man.* Jesus clarifies God's purpose in establishing the Sabbath: this day of rest was primarily intended to restore people, not make them slaves of arbitrary rules. In worship

God comes to instruct and feed us with His Word and Sacraments. Luther reflects on this, saying, "Man was especially created for the knowledge and worship of God; for the Sabbath was not ordained for sheep and cows but for men, that in them the knowledge of God might be developed and might increase" (LW 1:80).

2:28 Jesus' reason for referring to the story of David eating the holy bread (vv. 25–26) comes clear: the Lord of the Sabbath—Jesus—is greater than King David. Over the course of ch. 2, Jesus takes on the exclusively divine work of forgiveness (2:7–10), shows that He is free from following the practice of John (2:18), and parallels His actions with that of David. This bold claim to divinity is not lost on Jesus' critics, as 3:2, 6 show. Bengel notes that Jesus' remark had a present sense for those who first heard Him but a prophetic sense as well:

> [Jesus meant that] Whatever right as regards the Sabbath any man hath, I also have. The more august sense, though one kept hidden . . . is this, The [goal] of the institution of the Sabbath is the [welfare] of man as to his soul and body. The Son of Man is bound to ensure this salvation; and, in order to bring about this end, He . . . has also authority over all things, and expressly over the Sabbath. (Bengel 506)

Son of Man. This is the second use of this phrase, found here, as is typical, in a conflict setting. See the note on 2:10.

2:23–28 in Devotion and Prayer When the Pharisees accuse Jesus' disciples of violating the Sabbath, Jesus uses the opportunity to claim divine authority and assert His messianic status. Sadly, there are people today who still level criticisms like the Pharisees of old, censuring Jesus' followers when they really wish to criticize the authority and status of the Lord. But neither Jesus nor His Church can be dismissed. Through these same disciples, Jesus spread the good news of peace, rest, and comfort. Jesus defends His own divinity, but does so by providing for the good of His followers. • Lord, defend Your people from those who hate You and do harm to Your Church. Help the Church to see that the battle is Yours and that You can do all things. Amen.

3:1 *entered the synagogue*. Jesus enters the synagogue again, knowing the dangers waiting for Him. Jesus said that the physician needed to go to the ill (2:17) and He fulfills that here by seeking the place of the physically and spiritually ill. His daring to enter the synagogue also demonstrates the previous point that He is the Lord of the Sabbath and therefore also of the synagogue (2:28). See the note on 2:23 concerning conflicts on the Sabbath. *withered.* This word, *eksaraino* means to dry up or to wither. It is used of plants dried beyond any use (4:6; 11:20–21) and also describes the ending of the woman's bleeding (5:29). The man's hand was reduced in size and ability, most likely by an accident or illness.

3:2 *they.* Presumably the Pharisees from vv. 23–28 who accused Jesus' disciples of breaking the Sabbath. *watched Him.* This word, *paratareo,* is used in the Gospels only to describe the scheme-filled watching of Jesus by His enemies (Mk 3:2; Lk 6:7; 14:1; 20:20). Sadly, while they watch Him closely, their plot against Him blinds them. They can't see His identity as the Son of God or His purpose of bringing the good news (1:1). *accuse Him.* The Pharisees hoped to catch Jesus healing and then accuse Him of breaking the Sabbath. In so doing, they would ironically prove the very point they were trying to deny, that Jesus was divine. Here the issue is when Jesus does miracles. Next the argument will shift to how He does them (3:22–30).

3:3 *come here.* Jesus calls the man into the middle of the synagogue. This miracle will not be done privately nor will there be any caution against speaking of it later. Jesus knows the plot against Him and He intends to meet His enemies directly. This is a long, bold step on the road leading straight away to the cross.

3:4 *Is it lawful.* This was a rhetorical question, since everyone knew that Jewish tradition allowed for the Sabbath to be broken if life was threatened. See 2:24 for notes on the word *eksestin,* "lawful." *to save life or to kill.* Jesus raises the question to a level beyond the healing of this man. The man likely had his withered hand for some time and was not in mortal danger from it. Jesus however takes the question of the Sabbath's purpose to an extreme case of life and death. *they were silent.* Their silence shows the weakness of their argument. Their minds were closed to any discussion and fixed on His guilt.

3:5 *looked around.* This word, *periblepomai,* is used six times in Mark. He uses it generally of Jesus, often at the beginning of a teaching moment (3:34; 5:32; 10:23; 11:11). It also describes the searching look of the disciples after the Transfiguration (9:8). *anger, grieved.* Unlike Matthew and Luke, Mark tends to emphasize Jesus' emotions (cf. 7:34; 8:12; 10:21). Jesus' scanned the crowd with a hard, yet sorrowful look. *hardness of heart.* Jesus' adversaries did not care for the disabled man. So intent on being right, they were dreadfully wrong. They would not see that Jesus had come to have mercy on all people, including them. *restored.* The hand, restored to full size and power, began to function normally.

3:6 *immediately.* It would be expected that the "immediately" would occur in 3:5 to describe the instant healing of the man. However, the key point is not that Jesus can heal in an instant, even an illness that has lingered for years. Rather, the crucial action is the instant rejection of His miracle and the plot against Him. *Pharisees . . . held counsel with the Herodians.* Pharisees would not normally ally themselves with the Herodians, since they considered Herod's family to be an illegitimate dynasty. However, a shared hatred for Jesus drove these two parties together. *counsel.* Gk *symboulion*, appears in Mk only here and in 15:1, when the Jews take counsel against Jesus on Good Friday. Note how quickly Jesus' enemies oppose Him in Mark!

3:1–6 in Devotion and Prayer Again, Jesus demonstrates His authority over the Sabbath, this time by restoring a man's hand. He knows all our burdens and desires to grant us rest. His gift of rest and healing came at the cost of His own life and yet He never shrank away from that price. • Lord, lead us to take Your Word to heart. By Your Holy Spirit, work in us a faith that knows You as the way, the truth, and the life. Amen.

Large crowds follow Jesus (3:7–12)

ESV	KJV
7 Jesus withdrew with his disciples to the sea, and a great crowd followed, from Galilee and Judea 8 and Jerusalem and Idumea and from beyond the Jordan and from around Tyre and Sidon. When the great crowd heard all that he was doing, they came to him. 9 And he told his disciples to have a boat ready for him because of the crowd, lest they crush him, 10 for he had healed many, so that all who had diseases pressed around him to touch him. 11 And whenever the unclean	7 But Jesus withdrew himself with his disciples to the sea: and a great multitude from Galilee followed him, and from Judaea, 8 And from Jerusalem, and from Idumaea, and from beyond Jordan; and they about Tyre and Sidon, a great multitude, when they had heard what great things he did, came unto him. 9 And he spake to his disciples, that a small ship should wait on him because of the multitude, lest they should throng him.

spirits saw him, they fell down before him and cried out, "You are the Son of God." 12And he strictly ordered them not to make him known.

10For he had healed many; insomuch that they pressed upon him for to touch him, as many as had plagues.
11And unclean spirits, when they saw him, fell down before him, and cried, saying, Thou art the Son of God.
12And he straitly charged them that they should not make him known.

Introduction to 3:7–12 While the enemies of Jesus retreat to plot His destruction (3:6), Jesus retreats also, but with an enormous crowd. His fame grows despite His warning that they say nothing. However, the good news of His teaching and healing make straight paths for the crowds from every corner of the region.

3:7 After the conflicts described in 2:1–3:6, Jesus withdrew to a remote area along the sea. Conflicts in the synagogue, common so far, will not return until He goes to Nazareth (6:1). For now, Jesus travels along the Sea of Galilee and the hills surrounding it. People from all over flocked to Him. Jesus' popularity among the common people contrasts sharply with disapproval from His opponents. *great crowd.* Mark uses the adjective "large" (*polu*) along with the noun "crowd" (*plathos*) to describe the size of this crowd here and in v. 8. These two words are used together in the Gospels only here, in a parallel setting in Lk 6:17, and to describe the crowd that gathered on Good Friday to watch Jesus' death (Lk 23:27).

3:8 The range of places noted in vv. 7 and 8 shows Jesus' extraordinary fame. His enemies had reason to worry, not only because of His power but because the report of His work reached everywhere. Just as John the Baptist had gathered people from all Judea and Jerusalem (1:5), so Jesus brings people from these places and even beyond. *Idumea.* This was the region south of Jerusalem, the southern border of the crowd's source. *Beyond the Jordan.* This refers to the region east of the Jordan river. *Tyre and Sidon.* These were Gentile cities northwest of the Sea of Galilee on the Mediterranean coast. With these locations—Idumea, beyond the Jordan, and Tyre and Sidon—a triangle is drawn from the southeast, to the far east, to the northwest. A greater One than John has come indeed and His followers come from a greater area.

3:9 The crowds, for all their affection, were about to trample Jesus. For His own safety, as well as for the welfare of those around Him, Jesus sought refuge in a boat. It is ironic that while His enemies plot His destruction (3:6), Jesus' immediate danger came from the crushing crowds. Yet, despite the danger of the moment, and the larger danger of the crowds advancing His enemies' plot, Jesus remained in the center of the crowd. Their needs overrode His safety and any chance of rest.

3:10 *touch Him.* Jesus repeatedly healed by touch (1:31, 41; 5:28–29; 7:33; 8:23). Jesus' touch showed His compassion and willingness to cross boundaries for the good of others. We might expect nothing less of the incarnate Son of God, willing to take upon Himself our human flesh. He redeemed the world by carrying our flesh. He healed the sick by the touch of His hand.

3:11 *You are the Son of God.* The demons again show their knowledge of His identity. Their frightened shriek contrasts to the fearless plotting of Jesus' enemies (3:6) See notes on the Son of God at 1:1 and 1:24.

3:12 *not to make Him known.* This warning continues the theme of secrecy. See the notes on 1:25, 1:33–34. The identity of Jesus as the Son of God has been known to the readers since 1:1, but so far, the crowds have not expressed it. The Father will declare it in the Transfiguration. Jesus, on trial, will affirm that He is the Son of the Blessed One (14:61–62). Finally the centurion at Jesus' death will speak for the crowd when he declares Jesus to be the Son of God (15:39).

3:7–12 in Devotion and Prayer In contrast to the Pharisees' and Herodians' hostility, the crowds enthusiastically press around Jesus. The mixed reaction to Jesus has not changed. Many still reject Him while others desperately seek His help. He nonetheless attends to people's physical and spiritual needs. He continues to bless those who seek Him today. • Lord, draw us to You, that we might learn from You and be healed by You. Count us among the eager crowds who leave everything else to be near You. Amen.

Jesus Is Received with Both Unbelief and Faith (3:13–6:6)

Jesus appoints the twelve apostles (3:13–19)

ESV	KJV
13And he went up on the mountain and called to him those whom he desired, and they came to him. 14And he appointed twelve (whom he also named apostles) so that they might be with him and he might send them out to preach 15and have authority to cast out demons. 16He appointed the twelve: Simon (to whom he gave the name Peter); 17James the son of Zebedee and John the brother of James (to whom he gave the name Boanerges, that is, Sons of Thunder); 18Andrew, and Philip, and Bartholomew, and Matthew, and Thomas, and James the son of Alphaeus, and Thaddaeus, and Simon the Zealot, 19and Judas Iscariot, who betrayed him.	13And he goeth up into a mountain, and calleth unto him whom he would: and they came unto him. 14And he ordained twelve, that they should be with him, and that he might send them forth to preach, 15And to have power to heal sicknesses, and to cast out devils: 16And Simon he surnamed Peter; 17And James the son of Zebedee, and John the brother of James; and he surnamed them Boanerges, which is, The sons of thunder: 18And Andrew, and Philip, and Bartholomew, and Matthew, and Thomas, and James the son of Alphaeus, and Thaddaeus, and Simon the Canaanite, 19And Judas Iscariot, which also betrayed him: and they went into an house.

Introduction to 3:13–19 The previous actions reach a new peak here. Jesus has called several disciples to follow but now He sets apart the crucial Twelve and gives them their work of preaching and healing. However, the growing ministry is darkened by the inclusion of Judas as we see his work of betrayal coming.

3:13 *He went up on the mountain.* The solitude of the mountain and the evening spent in prayer (Lk 6:12) gives a solemn tone to this call. These men will not only represent Jesus but will also follow Him on the entire road to their own deaths. This is the first use of the word "mountain" in Mark and it will especially appear at the end as Jesus gathers His disciples on the Mount of Olives in Passion Week (13:3; 14:26). See note, 1:4, for the wilderness as a setting for the ministry of John and Jesus.

3:14 *twelve.* The number twelve links the disciples with the twelve tribes of Israel. Ephesians 2:20 notes the church's foundation of apostles and prophets. *apostles.* The word (Gk *apostolos*) means to be "sent out." Their mission is in tension within this verse. They will be sent out eventually but their first duty is to be with Jesus. The disciples need Jesus' training in order to have a clear message when they are sent out. Calvin writes, "The apostleship was not bestowed on account of any human merits; but, by the free mercy of God, persons, who were altogether unworthy of it, were raised to that high rank" (*Harmony* 1:255).

3:15 *cast out demons.* Because the disciples share in Jesus' ministry and its authority, they are even able to cast out demons. These exorcisms confirm the truth and power of their preaching, as Jesus' three distinct exorcisms did (1:26; 5:13; 9:25). Healing of the ill has been a major part of Jesus' ministry that is not listed as part of their call, though they will heal many (6:13).

3:16 *Peter.* Peter's name was a transliteration of the Gk adjective *petros*, which is related to the word for "rock." However, Peter was not always the stable man his name implied. Along with his brother Andrew, he was among the first disciples called to follow Jesus (1:16–18) but he sometimes acted rashly (e.g., 14:29, 66–72). After the resurrection, however, Peter became a much more stable support for the believers.

3:17 *James . . . John.* The prominent listing of the brothers corresponds with their being the next called after Peter and Andrew (1:17–18) and their being, with Peter, the leading trio among the disciples. They are with Jesus alone on the Mount of Transfiguration (9:2) and in prayer in the Garden (14:33). *sons of thunder.* Only Mark includes this title for James and John. There is no explanation to this name at this early moment in Jesus' ministry. It seems appropriate later given their fiery response to the rejection by a Samaritan village (Lk 9:54). The contrast between the two descriptive names of vv. 16–17 is interesting. Peter is the Rock and James and John echo the thundering heavens.

3:18 The next eight disciples are listed without distinction other than differentiating between the second James and the second Simon. This is the last time that these men will be mentioned by name in Mark.

3:19 *Judas Iscariot . . . who betrayed Him.* This important detail reinforces that Jesus is a marked man, destined to suffer from wicked intrigues (cf. v. 6). The meaning of "Iscariot" is unclear, though "man from Kerioth," a town approximately twenty miles east of the Dead Sea, is a likely meaning. However, the thing that truly distinguishes Judas is not his origin but his betrayal. Jesus calls the disciples with a clear view of His own end upon the cross.

3:13–20 in Devotion and Prayer Jesus calls the disciples both to a close relationship with Him and to a daring mission with His Word. As with all believers, the first necessity is an ongoing nearness to Jesus. Then filled with His truth, believers can join the apostles in being sent out to teach. • Lord, thank You for the call of faith and forgiveness that You give to all believers. Help us to go fearlessly with the message You daily teach us.

Jesus confronts the unbelief facing His ministry (3:20–4:34)

Jesus confronts unbelief both from the scribes and His family (3:20–35)

ESV	KJV
[20]Then he went home, and the crowd gathered again, so that they could not even eat. [21]And when his family heard it, they went out to seize him, for they were saying, "He is out of his mind." [22]And the scribes who came down from Jerusalem were saying, "He is possessed by Beelzebul," and "by the prince of demons he casts out the demons." [23]And he called them to him and said to them in parables, "How can Satan cast out Satan? [24]If a kingdom is divided against itself, that kingdom cannot stand. [25]And if a house is divided against itself, that house will not be able to stand. [26]And if Satan has risen up against himself and is divided, he cannot stand, but is coming to an end. [27]But no one can enter a strong man's house and plun-	[20]And the multitude cometh together again, so that they could not so much as eat bread. [21]And when his friends heard of it, they went out to lay hold on him: for they said, He is beside himself. [22]And the scribes which came down from Jerusalem said, He hath Beelzebub, and by the prince of the devils casteth he out devils. [23]And he called them unto him, and said unto them in parables, How can Satan cast out Satan? [24]And if a kingdom be divided against itself, that kingdom cannot stand. [25]And if a house be divided against itself, that house cannot stand. [26]And if Satan rise up against himself, and be divided, he cannot stand, but hath an end.

der his goods, unless he first binds
the strong man. Then indeed he may
plunder his house.
[28]"Truly, I say to you, all sins will
be forgiven the children of man, and
whatever blasphemies they utter,
[29]but whoever blasphemes against
the Holy Spirit never has forgiveness,
but is guilty of an eternal sin"—[30]for
they were saying, "He has an unclean
spirit."
[31]And his mother and his brothers came, and standing outside they
sent to him and called him. [32]And a
crowd was sitting around him, and
they said to him, "Your mother and
your brothers are outside, seeking
you." [33]And he answered them, "Who
are my mother and my brothers?"
[34]And looking about at those who sat
around him, he said, "Here are my
mother and my brothers! [35]For whoever does the will of God, he is my
brother and sister and mother."

[27]No man can enter into a strong man's house, and spoil his goods, except he will first bind the strong man; and then he will spoil his house.

[28]Verily I say unto you, All sins shall be forgiven unto the sons of men, and blasphemies wherewith soever they shall blaspheme:

[29]But he that shall blaspheme against the Holy Ghost hath never forgiveness, but is in danger of eternal damnation.

[30]Because they said, He hath an unclean spirit.

[31]There came then his brethren and his mother, and, standing without, sent unto him, calling him.

[32]And the multitude sat about him, and they said unto him, Behold, thy mother and thy brethren without seek for thee.

[33]And he answered them, saying, Who is my mother, or my brethren?

[34]And he looked round about on them which sat about him, and said, Behold my mother and my brethren!

[35]For whosoever shall do the will of God, the same is my brother, and my sister, and mother.

Introduction to 3:20–30 As expected, the crowds continue to grow but their numbers make new demands. Jesus has no time even to eat, leading to a new, serious charge that He is demon-possessed Himself. The central question is "To whom does Jesus belong?" Is He the servant of Satan, the son of the carpenter's family, or the personal healer of the crowd? Jesus gives a wider answer. He welcomes all who hear His word by which He includes all of us as His family.

3:20 *home.* It is not clear whether Jesus was in His own house or perhaps that of Simon Peter. The gathering crowd suggests Peter's house, much as in 1:29–34. *not even eat.* Again, Mark emphasizes Jesus' popularity with the masses. The demanding crowd left no time for a meal. This problem of the crowd and the food is a prelude to the two feeding miracles of the 5,000 and 4,000 when it is the crowd that has no food.

3:21 Jesus' immediate family thought He was delusional. The reason for this concern is not clear. However, as firstborn son, He would have important family duties that may have fallen to His siblings which could cause tension (cf. vv. 31–35). *His family.* The tie with His family will come again in Mk 6 when it is asked to whom He belongs. The KJV translates this phrase as "His friends," a possibility given that the Greek literally reads "those who were with Him." However, with his family coming in v. 31, "family" appears to be the intended meaning. *He is out of His mind.* When the family says this, they likely mean that Jesus is being overwhelmed by the crowd's demands. The scribes however in the next verse take this theme to a deeper, demonic level.

The family of Jesus will appear again in the near context at 3:31–35, a section which completes the issue begun in vv. 20–21. Mark frequently begins a narrative, then introduces a new person and conflict, and finally returns to finish the story first begun. This pattern, often called A-B-A, is more prominent in Mk than other Gospels. Other clear examples occur at 5:22–24 (A), 25–34 (B), 35–43; next at 6:7–13 (A), 14–29 (B), 30 (A); next at 11:12–14 (A), 15–19 (B), 20–26 (A); also at 14:1–2 (A), 3–9 (B), 10–11 (A). By doing this, Mark holds the first story in tension and often shows a connection between the two events that we might miss. The second story often supplies the resolution needed for the first conflict, or shows an action that is the opposite of the first event.

3:22 Because Jesus' opponents cannot deny His many miracles, they impugn their divine origin. They claim that He performed exorcisms by the power of Satan and thus question His identity. He was declared the Son of God in 1:1, but challenged in 2:8 on account of His divine forgiving of the paralyzed man, and also on account of His work on the Sabbath (2:28; 3:5). *Beelzebul.* Beelzebul was the name of an idol of Canaan, whose name meant "Baal is prince." See 2Ki 1:2 where the writer dismisses this god of the Canaanites by calling him Baal-zebub, "the lord of the flies." *prince of demons.* Satan, not Beelzebul, leads the demonic host. But Jesus' adversaries were more interested in heaping scorn than in being precise.

3:23 *parables.* Here "parable" means something like "metaphor" or "illustration." This is the first use of the word "parable" in Mark and it will characterize Jesus' teaching (Mk 4:33–34). Parables are narratives of varied length, generally with few characters, focused on brief action, using few emotions, with an emphasis on the ending. Often Jesus supplied the meaning of either the entire parable (Lk 18:1) or the significance of each important character and action (Mk 4:13–20). Here the divided house is explained immediately in the next verse. See Nathan's dramatic parable unveiling David's crime (2Sm 12:1–7) and also Jgs 9:8–15 for OT examples. *How can Satan cast out Satan?* This is a rhetorical question, with no expectation of answer, similar to Jesus' question of the Sabbath in 3:4. Jesus shows the folly of claiming that He defeated the demons by Satan's power. Since the fall, Satan may properly be understood as "the ruler of this world" (Jn 12:31). At the same time, his authority is only what God allows (cf. Jb 1:12; Jn 16:11; 1Pt 3:18–19). Jesus' point is that Satan cannot be divided against himself and yet retain some measure of power on earth.

3:24 *kingdom . . . divided.* Jesus shows that the exorcism of demons is not an administrative reshuffling by Satan. If it were, Jesus would simply be middle management. Casting out demons from their established places is a frontal assault on Satan's toehold on earth. Satan could not imagine or agree to this.

3:25 *house is divided.* This parallel example repeats the point made in v. 24 ("a kingdom divided"), but is even more pointed within this context of the division within Jesus' own family (v. 21). What father deliberately divides his house and expects it to stand strong? If the kingdom example is too far from His hearers' experience, then a divided house is easily known by all.

3:26 As noted in v. 23, Jesus often gives the direct meaning of a parable, as He does again here. *coming to an end.* It was not through Satan's wish or work, but Satan's kingdom was coming to an end through the arrival of Jesus' kingdom. Upon the return of the seventy-two disciples, Jesus said, "I saw Satan fall like lightning from heaven" (Lk 10:18). The death and resurrection of Jesus was the central judgment of God over Satan. "Now is the judgment of this world; now will the ruler of this world be cast out" (Jn 12:31).

3:27 *strong man's house.* While referring to Satan as the strong man, this comparison doesn't give Satan true authority over the world. It speaks to our perception rather than the spiritual truth. Satan claims ownership of the world (Mt 4:9), just as he promised the knowledge and equality of God to Adam and Eve. However, even if Satan appears to us as the strong owner of the created world, Jesus' parable speaks of His overpowering of Satan. The strong man is bound and his house is plundered while he, Satan, grinds his teeth in fruitless anger. Each demon cast out was another limb of the strong man being bound. Each man delivered from a demon was Satan's former prize taken away.

3:28 *children of man*. This is a Semitic way of referring to human beings (e.g., Ps 11:4; 12:1, 8; 14:2; 31:19). This phrase is also used frequently in the LXX. In the NT, it is used only here and in Eph 3:5. See notes on the use of the "Son of Man" at 2:10. *blasphemies*. The issue of blasphemy was first raised in 2:7 when Jesus forgave the man with divine authority. Blasphemy is falsely charging God or taking on the actions of God. When Jesus declares He is the Christ, He is charged with blasphemy (14:64). Blasphemy is the word also used to describe the insults heaped on Him while He dies (15:29). The identity of Jesus, a central theme of Mark since 1:1, is at the heart of blasphemy. Those who are ignorant of Him as the Son of God inevitably blaspheme His power and work. *forgiven*. Despite the opposition and ignorance which Jesus faced, He came to forgive even the harshest attacks upon Himself.

3:29–30 This is a famously difficult passage as it equates blasphemy of the Holy Spirit with the unpardonable sin. The sin against the Holy Spirit is the unyielding refusal to believe the Gospel and a rejection of the Holy Spirit's work to create faith in Jesus. Blasphemy against the Son is an attack against His work and being as the Son of God. Blasphemy against the Spirit is resistance against God's work within the blaspheming person. This resistance blocks the gift of faith and the reception of eternal life. This passage was of special interest to Wesley due to the outbursts that occurred during the sermons of eighteenth century revival preachers. He wondered whether the devil or the Spirit caused the outbursts. Wesley leaned toward attributing the outbursts to the Spirit, who was driving out demons. His conclusions may have opened the way for new extremes. Revivalists came to depend on such outbursts as evidence that the Spirit was present rather than holding to the Reformation emphasis on the Spirit working through the Word (Wesley 105). *eternal sin*. Guilt of this sin brings one into the everlasting condemnation and punishment established for Satan and his evil angels (cf. Mt 25:41). John wrote of a sin which leads to death for which one is not to pray (1Jn 5:16). Luther speaks of this sin against the Spirit:

> He calls the sin against the Holy Spirit a mortal sin. All of this is tantamount to saying: "Whoever despairs in his sin or relies on good works sins against the Holy Spirit and against grace." Of course, I should intercede for such people and pray that they may be freed from that sin and be converted; but it is impossible that God be gracious to them so long as they are given to that sin, it is impossible that God's grace be of greater effect in their hearts than that sin, as is true of other sins. . . . No, I must pray against that sin, as Moses did in Num. 16:15, against Korah, saying: "Do not respect their offering." For Korah, too, aspired to esteem before God by reason of his works, and so he sinned against grace. That is an intolerable sin. All other sins which let grace triumph and reign are forgivable. (LW 19:48–49)

3:20–30 in Devotion and Prayer Those who refuse to recognize Jesus as God's Son and acknowledge His works as signs of the Holy Spirit remain under the dominion of Satan. But Jesus has overcome Satan and brought freedom to those formerly imprisoned. Those baptized into Christ have received not only Him but also His promised Holy Spirit. • Lord, preserve us from the power of Satan. Remove any lingering doubts that we might be confident in the fact that You have bound him and rescued us from his dominion. Amen.

Introduction to 3:31–35 Having answered the charges of His enemies, Jesus now directs attention to His family and their fears. This recalls their early worry that He had lost His mind (3:21). The dark charges of blasphemy and the eternal scope of Satan's kingdom are reduced to the simple concerns of a mother and brothers. Going beyond that immediate circle, Jesus expands His family through the hearing of His Word and will.

3:31 *brothers.* Four brothers of Jesus, most likely the natural children of Mary and Joseph born after Jesus, are listed in Mk 6:3, along with the mention of sisters. There is also a tradition that these might be Joseph's children from an earlier marriage. Regardless, they are left outside because of the crowd, much as the paralyzed man was excluded in 2:2–3. Rather than physically entering, they called to Him, summoning Him to come out to them.

3:32 Note the irony. People who barely know Jesus are seated next to Him, eagerly listening, while His family is outside, trying to get close enough to make Him stop. Evidently since no one wished to give up the choice places near Jesus, the most the family could do was send a message: "Tell Him to stop and come out to us." Likely those who repeated this message to Jesus were curious as to His answer but hopeful that He would remain with the crowd.

3:33 *Who are My mother and My brothers?* Jesus' question perhaps paralleled the family's initial questions: "Where is my son? Where is our brother?" Jesus is not despising family ties and their importance. We see His devotion to His parents following the trip to the temple (Lk 2:51). Jesus' following answer does not mean that He might not have had private time with His mother and siblings after the crowd left. Though earthly relations are crucial, one's relationship to God and His family of faith is even more important, since they form an eternal communion.

3:34 *Here are My mother and My brothers.* Jesus' identification of those in the crowd affirms their desire to be near Him. He more than tolerates them; He gives them the closest ties to Himself. These people were not a millstone nor was His ministry a necessary burden. He came to be truly with His own.

3:35 *does the will of God.* Jesus has a similar definition of close relationship with Himself in Jn 15:14 "You are My friends if you do what I command you." However, this relationship is not our work or done by our initiative. Jesus says further in Jn 15:16, "You did not choose Me, but I chose you and appointed you . . ." Those who hear the call of Jesus to follow Him, whether the twelve disciples of Mk 3:14–19, or those who hear Him today, all are brought into the circle around Him by the gift of faith through the Spirit. That faith is the work of God in action (Jn 6:29).

3:31–35 in Devotion and Prayer Loyalty to God takes precedence over loyalty to blood relations. This is still hard to hear today, as the temptation to put relationships with family and friends above God can be overwhelming. But the Lord wants us to have both relationships, and have them as healthy as they can be. He stands first in our lives because He placed Himself last, to humbly bear our sins and make us children of God. • Lord, thank You for the privilege of being included in Your eternal family. Keep us in this faith and life forever. Amen.

Jesus teaches the crowds and His disciples in light of the unbelief of the religious authorities ("The Parabolic Discourse"; 4:1–34)

ESV

4 1 Again he began to teach beside
the sea. And a very large crowd gathered about him, so that he got into
a boat and sat in it on the sea, and
the whole crowd was beside the
sea on the land. 2 And he was teaching them many things in parables,
and in his teaching he said to them:
3 "Listen! A sower went out to sow.
4 And as he sowed, some seed fell
along the path, and the birds came
and devoured it. 5 Other seed fell on
rocky ground, where it did not have
much soil, and immediately it sprang
up, since it had no depth of soil. 6 And
when the sun rose, it was scorched,
and since it had no root, it withered
away. 7 Other seed fell among thorns,
and the thorns grew up and choked
it, and it yielded no grain. 8 And other
seeds fell into good soil and produced
grain, growing up and increasing and
yielding thirtyfold and sixtyfold and a
hundredfold." 9 And he said, "He who
has ears to hear, let him hear."

10 And when he was alone, those
around him with the twelve asked
him about the parables. 11 And he said
to them, "To you has been given the
secret of the kingdom of God, but for
those outside everything is in parables, 12 so that

"they may indeed see but not perceive,
and may indeed hear but not understand,
lest they should turn and be forgiven."

KJV

4 1 And he began again to teach by the sea side: and there was gathered unto him a great multitude, so that he entered into a ship, and sat in the sea; and the whole multitude was by the sea on the land.

2 And he taught them many things by parables, and said unto them in his doctrine,

3 Hearken; Behold, there went out a sower to sow:

4 And it came to pass, as he sowed, some fell by the way side, and the fowls of the air came and devoured it up.

5 And some fell on stony ground, where it had not much earth; and immediately it sprang up, because it had no depth of earth:

6 But when the sun was up, it was scorched; and because it had no root, it withered away.

7 And some fell among thorns, and the thorns grew up, and choked it, and it yielded no fruit.

8 And other fell on good ground, and did yield fruit that sprang up and increased; and brought forth, some thirty, and some sixty, and some an hundred.

9 And he said unto them, He that hath ears to hear, let him hear.

10 And when he was alone, they that were about him with the twelve asked of him the parable.

11 And he said unto them, Unto you it is given to know the mystery of the kingdom of God: but unto them that

13And he said to them, "Do you not understand this parable? How then will you understand all the parables? 14The sower sows the word. 15And these are the ones along the path, where the word is sown: when they hear, Satan immediately comes and takes away the word that is sown in them. 16And these are the ones sown on rocky ground: the ones who, when they hear the word, immediately receive it with joy. 17And they have no root in themselves, but endure for a while; then, when tribulation or persecution arises on account of the word, immediately they fall away. 18And others are the ones sown among thorns. They are those who hear the word, 19but the cares of the world and the deceitfulness of riches and the desires for other things enter in and choke the word, and it proves unfruitful. 20But those that were sown on the good soil are the ones who hear the word and accept it and bear fruit, thirtyfold and sixtyfold and a hundredfold."

21And he said to them, "Is a lamp brought in to be put under a basket, or under a bed, and not on a stand? 22For nothing is hidden except to be made manifest; nor is anything secret except to come to light. 23If anyone has ears to hear, let him hear." 24And he said to them, "Pay attention to what you hear: with the measure you use, it will be measured to you, and still more will be added to you. 25For to the one who has, more will be given, and from the one who has not, even what he has will be taken away."

26And he said, "The kingdom of God is as if a man should scatter seed on

are without, all these things are done in parables:

12That seeing they may see, and not perceive; and hearing they may hear, and not understand; lest at any time they should be converted, and their sins should be forgiven them.

13And he said unto them, Know ye not this parable? and how then will ye know all parables?

14The sower soweth the word.

15And these are they by the way side, where the word is sown; but when they have heard, Satan cometh immediately, and taketh away the word that was sown in their hearts.

16And these are they likewise which are sown on stony ground; who, when they have heard the word, immediately receive it with gladness;

17And have no root in themselves, and so endure but for a time: afterward, when affliction or persecution ariseth for the word's sake, immediately they are offended.

18And these are they which are sown among thorns; such as hear the word,

19And the cares of this world, and the deceitfulness of riches, and the lusts of other things entering in, choke the word, and it becometh unfruitful.

20And these are they which are sown on good ground; such as hear the word, and receive it, and bring forth fruit, some thirtyfold, some sixty, and some an hundred.

21And he said unto them, Is a candle brought to be put under a bushel, or under a bed? and not to be set on a candlestick?

22For there is nothing hid, which shall not be manifested; neither was

the ground. 27 He sleeps and rises
night and day, and the seed sprouts
and grows; he knows not how. 28 The
earth produces by itself, first the
blade, then the ear, then the full
grain in the ear. 29 But when the grain
is ripe, at once he puts in the sickle,
because the harvest has come."
30 And he said, "With what can
we compare the kingdom of God,
or what parable shall we use for it?
31 It is like a grain of mustard seed,
which, when sown on the ground, is
the smallest of all the seeds on earth,
32 yet when it is sown it grows up and
becomes larger than all the garden
plants and puts out large branches,
so that the birds of the air can make
nests in its shade."
33 With many such parables he spoke
the word to them, as they were able
to hear it. 34 He did not speak to them
without a parable, but privately to his
own disciples he explained everything.

any thing kept secret, but that it should come abroad.

23 If any man have ears to hear, let him hear.

24 And he said unto them, Take heed what ye hear: with what measure ye mete, it shall be measured to you: and unto you that hear shall more be given.

25 For he that hath, to him shall be given: and he that hath not, from him shall be taken even that which he hath.

26 And he said, So is the kingdom of God, as if a man should cast seed into the ground;

27 And should sleep, and rise night and day, and the seed should spring and grow up, he knoweth not how.

28 For the earth bringeth forth fruit of herself; first the blade, then the ear, after that the full corn in the ear.

29 But when the fruit is brought forth, immediately he putteth in the sickle, because the harvest is come.

30 And he said, Whereunto shall we liken the kingdom of God? or with what comparison shall we compare it?

31 It is like a grain of mustard seed, which, when it is sown in the earth, is less than all the seeds that be in the earth:

32 But when it is sown, it groweth up, and becometh greater than all herbs, and shooteth out great branches; so that the fowls of the air may lodge under the shadow of it.

33 And with many such parables spake he the word unto them, as they were able to hear it.

34 But without a parable spake he not unto them: and when they were alone, he expounded all things to his disciples.

Introduction to 4:1–34 Chapter four gives the first of two extended sections of teaching in Mark (cf. 13:3–37). Three parables of seeds and soil along with other comparisons repeatedly draw comparisons with things from everyday life in order to clarify how God plants and grows His kingdom. Jesus reveals both grace and judgment in these parables. Overall, the message is the assurance of God's powerful Word bearing fruit in a daunting world.

4:1–9 Though typically called "the parable of the sower," this story's main point has more to do the four kinds of soil than with the one sowing seed. The parable's interpretation comes in vv. 14–20 which may serve as a model for understanding the other parables in ch. 4.

4:1 *teach.* In a way similar to the beginning of His ministry in 1:21, Jesus teaches. But, unlike ch. 1, the content of His teaching is given in some detail for the first time. *sea.* This is the Sea of Galilee, which has been (1:16ff.), and will continue to be the center of His travels. *very large crowd.* It is to be expected that another crowd will gather, especially after His gracious definition of them as His family (3:34–35). The abundance of the crowd matches the fruitfulness of the Word in the fourth soil (v. 8). *into a boat.* See the similar problem and solution at 3:9.

4:2 *parables.* As noted in 3:23, Jesus' teaching was characterized by parables that show the close tie between creation and salvation. Jesus' parables give Him two opportunities to teach, first in the telling of the parable and, secondly, in the relationship with the disciples who then seek the meaning from Him. *teaching.* The Gk noun here is *didache* which the KJV translates as "doctrine." The word is used four other times in Mark as a summary of His teaching which raised either joyous astonishment (1:22, 27; 11:18) or as a point of conflict with His enemies (cf. 11:18; 12:38). His teaching was intended to stir His hearers into action.

4:3 *Listen.* Jesus begins His formal teaching, signaling to the growing crowd that a new dimension of His instruction was beginning. In 4:24, using the same word for "listen" or "hear," Jesus reminds them to pay attention to what they hear. *sower.* A farmer planting seed was a familiar sight, either easily remembered or perhaps even seen in the distance. *sow.* After seed was sown, an ox-drawn harrow (or even a flock of sheep or goats) was driven through the field to turn the soil over the seed.

4:4 *the path*. This was the packed down soil that bordered the field. The sower broadcast the seed with a sweep of his arm and inevitably some seed flew beyond the field. But this action hints at the abundance of the Word which is cast even among the hardened. *birds*. The KJV picturesquely translates this as "the fowls of the air."

4:5 Shallow soil over large stones warms up quickly after the winter cold, and so helps the seeds germinate and sprout quickly. Because such soil has no depth, however, the seedlings cannot sink healthy roots. *immediately*. In the telling of the parable and in the following explanation, Mark's familiar word "immediately" (*euthus* in Gk), appears with each of the three soils—the snatching of the seed on the path (v. 15), the quick emergence of the seed in the rocky soil (v. 5), and the falling away from faith of the weedy soil (v. 17). Only the good soil bears lasting fruit, but it does so without the impatience of "immediately."

4:6 *scorched*. This Gk word, *kaumatidzo*, is used only here, in the parallel passage in Mt 13:6, and in Rv 16:8–9 where it describes the scorching of earth's people with the fourth bowl. *withered*. The same word was used in 3:1 to described the withered man's hand. (In a fortunate parallel, I'm writing this on a hot July day at a wildlife preserve, Huiras Lake, in southeastern Wisconsin. I just spoke to the caretaker who told me that thousands of trees were once planted on the bare western hillside next to where I'm sitting. Unfortunately virtually all the trees have died due to the thin, rocky soil. Jesus' parable continues its timeless character two thousand years later.)

4:7 *choked*. This word, Gk *sumpigno*, gives the image of choking or strangling with both hands together. This collision of the weeds against the seed is not a mild shouldering aside but a violent attack. A variety of thorny weeds grow in Israel, some as tall as six feet. Like all weeds, these deplete the soil of nutrients, leaving little for the plants being cultivated.

4:8 *And*. This is the crucial moment of change in the parable, a turn from the failure of the first three to the abundance of the good soil. The tone of the introduction to this fourth step would be, "But then, finally, perhaps when it seemed there was no hope, other seeds fell into good soil. . . ." This plant produces grain abundantly in comparison to the single grain sown. Even a hundredfold increase is attested! While such abundance is not found in ordinary grainfields either then or now, the point is that the Word of God is beyond comparison in its yield. If someone says of this multiplication of one hundred-fold, "I've never seen anything like that," that is exactly the nature of the Word of God.

4:9 Just as Jesus began the parable with a call to listen, so He ends it in the same way. Jesus challenges the hearer to consider carefully what has just been said and apply it to his or her life. This saying appears frequently in the NT (e.g., v. 23; Mt 13:43; Lk 14:35; Rv 2:7, 11, 17, 29; 3:6, 13, 22).

4:1–9 in Devotion and Prayer The parable of the sower helps explain why not everyone who hears the Gospel believes it and bears the fruit of faith. Such failures are seemingly more common today than ever, even among traditionally Christian peoples. At the same time, the Word of the Lord accomplishes His good purpose. It works miracles in lives where the Spirit has His way. • Lord, continue to plant Your Word richly in us. Remove the stones and weeds that impede Your Word, and thereby bring forth a harvest of mature fruit in all who believe. Amen.

Introduction to 4:10–20 Not only does Mark record the actual teaching of Jesus in the telling of the parable (vv. 3–9), but we are brought into the circle of the twelve disciples to hear the parable's meaning (vv. 14–20). Jesus expects the disciples to understand at least some measure of the parable (v. 13), but He shows His mercy and patience to all believers in giving us the meaning through each of the four soils.

4:10 *when He was alone.* Only Mark includes this detail, perhaps as a part of Peter's recollection and retelling of the event. The disciples and those with them still do not have "ears to hear" (v. 9), and so must ask Jesus for an explanation. Perhaps they were too embarrassed to reveal their lack of understanding in public and so they asked Jesus for an explanation in private.

4:11 *To you has been given.* Before interpreting the parable of the sower for His disciples, Jesus first made clear that human beings cannot understand divine revelation unless given insight by God Himself. *secret of the kingdom.* The word for "secret" in Gk is *mysterion,* from which we derive "mystery," the word used here by the KJV. Here, and in the parallel passages in Matthew and Luke, are the only places where this noun is used in the Gospels, though it is often used by Paul (e.g. Rm 11:25; 1Co 2:1, 7; Eph 1:9; 3:3, 4, 9), and in the LXX translation of Dn. It fits well with the following quotation

(Is 6:9–10). This mystery has everything to do with a proper understanding of Jesus and His mission. Jesus' identity as the Son of God has been proclaimed repeatedly since 1:1. Unfortunately, the disciples have still not fully understood Jesus' divinity and the nature of His mission. Particularly difficult for them will be the idea that their Messiah has to suffer in order to complete His mission (cf. 8:31–33; 9:30–32; 10:35–45). *for those outside everything is in parables.* By teaching in parables, Jesus is not shutting out others, but invites them to see the link between creation and the saving kingdom of God. Parables also reveal their meaning through a relationship with Jesus Himself. Hearing and understanding the parables is part of the path that prepares for the coming king (1:2–3).

4:12 *see but not perceive . . . hear but not understand.* Jesus quotes Is 6:9–10 in a challenging manner. At first, it appears that He has no intention of enlightening the crowd and that the parables are a deliberate method of confusing their minds and hearts. However, God desires none to be lost, but all to be saved and come to the knowledge of the truth (1Tm 2:4). The failure to perceive and understand is the result of man's fallen nature clouded by rebellious sin (1Co 1:18; 2:6–14). While God could dismiss all people to a doomed silence and hardness of heart, He instead continues to speak through creation and parables. Calvin writes,

> When persons of a weak sight come out into sunshine, their eyes become dimmer than before, and that defect is in no way attributed to the sun, but to their eyes. In like manner, when the word of God blinds and hardens the reprobate, as this takes place through their own depravity, it belongs truly and naturally to themselves, but is accidental, as respects the word. (*Harmony* 2:108)

4:13 *How then will you understand.* While the hearers outside this circle are expected to struggle, the disciples should get the meaning. However, until the disciples believe that Jesus is the Messiah and interpret His teachings in light of His sacrificial suffering and death, they will never comprehend anything about Him. In fact, much of the unfolding plot in Mark involves the struggle of the disciples to accept that the Messiah will be rejected and crucified.

4:14 *sower.* Those sowing God's Word include Jesus Himself, the first disciples, and all subsequent teachers and preachers of the Gospel. The administration of Baptism and the Lord's Supper are included in this sowing activity. The analogy of the spread of the Word as a seed is frequent in Scripture with a call for workers (Mt 9:37), into a field already white unto harvest (Jn 4:35), with the certainty that the Word will have an unfailing return (Is 55:10–11).

4:15 *Satan immediately comes.* The power of the Word is seen in that even on a hardened heart, Satan immediately has to remove the Word. (See the note on 4:5 for the use of "immediately" in the parable.) Just as Jesus can and will be rejected, so also His Word will suffer opposition. The human ego is not the only obstacle to the Word's reception. Satan and his evil hosts also work vigorously against the Word.

4:16 *receive it with joy.* The expected beginning of faith is such joy, but this person's joy is too instant to last, too giddy to grow. Often this person expects no difficulty in the walk of faith.

4:17 *no root.* Shallow soil prevents a deep root. Such a root comes only with time and with the necessity of seeking water far below the surface. Many converts joyfully begin a walk in the faith but then turn away when difficulties come. The demand for immediate, easily found reward prevents the deepening of faith. *tribulation or persecution.* Difficulties and troubles will come to all believers, even as they once came to Christ. That is why Jesus repeatedly warns people of the perils of following Him (8:34–35; Mt 10:22) and why His apostles repeatedly urge believers to persevere, despite trials (Gal 6:9; 2Tm 2:1–7; Heb 12:3–11; Jas 1:12; 1Pt 1:13–16; Rv 2:10; 3:11).

4:18 Sowing among the thorns seems to repeat the futility of sowing upon the path and among the stones. Sowing in all these places shows the abundance of the Word as seed and the desire of God that all are touched by His message. *hear the word.* These hearers hear the word with the same eagerness with which they hear so many offers in life. They are busy, capable people who do many, many things well, and that very success can become the problem for the Word.

4:19 *cares . . . deceitfulness of riches . . . desires of other things.* Three distinct types of weeds surround the Word. The cares of the world are the worries that demand constant, instant attention, tearing a person from hearing and cultivating the Word (Lk 10:38–42). The deceitfulness of riches is the tempting claim of wealth which promises ease and security. However, the very next hours could bring life to an end for an unprepared soul (Lk 12:16–21). The desire of other things is the restlessness which unendingly seeks more, even while what is already owned is too much to bear (1Tm 6:9). *unfruitful.* Here, as in other places, Jesus makes clear that the barometer of one's faith is not what one says, but rather what one does. The fruits of faith (good works) are indicators of the sincerity of belief. Cf. Mt 7:15–20; 12:33; Mk 12:1–9. In contrast to the intentions and plans of this person for their own growth, real fruitfulness comes as the fruit of the Spirit (Gal 5:22–23).

4:20 *accept it and bear fruit.* Elsewhere, Scripture teaches that believers must be given grace in order to accept the Word and bear the fruit of faith (cf. 1Co 12:3). That reality corrects any thought that the productive soil is inherently better than the other, unproductive soils. Luther writes, "The Word is so effective that whenever it is seriously contemplated, heard, and used, it is bound never to be without fruit" (LC I 101). *hundredfold.* The abundance of the fruit reflects the power of God's Word beyond the soil in which it grows. This hundredfold increase more than makes up for what was lost in the first soils. God's abundant sowing, though seemingly futile at first, returns more than could be imagined. Jesus likened His death to a single seed which, if planted, would result in life multiplied for many (Jn 12:24).

4:10–20 in Devotion and Prayer Jesus interprets the parable of the sower for His disciples. The failures of the various soils to produce for the Lord are still common: people refuse to hear, fall away when hardship comes, and allow worldly concerns to overwhelm their faith. Yet, by God's grace, many receive the Word in good faith and produce richly. • Lord, help us to see and perceive, to hear and understand. Remove every impediment to our faith. Let Your Word bring forth lasting fruit in our lives. Amen.

Introduction to 4:21–25 Jesus points out that light is made to be seen, and that nothing can be truly hidden. These challenging truths remind His hearers to make full use of the light of His Word. The understanding and use of this Word will lead to even more light.

4:21 *Is a lamp . . . put under.* It is obviously self-defeating to light a lamp and then hide it. The light here is parallel to the seed which is the Word of God in the previous parable. However, the placement of the two is opposite. The seed must be buried and hidden to grow, but the light must be left out on the stand. Jesus' followers are supposed to bring the light of the Gospel to the darkness surrounding them.

4:22 *nothing is hidden.* If someone hopes to bury his sins, like a weed seed, this verse warns that nothing buried can remain hidden. Weeds will rise up and the piercing light will expose them. Bengel writes, "This [revealing] is done in successive stages in this present order of things; and it shall be done fully, when the light shall make manifest all secrets on the last day; 1 Cor. iv. 5" (Bengel 514). The records of God detailing the lives of everyone are complete, as Rv 20:12 shows. However, believers' names are written in the Book of Life by grace (Rv 20:12; Lk 10:20).

4:23 *let him hear.* As noted in 4:9, Jesus often ends a parable with this command to hear and act. In v. 9, plant carefully the seed of the Word. In v. 23, shine brightly the light that has been given.

4:24 *the measure you use.* As a general rule of life, Jesus assures His followers that, when they act graciously and righteously toward others, an even greater measure of goodness will come back to them (cf. Gal 6:9). This also applies to their hearing and using of the Word. As it is used, so it will prove to be life-giving and growing. The more the seed is planted, the greater the harvest. The more the light is shone, the greater the insights.

4:25 *more will be given . . . taken away.* At first, this principle seems harsh. However, this is the outcome of v. 24. Either there is a generous sowing of the seed and therefore a large harvest. Or, if one has only a small knowledge of the Word and that is neglected, then even that little is lost. The parable of the talents (Mt 25:14–30) uses this same phrase and demonstrates it through taking a man's single, hidden talent and giving it to one with ten talents.

4:21–25 in Devotion and Prayer Jesus continues the theme of producing for the Kingdom by comparing His people to lamps set on a stand and by promising that faithfulness will be rewarded. It is a great pity, therefore, that so many Christians block God's desire to bless faithfulness by failing to put their faith into practice wholeheartedly. The Lord forgives those who repent, and He calls us to focus on His mission. Even if we are generous, He is more generous still and blesses more and more. • Lord, thank You for graciously rewarding our small kindnesses with outpourings of even more precious blessings. Amen.

Introduction to 4:26–29 Although this parable and the one in vv. 1–20 both involve the sowing of seed and its growth, this one makes a different point. The opposition to the seed found in the first three soils is replaced in this parable by the mystery of growth. Only Mark records this parable.

4:26 *kingdom of God.* This is the introduction used for many of Jesus' parables (Mk 4:30; Mt 13:31, 33, 44, 45, 47). See the note on 1:15 concerning the first time this is used in Mark. *man.* The parable begins similarly to the parable of the four soils with the broadcasting of the seed. The one who sows represents again the disciples and all believers who spread the Word of God. However, in the four soils parable, the emphasis is on the different soils; here the stress is the man's understanding of the mystery of the seed sprouting and growing. Calvin writes, "Though the seed of the word be concealed and choked for a time, Christ enjoins pious teachers to be of good courage, and not to allow their alacrity to be slackened through distrust" (*Harmony* 2:128).

4:27 *sleeps and rises.* Although the farmer plays an important role in the cultivation of his field—after all, he sows the seed—its growth occurs apart from his efforts, even as he sleeps. The kingdom of God comes without our watching and grows without our urging. This doesn't separate believers from the Kingdom but reminds us that God's work is not dependent on our constant effort. In contrast to the Reformers' emphasis on the Word and grace, Wesley uses this passage to teach the power of the soul, which like soil brings forth its fruitfulness, becoming progressively stronger until it reaches "full holiness" (Wesley 107). *sprouts and grows; he knows not how.* Even today, many aspects of horticulture remain a mystery. The more one studies nature, the more one marvels at its intricacy, as well as the wisdom and power of its Lord.

4:28 *by itself.* The Gk word for this phrase, *automate*, is used only here and Ac 12:10 and might be rendered as "automatically." This automatic growth is how it appears to the farmer—a wonderful mystery. However, the earth does not actually produce growth "by itself." The plant owes its growth to the power of God, who both creates and sustains the natural order (cf. v. 27). Growth in the Kingdom is similarly the result of God's Word and Spirit, not the speaker or hearer (Rm 10:17). Believers who see the Word grow within themselves and others share the farmer's joy over this mystery.

4:29 *harvest has come.* This image is frequently used to describe judgment at the end of time (cf. Is 17:5; Rv 14:14–19). By concluding this parable with a reference to the final judgment, Jesus underscores the idea that the Kingdom is moving toward a goal. The growth of the seed, as wonderful as it is, reaches its final purpose when mature believers are brought into their eternal homes.

4:26–29 in Devotion and Prayer God's kingdom grows mysteriously of itself, at its own pace, and through the power of the Word. This reality often causes frustration among those who eagerly long for a rapid expansion of the Kingdom, and all the more as we only have a short-term view of things. But God's kingdom grows according to His plan and timetable. And it is a great blessing that things ultimately depend on Him and not us, for only He is able to bring home a great harvest for life eternal. • Lord, as You have begun a good work by planting Your kingdom in our world, bring it to a full harvest in Your own good time. Amen.

Introduction to 4:30–34 The progression of the three seed parables is complete with the mustard seed. The parable of the sower focuses on the four different soils; the parable of the seed growing centers on the action and surprise of the farmer. Now the parable of the mustard seed highlights the nature of the seed itself, its initial size and eventual growth. Overall, the three parables summarize the kingdom of God: its fruitfulness will far outdo the losses in some soils; its growth is a blessed mystery that does not depend on the sower's knowledge and work; its final size is all the more impressive given the tiny beginning of a single seed buried and reborn. So the kingdom of God comes by the work of Jesus, often rejected by men, but working beyond the reason of men to rise from the dead. In His rising, He makes a lasting home for all.

4:30 *compare the kingdom.* This is the only instance of this phrase in Mark but note that in Matthew Jesus uses a similar phrase to begin parables (Mt 13:24; 18:23; 22:2; 25:1). Jesus question invites His listeners to consider all of creation as a possible point of comparison with the kingdom of God. Jesus could have used countless parallels in creation to demonstrate His work and to show that creation itself is eager to speak of its Creator (Ps 19:1; Rm 1:19–20).

4:31 *mustard seed.* The comparison of the Kingdom with the mustard seed, which will grow into a small tree, follows OT images. The kingdom of God is compared to a cedar planted on a mountain (Ezk 17:22–23), and also a vineyard (Is 5:1ff.). With the mustard seed and tree, this trio of planting parables stresses the extremes in the size of the seed and the resulting plant. *smallest of all seeds.* Technically this is a hyperbole, since the mustard seed is not actually the smallest seed known, though Jesus likely refers to the experience of His hearers rather than to botanists. The tiny size is in contrast to the later growth. Jesus used the tiny mustard seed again in Mt 17:20; Lk 17:6 as a picture of the sufficient size of faith. In both cases, the size of the mustard is both warning and encouragement. Don't discount the Kingdom or faith because of its outward size, but be amazed at the astonishing life hidden within it.

4:32 *larger than all the garden plants.* One variety of mustard (*sinapis nigra*) can reach a mature height of ten feet, making it the largest plant in an herb garden. *birds.* The birds found not only shelter in the branches but also ate the seeds of the tree. In contrast to v. 15, here the birds represent people of every nation who are welcomed in the parable. The birds demonstrate the maturity and fruitfulness of the plant. This also alludes to a prophecy comparing the Messiah's rule to a great tree in whose shadow "birds of every sort will nest" (Ezk 17:23).

4:33 *able to hear it.* Jesus taught with gracious restraint. He could have overwhelmed His listeners with the mind of God which none can know (Rm 11:33–35). However, as a wise and kind teacher, He limits His message and method to the ability of the hearers. Yet, despite their apparent simplicity, His parables yield a lifelong harvest of thought. On the ability of His listeners to understand, see the notes on vv. 9, 11.

4:34 *did not speak . . . without a parable.* This hyperbole doesn't contradict other teachings such as the Sermon on the Mount (Mt 5–7), but concentrates on this body of teaching and the perception of these hearers. *privately.* Jesus did not purposely make His teaching confusing. Rather, it was the people's preconceptions that made His teachings seem hard. The parables require a relationship with Jesus for full explanation as 2Pt 1:20 states that "no prophecy of Scripture comes from someone's own interpretation."

4:30–34 in Devotion and Prayer Jesus' parables reassure believers that over time the kingdom of God will grow incredibly large, far beyond its unassuming beginnings. Precisely because the Kingdom grows so slowly and its Lord is so patient, believers tend to become discouraged and its enemies are emboldened. But in the end, the Kingdom alone will stand, and everything else will be overthrown. Thank God, He shelters His people of every nation in its eternal shade. • Lord, let us see both in fact and by faith that Your kingdom will someday be all in all. Keep us ever sheltered safely within its branches. Amen.

Jesus performs miracles on and around the Sea of Galilee (4:35–5:43)

Jesus calms a storm (4:35–41)

ESV	KJV
35 On that day, when evening had come, he said to them, "Let us go across to the other side." 36 And leaving the crowd, they took him with them in the boat, just as he was. And other boats were with him. 37 And a great windstorm arose, and the waves were breaking into the boat, so that the boat was already filling. 38 But he was in the stern, asleep on the cushion. And they woke him and said to him, "Teacher, do you not care that we are perishing?" 39 And he awoke and rebuked the wind and said to the sea, "Peace! Be still!" And the wind ceased, and there was a great calm. 40 He said to them, "Why are you so afraid? Have you still no faith?" 41 And they were filled with great fear and said to one another, "Who then is this, that even the wind and the sea obey him?"	35 And the same day, when the even was come, he saith unto them, Let us pass over unto the other side. 36 And when they had sent away the multitude, they took him even as he was in the ship. And there were also with him other little ships. 37 And there arose a great storm of wind, and the waves beat into the ship, so that it was now full. 38 And he was in the hinder part of the ship, asleep on a pillow: and they awake him, and say unto him, Master, carest thou not that we perish? 39 And he arose, and rebuked the wind, and said unto the sea, Peace, be still. And the wind ceased, and there was a great calm. 40 And he said unto them, Why are ye so fearful? how is it that ye have no faith? 41 And they feared exceedingly, and said one to another, What manner of man is this, that even the wind and the sea obey him?

Introduction to 4:35–41 The three preceding seed parables of death and rebirth come to life with the storm and following calm. The disciples fear that they will be buried beneath the waves while it appears to them that Jesus, like the farmer of 4:27, is sleeping without knowing what is happening. But Jesus instantly calms the storm and asks where their faith is, even if that were as tiny as a mustard seed.

4:35 *other side.* Jesus is traveling from the western side of the Sea of Galilee to the eastern shore, leaving the predominantly Jewish region of Galilee for the more Gentile region of the Gerasenes. See the note on 5:1 for more details. *He said to them.* Jesus continues the close relationship with the disciples shown throughout ch. 4 by His explanations of the parables. After dealing with the massive crowds, this journey promised to be a quiet rest. Mk 6:32 is a similar setting of escape from the crowds by boat.

4:36 *just as He was.* Jesus had entered the boat to teach (v. 1) and so without any further preparations, they began the journey. *other boats.* Only Mark notes the presence of other boats, though Jesus and the Twelve were evidently all in a single boat.

4:37 *windstorm.* The Sea of Galilee is about 700 feet below sea level. Mount Hermon, a 9,200 foot peak, sits only thirty miles northeast. When the westerly winds coming off this mountain collide with the warm air over the lake, sudden and violent storms are sometimes produced. The rare Gk word *lailaps,* meaning "storm," is a cyclone of wind, conveying the extreme conditions even for these experienced sailors. *waves were breaking into the boat.* Whipped by the wind, the waves crashed over the bow and sides. We can imagine the disciples furiously working to keep the bow into the waves and also bailing the boat.

4:38 *asleep.* Jesus' peaceful rest is a complete contrast to the wind, waves, and desperate disciples. His knowledge of the storm and His power over the wind is complete even when sleeping. *cushion.* Only Mark notes that Jesus' head was on a pillow, perhaps as a distinct memory of Peter. *Teacher.* While the word for teacher, *didaskalos,* is used by the disciples occasionally (9:38; 10:35; 13:1) it is most often used of Jesus by those first coming to Him, either seeking help or by His enemies hoping to trap Him (Mk 9:17; 10:17, 20; 12:14, 19, 32). The title "teacher" is especially appropriate here as Jesus had just finished the extended teaching of ch. 4 and another crucial lesson was about to be given. *do you not care.* Only Mark has this question which is beautifully asked in KJV, "Carest Thou not that we perish?" They could only imagine that His sleep equaled a callous ignorance of their need.

4:39 *rebuked . . . Peace! Be still!* Jesus addresses creation by speaking to the storm as if it were a person. By His authoritative word, He masters the wind and waves just as easily as illnesses and demons. The word for "rebuke," *epitimao,* occurs often in Mark, as Jesus corrects and warns disciples and others (3:12; 8:30, 33) and rebukes the demon (1:25). *calm.* The resulting calm is remarkable because it is instantaneous and complete.

4:40 *still no faith?* Jesus had assured the Twelve not much earlier that "the secret of the kingdom" had been given to them (v. 11). However, they had yet to internalize His teaching and self-revelation. Their lack of understanding is a theme for almost all of Mark. They were unnerved more by the calm than by the storm, just as the people of the area of the Gerasenes will be frightened when the demonized man is healed and restored to a peaceful mind (5:15–16).

4:41 *Who then is this.* This is the theme of much of Mark from 1:1 and continued through conflicts with demons and enemies. The identity of Jesus as Son of God, master over demons, and Lord of the Sabbath, now expands to the ruler of wind and wave. The disciples may have been wondering if Jesus was a miracle worker, such as Honi the Circle-Drawer and Hanina ben Dosa. They still did not understand that Jesus is more than a miracle worker; He is the Messiah and Son of God. None of them will acclaim Jesus as Messiah until 8:29. *even the wind and the sea obey Him.* The disciples see this miracle as a unique, third level beyond healing and exorcism. Physicians also heal and demons might depart on their own. But who can instantly calm the sea and wind but their Creator?

4:35–41 in Devotion and Prayer When Jesus rebukes the wind and waves, the lifeless storm shows a greater recognition of His divine power than the disciples. The brute forces of nature invariably obey the Lord's commands better than people, including God's own children, obey them. But the Lord nonetheless continues to love and care for us, despite our dullness and doubts. He not only calms all of the storms in our lives but actually does so in ways that mature our faith and lead us to trust Him more deeply. He may appear to sleep through our struggles but He always hears our cry. • Lord, forgive our doubts, for we sometimes take Your silence as nothing more than sleepy indifference. Remind us that You never sleep nor slumber, but always keep us under Your watchful eye. Amen.

Jesus heals a Gerasene demoniac (5:1–20)

ESV

5 1 They came to the other side of the
sea, to the country of the Gerasenes.
2 And when Jesus had stepped out
of the boat, immediately there met
him out of the tombs a man with an
unclean spirit. 3 He lived among the
tombs. And no one could bind him
anymore, not even with a chain, 4 for
he had often been bound with shackles and chains, but he wrenched the
chains apart, and he broke the shackles in pieces. No one had the strength
to subdue him. 5 Night and day among
the tombs and on the mountains he
was always crying out and cutting
himself with stones. 6 And when he
saw Jesus from afar, he ran and fell
down before him. 7 And crying out
with a loud voice, he said, "What
have you to do with me, Jesus, Son
of the Most High God? I adjure you
by God, do not torment me." 8 For he
was saying to him, "Come out of the
man, you unclean spirit!" 9 And Jesus
asked him, "What is your name?"
He replied, "My name is Legion,
for we are many." 10 And he begged
him earnestly not to send them out
of the country. 11 Now a great herd
of pigs was feeding there on the hillside, 12 and they begged him, saying,
"Send us to the pigs; let us enter
them." 13 So he gave them permission.
And the unclean spirits came out, and
entered the pigs, and the herd, num-
bering about two thousand, rushed
down the steep bank into the sea and
were drowned in the sea.

14 The herdsmen fled and told it in
the city and in the country. And people came to see what it was that had

KJV

5 1 And they came over unto the other side of the sea, into the country of the Gadarenes.

2 And when he was come out of the ship, immediately there met him out of the tombs a man with an unclean spirit,

3 Who had his dwelling among the tombs; and no man could bind him, no, not with chains:

4 Because that he had been often bound with fetters and chains, and the chains had been plucked asunder by him, and the fetters broken in pieces: neither could any man tame him.

5 And always, night and day, he was in the mountains, and in the tombs, crying, and cutting himself with stones.

6 But when he saw Jesus afar off, he ran and worshipped him,

7 And cried with a loud voice, and said, What have I to do with thee, Jesus, thou Son of the most high God? I adjure thee by God, that thou torment me not.

8 For he said unto him, Come out of the man, thou unclean spirit.

9 And he asked him, What is thy name? And he answered, saying, My name is Legion: for we are many.

10 And he besought him much that he would not send them away out of the country.

11 Now there was there nigh unto the mountains a great herd of swine feeding.

12 And all the devils besought him, saying, Send us into the swine, that we may enter into them.

happened. [15]And they came to Jesus and saw the demon-possessed man, the one who had had the legion, sitting there, clothed and in his right mind, and they were afraid. [16]And those who had seen it described to them what had happened to the demon-possessed man and to the pigs. [17]And they began to beg Jesus to depart from their region. [18]As he was getting into the boat, the man who had been possessed with demons begged him that he might be with him. [19]And he did not permit him but said to him, "Go home to your friends and tell them how much the Lord has done for you, and how he has had mercy on you." [20]And he went away and began to proclaim in the Decapolis how much Jesus had done for him, and everyone marveled.

[13]And forthwith Jesus gave them leave. And the unclean spirits went out, and entered into the swine: and the herd ran violently down a steep place into the sea, (they were about two thousand;) and were choked in the sea.

[14]And they that fed the swine fled, and told it in the city, and in the country. And they went out to see what it was that was done.

[15]And they come to Jesus, and see him that was possessed with the devil, and had the legion, sitting, and clothed, and in his right mind: and they were afraid.

[16]And they that saw it told them how it befell to him that was possessed with the devil, and also concerning the swine.

[17]And they began to pray him to depart out of their coasts.

[18]And when he was come into the ship, he that had been possessed with the devil prayed him that he might be with him.

[19]Howbeit Jesus suffered him not, but saith unto him, Go home to thy friends, and tell them how great things the Lord hath done for thee, and hath had compassion on thee.

[20]And he departed, and began to publish in Decapolis how great things Jesus had done for him: and all men did marvel.

Introduction to 5:1–20 The disciples sail from one storm into another. The calm of 4:39 is broken by the shrieking of the demon. However, Jesus again shows His complete and immediate power. Mark records three episodes in which Jesus casts out unclean or demonic spirits (1:21–28; 5:1–20; 9:14–29). Each account exhibits a similar structure: opening conflict; exorcism; and, finally, dismay and praise.

5:1 *Gerasenes.* Gerasa was a city c. 35 miles southeast of the Sea of Galilee. These events do not take place within the city proper but in the outlying regions near the seashore. Yesterday had been a day of teaching the crowd and a night of battling the storm. The disciples likely yearned for a quiet, anonymous day on this new shore.

5:2 *immediately there met Him . . . a man with an unclean spirit.* The disciples and Jesus find no rest on this beach. The demon-possessed man approaches Jesus with the same immediacy of the demon of 1:23. The man comes towards Jesus even though the demons know His identity, His power, and their hopeless situation. The man's approach might show a conflict between the man himself and the controlling demons. The man seeks relief while the demons dread the encounter. *unclean spirit.* Contact with tombs was likely regarded as ritually defiling (cf. Lv 21:1). In folk piety, graveyards were believed to be the haunts of ghosts and disembodied spirits.

5:3 *tombs.* In this region, archaeologists have unearthed "cavern tombs" (man-made caves carved out of rocky outcroppings). They are large enough to provide living space. The disciples have just escaped being entombed in the sea and they now meet a man who lives among the dead.

5:4 Apparently, the townspeople feared the man's violent strength and had tried to bind him. The extent to which they had tried to restrain the man makes the exorcism all the greater. Just as no one could still the storm of the previous night, no one could still this man's torment. The town's attempts to control him makes their fear all the more remarkable when he is restored, vv. 15–16.

5:5 *always crying out and cutting himself.* Demons drove this man to inflict wounds on himself. This suffering is in contrast to the mercy the demons desire for themselves (v. 7). See similar torment with the demon-possessed boy in 9:18, 20, 22.

5:6 *he saw Jesus from afar, he ran.* Here is a race for life itself! What a scene it was as he approached. He was barely dressed, perhaps with the remains of the shackles on his ankles and wrists, lean and desperate. What a challenge for the faith of the disciples who saw him approach. Did they welcome him as another opportunity for Jesus' healing power, or did they shrink backward from this demonic storm?

5:7 *Jesus, Son of the Most High God?* See the notes on 1:24 on the demon's use of Jesus' title. The knowledge of a demon's name was considered to give one power over the demon. The demon's use of Jesus' name and title might have been an attempt to gain leverage for its request of mercy. *I adjure you by God.* The word for "adjure" (*orkidzo*) is used only here and in Ac 19:13 when magicians attempt an exorcism. It may mean either to command or to beg, both meanings fitting here as the demons attempt this demand though they are powerless. It is ironic that the demon invokes the name of God for his own purpose. *do not torment me.* The demon rightly expects a final torment which is foreseen in Rv 20:10 with the lake of eternal fire. The coming immersion of the demons in the Sea of Galilee was a small punishment compared to the fierce, eternal lake to come.

5:8 *for He was saying.* This phrase captures the ongoing, simultaneous speaking of Jesus. Here was a striking contrast: while the legions of demons shriek, perhaps in a cacophony of sounds, Jesus powerfully, insistently commands them to come out. Here is the quiet voice of 4:39 calming another storm. As with 1Ki 19:11–12, God speaks not with earthquake, wind, or fire, nor is He silenced by them, but His still, small voice is greater than all.

5:9 Jesus forces these demons to reveal their name! Jesus' omniscience clearly knows this, but He gains control over their demands with His question. *Legion.* Roman military units containing 4,000–6,000 soldiers. Roman legions were legendary for their ferocity and ability to impose their will upon others. A whole host of demons possessed this man. The name "Legion" might have been their attempt to impress with their large number or their harsh treatment of the man. Bengel writes,

> There was one principal leader among them, and the rest were conjoined with him, constituting thus the legion. . . . If in one [dwelling] there can be so many [demons], how many there must be in the whole aggregate throughout the world! (Bengel 518)

5:10 *they begged Him.* In one moment, the demons tried to gain control over Jesus by invoking His name (v. 7); in the next, they begged Jesus not to expel them too far away. Even when clearly doomed, they, without apology or remorse, seek their own advantage. See a similar selfishness shown by the rich man in the parable of Lk 16:22–27. *send them out of the country.* In Mark their focus is remaining in the region while in Lk 8:31 they beg not to be sent into the abyss, their eternal torment. Both requests and other appeals likely came repeatedly from the host of demons.

5:11 *great herd of pigs.* Both the large number and the unclean nature of the pigs matched the demons and their deserved end. Here is a fitting end since the demons have driven this man to live among the unclean tombs with the dead. Now the demons are themselves driven into the ritually unclean swine which will soon perish.

5:12 *begged.* The earlier tone of command in v. 7 conveyed with the verb "adjure" is replaced here and in v. 10 with begging. The bravado of the demons, even with being a legion, disappeared as their destruction came near. How often the possessed man must have also begged for mercy, but none was shown to him. Yet the demons expected divine compassion for themselves.

5:13 *He gave them permission.* Jesus agrees with their request in light of His foresight and judgment. This brief respite in the swine will be no true escape for the demons. *rushed down.* Just as the demon-possessed man sprinted to meet Jesus, so the demons race away from Him. But what a contrast. The man ran for his life and received it, but the demons dashed to their death. *drowned.* The death of the pigs powerfully confirms that the demons' hold over this poor man was finally loosed.

5:14 *herdsmen . . . told.* Running continues to energize this narrative. The herdsmen tell their story repeatedly in both city and country, to anyone they meet. As with many of the miracles of Jesus, the news explodes (1:28, 32, 45; 2:12–13; 4:1), but here there is no restriction on its retelling. An event of this size, unlike the private healing of the leper, 1:44, could never be hidden. It was time for the news of Jesus' power to expand, especially in this new region. *people came.* As the news goes out, the crowd comes in. They likely came with some of the same breathless urgency that has characterized this entire narrative.

5:15 *the demon-possessed man, the one who had the legion.* Mark doubles the description of the man, stressing that it was this very man. His former tormented state is stunning compared to his restored life. *sitting there . . . in his right mind.* The sudden change in the man recalls the instant calm that Jesus brought to the storm in 4:39. *afraid.* Here is the typical reaction to a stunning show of divine power. The disciples had similar fear in the boat following the storm (4:41).

5:16 *those who had seen it.* Though Jesus and the man are present, the story is retold by the witnesses. They likely were too excited to be silenced and their retelling had greater effect than what the man might have said. Also the man had not spoken coherent words for some time so no one expected an explanation from him.

5:17 *began to beg.* This is the third of the four times in this narrative (5:10, 12, 18) for the verb "beg" (*parakaleo*). Jesus was begged by the demons that they might not be forced to leave the region and now the townspeople beg Jesus to leave. The loss of the pigs and the complete reversal of the man's life were too unsettling. They feared what might next be upended.

5:18 *as He was getting into the boat.* Though Jesus' presence would have been a blessing, He left when asked. This is similar to His performing few miracles in Nazareth because of their disbelief. Jesus did not force faith upon the doubting, nor did He stay with the rejecting. *begged Him that He might be with him.* The man might have worried over a return of the demons, or been anxious of rejection from the townspeople. While the miracles have often brought crowds around Jesus, this is the first time that the one healed has asked to go with Jesus. We might have expected him to come along as a new disciple, one who volunteered without a personal directive from Jesus.

5:19 *He did not permit him.* This refusal was certainly done with kindness and understanding. Jesus reassured the man that he was permanently free from the demons and that he had an important mission. *Go home to your friends.* Given that the man had been living in the tombs, this first step had to be a welcome gift. Rather than detaining the man any longer from home, Jesus restored him to his family as completely healed. *tell them.* Though Jesus has commanded silence after healing others (e.g., 1:44; 5:43; 7:36; 8:26), He encourages this man to share the good news of his deliverance. The man does so enthusiastically, spreading the word in numerous communities (Decapolis means "10 cities"). Jesus will not remain in this area (5:21), and so this man's news will not bring a hampering crowd. *mercy on you.* The word for mercy, *eleeo*, occurs only here and in the cry for mercy by the blind man Bartimaeus (10:47–48). It is the word behind the liturgical prayer, "Lord, have mercy." While rare in Mark, it is frequently used in Matthew (Mt 5:7; 9:27; 15:22; 17:15; 18:33; 20:30–31), most often as appeal for healing from Jesus.

5:20 *began to proclaim.* The man's testimony must have been extensive as he detailed not only the moment of healing but also the great change between his life before and after the exorcism. This was a story of which he must have never tired. *everyone marveled.* The Gk word for "marveled" is *thaumadzo* which means to wonder, marvel and be astonished at. It is used four times in Mark, demonstrating a range of amazement. Here is the wonder that we expect, people astonished over the power of Jesus. In contrast, Jesus marvels over the lack of faith shown by the people of Nazareth (6:6). Pilate is amazed over the silence of Jesus while on trial (15:5), and finally Pilate is again stunned to hear that Jesus had died so quickly (15:44). Astonishment fits the theme of sudden miracles in Mark and continues even through Jesus' death.

5:1–20 in Devotion and Prayer Despite Jesus' magnificent work of deliverance, the reaction to Him is mixed. The man eagerly wishes to follow Jesus and then enthusiastically furthers His cause, while the townspeople ask Jesus to go away. The Lord still receives the same kind of mixed reaction today, even among those who follow Him, especially when doing so requires a change from established ways. But what remarkable kindness Jesus shows! He rescues people from the devil's power and even the grave itself, and then allows them to be witnesses to the wonders of His grace. • Lord, rescue us from the power of Satan, and draw us from the grave through Your resurrection. May we learn joyfully to tell our neighbors what good things the Lord has done. Amen.

Jesus heals a sick woman and raises a dead girl (5:21–43)

ESV	KJV
21 And when Jesus had crossed again in the boat to the other side, a great crowd gathered about him, and he was beside the sea. 22 Then came one of the rulers of the synagogue, Jairus by name, and seeing him, he fell at his feet 23 and implored him earnestly, saying, "My little daughter is at the point of death. Come and lay your hands on her, so that she may be made well and live." 24 And he went with him. And a great crowd followed him and	21 And when Jesus was passed over again by ship unto the other side, much people gathered unto him: and he was nigh unto the sea. 22 And, behold, there cometh one of the rulers of the synagogue, Jairus by name; and when he saw him, he fell at his feet, 23 And besought him greatly, saying, My little daughter lieth at the point of death: I pray thee, come and lay thy hands on her, that she may be healed; and she shall live.

thronged about him. 25 And there was a woman who had had a discharge of blood for twelve years, 26 and who had suffered much under many physicians, and had spent all that she had, and was no better but rather grew worse. 27 She had heard the reports about Jesus and came up behind him in the crowd and touched his garment. 28 For she said, "If I touch even his garments, I will be made well." 29 And immediately the flow of blood dried up, and she felt in her body that she was healed of her disease. 30 And Jesus, perceiving in himself that power had gone out from him, immediately turned about in the crowd and said, "Who touched my garments?" 31 And his disciples said to him, "You see the crowd pressing around you, and yet you say, 'Who touched me?'" 32 And he looked around to see who had done it. 33 But the woman, knowing what had happened to her, came in fear and trembling and fell down before him and told him the whole truth. 34 And he said to her, "Daughter, your faith has made you well; go in peace, and be healed of your disease."

35 While he was still speaking, there came from the ruler's house some who said, "Your daughter is dead. Why trouble the Teacher any further?" 36 But overhearing what they said, Jesus said to the ruler of the synagogue, "Do not fear, only believe." 37 And he allowed no one to follow him except Peter and James and John the brother of James. 38 They came to the house of the ruler of the synagogue, and Jesus saw a commotion, people weeping and wailing loudly. 39 And when he had entered, he said

24 And Jesus went with him; and much people followed him, and thronged him.

25 And a certain woman, which had an issue of blood twelve years,

26 And had suffered many things of many physicians, and had spent all that she had, and was nothing bettered, but rather grew worse,

27 When she had heard of Jesus, came in the press behind, and touched his garment.

28 For she said, If I may touch but his clothes, I shall be whole.

29 And straightway the fountain of her blood was dried up; and she felt in her body that she was healed of that plague.

30 And Jesus, immediately knowing in himself that virtue had gone out of him, turned him about in the press, and said, Who touched my clothes?

31 And his disciples said unto him, Thou seest the multitude thronging thee, and sayest thou, Who touched me?

32 And he looked round about to see her that had done this thing.

33 But the woman fearing and trembling, knowing what was done in her, came and fell down before him, and told him all the truth.

34 And he said unto her, Daughter, thy faith hath made thee whole; go in peace, and be whole of thy plague.

35 While he yet spake, there came from the ruler of the synagogue's house certain which said, Thy daughter is dead: why troublest thou the Master any further?

36 As soon as Jesus heard the word that was spoken, he saith unto the ruler of the synagogue, Be not afraid, only believe.

to them, "Why are you making a
commotion and weeping? The child
is not dead but sleeping." 40 And they
laughed at him. But he put them all
outside and took the child's father
and mother and those who were with
him and went in where the child was.
41 Taking her by the hand he said to
her, "Talitha cumi," which means,
"Little girl, I say to you, arise." 42 And
immediately the girl got up and began
walking (for she was twelve years of
age), and they were immediately
overcome with amazement. 43 And
he strictly charged them that no one
should know this, and told them to
give her something to eat.

37 And he suffered no man to follow him, save Peter, and James, and John the brother of James.

38 And he cometh to the house of the ruler of the synagogue, and seeth the tumult, and them that wept and wailed greatly.

39 And when he was come in, he saith unto them, Why make ye this ado, and weep? the damsel is not dead, but sleepeth.

40 And they laughed him to scorn. But when he had put them all out, he taketh the father and the mother of the damsel, and them that were with him, and entereth in where the damsel was lying.

41 And he took the damsel by the hand, and said unto her, Talitha cumi; which is, being interpreted, Damsel, I say unto thee, arise.

42 And straightway the damsel arose, and walked; for she was of the age of twelve years. And they were astonished with a great astonishment.

43 And he charged them straitly that no man should know it; and commanded that something should be given her to eat.

Introduction to 5:21–43 Both stories here center on females, and both mention a span of twelve years: the girl was twelve years old, and the woman had suffered from a hemorrhage for twelve years. As discussed in the notes on 3:21, this is one of the A-B-A sections in Mark where the first story begins, then a second person and action comes, and finally the first story concludes. While both women are ill, there is a great contrast between the urgent, fatal illness of the girl versus the woman whose bleeding has gone on for twelve years. Yet the woman's faith in Jesus' instant, healing power is what both need.

5:21 *He was beside the sea.* This is the fourth narrative unit in a row that has begun beside or on the sea. Jesus began teaching in the boat (4:1), concluding that day with the voyage through the storm (4:35–41). He arrived on the far coast (5:1) where He healed the demoniac, and now He returns to the west bank of the Sea where He faces illness and death. The full range of Jesus' ministry is held in these two chapters centered around the Sea. In this short time and space, Jesus teaches, controls nature's rage, heals illness, casts out demons, and even raises the dead.

5:22 *rulers of the synagogue.* Jairus was one of the laymen responsible for the upkeep of the synagogue. *he fell at his feet.* As a recognized local leader, Jairus' respect for Jesus was especially noteworthy. He likely had heard of the previous healings by Jesus. In light of his daughter's serious condition, he must have rushed towards Jesus as soon as he could reach Him. This urgent approach matches well the race towards Jesus by the demoniac (5:1, 6–7), but is the opposite of the stealthy approach by the woman (5:27).

5:23 *implored Him earnestly.* The verb "implored" is *parkaleo,* the same verb used four times in the previous miracle of the healing of the demon-possessed man. See the notes on 5:17–18. The theme of earnest, vocal pleading continues, but will be contrasted by the woman's quiet confidence that makes no outward request (5:28). *lay Your hands on her.* Jesus had healed with a touch before (1:31, 41) and so would do again several times (6:5; 7:32; 8:23, 25; 9:27). The touch by Jesus seemed a natural way to convey His power and His courageous compassion. That said, Jesus was perfectly capable of effecting cures simply by saying the word (7:29; Mt 8:13). *point of death.* Only Mark describes her condition in this way, essentially saying that she was at the very end. However, Jairus was hopeful that Jesus could outrace death by coming quickly.

5:24 The account of Jairus and his daughter is interrupted by a story about the healing of the woman with a discharge of blood. This is one of several similar arrangements of two stories occurring simultaneously (cf. 3:21–35; 6:7–30; 11:12–25; 14:1–12). In this case and most others, the two events occur in this sequence while with 6:7–30, the death of John is reported purposefully within the disciples' journey. *He went with him.* Jesus could have easily dismissed Jairus with the assurance that his daughter would be well, as He did with the centurion and the Syro-Phoenician woman (Mt 8:13; Mk 7:29). However, Jesus compassionately goes with Jairus who needs His reassuring presence. Jesus also knows the approach of the woman and the lesson her faith will be for Jairus. *a great crowd followed him.* Jesus' ministry has been marked by such crowds since ch. 1, coming to be healed or taught (1:32, 45; 2:2, 13; 3:7, 20, 32; 4:1; 5:14). Here a crowd gathers primarily to watch what will happen more than to receive something themselves. *thronged about Him.* The verb for "thronged about" is *synthlibo*, and is used only here and Mk 5:31 in the New Testament. It means to "press together, to surround thoroughly." Given the many previous crowds which pressed upon Jesus, this crowd, described in this way, must have been extraordinary.

5:25 *discharge of blood.* This was likely a uterine hemorrhage. See Lv 15:25–30 for the restrictions upon a woman with such a condition. According to the rules of ritual cleanliness, she should not have been in the midst of the crowd and certainly should not have touched Jesus as this would have made Him also ritually unclean. *twelve years.* Our sympathy goes out to her upon learning of this long illness. She is the complete opposite of Jairus, being a woman, ritually unclean, unable to approach Jesus openly, and herself having the illness. Though her illness is not immediately fatal, as Jairus daughter's is, yet given that it has lasted twelve years, it has clearly lasted long enough. Both women are at a crucial moment.

5:26 *had suffered much from many physicians.* The woman had tried all kinds of remedies. The Talmud lists eleven cures for such ailments, all of which we would consider superstitious; she likely tried such remedies and anything that promised relief. *was not better but rather grew worse.* Her gradual decline matches the condition of the little girl as her family must have also watched her get no better but only worse. This phrase captures the state of the world upon Jesus' arrival and the ultimate futility of our own remedies for body and soul.

5:27 *came up behind Him.* As she had repeatedly gone from doctor to doctor, now she went with even greater resolve towards Jesus. Where her efforts had once been broadcast among many and any, now they could be focused on this one hope. *touched His garment.* The touch was her appeal and the conduit of His healing. Even in the midst of the pressing crowd, she was sure that there was distinctive healing power for her in this secret touch. No one else in the crowd needed to be healed for her to believe in His power for her. Her secret approach from behind and her modest thought of merely touching His cloak are the opposite of Jairus, who lead Jesus to his home.

5:28 *I will be well.* How often she must have had this hope and heard this promise as she went to one physician after another. However, she had likely heard the growing news of Jesus' authentic healings. Given the serious illnesses that He had overcome, she had reason to believe that He could heal her. In turn, her faith and healing would become the foundation for Jairus' hope (v. 36).

5:29 *immediately.* In contrast to Jairus's anxious waiting (vv. 22–24, 35), healing came instantaneously to this woman, who had waited so many years. "Immediately," Mark's familiar word, *euthus* in Gk, often describes the instantaneous effect of Jesus' power (1:42; 2:12; 5:42; 10:52). She believed correctly that His power and compassion would end these twelve years of suffering without delay. *She felt in her body.* Her instant knowledge was matched simultaneously with Jesus' own knowledge (v. 30). What a relief for her to know, finally and fully, that her illness was gone. She didn't need to imagine being a bit better, or hope that tomorrow would bring relief. The twelve-year ordeal was over.

5:30 *power . . . from Him.* This does not mean Jesus performed this miracle unawares or involuntarily. He had known of her approach, put Himself into her grasp, and knew the healing which she had just felt. *immediately turned about.* Jesus' knowledge has a corresponding instant action, just as her touch had brought an immediate inner healing and knowledge. *Who touched My garments?* This was not an accusatory question but an invitation for the woman to confess her faith. She alone knew the meaning of the question since He had not mentioned the healing to the disciples.

5:31 *you see the crowd pressing.* The disciples are asking, in essence, "You see the crowd, don't you? How can you ask this?" Countless people had accidentally or intentionally touched Him. With Jesus' sudden stop and question, the crowd must have ground to a ragged halt, pressing upon Jesus all the more. Yet Jesus and the woman knew that there was only one touch that day which brought healing. Jesus was waiting for her to have faith not only in His healing power, but in His loving grace. Faith trusts that God can heal, and also that He knows our needs and graciously gives help without reproach.

5:32 *looked around.* This word, *periblepo* in Gk, is used almost exclusively by Mark in the NT, appearing six times. (Only Lk uses it otherwise, Lk 6:10.) In Mark, five times it describes Jesus' look which surveys the crowd around Him, sometimes in anger (3:5), or in appreciation (3:34), or in response to rejection (10:23). The final look is His scan of the temple in 11:11 which had to be a poignant look at what would be eventually destroyed. Here Jesus is not so much searching the crowd as waiting patiently for the woman to come forward. Since Jesus knows all, His look asks not, "Who did this?" or "Where is she?" but "When will you come forward?"

5:33 *knowing what had happened.* Jesus' all-knowing power often reveals a portion of a person's thoughts and past, leaving him or her the opportunity to express and to act upon what He knows. See 2:8–12 for an example of Jesus' knowledge of His enemies, and 10:17–22 for His knowledge of the beloved riches of the young man. Here, only the woman shares with Jesus the knowledge of her illness, faith, and healing. The KJV interestingly summarizes all she knew with, "knowing what was done in her." *fear and trembling.* The woman's illness involved impurity and thus left her open to the charge that she had defiled Jesus by touching Him. She might have worried that the illness or even worse might return, but her faith in Jesus' mercy overcame that fear. *the whole truth.* What a rush of words this was, covering twelve years of suffering ending with this moment of blessed healing, all told with faith and gratitude.

5:34 *Daughter.* Jesus' title of close relationship is the opening word of kindness needed for her anxiety. It reminds of His declaration that anyone who does the will of God is His brother, sister, and mother (Mk 3:35). *faith has made you well.* To be clear, this woman's faith was not the main cause of her healing. Rather, her faith was the means whereby healing was received from the outpouring of Jesus' power and grace. *go in peace and be healed of your disease.* Jesus assures her that her illness was permanently gone. This lasting health is the perfect counterpart to her instant healing. In this way, her bodily health and spiritual peace are a blessed match, as in 3Jn 2, John prays "that you may be in good health, as it goes well with your soul." Peace comes as a result of justification by faith (Rm 5:1). Such peace overcomes any future difficulties since it is founded on the bedrock of God's forgiveness by the sacrifice and resurrection of Jesus.

5:35 *your daughter is dead.* Their blunt announcement offers no comfort and even goes on to accuse Jairus of troubling Jesus uselessly. *trouble the teacher.* The title "teacher" is usually used by Jesus' opponents, or, as here, by those who interrupt His speaking to announce that His help is too little and too late. While Jesus spent many hours teaching, He was far more than an instructor, as His miracles forcefully underscored. See the note on 4:38 for further details concerning the use of "teacher" in Mark. The word "trouble," *skullo,* is used to describe the harassed people of Mt 9:36 and is in the reply of the centurion who says that Jesus need not be troubled to come to his house (Lk 7:6). Here Jesus insists that His coming with Jairus is neither useless nor a bother. Jairus' fears need the reassuring presence of Jesus.

5:36 *overhearing what they said.* Jesus waits until they have reported all of their news before reclaiming the moment as the Teacher. *Do not fear, only believe.* The fear and despair naturally falling over Jairus could be overcome only through faith. The woman's example comes into play here even as she slips back into the crowd. As she trusted a mere touch of Jesus, so Jairus can trust that Jesus' presence and power can overcome death. The command to believe brings faith with it. Calvin writes, "We are taught by this passage, that we cannot go beyond bounds in believing: because our faith, however large, will never embrace the hundredth part of the divine goodness" (*Harmony* 1:414).

5:37 *Peter and James and John.* Jesus takes only the inner circle of these three disciples, perhaps due to the small size of the house and the girl's room. The commotion in Jairus' house would only have increased if a large entourage had come in with Jesus. Jairus needed to focus on Jesus alone during this time. These three disciples will be set apart two more times at the Mount of Transfiguration (9:2), and also during the Garden prayer (14:33). The Transfiguration is a moment of glory, while the Garden is under the dark shadow of the cross. The journey to Jairus' house has both elements as Jesus comes to people in despair over death but leaves them with the joy of the resurrection.

5:38 *commotion.* The word for "commotion" is *thorubos,* a tumult or even riot. This word describes also the uproar of the crowd that the enemies of Jesus feared if He had been openly arrested (Mk 14:2), and it was the very riot that Pilate saw forming during Jesus' trial (Mt 27:24). Jesus has left outside the anxious crowd that came with Him but now steps into even greater tension. Jairus' faith is even more severely tried when he hears and sees this confirmation that his daughter is truly dead.

5:39 *why are you making a commotion and weeping?* Jesus' question expects faith even in the face of death. In a similar way He had asked the disciples about their fear of the storm, "Why are you so afraid?" (Mk 4:40). He shows a similar calm expectation of faith when approaching the grave of Lazarus (Jn 11:4, 14, 25–26). When confronting death, believers are to grieve with the certainty that Jesus has overcome death (1Th 4:13). *not dead but sleeping*. The girl had, in fact, died, but Jesus was about to awaken her as easily as from a natural sleep. Because of the Lord's mastery over death and the resurrection promise, the NT repeatedly speaks of death in terms of "sleeping" (Mt 27:52; Jn 11:11, 13; Ac 7:60; 13:36; 1Co 11:30; 15:6, 18, 20, 51; 1Th 4:13–15). The image of sleep is a beautiful picture of death as an outward rest which ends with the touch of the Master and His call.

5:40 *laughed*. The word for "laughed" is *katagelao* which is used only here and the parallel verses in Mt 9:24 and Lk 8:53. The KJV expresses it as "they laughed him to scorn." This is a ridiculing, scornful derision. The mourners knew death. How could this man, without even seeing the girl, say that she was only sleeping? Why would Jairus bring someone like this, especially at this time? However, Jesus knew the true state of the girl. Usually Jesus' omniscience uncovered the hidden thoughts of others (2:8), but here He knows the hidden, forthcoming life of the girl. *He put them all outside.* The parents needed to hear and see only Jesus, and so He took them and the three disciples into the room. The grieving parents must face their daughter's death, but they do so in the presence of the Lord of Life.

5:41 *Talitha cumi.* These words are Aramaic, meaning "young one" (feminine), "arise." The power of these simple words from Jesus' lips was such that those witnessing their effect never forgot them. Peter likely included the exact words in his preaching and Mark passes them on here. St. Ambrose writes: "How quickly at the word of the Lord does the spirit return, the reviving body rise up, and food is taken, that the evidence of life may be believed!" (*NPNF*2 10:187). As Adam was brought to life by the breath of God (Gn 2:7), so this girl comes to life by the words of Him who created all things (Jn 1:3). In a similar way, Jesus raised the son of the widow of Nain and Lazarus with a brief word (Lk 7:14; Jn 11:43).

5:42 *immediately.* This is the only verse in Mark in which "immediately," *euthus,* is used twice. Such an emphasis fits the drama of the resurrection and the astonishment of the family. Just as the woman was healed of her twelve years of bleeding (v. 29), so the little girl's life is renewed instantaneously as a sign of Jesus' power. *began walking.* Often the miraculous healings of Jesus are demonstrated by renewed action, such as the paralytic rolling up his mat and leaving (2:12), and Peter's mother-in-law beginning to serve Jesus and the others (1:31). So the girl is more than just conscious. She is fully restored, ready to leave the bed and room. *overcome with amazement.* Mark uses an unusual construction by using the same root word for both the verb and noun, essentially saying that they were amazed with a great amazement. The noun "amazement," *ekstasis,* is used only here and in 16:8 where it describes the amazement of the women racing back from Jesus' empty tomb. We are left to imagine the confused amazement of the scoffers (v. 40), when the girl walked out perfectly well.

5:43 *no one should know.* This continues the note of secrecy that has often been found. See the notes on 1:25; 1:44. Mark doesn't record if the miracle was kept secret but it is hard to imagine how the girl and her parents could say nothing. *give her something to eat.* Jesus' concern for the girl goes beyond the miracle. Also, her eating demonstrated her complete restoration.

5:21–43 in Devotion and Prayer Jesus heals Jairus's daughter and a woman with a chronic ailment. Like Jairus, we often worry that the Lord's delay in answering our prayers may end up in catastrophe. But the Eternal One, who overcame death by rising from the dead, never runs out of time. In fact, His gracious promise is that we shall share eternal life with Him. • Lord, grant us to believe without doubting that You can heal every illness. Give us patience as well, while we wait for You to act in Your good time, according to Your gracious will. Amen.

Jesus is rejected at Nazareth (6:1–6)

ESV	KJV
6 [1]He went away from there and came to his hometown, and his disciples followed him. [2]And on the Sabbath he began to teach in the synagogue, and many who heard him were astonished, saying, "Where did this man get these things? What is the wisdom given to him? How are such mighty works done by his hands? [3]Is not this the carpenter, the son of Mary and brother of James and Joses and Judas and Simon? And are not his sisters here with us?" And they took offense at him. [4]And Jesus said to them, "A prophet is not without honor, except in his hometown and among his relatives and in his own household." [5]And he could do no mighty work there, except that he laid his hands on a few sick people and healed them. [6]And he marveled because of their unbelief. And he went about among the villages teaching.	6 [1]And he went out from thence, and came into his own country; and his disciples follow him. [2]And when the sabbath day was come, he began to teach in the synagogue: and many hearing him were astonished, saying, From whence hath this man these things? and what wisdom is this which is given unto him, that even such mighty works are wrought by his hands? [3]Is not this the carpenter, the son of Mary, the brother of James, and Joses, and of Juda, and Simon? and are not his sisters here with us? And they were offended at him. [4]But Jesus, said unto them, A prophet is not without honour, but in his own country, and among his own kin, and in his own house. [5]And he could there do no mighty work, save that he laid his hands upon a few sick folk, and healed them. [6]And he marvelled because of their unbelief. And he went round about the villages, teaching.

Introduction to 6:1–6 Jesus completes His travels by returning to Nazareth. News of His miracles preceded Him, but instead of praise, it creates confusion and rejection. Nazareth acknowledges the miracles were done, but they reject that Jesus, the carpenter, the brother of all those they know, could or should have done them. So instead of a joyous welcome, Jesus is given a faithless rejection. This is a prelude to His final rejection at Jerusalem, but despite rejection, Jesus continues on with His ministry.

6:1 *hometown.* Nazareth, the town where Jesus was raised (Mt 2:19–23), not Capernaum, from which He conducted His ministry (Mt 4:13). The disciples coming with Jesus recalls the earlier attempt by His family to encircle Him (3:21, 31–32). As He returns to Nazareth, the presence of the disciples shows His ministry is ongoing.

6:2 *teach in the synagogue.* It appears that Jesus had not yet preached in the Nazareth synagogue, as He had in Capernaum. While He might have come to Nazareth for some rest, this opportunity couldn't be missed. Given the conflicts on two previous Sabbaths in synagogues (1:21; 3:1), another clash could be expected here. *teach.* See notes on 1:21 concerning Jesus' teaching in the synagogue. As often with Mark, the content of the teaching is not given, but rather the conflict that follows. *What is the wisdom.* The wisdom of Jesus' teaching is not the key question. Like His miracles, His teaching's power is undeniable. The issue will be the identity of Jesus, the very point on which Mark began the Gospel (1:1). *mighty works done by His hands.* The word for "mighty works" is *dynamis,* used in this chapter at 6:5 and 6:14 where there is conflict over His power. Jesus uses the word twice as a sign of His return and identity as the Son of God (13:26; 14:62). Nazareth cannot grasp how the carpenter who simply worked with wood now creates miracles by the same hands.

6:3 *carpenter.* The word for "carpenter" in Greek is *tekton* and applied not only to carpenters and woodworkers but also to those who fashioned goods from a combination of wood and stone. Such a carpenter could work with all the materials found in the homes which Jesus often mentions in His teaching. Perhaps Jesus' work was there to be seen even at that moment. Perhaps Jesus' old neighbors mentioned His days as a tradesman in order to draw an unflattering contrast with His new role as teacher. No one expected a tradesman to have such wisdom and to leave his trade. But just as Jesus called the brothers to leave fishing and follow Him (1:16–20), so He had earlier left His carpentry for the ministry of the Kingdom. *brother.* See the notes on 3:31 where the family of Jesus first comes prominently in Mark. Though none of these four brothers of Jesus believed in Him as Savior during His earthly ministry (Jn 7:5), James and Jude did so after His resurrection. *James.* He saw the resurrected Jesus (1Co 15:7) and became a leader in the Jerusalem Church (cf. Ac 12:17; 15:13; 21:18; Gal 1:19; 2:9, 12; Jas 1:1). He wrote the short Epistle that bears his name. *Judas.* He wrote the short Epistle called Jude. *sisters.* Unfortunately, Jesus' sisters go unnamed and unnumbered. Consequently, nothing else is known of them. *took offense.* His wisdom in teaching, His demonstrated power in miracles, and

His gathering of many followers all set Him apart from His past in Nazareth. Jesus did not give offense; rather, the people took offense at His words and actions. *took offense.* The Gk word for "taking offense" is *skandalidzo,* which means originally to set a trap, or to cause someone to fall. The word is used in 4:17 of the seed which fails to endure, and often describes those who took offense at Jesus (Mt 11:6; 13:57; 26:31, 33). The people of Nazareth sense a trap in believing in the words and miracles of Jesus and so they sheer away from Him in fright.

6:4 *prophet is not without honor.* Jesus had sought no honor for thirty years but was content being the carpenter. There was enough for Him in that simple, creative work while He waited to begin His ministry. But when that ministry came, He was recognized as a prophet worthy of honor in any place but home. The rejection Jesus faces echoes the rejection of the prophets, such as Jeremiah, by the people of Israel, and the death of John the Baptist, the account of which is soon to be told (6:14–29). *hometown . . . relatives . . . own household.* Jesus gives three fields of disappointment, from the widest—the whole town—down to His own family circle. The KJV puts it, "his own country and among his own kin and in his own house." One would expect at least His immediate family would give Him that honor, but it was missing even there.

6:5 *could do no mighty works.* Jesus was fully capable of performing miracles in Nazareth, had He wanted to. Yet, He chose not to give any signs of His divinity to those who scoffingly dismissed Him. Jesus' miracles were gifts He freely gave, not proofs demanded of Him. The woman in the crowd (5:28), never having met Jesus, knew that the slightest touch by faith would heal her. And yet these who knew Him for decades received nothing since their hearts, minds, and hands were clenched shut against Him. *He laid His hands on a few sick people.* Jesus' compassion reached beyond their rejection. He could have justifiably refused giving any help just as He was refused. He could have done miracles to force people to acknowledge His power and identity. But these miracles are done for the sake of other's needs: a quiet sympathy. He came to be rejected rather than to reject the needs of others.

6:6 *marveled because of their unbelief.* The word for "marvel," *thaumadzo,* is generally used for the astonishment of the crowd after a miracle of Jesus (5:20; Mt 8:27; 9:33; 15:31). However, here

Jesus marvels over the lack of faith and scarcity of miracles in Nazareth. The callous unbelief of Jesus' hometown contrasts starkly with the humble but dogged examples of faith in 2:2–5 and 5:34. *teaching*. Jesus continues His teaching despite the failure of Nazareth. As before, the teaching is announced in one verse without detail as to what was taught (1:21; 2:2; 6:2). Mark's emphasis is on the act of teaching and either the faith or rejection that follows.

6:1–6 in Devotion and Prayer Two very different astonishments stand side by side: Jesus' teachings amaze His hometown neighbors; yet their hard-heartedness leaves Jesus amazed. We see similar contrasts today as people experience so much goodness from God and yet remain unthankful and unbelieving. But Jesus did not retaliate or write people off, even when they scornfully dismissed Him. He took the world's rejection and, through His sacrificial death, reconciled all people to God. • Lord, give us eyes to recognize You, ears to receive Your Word, and hearts to believe its promises. By Your grace, bring us to the fullness of Your glory in heaven. Amen.

Jesus Withdraws from His Public Ministry in Galilee (6:7–8:30)

Jesus sends the 12 apostles; John the Baptist dies (6:7–30)

ESV	KJV
7And he called the twelve and began to send them out two by two, and gave them authority over the unclean spirits. 8He charged them to take nothing for their journey except a staff—no bread, no bag, no money in their belts—9but to wear sandals and not put on two tunics. 10And he said to them, "Whenever you enter a house, stay there until you depart from there. 11And if any place will not receive you and they will not listen to you, when you leave, shake off the dust that is on your feet as a testimony against them." 12So they went out and proclaimed that people should repent. 13And they cast out many demons and anointed with	**7And he called unto him the twelve, and began to send them forth by two and two; and gave them power over unclean spirits; 8And commanded them that they should take nothing for their journey, save a staff only; no scrip, no bread, no money in their purse: 9But be shod with sandals; and not put on two coats. 10And he said unto them, In what place soever ye enter into an house, there abide till ye depart from that place. 11And whosoever shall not receive you, nor hear you, when ye depart thence, shake off the dust under your feet for a testimony against them.**

oil many who were sick and healed them.

14 King Herod heard of it, for Jesus' name had become known. Some said, "John the Baptist has been raised from the dead. That is why these miraculous powers are at work in him." 15 But others said, "He is Elijah." And others said, "He is a prophet, like one of the prophets of old." 16 But when Herod heard of it, he said, "John, whom I beheaded, has been raised." 17 For it was Herod who had sent and seized John and bound him in prison for the sake of Herodias, his brother Philip's wife, because he had married her. 18 For John had been saying to Herod, "It is not lawful for you to have your brother's wife." 19 And Herodias had a grudge against him and wanted to put him to death. But she could not, 20 for Herod feared John, knowing that he was a righteous and holy man, and he kept him safe. When he heard him, he was greatly perplexed, and yet he heard him gladly.

21 But an opportunity came when Herod on his birthday gave a banquet for his nobles and military commanders and the leading men of Galilee. 22 For when Herodias's daughter came in and danced, she pleased Herod and his guests. And the king said to the girl, "Ask me for whatever you wish, and I will give it to you." 23 And he vowed to her, "Whatever you ask me, I will give you, up to half of my kingdom." 24 And she went out and said to her mother, "For what should I ask?" And she said, "The head of John the Baptist." 25 And she came in immediately with haste to the king and asked, saying, "I want you to give

Verily I say unto you, It shall be more tolerable for Sodom and Gomorrha in the day of judgment, than for that city.

12 And they went out, and preached that men should repent.

13 And they cast out many devils, and anointed with oil many that were sick, and healed them.

14 And king Herod heard of him; (for his name was spread abroad:) and he said, That John the Baptist was risen from the dead, and therefore mighty works do shew forth themselves in him.

15 Others said, That it is Elias. And others said, That it is a prophet, or as one of the prophets.

16 But when Herod heard thereof, he said, It is John, whom I beheaded: he is risen from the dead.

17 For Herod himself had sent forth and laid hold upon John, and bound him in prison for Herodias' sake, his brother Philip's wife: for he had married her.

18 For John had said unto Herod, It is not lawful for thee to have thy brother's wife.

19 Therefore Herodias had a quarrel against him, and would have killed him; but she could not:

20 For Herod feared John, knowing that he was a just man and an holy, and observed him; and when he heard him, he did many things, and heard him gladly.

21 And when a convenient day was come, that Herod on his birthday made a supper to his lords, high captains, and chief estates of Galilee;

22 And when the daughter of the said Herodias came in, and danced, and pleased Herod and them that sat with

**me at once the head of John the Bap-
tist on a platter." 26And the king was
exceedingly sorry, but because of his
oaths and his guests he did not want
to break his word to her. 27And immediately the king sent an executioner
with orders to bring John's head. He
went and beheaded him in the prison
28and brought his head on a platter
and gave it to the girl, and the girl
gave it to her mother. 29When his disciples heard of it, they came and took
his body and laid it in a tomb.**

**30The apostles returned to Jesus and
told him all that they had done and
taught.**

**him, the king said unto the damsel,
Ask of me whatsoever thou wilt, and
I will give it thee.**

**23And he sware unto her, Whatso-
ever thou shalt ask of me, I will give
it thee, unto the half of my kingdom.**

**24And she went forth, and said unto
her mother, What shall I ask? And she
said, The head of John the Baptist.**

**25And she came in straightway with
haste unto the king, and asked, saying, I will that thou give me by and
by in a charger the head of John the
Baptist.**

**26And the king was exceeding sorry;
yet for his oath's sake, and for their
sakes which sat with him, he would
not reject her.**

**27And immediately the king sent
an executioner, and commanded his
head to be brought: and he went and
beheaded him in the prison,**

**28And brought his head in a char-
ger, and gave it to the damsel: and the
damsel gave it to her mother.**

**29And when his disciples heard of
it, they came and took up his corpse,
and laid it in a tomb.**

**30And the apostles gathered them-
selves together unto Jesus, and told
him all things, both what they had
done, and what they had taught.**

Introduction to 6:7–30 The combination of teaching and miracles, accomplished but rejected, continues with the sending of the Twelve and the end of John's life. The disciples go out with the message of the kingdom of God, having the ability to do the miracles done by Jesus. However, John's death, told in detail, is a forecast that the ministry of Jesus and the disciples will also end with rejection and death.

6:7 *began to send them out two by two.* Jesus multiplies His preaching and healing by doing this. Sending them in pairs gives them the support of each other. As Jesus did not do His ministry alone, but gathered others to Himself, so also no disciple was sent alone. It was particularly daring to send them out now with the rejection in Nazareth and the death of John as the bookends of their travels. Many see the sending of the disciples (vv. 7–13), the death of John (vv. 14–29), and the return of the disciples (v. 30), as one of the A-B-A sections of Mark. The account of the disciples' journey is held in suspense while the death of John is told. See the notes on 3:21 for more on this feature of Mark. *authority over the unclean spirits.* Jesus had appointed the Twelve (3:13–19); then they were with Him for some time, learning from His teaching and observing how He exercised authority. Now, He gives them a more active role in His ministry. Chief among the powers He gives them is the authority to cast out demons. As with Jesus' first public teaching in the synagogue (1:21–23), their teaching is linked with casting out of demons. See the notes on 3:14–15 for the first listing of the disciples and their calling to preach and cast out demons.

6:8 The apostles were to depend wholly upon the kindness of others and the provisions of God. Given the shabby treatment Jesus just received in Nazareth (vv. 1–5), this command must have sounded quite perilous. *their journey.* The word for "journey," *hodos,* is the same used in 1:3 for "way," "prepare the way of the Lord." The disciples walk on the same path as the Savior and trust that it is prepared also for them. They will find what is needed waiting for them.

6:9 *sandals.* The one item to be taken suggests that the men will travel a considerable distance. They were to spread the Word, not comfortably settle into one safe place. *not to wear two tunics.* The limited clothes signaled that the trip would be relatively short and that these men were far from the extravagantly dressed Pharisees who Jesus opposed in Mt 23:5–7, 27. As they went out, likely the words said by Jesus to Jairus (5:36) would apply to the disciples also: "Do not fear, only believe." Wesley writes,

> Our Lord intended by this mission to initiate them into their apostolic work. And it was doubtless an encouragement to them all their life after, to recollect the care which God took of them, when they had left all they had, and went out quite unfurnished for such an expedition. (Wesley 110)

6:10 *whenever you enter a house.* If they were accepted at a house, they were to stay there instead of moving on to find a better place. Their contentment reflects Jesus' own as He stayed thirty years in small Nazareth, a town which, in the end, didn't recognize Him as a prophet, let alone as the Son of God. Jesus' sending of the disciples to find a welcoming home is repeated in the preparations for the Lord's Supper when two disciples find a large room ready for them (14:13–15).

6:11 *shake off the dust.* Shaking dust off showed a complete rejection. In a similar way, Nehemiah shook out his garment as a sign, and Paul also shook out his garments (Ac 18:6), and the dust from his sandals (Ac 13:51). The dust left behind was a witness that the Word of Life had come, but, because of their rejection, this town was left with only choking dust. As in Ps 1, the Word which could have brought lasting life was thrown away and only the chaff was left.

6:12 *proclaimed . . . repent.* Repentance lay at the heart of both John's and Jesus' proclamations of the Kingdom (1:4, 14–15). The Twelve, therefore, continued and extended the ministries of John and Jesus. The preaching itself brings about both the recognition of sin and the receiving of forgiveness by faith. Repentance is not only the recognition of sins, but also the appeal for forgiveness and the faith that forgiveness has already been won through Christ. Disciples then and now are more than speakers of the Law when they preach repentance. They point beyond the failings of men to the saving work of Christ.

6:13 *cast out many demons.* As expected, given the conflicts seen with demons in 1:23 and 5:1ff., the proclamation of repentance brought assaults from the demons. The demons' attacks showed the seriousness of the disciples' ministry; the exorcisms demonstrated the power given by Jesus even from a distance. *anointed with oil.* Christian fellowships today still practice anointing rituals for healing (Lk 10:34). See 1Sm 10:1 and Jas 5:14. Recall also the beautiful blessing of Ps 23:5, "You anoint my head with oil." See also *LSB Pastoral Care Companion*, p. 34 for more information about how the people are anointed today. Calvin writes that this was "a visible token of spiritual grace, by which the healing that was administered by them was declared to proceed from that secret power of God; for under the Law *oil* was employed to represent the grace of the Spirit" (*Harmony* 2:6). *healed them.* The final of the three signature actions of Jesus within His kingdom ministry. With preaching, exorcisms, and healing, the disciples repeat the actions done by Jesus repeatedly since ch. 1. While Jesus often healed with His touch, the healings by the disciples demonstrate the power by which He could bring healing far from His personal presence. See also Mt 8:5–13 and Mk 7:25–30 for healings done at a distance by Jesus.

6:7–13 in Devotion and Prayer The disciples multiply Jesus' healing and revealing ministry. They build on the foundation of John the Baptist while anticipating their own ministries after Jesus' ascension. Even as Jesus sends the Twelve, He anticipates that not everyone will welcome the Gospel. But God unfailingly opens hearts to their ministry, and He promises to do the same until the end of time. We might wish to have lived at the time of Jesus and to have heard Him directly. However, the ministry of these disciples reminds us that the full power of His Word and even healing was at work through the disciples. His Word preached today still gives men the repentance that leads to life. • Lord, give us courage to share Your Word with a dying world in these uncertain times. Open hearts to repentance and faith in the Gospel. Amen.

6:14 *heard of it.* Exactly what Herod heard is unclear, though it was likely both the expanded ministry of the disciples and especially the preaching and miracles of Jesus. Bengel wrote,

> Jesus had not come to be known by many before . . . John's death become known, otherwise they would not have supposed Him to be John. . . . Except for the public rumor, Herod would not have known of Him. A palace is generally late in hearing spiritual news. (Bengel 522)

King. Matthew and Lk use the more specific term "tetrarch" (Mt 14:1; Lk 9:7) because the Roman emperor did not recognize Herod Antipas's claim to royalty. *raised from the dead.* Herod's fear and guilt over John's death likely caused his suspicion that the Baptizer had returned from the dead. While Jesus only healed and never harmed anyone, Herod's guilty conscience viewed Jesus' miracles as a sign of judgment. Others also suspected that Jesus might be John raised from the dead (8:28). The reasonable belief was that someone raised from the dead would be able to do miracles, and that they would do so in a fearless manner such as Jesus was doing. Herod's fear that Jesus was a man raised from the dead was a small foreshadowing of the coming truth. Jesus would be the One raised from the dead, not to become someone else, but to demonstrate that He was and is always the Son of God.

6:15 *Elijah.* See notes on 1:6–8 for John's ministry and parallels to Old Testament prophets. It was understood that one would come in the spirit of Elijah and Jesus' many miracles recalled the miracles of Elijah which included healings and even resurrections. *like one of the prophets.* The third possibility of Jesus' identification becomes the most general. Attempts to recognize Jesus went from a single contemporary, John, to the most general and distant, one of the prophets. This pattern is repeated in 8:28–29 when Jesus asks the disciples who men thought He was. Peter however gives the single correct answer: "You are the Christ."

6:16 *John, whom I have beheaded, has been raised.* Herod returned to a single answer as to the identity of Jesus. Herod's guilt gave him no easy rest; he could only believe that Jesus was the returned, and likely vengeful, John. This discussion on the identity of Jesus continues the theme begun in 1:1 and which is also found in 8:28–29 where Jesus asks the disciples who people think He is. After the same survey of possible identities for Jesus 6:14–15; 8:28–29, Herod and Peter reach opposite conclusions. Herod sees Jesus with guilt, believing Him to be the accusing John. Peter sees Jesus with faith, knowing Him to be the saving Christ.

6:17 *Herodias, his brother Philip's wife.* Herodias was the granddaughter of Herod the Great. Her present husband, Herod Antipas, was a son of Herod the Great. She had been previously married to Philip, another son of Herod the Great (Philip was also the half-brother of Herod Antipas). In other words, both of Herodias's husbands were also her uncles. As bad as this arrangement was, Herod's greater fear was what he had done to John and how that would be judged against him.

6:18 *not lawful.* Herod divorced his first wife, the daughter of a Nabataean king, in order to marry Herodias. (Nabataea was the region east of the Dead Sea.) However, it was not lawful for him to marry his brother's wife (cf. Lv 18:16; 20:21). Furthermore, Herodias had divorced her husband, also forbidden by Jewish law. While we generally think of John living alone in the desert (1:4), or preaching on river's edge (1:5), this shows a ministry that also reached to the king's palace. John's fearless attacks against the Pharisees (Mt 3:7–12) continued also against Herod. John proved that he feared God but no man.

6:19 *Herodias had a grudge.* Given her shameful behavior (see notes, vv. 17–18), Herodias was understandably angry that John called attention to her divorce and remarriage. This bitterness grew with her inability to destroy John. Her anger is a preview of the similar anger and plots of the enemies of Jesus. See Lk 11:53 where the same verb, used here for bearing a grudge, is found as His enemies "began to press Him hard." Herodias' desire to kill John had the same problem that Jesus' enemies would face. Both John and Jesus were considered to be righteous. Herodias however cared nothing for the public's opinion and had only to overcome Herod's reluctance.

6:20 *Herod feared John.* As seen in v. 14, Herod considered Jesus to be John resurrected. While he had feared John when he was still living, this fear must have magnified greatly when he thought John had returned for vengeance through the miraculous power of Jesus. *righteous and holy man.* John was a prophet who sought neither riches nor political power. Prophets often rebuked kings for their sins (e.g., 2Sm 12:1–14). Herod's vacillation between John and Herodias remind one of King Ahab who listened to the preaching of Elijah and saw his miracles and yet returned to his wife Jezebel who vowed to kill Elijah at all cost (1Ki 18:1–19:2). *kept him safe.* Jewish historian Josephus wrote that Herod imprisoned John at Machaerus, a fortress overlooking the Dead Sea. There, the prophet was relatively safe from the hatred of Herodias. *heard.* John preached the Law but also that the Gospel of the kingdom of God was at hand. *greatly perplexed.* The whole of John's life and message must have confused Herod since John had no fear of him as king, but attacked his sins as he did those of any man. Furthermore, John's message was not about himself but of the Greater One who was to come. The verb for "perplexed," *aporeo,* is relatively rare in the NT and is used in Lk 24:4 to describe the confusion of the women at the tomb on Easter. Despite the harsh message of John, and the tense uncertainty Herod had, he gladly listened to John, as the crowds would listen to Jesus (12:37). Herod's welcome of John must have infuriated Herodias all the more.

6:21 *an opportunity came.* Herod's life was torn between the holiness of John and the hatred of Herodias. The opportune day came on Herod's birthday, the day fit for John's death. *nobles.* These men were part of the wealthy class, whose support Herod needed. *military commanders.* Along with the nobles, these people formed the backbone of Herod's support. *leading men.* There were likely second-level rank of officials and civilian leaders. Herodias carefully chose this audience for her plot since Herod couldn't afford to retract his vow before the men upon whom he depended.

6:22 *danced.* The dance was likely suggestive, in a manner calculated to gain favor. All this was planned by her mother Herodias (vv. 24–26), whose long experience in manipulating men now included the exploitation of her daughter. The dance came at the end of the dinner when the drinking had also had its effect.

6:23 *up to half of my kingdom.* Herod did not have authority to dispense with half of his kingdom, but used the phrase as an extravagant expression. The exaggerated vow recalls the similar promise made by Xerxes to Queen Esther (Est 7:2). However, the virtuous Esther, seeking to save the lives of the people of Israel, was the complete opposite of the murderous Herodias and her daughter. Furthermore, in the book of Esther, Haman, who was plotting to kill all the Jews, was rightly destroyed. Mark however must record that John, whose virtuous life and preaching angered Herodias, was destroyed.

6:24 *"For what should I ask?"* She likely had hopes of things for her own personal pleasure or which would advance her position in the court directly. But her mother's selfishness and hatred of John took those hopes away. By having to go ask Herodias, she seems unaware of her mother's plot. While the girl's mind might have raced with possibilities, Herodias had a long-planned and immediate answer—the head of John.

6:25 *immediately with haste.* The girl returns without delay, likely without any argument with her mother. The phrase "with haste" is *meta spoudas* in Gk, an unusual phrase in the NT. The only other time it is used in the Gospels is Lk 1:39 where it describes Mary, after being visited by the angel Gabriel, traveling with haste to visit Elizabeth. What a contrast of these two pairs of women: Mary races to visit her older relative Elizabeth, both rejoicing over the coming birth of their miraculous sons, Jesus and Joseph, versus the daughter of Herodias, quickly leaving her mother with news of the death of John.

6:26 *exceedingly sorry.* Herod ironically attempts to save his honor by taking John's life. Ambrose says: "[This] is not repentance on the part of the king, but a confession of guilt" (*NPNF*2 10:385). *because of his oaths and his guests.* Herod is trapped by the political situation and must order John's death. Pilate will later feel similar pressure when the Jewish leaders demanded Jesus' death (Jn 19:12–

16). Both Herod and Pilate wanted to spare John and Jesus, but the crowd demanded moving ahead with the deaths. In one point of difference, while Herod was driven by murderous Herodias, Pilate was pressured by his wife's dreams and her warnings to have nothing to do with Jesus, a righteous man (Mt 27:19).

6:27 *immediately.* This unusual double use of immediately (vv. 25, 27), was last seen at 5:29–30 where the immediate healing of the woman was simultaneously known by Jesus. Now the girl's request is instantly fulfilled. Herod, while inwardly reluctant, cannot show that he is being manipulated. So he regains some small control by ordering the beheading as though he was in whole-hearted agreement.

6:28 *head on a platter.* This grisly display of John's severed head—at a meal, no less—illustrates the extreme corruption of Herod and his high society friends. Herod might have fulfilled the girl's request literally, giving her the head to deal with herself, to force the reality of the deed upon her and Herodias. Whatever the girl's reaction, we can imagine that Herodias welcomed the moment of conquest over John. Herod tried to give the head and responsibility of John's death to Herodias, but he remained haunted by his guilt. He was a prisoner to Herodias and a captive to his fears of a resurrected John.

6:29 Herod tries to salvage his reputation by allowing John's disciples to bury John's body. John's burial prefigures the interment of Jesus (15:42–47). The whole narrative of John's death began with Herod's fear that Jesus was John returned to life (v. 16). The disciples who buried John did so with no promise or hope that John would return. However, the burial of Jesus could have been done with the complete confidence that He would come back to life in just three days. Calvin writes, "Though the honour of burial is of no importance to the dead, yet it is the will of the Lord that we should observe this ceremony as a token of the last resurrection" (*Harmony* 2:228).

6:14–29 in Devotion and Prayer Coming just after the story about Jesus' rejection in Nazareth, the tragic story of John gives an unmistakable foreshadowing of what awaits Jesus: rejection and even violent hostility. But rejection and violence cannot overcome the risen Lord. His victory over death and the grave shows how wonderfully He can turn such antagonism into life and salvation. • Lord, give us a faith like John's, especially his integrity and trust. Deliver us from the weakness and fear shown by Herod. Help us to believe unquestioningly that faithfulness unto death will receive the crown of eternal life. Amen.

6:30 *The apostles returned.* The story begun in vv. 7–13 resumes after the narrative of John's death. The intervening account of John's death (vv. 14–29) is a somber reminder that Jesus and His disciples will face the wrath of rulers like Herod. *told him all that they had done and taught.* The gathering of the disciples was completely opposite of the mournful gathering of the disciples of John who came to bury John (v. 29). John's ministry, ended dramatically, has been multiplied by the travel, teaching, and healing miracles of the disciples. Like a seed planted and growing, John's life and ministry was fully expressed in the work of the disciples and the Kingdom brought by Jesus.

A first cycle of parallel events (6:31–7:37)

Jesus feeds 5,000 in the wilderness and walks on water (6:31–56)

ESV	KJV
[31]And he said to them, "Come away by yourselves to a desolate place and rest a while." For many were coming and going, and they had no leisure even to eat. [32]And they went away in the boat to a desolate place by themselves. [33]Now many saw them going and recognized them, and they ran there on foot from all the towns and got there ahead of them. [34]When he went ashore he saw a great crowd, and he had compassion on them, because they were like sheep without a shepherd. And he began to teach them many things. [35]And when it grew late, his disciples came to him and said, "This is a desolate place, and the hour is now late. [36]Send them away to go into the surrounding countryside and villages and buy themselves something to eat." [37]But he answered them, "You give them	**[31]And he said unto them, Come ye yourselves apart into a desert place, and rest a while: for there were many coming and going, and they had no leisure so much as to eat.** **[32]And they departed into a desert place by ship privately.** **[33]And the people saw them departing, and many knew him, and ran afoot thither out of all cities, and outwent them, and came together unto him.** **[34]And Jesus, when he came out, saw much people, and was moved with compassion toward them, because they were as sheep not having a shepherd: and he began to teach them many things.** **[35]And when the day was now far spent, his disciples came unto him, and said, This is a desert place, and now the time is far passed:**

something to eat." And they said to
him, "Shall we go and buy two hundred denarii worth of bread and give
it to them to eat?" 38And he said to
them, "How many loaves do you
have? Go and see." And when they
had found out, they said, "Five, and
two fish." 39Then he commanded
them all to sit down in groups on
the green grass. 40So they sat down
in groups, by hundreds and by fifties.
41And taking the five loaves and the
two fish he looked up to heaven and
said a blessing and broke the loaves
and gave them to the disciples to set
before the people. And he divided the
two fish among them all. 42And they
all ate and were satisfied. 43And they
took up twelve baskets full of broken
pieces and of the fish. 44And those
who ate the loaves were five thousand men.

45Immediately he made his disciples
get into the boat and go before him to
the other side, to Bethsaida, while he
dismissed the crowd. 46And after he
had taken leave of them, he went up
on the mountain to pray. 47And when
evening came, the boat was out on
the sea, and he was alone on the land.
48And he saw that they were making
headway painfully, for the wind was
against them. And about the fourth
watch of the night he came to them,
walking on the sea. He meant to pass
by them, 49but when they saw him
walking on the sea they thought it
was a ghost, and cried out, 50for they
all saw him and were terrified. But
immediately he spoke to them and
said, "Take heart; it is I. Do not be
afraid." 51And he got into the boat
with them, and the wind ceased. And
they were utterly astounded, 52for

36Send them away, that they may
go into the country round about, and
into the villages, and buy themselves
bread: for they have nothing to eat.

37He answered and said unto them,
Give ye them to eat. And they say
unto him, Shall we go and buy two
hundred pennyworth of bread, and
give them to eat?

38He saith unto them, How many
loaves have ye? go and see. And when
they knew, they say, Five, and two
fishes.

39And he commanded them to make
all sit down by companies upon the
green grass.

40And they sat down in ranks, by
hundreds, and by fifties.

41And when he had taken the five
loaves and the two fishes, he looked
up to heaven, and blessed, and brake
the loaves, and gave them to his disciples to set before them; and the two
fishes divided he among them all.

42And they did all eat, and were
filled.

43And they took up twelve baskets full of the fragments, and of the
fishes.

44And they that did eat of the loaves
were about five thousand men.

45And straightway he constrained
his disciples to get into the ship, and
to go to the other side before unto
Bethsaida, while he sent away the
people.

46And when he had sent them away,
he departed into a mountain to pray.

47And when even was come, the
ship was in the midst of the sea, and
he alone on the land.

48And he saw them toiling in rowing; for the wind was contrary unto
them: and about the fourth watch of

they did not understand about the loaves, but their hearts were hardened.
**53When they had crossed over, they came to land at Gennesaret and moored to the shore. 54And when they got out of the boat, the people immediately recognized him
55and ran about the whole region and began to bring the sick people on their beds to wherever they heard
he was. 56And wherever he came, in villages, cities, or countryside, they laid the sick in the marketplaces and implored him that they might touch even the fringe of his garment. And as many as touched it were made well.**

the night he cometh unto them, walking upon the sea, and would have passed by them.
49But when they saw him walking upon the sea, they supposed it had been a spirit, and cried out:
50For they all saw him, and were troubled. And immediately he talked with them, and saith unto them, Be of good cheer: it is I; be not afraid.
51And he went up unto them into the ship; and the wind ceased: and they were sore amazed in themselves beyond measure, and wondered.
52For they considered not the miracle of the loaves: for their heart was hardened.
53And when they had passed over, they came into the land of Gennesaret, and drew to the shore.
54And when they were come out of the ship, straightway they knew him,
55And ran through that whole region round about, and began to carry about in beds those that were sick, where they heard he was.
56And whithersoever he entered, into villages, or cities, or country, they laid the sick in the streets, and besought him that they might touch if it were but the border of his garment: and as many as touched him were made whole.

Introduction to 6:31–44 A new miracle enlarges the scope of Jesus' ministry and demonstrates his compassion in a remarkable way. The feeding of the 5,000 comes when Jesus and the disciples need time alone. But instead, they meet their largest crowd yet. Jesus teaches as expected, but when the day ends, His miracle which confirms His power is completely new. Instead of healing the sick or casting out demons, He feeds the crowd with an amazing abundance.

6:31 Despite an unending list of ministry tasks to get done, Jesus made time for Himself and His disciples to rest and recover. Presumably, this time of rest included instruction and prayer (cf. 1:35; 7:17). The press of the crowds and the lack of time even to eat had already been seen in 3:20–21. Here Jesus sees the disciples' need for rest. While their private time with Jesus and their rest from the crowd didn't come as they hoped, Jesus gives true rest still to those who are weary and heavy-laden (Mt 11:28).

6:32 *desolate place.* This was not a true desert such as the Wilderness of the Dead Sea region, since there was green grass (v. 39). See 1:35 and the notes there for the use of the same phrase when Jesus alone retreated after the first gathering of crowds. The disciples had experienced enough crowds during their ministry travels and so they needed a place to rest, to tell Jesus of their individual experiences, and to relish private time with Jesus. This move to a desolate place continues the theme of secrecy begun in ch. 1 and repeated through the Gospel.

6:33 *recognized them.* Even though safely isolated by the Sea, the disciples couldn't escape being noticed. The crowds recognized not only who they were, but also where they were likely going. *they ran there on foot.* Luke 9:10 identifies this as Bethsaida, a city on the northeast shore of the Sea of Galilee. The crowd likely flowed together, like several small streams all leading downward to the Sea, gathering souls ever faster as they came to Jesus. The KJV adds the image of their coming together as a waiting crowd.

6:34 *when he went ashore.* The compassion of Jesus begins with His landing. He knew the crowd would come, that the entire day would be spent on them, and that they would even need food. There would be no rest if He came ashore. The disciples might have suggested sailing on, but Jesus was drawn to the crowd as they were drawn to Him. *compassion.* This word, *splanchnidzomai*, refers to the center or heart of emotion, the depth of one's feeling and pity. See the note on 1:41 where this word is first used in Mark and also 8:2 where Jesus has similar compassion on the crowd of 4,000. *shepherd . . . teach.* Jesus, the Good Shepherd, fulfills the needs of His flock. See Mt 9:36 where the same phrase, "sheep without a shepherd" is used. Here, He provides instruction as well as an unforgettable meal (vv. 37–44). Still today, Christian worship services have Jesus' teaching and a miraculous meal as their most important elements.

6:35 *the disciples came to Him.* It is always interesting when humans feel it necessary to tell the omniscient God what He appears to have forgotten. Though they have listened to Jesus all day, their response to His teaching is this short lesson of their own concerning geography and time. As often is the case in Mark, the actual teaching of Jesus is not recorded. See the notes on 1:21. However, in this case the result of Jesus' teaching was not furious opposition, as in 1:27 and 6:2, but the opportunity for Jesus to demonstrate His power through unexpected compassion. The crowd that ran to be with Jesus would have few ill among them, and so His confirming miracle would not be healing but feeding.

6:36 *Send them away.* The disciples' advice was not entirely heartless. Since it was likely late afternoon, the people would have time to buy food at the market. The disciples knew that only Jesus' command would dismiss the crowd. As long as He chose to speak, He would continue to hold the crowd. However, on the day following this miracle, after Jesus had spoken extensively about Himself being the bread of life (Jn 6:26–59), then the crowd dispersed themselves by grumbling that His teaching was too difficult (Jn 6:60, 66). Jesus would not send the crowd away without bread and fish, but many of them would later leave on their own without the bread of life.

6:37 *You give them something to eat.* Just as Jesus had sent the disciples out to teach and heal in His place (6:7), so He invites them to continue to be His miraculous hands here. As they were cared for by strangers during their journey (6:10), so they could now return the kindness to this crowd. *two hundred denarii.* This amounted to over half a year's salary, a substantial amount. The disciples questioned both the logistics of their going and the cost of the buying. How were they to find so much food and bring it all the way out to this desolate place? And how would they ever pay for it? Though they had just come from the miracles of their travels, they are certain that none of this could be done.

6:38 *Five, and two fish.* Obviously, this amount of food was insufficient for Jesus and the Twelve, let alone the multitude. This miracle of multiplication recalls Jesus' first miracle of changing water into wine, another feeding miracle of transformation. Given God's creation of all things simply by a spoken word, and the model of manna as bread from heaven, we might have expected Jesus to speak and to have bread suddenly appear out of the air. However, this bread which feeds the 5,000 will be a way for Him to teach about Himself as the bread of life (Jn 6:26–59). Therefore, He begins with the bread they know and then shows what wonders He can perform with it. So also He is the familiar carpenter to many in Nazareth (6:2–3), but the true Bread of Life for those with faith.

6:39 *green grass.* Only Mark records this detail, possibly a vivid recollection from Peter's memory. The green grass shows that this was a remote place but not a forbidding, lifeless desert. The feeding of so many on green grass recalls the beautiful image of Ps 23:2 "He makes me lie down in green pastures." Jesus as the Good Shepherd saw the harassed condition of His sheep, gathered them, trained them with His teaching, and settled them with their evening meal.

6:40 *by hundreds and by fifties.* The people showed remarkable patience and trust to organize this way. This detail of Mark again suggests the vivid preaching of Peter and the lasting memory of the event. As this is the only miracle recorded in all four Gospels, it was striking for all the disciples for the number fed, the likeness to manna and Moses, the public nature of the miracle, and the abundance that was left over.

6:41 *taking the five loaves and two fish.* There is a great contrast between the numbered, expectant crowd and this tiny supply of bread and fish. However, by lifting the meal towards heaven, Jesus reminds everyone of the power and presence of God. These loaves and fish are not the meager scrapings of a borrowed meal; they are a potential feast in the hands of the One who made all the world from nothing. *blessing . . . broke . . . gave.* This sequence—taking the bread, speaking a blessing, breaking, and then giving—also occurs in the institution of the Lord's Supper (14:22), which may be foreshadowed here. We hear echoes of the Lord's Supper also in Jesus' words concerning Himself as the bread of life (Jn 6:51–58). Jesus is the new Moses and greater is His gift than that given by Moses. Moses returned to the people from forty days on Mt. Sinai and broke the tablets of Law over their sinfulness. Jesus lifted these loaves to heaven in peaceful blessings and broke the loaves to fill their hunger. *gave them to the disciples.* Just as Jesus sent the disciples out to preach and heal (6:7, 12), so He gives them the crucial, inter-personal work of giving out the meal. Jesus remains at a distance, out of sight from many receiving the meal. This forecasts His dismissal of the crowd and retreat from them (vv. 45–46). Jesus intended to fill their hunger, not fall into their hands.

6:42 *all ate . . . satisfied.* The Lord's superabundant provision was such that, despite the overwhelming number of people, no one went away hungry. The patience and faith of the people were completely satisfied. No one was so hungry that he couldn't be filled. No one was so distant that he couldn't be reached. This was more than a kind sharing of what was already there; it was the magnificent blessing by the One who was the Bread of Life.

6:43 *they took up twelve baskets.* The complete filling of everyone was proven by these baskets of leftover pieces. This crowd would have snatched up any fragment of bread before the meal. Now they are so content, they cannot stand another bite, nor do they even want to take the extra pieces with them. This is a fullness that cannot imagine being hungry again. The boundless feast recalls Ps 23:5, and God's provision of a banquet table and overflowing cup. The exact number of these baskets, and the abundance which they represent, will be important soon (8:14–21), when Jesus cautions the disciples against the teaching of the Pharisees. The leftover pieces should remind them that a momentary lack of food is no obstacle for Jesus. Already in 6:52 it is noted that they didn't understand about the loaves, and thereby they failed to understand Jesus' divine power.

6:44 *five thousand men.* Women and children were fed but not included in the number. This was a day of both careful counting and boundless multiplication. The day began with the twelve disciples hoping to be alone with Jesus. However, those Twelve were multiplied to more than 5,000, and five loaves and two fish became limitless pieces. This miracle is noted by all four Gospels in part because of this large number involved. The miracle also points to Jesus as the One greater than Moses who will give the lasting bread of Himself.

6:30–44 in Devotion and Prayer When a multitude of Jesus' followers have too little food for all to eat, Jesus multiplies five loaves and two fishes so that all are satisfied. When problems threaten us and needs overwhelm our resources, what is our reaction? Do we magnify our troubles and remind God that nothing can be done? Or, do we turn first to the Lord, expecting His help and even His amazing multiplication of what formerly seemed too little? His Word makes clear that we can come to Him for what we lack with what little we have. He still treats His flock with compassion and more than provides for every need of body and soul. His gifts are beyond counting, overflowing past our need. • Lord, thank You for providing so abundantly and for graciously sustaining our bodies and souls. Teach us to turn to You first in every want and need. Amen.

Introduction to 6:45–52 After such a magnificent miracle, with an enthusiastic crowd ready to remain with Him, Jesus dismisses both the crowd and the disciples. While Jesus is in peaceful prayer on the mountain, the disciples struggle with the sea's raging storm. While it seems to them that He has forgotten them, He immediately reassures them with His presence and power. Yet, their greatest fear and confusion come with the calm as they struggle to understand Him.

6:45 *Immediately He made His disciples.* Jesus directed the disciples to embark for the other shore. He certainly knew they would face an all-night struggle against the wind. This is the second time in the day that Jesus commanded the disciples to do something difficult or even impossible (cf. v. 37). *He dismissed the crowd.* Jesus separates the disciples from the crowd. He did not come for the secure embrace of a satisfied host but, finally, for the hatred of a murderous crowd.

6:46 *on the mountain to pray.* This retreat to pray recalls a similar night (1:35). There also Jesus had astonishing success with a crowd that continued to look for Him. Jesus needed distance from the crowd and nearness to the Father. Here finally was the rest that He had sought with the disciples at the beginning of the day (6:31). This time of prayer amplifies the brief prayer of blessing said at the start of the meal (6:41). Jesus' true meal was this extended time of communion with the Father which will also prepare Him for the next day's teaching (Jn 6:25–58), and the rejection by many (Jn 6:60, 66). John notes (6:64) that Jesus was also aware of Judas' coming betrayal. Jesus leaves the safety of a crowd that would protect Him if He would only feed them daily. He will also leave the safety of the mountain and the Father to walk on a stormy sea to save the one who will betray Him to death.

6:47 *out on the sea.* John 6:19 notes that they were three to four miles out. Considering the effort of the disciples against the storm, these were dearly fought miles. Yet each mile brought them farther from the safe shore and their protecting Lord. *He was alone.* Having come down from the mountain, Jesus was on the shore. Mark emphasizes the distance between Jesus and the disciples and also the effectiveness of His dismissal of the crowd. For once, Jesus is truly alone with no one else in view. However, this peaceful moment for Jesus will end because of His knowledge of the disciples' trouble.

6:48 *they were making headway painfully.* The disciples were in terrible distress. The KJV translates simply, "toiling in rowing" and the verb for "toiling" is the same used for tormenting. The demons in 5:7 feared that Jesus came to torment them. The shrieking of the storm must have matched the fearsome sounds of the legion of demons (5:5), except that it was now the disciples who were in its grasp. *fourth watch.* This was from 3 to 6 a.m. The disciples have been gone throughout the night with the joy of the meal and peaceful departure long forgotten. *walking on the sea.* Jesus comes to reveal Himself as the Lord of all creation. *pass by them.* In the OT, God passed by Moses (Ex 33:22; 34:6) and Elijah (1Ki 19:11–13). This was His way of presenting Himself to them. In going towards the disciples in the storm, Jesus was not going past the men, uncaring of their trouble. They might have imagined, when they first saw Him, that He was going past but He was walking purposefully to the point where they would meet.

6:49 *ghost.* The Gk word is *phantasma* and is used only here and in the parallel passage (Mt 14:26). The disciples are not far from the truth as they assume that the one walking on the water is more than a mere mortal, for Jesus' divinity is clearly manifest. Similar to the disciples thinking Jesus was a ghost, Herod had confused Jesus with John the Baptist coming back from the dead (6:14, 16). The theme of Jesus' true identity had begun already in 1:1 and is repeated even as near as 6:1–5 when Nazareth rejects Him. He is clearly seen as the Son of God in baptism (1:11), and in the Transfiguration (9:7). Also, Peter rightly answers that He is the Christ (8:29), and the centurion at Jesus' death declares Him to be the Son of God (15:39). Between these high points of clarity, however, there were many moments such as this evening where even the disciples questioned who He was.

6:50 *terrified.* They all saw Him so this was not just one man's delusion. Their terror is expressed by the verb *tarasso,* a word used often for the fear of men, such as at the announcement of Jesus' birth (Mt 2:3), at the appearance of an angel (Lk 1:12), at Jesus' Easter appearance (Lk 24:38). It is also used to describe Jesus' own turmoil and sorrow (Jn 11:33; 12:27; 13:21). However, because of Jesus' overcoming the shadow and fear of death, He can comfort those who are afraid (Jn 14:1, 27). *Immediately He spoke to them.* This is the second occurrence of "immediately" in this short narrative. It begins the evening (v. 45), as Jesus sends the disciples directly onto the lake, but just as immediately He calms their fear by His presence and identity (v. 50). *Take heart; it is I. Do not be afraid.* The latter command drives out fear, even as His first command, "take heart" fills them with hope. Such a fear-dispelling command will be echoed at another important moment of revelation—at the empty tomb (16:6). Courage comes by realizing that God is with us. See Ex 3:11–12 where Moses questions who he is that he should go to Pharaoh to free Israel. God calms his fear by saying that He will be with Moses. Courage is not found through new strength within ourselves, but by realizing that God, the Great I Am, is beside us.

6:51 *He got into the boat.* Jesus brought peace by getting into the boat. His presence in the boat must have reminded them of the previous storm where Jesus slept in the boat (4:38). *wind ceased.* Unlike the previous calming of the storm (4:39), there is no command by Jesus to the winds recorded. Mark records the end of the storm simultaneous with His entry to the boat. *they were utterly astounded.* Their astonishment had several reasons: the ability of Jesus to walk upon the water, His finding of them in the trackless storm, His instant calming of the storm, and the unfolding mystery of His true identity. Though the disciples had traveled with Jesus and had gone out with His message, they were still growing in their understanding of His power as the Son of God.

6:52 *did not understand about the loaves.* Despite the unmistakable ways Jesus had just displayed His divine nature and power, the disciples somehow remain in the dark. The miracles of feeding the 5,000 and 4,000 and the baskets of left-over pieces are brought up in 8:14–21. Jesus uses these miracles and the abundance of bread as proof of His identity and power. If He can multiply the bread, then He must be God. If so, nothing He does should surprise the disciples. *hearts were hardened.* It is somewhat surprising that the disciples and Jesus' opponents are described in the same way (cf. 10:5; 16:14). Early in the chapter the disciples preach and heal on the basis of their knowledge of Jesus as Lord and Messiah. However the following events reduce their understanding to little better than the rejection shown in Nazareth (6:1–5). The disciples' lack of comprehension will only worsen in the coming chapters (e.g. 9:32; 10:32). Jesus' predictions of His death will be the most difficult to grasp. However, the greatest wonder is not their hardened hearts, but Jesus' rescue of them and His patience with them.

6:45–52 in Devotion and Prayer Demonstrating mastery over the winds and waves for a second time, Jesus calms another storm. Even more amazing, however, is the fact that Jesus' disciples still do not recognize His divine nature. Too often, our eyes are also blind and our hearts are just as hard. It is a good thing, therefore, that He who walked on the water that night also died in Calvary's darkness to save us from our hard-heartedness. • Lord, save us when we are overcome by life's storms and our hearts are darkened by unbelief. Calm the tempest, open our eyes, and create within us the faith to recognize You. Amen.

Introduction to 6:53–56 Even while the disciples slowly struggle with understanding who Jesus is, and what He can do, the crowds here recognize Him instantly. Unlike His hometown of Nazareth, these people welcome Him and believe that He can heal with the slightest touch. This brief section summarizes the miraculous success possible within Jesus' ministry. It is a brief respite from the misunderstanding of the disciples and the coming opposition of His enemies.

6:53 *When they had crossed over.* John 6:21 says that when Jesus entered the boat, they arrived instantly at the shore. This is the central aspect of the miracle in John's account. Mark stresses Jesus' walking on the water and the immediate silencing of the storm. *Gennesaret.* This was a town on the northwestern shore of the Sea of Galilee, between Capernaum and Tiberius. See map, p. xxi.

6:54 *immediately recognized Him.* Note how this picture contrasts with the depiction of the disciples in vv. 50–51. The Twelve's hardened hearts had just failed to see Jesus' divine nature, even after He had multiplied the loaves and walked on the water. Further, these people know Him though the people of His own town, Nazareth, see Him as nothing more than the carpenter (6:2–3). The people do not need the miracle of the storm and crossing to recognize Him. They likely have heard the accumulated news of His miracles and teaching, just as the crowd did in 6:33. Given the size of that crowd and Jesus' gracious teaching and feeding of them, it might be expected that this crowd will reach the same size.

6:55 *ran about the whole region.* The spread of this news repeats the encompassing excitement seen before, beginning with John the Baptist's draw of the whole city of Jerusalem and the region of Judea (1:5). Since then Jesus has also gathered the surrounding areas to Himself (1:32–37, 45; 3:7–8; 6:33). He has also traveled extensively and sent the disciples out to cover a broad area (1:38–39; 3:14–15; 5:1, 21; 6:7–12). Jesus' ministry balanced His powerful draw of people to Himself with His and the disciples' travels to reach the untouched regions. *bring the sick people.* This crowd brings the ill, unlike the crowd of the 5,000 which appears to have come with great haste without the delay of carrying the ill (Mk 6:33).

6:56 *laid the sick in the marketplaces.* Instead of the usual goods on the market, Jesus found a multitude of desperately ill people, all asking for His touch and healing. The numerous healings here in Gennesaret contrast with the few that were healed in Nazareth (6:5–6). *touch even the fringe.* This confidence echoes that of the woman who touched Jesus' garment and was healed (5:28–29). The touch matches Jesus' boldness in touching many in order to heal (1:31; 3:10; 5:41; 6:5; 7:33; 8:23; 9:27), even the untouchable lepers (1:41).

6:53–56 in Devotion and Prayer Not long after Jesus' disciples failed to recognize an unmistakable display of His divinity, the people of Gennesaret show great faith by receiving Jesus and clamoring for His healing power. Even today, those new to the faith often exhibit more conviction than those who have known Jesus for a long time. It is good news, then, that Jesus remains devoted to us even when our commitment wavers or fails. His resolve to suffer and die for all is ample proof of that. • Lord, give us the zeal of the Gennesaret believers. May we ever press toward You, resolute in our conviction that You can heal and restore us. Amen.

Jesus confronts the Pharisees and scribes and teaches on the distinction between clean and unclean, but His disciples misunderstand (7:1–23)

ESV

7 [1]Now when the Pharisees gathered to him, with some of the scribes
who had come from Jerusalem, [2]they
saw that some of his disciples ate
with hands that were defiled, that is,
unwashed. [3](For the Pharisees and
all the Jews do not eat unless they
wash their hands, holding to the tradition of the elders, [4]and when they
come from the marketplace, they do
not eat unless they wash. And there
are many other traditions that they
observe, such as the washing of cups
and pots and copper vessels and dining couches.) [5]And the Pharisees and
the scribes asked him, "Why do your
disciples not walk according to the
tradition of the elders, but eat with
defiled hands?" [6]And he said to them,
"Well did Isaiah prophesy of you hypocrites, as it is written,

" 'This people honors me with their lips,
but their heart is far from me;
[7]in vain do they worship me,
teaching as doctrines the commandments of men.'

[8]You leave the commandment of
God and hold to the tradition of
men."

[9]And he said to them, "You have a
fine way of rejecting the commandment of God in order to establish your
tradition! [10]For Moses said, 'Honor
your father and your mother'; and,
'Whoever reviles father or mother
must surely die.' [11]But you say, 'If
a man tells his father or his mother,

KJV

7 [1]Then came together unto him the Pharisees, and certain of the scribes, which came from Jerusalem.

[2]And when they saw some of his disciples eat bread with defiled, that is to say, with unwashen, hands, they found fault.

[3]For the Pharisees, and all the Jews, except they wash their hands oft, eat not, holding the tradition of the elders.

[4]And when they come from the market, except they wash, they eat not. And many other things there be, which they have received to hold, as the washing of cups, and pots, brasen vessels, and of tables.

[5]Then the Pharisees and scribes asked him, Why walk not thy disciples according to the tradition of the elders, but eat bread with unwashen hands?

[6]He answered and said unto them, Well hath Esaias prophesied of you hypocrites, as it is written, This people honoureth me with their lips, but their heart is far from me.

[7]Howbeit in vain do they worship me, teaching for doctrines the commandments of men.

[8]For laying aside the commandment of God, ye hold the tradition of men, as the washing of pots and cups: and many other such like things ye do.

[9]And he said unto them, Full well ye reject the commandment of God, that ye may keep your own tradition.

[10]For Moses said, Honour thy father and thy mother; and, Whoso curs-

"Whatever you would have gained
from me is Corban"' (that is, given
to God)—12then you no longer permit him to do anything for his father
or mother, 13thus making void the
word of God by your tradition that
you have handed down. And many
such things you do."
14And he called the people to him
again and said to them, "Hear me,
all of you, and understand: 15There
is nothing outside a person that by
going into him can defile him, but the
things that come out of a person are
what defile him." 17And when he had
entered the house and left the people,
his disciples asked him about the parable. 18And he said to them, "Then are
you also without understanding? Do
you not see that whatever goes into
a person from outside cannot defile
him, 19since it enters not his heart but
his stomach, and is expelled?" (Thus
he declared all foods clean.) 20And he
said, "What comes out of a person is
what defiles him. 21For from within,
out of the heart of man, come evil
thoughts, sexual immorality, theft,
murder, adultery, 22coveting, wickedness, deceit, sensuality, envy, slander,
pride, foolishness. 23All these evil
things come from within, and they
defile a person."

eth father or mother, let him die the death:

11But ye say, If a man shall say to his father or mother, It is Corban, that is to say, a gift, by whatsoever thou mightest be profited by me; he shall be free.

12And ye suffer him no more to do ought for his father or his mother;

13Making the word of God of none effect through your tradition, which ye have delivered: and many such like things do ye.

14And when he had called all the people unto him, he said unto them, Hearken unto me every one of you, and understand:

15There is nothing from without a man, that entering into him can defile him: but the things which come out of him, those are they that defile the man.

16If any man have ears to hear, let him hear.

17And when he was entered into the house from the people, his disciples asked him concerning the parable.

18And he saith unto them, Are ye so without understanding also? Do ye not perceive, that whatsoever thing from without entereth into the man, it cannot defile him;

19Because it entereth not into his heart, but into the belly, and goeth out into the draught, purging all meats?

20And he said, That which cometh out of the man, that defileth the man.

21For from within, out of the heart of men, proceed evil thoughts, adulteries, fornications, murders,

22Thefts, covetousness, wickedness, deceit, lasciviousness, an evil eye, blasphemy, pride, foolishness:

23All these evil things come from within, and defile the man.

Introduction to 7:1–23 Even though the ministry of Jesus has grown through His travels, miracles, and disciples, some of the early disputes come up again. Just as in ch. 2, there are questions about true purity and what is lawful. Jesus explains that genuine holiness is not on the outside but within a person.

7:1 *Pharisees . . . scribes.* In contrast to the sincere throngs in Gennesaret, Jesus' adversaries renew their fight with Jesus. They don't come with the same number or urgency of the crowds in 6:54–56, but with a relentless pursuit to find Him wrong. They were sticklers for the observance of detailed interpretations of the Law. Since Jesus knows the purpose of their coming, it's remarkable that He remains where they can reach Him. While He leaves the crowds on several occasions, He remains ready to face the Pharisees. *from Jerusalem.* Cf. Mt 15:1.

7:2 *hands . . . unwashed.* These washings were not so much an issue of hygiene but of ritual observance. By increasing these laws of purity, the Pharisees stand out from others (Mt 23:5–7). They gained control over this measure of their lives in a world dominated by the Romans and their disregard for God and the people of Israel. The Pharisees' rituals were outwardly noticeable, but they did nothing to change the inner nature (Mt 23:26). Jesus described the Pharisees as white-washed tombs, beautiful outside but filled with dead men's bones inside (Mt 23:27).

7:3–4 See Ex 30:17–21 and Lv 22:4–7 for laws intended for priests. This lengthy aside explains that the Pharisees required ritual washings, not only of those returning from the market, but also of different cooking utensils and even furniture. *wash.* The verb to "wash" is the Gk *baptizo*. It is the same term used when referring to Christian Baptism. Though this verb may denote immersion, it also describes washings by pouring or sprinkling. The Didache describes the early Christian practice of Baptism, saying:

> Baptize into the name of the Father, and of the Son, and of the Holy Spirit, in living water. But if you have not living water, baptize into other water; and if you cannot in cold, in warm. But if you have not either, pour out water thrice upon the head into the name of Father and Son and Holy Spirit. (*ANF* 7:379)

This shows the flexibility of earliest Christian practice as it adapted the customs of Judaism. Archaeologists have discovered ritual washing pools or tanks (Hbr *miqwaoth*) that held c. sixty gallons of water, which would have been running or "living" (cf. Jn 4:10–11; 7:37–38) according to rabbinic custom. *dining couches*. These were the cushions on which diners would recline while eating.

7:5 *your disciples*. The Pharisees attack Jesus through the disciples' actions. The disciples had represented Jesus in their traveling ministry (6:12–13), and now are examples of the teaching of Jesus. Earlier the scribes of the Pharisees had questioned Jesus' eating with sinners and tax collectors (2:15–17). Jesus had explained that the ill needed a physician, and so their attack now descends to the disciples and their lack of ritual washing. *according to the tradition of the elders*. The Pharisees and scribes expected the disciples and Jesus to follow their ritual practices, especially those involving washings. The Pharisees passed on the accumulated teachings of earlier rabbis. They believed that these interpretations had equal weight with the OT laws themselves. Their teachings both explained the intent of the OT Law and also added to the restrictions of the Law. By this they hoped to safeguard the Law itself. In reality, their added restrictions added heavy burdens to others, though they did nothing to help carry those burdens (Mt 23:4).

7:6 *well did Isaiah prophecy*. Jesus quotes Isaiah to rebuke the hypocrisy of His pharisaical accusers. This passage contrasts lip service with heartfelt obedience. Since the Pharisees accused Jesus through the disciples, Jesus answers them through the words of Isaiah. *Isaiah*. Isaiah 29:13 is quoted from the LXX. See the notes on 1:2–3 where Isaiah is first quoted. In ch. 1, Jesus begins to fulfill the prophecy of one traveling a straight path. The Pharisees are some of the obstacles in His path to the cross. *hypocrites*. This is the only time Mk uses this word, though the noun "hypocrisy" is found once at 12:15, again directed against the Pharisees. Ironically, in 12:14, they try to trap Jesus by saying He cares nothing for the appearance of someone. Yet, in 7:5, it is the outward act that the Pharisees value, and it is the emptiness of their outward show that Jesus attacks through the Isaiah quote.

7:7 *in vain do they worship me*. The emptiness of the Pharisees' worship matches the vacuum of their hearts. When they added directions and restrictions upon the Law, they did so as a reflection of themselves. Neither their worship nor their teaching reflected God, but their worship and teaching display only the vanity with which they regard themselves.

7:8 *commandment of God . . . tradition of men.* Jesus' rebuke is aimed particularly at the Pharisees' lifting human tradition above divine commandment. Jesus contrasts the commandments, *entola,* versus the tradition, *paradosin,* handed down from men. Just as their words praise only themselves, so their commandments reflect only themselves. While the Pharisees might style themselves to be the interpreters of Moses, they did not deliver the words of God with the clarity and fixed truth of Moses' stone tablets. Instead, their increasing traditions came down only from themselves, rather than from the voice and mountain of God.

7:9 *you have a fine way of rejecting.* While v. 8 has the Pharisees merely leaving (*aphiami*), the commands of God, now their action is stronger. Now the Pharisees reject (*atheteo*), God's commands. They have uprooted the established commandments of God in order to establish their own commands. Jesus notes that they have done a thorough job of demolishing God's work in order to build their own house of cards in its place. They have moved from interpretation to outright challenge. Their action recalls the pattern of Satan's temptation of Eve (Gn 3), whereby he begins with the question, "Did God actually say . . . ?" but moves soon to outright denial of God's Word, "You will not surely die" (Gn 3:2, 4).

7:10 *Honor your father and your mother.* Jesus gives a concrete example of the Pharisees' hypocritical piety: He describes them as failing to obey the Fourth Commandment. Jesus states the commandment first in its positive manner, and then, quoting Ex 21:17, He shows the serious consequence if it is broken. Despite the promise of blessings if they honor their parents, and the warning of death if they do not, the Pharisees establish their own teaching against this commandment.

7:11 They consider it more important to give special offerings than to support elderly parents. Such piety is ultimately self-serving and a sham. *Corban.* An offering above and beyond the tithes required by Mosaic Law. *given to God.* This is an especially ironic claim since the Corban offering is prompted by their human tradition as an avoidance of divine command. The gift that could have been used to help a parent was kept by the man instead. It was supposed to be given as an offering to God. However, how quickly the man gave the gift was uncertain and so he might selfishly keep the money forever.

7:12 *you no longer permit him.* A man might use the Pharisees' teaching as an excuse for his own greed. "I would be glad to help, but this is their teaching!" Such trickery and excuse for selfishness would also gain disciples for the Pharisees. The Pharisees gave expression and excuse to the greed that lies in many.

7:13 *making void the word of God.* A mere appearance of piety does not please God. He prefers that people simply obey His Commandments. Their "making void" uses a relatively rare word, *akuruo,* used only in Mt 15:6; Gal 3:17 and here. It means to nullify, to deny the authority and lordship of someone or something. They deny the Word of God's power and its source as the expression of God. *And many such things you do.* Jesus assures everyone listening that He could give many more examples. The silence of His enemies confirms that He has uncovered their often-repeated method.

7:1–13 in Devotion and Prayer Jesus criticizes the Pharisees for being overly concerned with man-made observances while failing to fulfill God's Commandments. Such hypocrisy still abounds, as most people worry more about human opinions than what God thinks. Given our own failures in this regard, it is a good thing that the Lord not only commands in His Word, but also graciously forgives and promises goodness. • Lord, cleanse us each day from our sins. We thank You that Jesus was made a fragrant, sacrificial offering for us. Amen.

Introduction to 7:14–23 Jesus does not simply refute and criticize the Pharisees. He also teaches the people the correct understanding of God's will and human nature. Holiness is displayed by what comes out of a person's heart, not by what he avoids eating or touching.

7:14 *called the people to Him again.* The crowd likely retreated while the Pharisees debated with Jesus. However, they must have remained within hearing so that Jesus could call them forward. The Pharisees likely retreated out of sight and hearing. Jesus has often been pursued by the crowds and had to distance Himself from them (1:35, 45; 3:9; 6:31). Here, however, He deliberately calls them forward. The errors and authority of the Pharisees had to be challenged immediately.

7:15 *nothing outside a person . . . can defile him.* Jesus turns the pharisaical conception of impurity upside down. The Pharisee's outward practice of ritual washings (vv. 3–4), were aimed at mere food and utensils: items that had no bearing on actual purity. The word for "defile" is *koinoō,* a relatively rare word meaning to make common, impure, or to defile. It is related to the much more common noun, *koinonia,* meaning association or communion. While *koinonia* is a positive idea in the NT, the verb *koinoō* is a negative corruption. *things that come out of a person.* The words and actions that come from one's sinful heart demonstrate the defiled nature within. The sinfulness is already within so that these acts in themselves do not defile, but show the evil already in place.

7:16 The KJV has this verse, "If any man have ears to hear, let him hear." It is not found in the earliest manuscripts but is common in many later ones. It echoes 4:9, 23 where Jesus uses these words to conclude His teaching, and so it would fit this ending of public teaching also.

7:17 *left the people.* Jesus' teaching of the crowd likely went on longer than this brief statement. As is often the case, Mark reduces Jesus' teaching to the very core, or simply announces that He taught without giving the content (1:21, 39; 2:2; 4:2, 33; 6:2, 34). Jesus provided additional, private teaching for the disciples, away from the crowds (cf. 4:10, 34). *His disciples asked him about the parable.* As they did with the first parable of the Sower (4:10), the disciples take the initiative to learn more. Unfortunately, when Jesus tells them of the deeper truth of His coming death and resurrection, and marches resolutely towards Jerusalem, they do not ask for further explanation (9:32; 10:32).

7:18 *without understanding?* Jesus has already had to confront their hard-hearted confusion (6:52), when they were terrified after the storm. Now on a calmer, simpler matter, they are still puzzled. When He asks if they are also without understanding, He is likely referring to the Pharisees who left unchanged, confirmed in their errors. *whatever goes in to a person from outside.* Jesus has to show that the matters of the outside are mere food which can neither defile the pure nor demonstrate their purity. The true physician does not diagnose a man by his clothes, but by what lies within him.

7:19 *enters not his heart.* Jesus summarizes the argument of v. 15. Ritually impure food does not touch the heart and so cannot contaminate it. *all foods clean.* This sentence is Mark's summary of Jesus' point. It likely reflects Peter's own discovery in Ac 10:14–16 where, in a vision, he was commanded to kill and eat unclean animals. Peter learned again that day that purity was found not in food, nor in being of the line of Abraham, but that God welcomes any one from any nation who "fears him and does what is right" (Ac 10:35). Jesus' teaching will affect the future Christian mission. Simply put, Gentiles will not need to observe Jewish dietary laws. The question of food laws caused much controversy in the first-century Church (cf. Ac 15:1–35; Rm 14:1–3; 1Co 8:7–13).

7:20 *what comes out of a person defiles him.* Jesus clarifies that what does indeed defile is not what enters from the outside, but rather what lurks in the hearts of fallen people. This defiling has already taken place and been known by God who searches the heart. The words and actions that come out of the heart are the condemning display visible to men. The Pharisees sought to showcase their holiness through ritual washing, but by their hard hearts and refusal to acknowledge Jesus as the Son of God, they demonstrated only their true, fallen nature.

7:21–22 Beginning with sexual immorality, twelve kinds of evil thoughts and actions are combined in a dreadful list of vices. The first six are in the plural form and describe behaviors; the last six are in the singular and have more to do with attitudes. The dangerous nature of the first six—murder, adultery, etc.—is clear, but Jesus shows that even the last six—pride, foolishness, etc.—are equally serious. These twelve vices leave no doubt as to the wretched impurity of the human spirit. See Ps 51:5 for the original, fallen state of the heart from conception. *heart.* This is the center of human decision and, in Mark, is often what rejects the claim and power of Jesus (2:6, 8; 3:5; 6:52; 7:6; 8:17). It is more than emotion but is the center of the will and the springboard of action.

7:23 With this single verse, Jesus summarizes the argument for a third time (7:15, 18–20). These things rage first within the heart and then come out. These show that even the Pharisees were common sinners with no difference or separation between them and the worst. The astonishing Gospel is that Jesus, the only One with a completely pure heart and matching pure deeds, took down the separation between sinners and Himself. God "made Him to be sin who knew no sin so that in Him we might become the righteousness of God" (2Co 5:21).

7:14–23 in Devotion and Prayer Jesus teaches that people are not defiled by food or other things entering the body from the outside, but rather by their own evil inclinations and sinful behaviors. This teaching exposes the uselessness of our own excuse-making. However, Jesus does not merely condemn; He also sets free. Through His promises we are liberated from sin and reconciled to God. He takes our record and sin upon Himself and is condemned for them in our place. • Lord, renew us each day with clean hearts. By Your Spirit, give us joyous words, generous spirits, and behaviors that reflect Your glory. Amen.

Daughter near Tyre (7:24–30)

ESV	KJV
24 And from there he arose and went away to the region of Tyre and Sidon. And he entered a house and did not want anyone to know, yet he could not be hidden. 25 But immediately a woman whose little daughter had an unclean spirit heard of him and came and fell down at his feet. 26 Now the woman was a Gentile, a Syrophoenician by birth. And she begged him to cast the demon out of her daughter. 27 And he said to her, "Let the children be fed first, for it is not right to take the children's bread and throw it to the dogs." 28 But she answered him, "Yes, Lord; yet even the dogs under the table eat the children's crumbs." 29 And he said to her, "For this statement you may go your way; the demon has left your daughter." 30 And she went home and found the child lying in bed and the demon gone.	24 And from thence he arose, and went into the borders of Tyre and Sidon, and entered into an house, and would have no man know it: but he could not be hid. 25 For a certain woman, whose young daughter had an unclean spirit, heard of him, and came and fell at his feet: 26 The woman was a Greek, a Syrophenician by nation; and she besought him that he would cast forth the devil out of her daughter. 27 But Jesus said unto her, Let the children first be filled: for it is not meet to take the children's bread, and to cast it unto the dogs. 28 And she answered and said unto him, Yes, Lord: yet the dogs under the table eat of the children's crumbs. 29 And he said unto her, For this saying go thy way; the devil is gone out of thy daughter. 30 And when she was come to her house, she found the devil gone out, and her daughter laid upon the bed.

Introduction to 7:24–30 Jesus leaves the controversy with the Pharisees and the pressure of the crowds by retreating to Tyre and Sidon. But there is no rest even here as a woman of great need and insightful faith finds Him. She shows exceptional persistence along with humble trust, becoming a model for all.

7:24 *Tyre and Sidon.* These were cities northwest of Galilee along the Mediterranean coast. *did not want anyone to know.* As noted often before, Jesus seeks a refuge from the crowd both for Himself and also the disciples (1:35, 43; 3:9; 6:31, 45–46; 8:9–10). By going to this distant location, He should be outside the fame of His miracles.

7:25 *But immediately.* Despite His wishes, He has placed Himself deliberately in the path of this woman. Mark's use of "immediately" stresses the instant disruption, much as happened with coming of the demoniac (5:2), and the crowds (6:33–34). The urgent need of the woman's daughter pushed aside Jesus' schedule, just as He had known and planned. Bengel writes, "Jesus put Himself in her way. . . . He had undertaken this whole journey for her sake" (Bengel 528).

7:26 *Gentile.* Mark stresses this woman's Gentile background, probably because of Jesus' previous debate with the Pharisees over what is defiling (vv. 1–23). While the Pharisees avoided the slightest contamination from an unclean cup (7:3–4), Jesus purposefully surrounded Himself with the Gentiles, even the mother of a demon-possessed girl. *she begged . . . her daughter.* This is another case of one person's faithful intercession benefiting another (cf. 2:3–5; 5:22–24; 6:56). Like the centurion who asks for the healing of his servant (Mt 8:5–10), the woman believes that Jesus can heal from a distance with just a word.

7:27 *not right to take the children's bread.* Jesus' response to this woman appears to be discouraging to the woman on at least two counts. First, He implies she is a dog, which was a great insult (see 2Sm 3:8; Php 3:2). Second, He suggests that He will serve Jewish people first (the children at the table). He might never get to the Gentiles. *dogs.* This is the Gk *kunarion,* a diminutive form referring to family pets, not wild or street dogs.

7:28 *Yes, Lord; yet even the dogs.* The woman seizes upon her characterization as a family pet and expresses her willingness to assume even this modest place within the household. She recognizes that Jesus is not rejecting her but is giving her a chance to express her faith. She notes that the family dogs have a special place under the table, close to the family, and they eat the same food as even the children. They are treated as part of the family—as many pet owners know today.

7:29 *For this statement you may go.* The healing is all due to Jesus' compassion and power but her words express the faith and close relationship that receive His gift. This outsider's great faith contrasts sharply with that of the Pharisees and even the disciples, who fail to understand much of what Jesus is teaching. Such unswerving faith results in the daughter's full recovery.

7:30 *she went home and found.* We can expect that she went home with a mixture of trust, relief, and eagerness to see her daughter finally well. Her journey from Jesus was an echo of the woman with the bleeding who left Jesus' side with His life-giving words, "Your faith has made you well; go in peace." (5:34). She, her daughter, and her home can finally find peace and rest. Jesus gave up His own rest for the sake of her need. Far from getting a crumb, she received the whole of His care.

7:24–30 in Devotion and Prayer In the regions of Tyre and Sidon, Jesus reveals that He has come to save the Gentiles along with the Jews. Unfortunately, the all-encompassing nature of His Gospel is viewed today as a threat by many Christian communities who might feel more comfortable ignoring rather than welcoming some population into the Church; outreach to other cultures might be ignored. But Jesus calls us to repent of such notions, and He reaches out to all people. No one lies beyond the scope of His love and grace. Even those who feel that they are the lowest and beyond His care have a lesson here. Jesus welcomed and cared for this woman and her daughter as two of His beloved. • Lord, help us to share the Gospel with all people, especially those who are different from us, that all may be edified in the faith. Amen.

Jesus heals a deaf man in the region of the Decapolis (7:31–37)

ESV	KJV
[31]Then he returned from the region of Tyre and went through Sidon to the Sea of Galilee, in the region of the Decapolis. [32]And they brought to him a man who was deaf and had a speech impediment, and they begged him to lay his hand on him. [33]And taking him aside from the crowd privately, he put his fingers into his ears, and after spitting touched his tongue. [34]And looking up to heaven, he sighed and said to him, "Ephphatha," that is, "Be opened." [35]And his ears were opened, his tongue was released, and he spoke plainly. [36]And Jesus charged them to tell no one. But the more he charged them, the more zealously they proclaimed it. [37]And they were astonished beyond measure, saying, "He has done all things well. He even makes the deaf hear and the mute speak."	[31]And again, departing from the coasts of Tyre and Sidon, he came unto the sea of Galilee, through the midst of the coasts of Decapolis. [32]And they bring unto him one that was deaf, and had an impediment in his speech; and they beseech him to put his hand upon him. [33]And he took him aside from the multitude, and put his fingers into his ears, and he spit, and touched his tongue; [34]And looking up to heaven, he sighed, and saith unto him, Ephphatha, that is, Be opened. [35]And straightway his ears were opened, and the string of his tongue was loosed, and he spake plain. [36]And he charged them that they should tell no man: but the more he charged them, so much the more a great deal they published it; [37]And were beyond measure astonished, saying, He hath done all things well: he maketh both the deaf to hear, and the dumb to speak.

Introduction to 7:31–37 While Jesus has healed many, here He brings hearing and speech to one man. His healing comes through His personal touch, in contrast to the exorcism just accomplished at a distance for the Syrophoenician woman. Though Jesus is outside Galilee and away from the Sea, yet crowds hear and repeat His deeds.

7:31 *Decapolis.* This is literally "ten cities." This region lay southeast of the Sea of Galilee so that Jesus has traveled diagonally southeastward from the edge of the Mediterranean, across Galilee, past the Sea of Galilee, to reach another region associated with the Gentiles.

The man healed of the legion of demons was from this area and had filled it with news of his healing (5:20).

7:32 *deaf and had a speech impediment.* Because those unable to hear have difficulty learning to speak correctly, it is probable that this man had been handicapped from birth with both problems. *they.* His family likely brought him to Jesus. We might expect that they have tried every possible solution without success, much like the woman with the bleeding (5:26), and the Syrophoenician woman (7:25).

7:33 *privately.* As will become clearer in v. 36, this is another example of Jesus commanding silence in order to avoid misunderstanding about His identity. *touched.* Here, touch made communication easier with the man. Jesus tended to use touch in His healings (cf. 1:31, 41; 5:28–29, 41; 6:56; 8:25) as a sign of His compassion and power. Jesus touched the man on both ears and tongue to signal to the man what He was about to heal. With His gentle touch and calming look, Jesus prepared the man for his healing. With these touches, and the privacy of stepping from the crowd, the man would know that Jesus alone healed him.

7:34 *looking up to heaven.* Jesus looked up to heaven at the blessing and breaking of the bread for the 5,000 (6:41). The upward look was a further sign for the deaf/mute man that the coming healing was the gift of God. *sighed.* This physical sign of emotion recalls other moments of Jesus' feelings (1:43, 3:5, 6:6). Jesus, true God, also lived the full life of His human nature, complete with the emotions that connected with the people around Him. *Ephphatha.* Mark captures the moment by reporting the exact word. This Aramaic word was later used in the Church's baptismal liturgies in order to emphasize the Spirit's power to open ears to the Gospel.

7:35 *ears were opened . . . tongue was released . . . spoke plainly.* All three effects came immediately. Once the man's ears were healed, he was also able to speak clearly. He immediately put this gift to work in praise. The barriers to sound and speech were shattered in one moment and the pent-up words came out with astonishing clarity.

7:36 *tell no one.* How ironic that the new-found gift was to be silenced! Not only was the man to keep the secret, but so also his family and those who saw the miracle. This command to silence is one of the many times Jesus prohibits the spread of His work or identity (1:44; 3:12; 5:43; 8:30; 9:9). However, as it happened before (1:45), the more He commanded, the more they joyfully disobeyed. In contrast, earlier in the Decapolis, after Jesus had healed the demon-possessed man, He commanded the man to spread the news of what God had done for him (5:19–20). Jesus harnesses the spreading news of His power. He knows that the crowd's praise will eventually force His enemies to kill Him. However, He must have time also to do the miracles and teaching before the end. So He must generally limit the spread of the news until Palm Sunday when the crowds can sing out without restraint. Calvin writes,

> Many commentators torture these injunctions to an opposite meaning, as if Christ had purposely excited them to spread abroad the fame of the miracle; I prefer a more natural interpretation . . . that Christ only intended to delay the publication of it till a more proper and convenient time. (*Harmony* 2:272–73)

7:37 *astonished beyond measure.* The word for "beyond measure" *hyperperissos,* occurs only here in the NT. While many crowds have been impressed by Jesus, this crowd has reached a new level of astonishment. At the healing of the deaf and mute man, they themselves have become almost deaf and mute. They cannot believe what they have heard and cannot find the words to describe it. *done all things well.* This summarizes all of Jesus' works. The Pharisees will demand more signs (8:11–12). The crowds are awed and remain positive toward Jesus. But, like the disciples, they do not truly understand who Jesus is.

7:31–37 in Devotion and Prayer Jesus heals another person in a Gentile region, further emphasizing His love for every race and kind of people. This serves as yet one more example of why we need to avoid the temptation to narrow the scope of the mission and to ignore opportunities to reach out to those who are different than ourselves. Jesus' healing of this man, immediately after He restored the daughter of the Syrophoenician woman, underscores that He desires to love, cleanse, and heal all people. • Lord, You have done everything well. Help us also to see the depths of Your mercy and grace, that we understand them as gifts meant for all. Amen.

A second cycle of parallel events (8:1–26)

Jesus feeds 4,000 in the wilderness (8:1–10)

ESV	KJV
8 [1]In those days, when again a great crowd had gathered, and they had nothing to eat, he called his disciples to him and said to them, [2]"I have compassion on the crowd, because they have been with me now three days and have nothing to eat. [3]And if I send them away hungry to their homes, they will faint on the way. And some of them have come from far away." [4]And his disciples answered him, "How can one feed these people with bread here in this desolate place?" [5]And he asked them, "How many loaves do you have?" They said, "Seven." [6]And he directed the crowd to sit down on the ground. And he took the seven loaves, and having given thanks, he broke them and gave them to his disciples to set before the people; and they set them before the crowd. [7]And they had a few small fish. And having blessed them, he said that these also should be set before them. [8]And they ate and were satisfied. And they took up the broken pieces left over, seven baskets full. [9]And there were about four thousand people. And he sent them away. [10]And immediately he got into the boat with his disciples and went to the district of Dalmanutha.	8 [1]In those days the multitude being very great, and having nothing to eat, Jesus called his disciples unto him, and saith unto them, [2]I have compassion on the multitude, because they have now been with me three days, and have nothing to eat: [3]And if I send them away fasting to their own houses, they will faint by the way: for divers of them came from far. [4]And his disciples answered him, From whence can a man satisfy these men with bread here in the wilderness? [5]And he asked them, How many loaves have ye? And they said, Seven. [6]And he commanded the people to sit down on the ground: and he took the seven loaves, and gave thanks, and brake, and gave to his disciples to set before them; and they did set them before the people. [7]And they had a few small fishes: and he blessed, and commanded to set them also before them. [8]So they did eat, and were filled: and they took up of the broken meat that was left seven baskets. [9]And they that had eaten were about four thousand: and he sent them away. [10]And straightway he entered into a ship with his disciples, and came into the parts of Dalmanutha.

Introduction to 8:1–10 Jesus feeds the 4,000, demonstrating His compassion and power again. The disciples continue struggling to understand Jesus' miracles. Jesus repeats the feeding miracle, expecting that they will understand that He is the almighty God whose teaching is the true food (8:14–21).

8:1 *In those days.* The mention of several days maintains the tension described in the confrontations and miracles of ch. 7. The reader will easily recall the earlier feeding of the 5,000, though the disciples will soon have to be reminded (8:19–20). *when again a great crowd had gathered.* This is a familiar beginning for Mark's episodes. In this case, however, Jesus is not trying to avoid the crowd. He has encouraged their stay by His extended teaching.

8:2 *compassion.* This distinctive word for compassion and mercy which come from the center of one's being, *splagchnidzomai,* has been seen before as the reason for Jesus' actions of feeding and healing. See the notes on 1:41. *with me . . . nothing to eat.* Crowds were wildly enthusiastic for Jesus (cf. 1:37, 45; 3:9; 6:33, 54–55). They were so eager to stay with Him that they lost track of time and began to ignore basic necessities such as food. What little food they might have had must have been long gone by now. Given food and shelter, they likely would have stayed far beyond the three days.

8:3 Jesus has finished the lesson to the crowd and now begins teaching the disciples privately. He sets the parameters of the lesson by removing any suggestion that the crowd be simply dismissed hungry. Jesus already had in mind to feed the hungry multitude; nonetheless, He invited the disciples to reflect on the problem (cf. 6:37). He tested them to see whether they would have faith.

8:4 *how can one feed these people.* Once again, the disciples failed to recognize Jesus' true identity and lacked faith in His power. They had learned not to suggest dismissing the crowd, but they hadn't grasped Jesus' power to repeat the miracle of feeding. *desolate place?* The desolate place or wilderness is the scene for one of Jesus' most important actions. See the notes on 1:4 for further examples. The desert highlights the crowd's need and the magnificence of Jesus' feeding so many.

8:5 *Seven.* This may represent the number of Gentile nations surrounding Israel. This might be especially meaningful given Jesus' recent travels to the Gentile regions of Tyre and Sidon and the Decapolis. There were twelve baskets of leftovers collected in 6:43, a number representing Israel. *do you have.* The disciples might have volunteered these loaves at the start, but Jesus had to remind them of the loaves. Their focus on the crowd and the desert made the loaves seem almost worthless, certainly nothing to speak of.

8:6 *took . . . given thanks . . . broke . . . gave.* This repeats the essential actions before the feeding of the 5,000. See the notes for these words at 6:41 along with their resemblance to Jesus' actions at the Lord's Supper. There is a cross-like combination of movements here. Jesus' prayer vertically ascends to heaven and His distribution of food horizontally feeds the entire crowd. In the center of these actions is the broken bread. We recall Jesus' teaching of Jn 6:33 that He is the true bread that comes down from heaven, giving life to the world.

8:7 *small fish.* These were probably roasted until crisp and could be kept for an extended time. In contrast with 6:41, Jesus blessed the fish separately, after the bread had been distributed, thus making a second course that highlighted the bounty of the meal. *blessed.* Jesus' blessing is distinctive compared to the blessing of a meal by anyone else. Our ordinary blessing of a meal gives thanks for the meal and asks for its benefits to all who eat. Beyond this blessing, Jesus, as true God, bestows on the meal the miraculous multiplication which will feed everyone.

8:8 *satisfied.* See notes on 6:42 where similar words describe the filling of the 5,000. Jesus once again makes everyone fully content, even to the extent that much was left over. *they took up the broken pieces.* The abundance of the meal made these extra pieces seem superfluous to the crowd. Yet the disciples gathered them. The Twelve should have recognized the miraculous nature of the pieces and it would likely have seemed wrong to leave them as insignificant scraps. *seven baskets full.* The word here for "baskets" (*spuridas*), is different from that used for the twelve baskets of left-over pieces after the feeding of the 5,000 (*kophinon*). (See their contrast in 8:19–20.) The *spuridas* were larger, braided reed baskets while the *kophinon* were the more common traveling wicker baskets. Though only seven, the baskets of 8:8 likely held even more pieces than what was gathered in the feeding of the 5,000. *and He sent them away.* Though the crowd was fed sufficiently to stay longer, Jesus' teaching had been highlighted with this concluding miracle. It was time to move on and also to avoid the sheltering praise of the crowd.

8:10 Jesus' departure with the disciples is highlighted with "immediately" which contrasts with His remaining on the shore following the feeding of the 5,000 (6:45–46). *district of Dalmanutha.* This is the only NT mention. It was most likely on the western shore of the Sea of Galilee.

8:1–10 in Devotion and Prayer Jesus' compassion moves Him to feed another hungry crowd by means of a second miraculous multiplication of bread. When Jesus confronts the disciples with a directive to feed the crowds for a second time, they again fail to see that His power provides the way forward. How slowly we sometimes respond in faith! Yet how graciously Jesus continues to provide, both with His Word of forgiveness and with daily bread. He fully satisfies our bodies and souls. He provides repeated opportunities for us to ask for, and expect, His power to work. • Lord, deepen our hunger for Your Word, and so teach us to turn first to You in every need. Then feed us with Your multiple gifts. Amen.

Jesus confronts the Pharisees and warns against the yeast of the Pharisees and Herod, but His disciples misunderstand (8:11–21)

ESV	KJV
[11]The Pharisees came and began to argue with him, seeking from him a sign from heaven to test him. [12]And he sighed deeply in his spirit and said, "Why does this generation seek a sign? Truly, I say to you, no sign will be given to this generation." [13]And he left them, got into the boat again, and went to the other side.	[11]And the Pharisees came forth, and began to question with him, seeking of him a sign from heaven, tempting him. [12]And he sighed deeply in his spirit, and saith, Why doth this generation seek after a sign? verily I say unto you, There shall no sign be given unto this generation. [13]And he left them, and entering into the ship again departed to the other side.
[14]Now they had forgotten to bring bread, and they had only one loaf with them in the boat. [15]And he cautioned them, saying, "Watch out; beware of the leaven of the Pharisees and the leaven of Herod." [16]And they began discussing with one another the fact that they had no bread. [17]And Jesus, aware of this, said to them, "Why are you discussing the fact that you have no bread? Do you not	[14]Now the disciples had forgotten to take bread, neither had they in the ship with them more than one loaf. [15]And he charged them, saying, Take heed, beware of the leaven of the Pharisees, and of the leaven of Herod. [16]And they reasoned among themselves, saying, It is because we have no bread.

yet perceive or understand? Are your hearts hardened? [18]Having eyes do you not see, and having ears do you not hear? And do you not remember? [19]When I broke the five loaves for the five thousand, how many baskets full of broken pieces did you take up?" They said to him, "Twelve." [20]"And the seven for the four thousand, how many baskets full of broken pieces did you take up?" And they said to him, "Seven." [21]And he said to them, "Do you not yet understand?"

[17]And when Jesus knew it, he saith unto them, Why reason ye, because ye have no bread? perceive ye not yet, neither understand? have ye your heart yet hardened?

[18]Having eyes, see ye not? and having ears, hear ye not? and do ye not remember?

[19]When I brake the five loaves among five thousand, how many baskets full of fragments took ye up? They say unto him, Twelve.

[20]And when the seven among four thousand, how many baskets full of fragments took ye up? And they said, Seven.

[21]And he said unto them, How is it that ye do not understand?

Introduction to 8:11–21 When Jesus leaves the 4,000, He sails not into a physical storm as when leaving the 5,000 (6:48), but He faces a spiritual squall with the Pharisees. The Pharisees want to see more signs than have been given, while the disciples cannot see the significance of the signs that have already come. Jesus closes the door on the Pharisees' demands and gives the disciples a chance to review what should have been obvious. But the full meaning of the feeding miracles remains just out of their grasp.

8:11 *the Pharisees came.* Mark most often begins an episode by describing the travel of Jesus (1:16, 21, 29; 2:1), or the gathering of a crowd (2:2, 18; 3:7, 31–32). Here it is the Pharisees' action that starts the scene. The Pharisees had already decided that Jesus must die (3:6). Thus, their behavior here is pure hypocrisy. *sign from heaven.* Such a sign, *semeion*, if performed, may have been used as evidence in their case against Jesus. No amount of miracles would be enough to create faith. In the end, Jesus' miracles would only create enough hatred within the Pharisees to deliver Jesus to the cross.

8:12 *sighed deeply.* This word (*anastenacksas*) is used only here in the NT. Jesus' sigh was in the privacy of His spirit, much as His knowledge in 2:8. It was likely not a loud, demonstrative moan, but an inner sorrow over their hardened hearts. See the notes on 3:5 for Jesus' emotions. Calvin writes,

> Certainly all who are desirous to promote the glory of God, and who feel concern about the salvation of men, ought to have such feelings that nothing would inflict on their hearts a deeper wound than to see unbelievers purposely blocking up against themselves the way of believing, and employing all their ingenuity in obscuring by their clouds the brightness of the word and works of God. (*Harmony* 2:278)

no sign. Jesus refused to provide a gratuitous show of power. The only sign given to such unbelief will be Jesus' death and resurrection. In Mt 16:4, Jesus says the only sign will be the sign of Jonah. Jesus is the fulfillment of Jonah, the one willing to die for the well-being of all others, dead for three days and risen again. The disciples will ask for the sign of the end of time (13:4), and there Jesus will focus them on the necessity of knowing the true Christ. The sign that is needed for eternal life is the knowledge of Jesus as the Messiah.

8:13 *he left them.* How different this leaving is from the leaving of the 5,000 and the 4,000 (6:45–46; 8:9–10). To those crowds, Jesus gave days of teaching and a feast at the end. They left filled in body and soul. But the Pharisees, with minds and hearts already filled against Him, get only a sentence and leave unchanged.

8:11–13 in Devotion and Prayer Even though the Pharisees have already rejected Jesus, they still try to demand that He prove His identity. Scoffers continue to do as much today, denying God, but at the same time hurling demands for proof toward Him. Believers, however, know that God is real, and they see the depth of His love in Christ's suffering and the glory of His promises in the resurrection. • Lord, when we hunger for a sign of Your presence and power, focus our eyes on Your empty tomb. Make this the lasting, satisfying sign that opens our eyes to You. Amen.

Introduction to 8:14–21 By now, the disciples should have gotten the idea that a shortage of food was no problem for Jesus. However, they remain as blind to Jesus' true identity as ever. Jesus uses their lack of bread as a teaching moment, warning of the Pharisees' teaching. However, the disciples show a slowness of understanding that's almost as dense as the hard hearts of the Pharisees.

8:14 *they had forgotten . . . only one loaf.* We can imagine the finger-pointing among the Twelve when only one loaf is found. "Who is to blame? What are we going to do?" The questions, accusations, and self-defenses grow like the yeast in rising bread. Jesus likely waited to hear if just one would say, "It doesn't matter. We're with Jesus! He can feed us." The Pharisees sought a sign, but none was given them. The disciples had handled the miracle of multiplied bread twice and now had a chance to see His sign at work again. But they couldn't imagine it.

8:15 *leaven.* Bread rises through yeast and such leavened bread was often viewed as a metaphor for evil. See the unleavened bread of Passover and the images of 1Co 5:6, 7; Gal 5:9. But yeast can also be an image of growth as in the parable of Mt 13:33. Here the inflated self-worth and empty posturing of the Pharisees is the point. Like raised dough, they can be reduced with a single blow. *Pharisees.* It is ironic that Jesus must warn the disciples about contact with the Pharisees' teaching. The Pharisees, scrupulous about their own ritual purity, had recently accused Jesus of His own lack of ritual cleansing (7:1–8). Jesus shows that the true danger is in a teaching which comes from a wicked heart. *Herod.* See the notes on 3:6 and the council of the Pharisees and Herodians which first planned the death of Jesus.

8:16 *no bread.* The problem is not a shortage of food, but a lack of faith in the One who can provide for this and every need. The discussion likely was heated given the disciples' tendency to compete with each other when they didn't understand Jesus' teaching (9:32–34). That accusing tone echoed the contentious nature of the Pharisees whose argument with Jesus just ended. But a similar spirit of defensive pride remained on the boat with the Twelve.

8:17 *Jesus, aware of this.* Jesus' knowledge of their thoughts matches His knowledge of an argument by the Pharisees (2:8). Jesus must warn them against both the teaching and the argumentative thoughts of the Pharisees. *Do you not yet perceive.* The Twelve had seen the clear testimony of Jesus' miraculous feedings—to say nothing of His many other miracles—yet they do not grasp that Jesus is the Messiah. *hearts hardened?* Jesus warns against a failure to see His true identity and a lack of faith in Him as Lord. Significantly, His adversaries already know, but reject, His claims to be the Messiah. His disciples, on the other hand, are depicted as merely oblivious to His true identity.

8:18 *having eyes . . . having ears.* These questions echo Jesus' words of 4:11–13 when He said that the disciples had been given the secret of the Kingdom but others would see but not perceive, hear but not understand. The disciples have fallen to the level of the untrained crowd. *do you not remember?* Jesus stresses the experiences that the disciples alone have which should enlighten them.

8:19 *when I broke the five loaves for the five thousand.* The contrast between the few loaves and the thousands of people, one loaf for each thousand men, should reassure them that one loaf in Jesus' hands would be enough. *twelve.* The disciples were likely relieved to be able to give a clear answer. The twelve baskets were smaller traveling baskets compared to the larger baskets of 8:20. See notes on 8:8.

8:20 *seven . . . seven.* The parallel between seven loaves and seven baskets matches the correspondence between the five loaves and the five thousand men. Jesus repeats the question as He will also repeat the question about His identity in 8:27, 29. These questions are simple memory and arithmetic, but the next ones will require the Father's revelation. The overall point of the questions on the bread is the abundance of pieces left over provided an extraordinary supply for the disciples. After the crowds were filled, the disciples had their meal plus all that was left over. They did not need to worry about this short time in the boat.

8:21 *do you not yet understand?* Mark leaves this question unanswered. Matthew 16:12 notes that the disciples then understood that Jesus was speaking about the teaching of the Pharisees. The understanding likely didn't come to all immediately but eventually, perhaps with further teaching. By leaving the disciples without understanding, Mark prepares the reader for the blindness of the man next healed (8:22–26) the challenge of understanding Jesus' identity (8:27–30), and acceptance of His death (8:31–33). The disciples are entering a long period of darkness in which they will struggle to see Jesus and His mission clearly.

8:14–21 in Devotion and Prayer The disciples remember their lack of bread but forget about the One who is with them, the very Lord and Creator of all. At times, we are similarly hard-hearted and shortsighted, focusing so much on our need for daily bread that we forget to call upon Jesus, the very bread of life. Nevertheless, Jesus patiently teaches His disciples, showing over and over that He alone can satisfy our deepest needs. • Lord, open the eyes of our hearts, so that we see You as the very bread from heaven, the answer to all our wants and needs. Amen.

Jesus heals a blind man in Bethsaida (8:22–26)

ESV	KJV
[22]And they came to Bethsaida. And some people brought to him a blind man and begged him to touch him. [23]And he took the blind man by the hand and led him out of the village, and when he had spit on his eyes and laid his hands on him, he asked him, "Do you see anything?" [24]And he looked up and said, "I see men, but they look like trees, walking." [25]Then Jesus laid his hands on his eyes again; and he opened his eyes, his sight was restored, and he saw everything clearly. [26]And he sent him to his home, saying, "Do not even enter the village."	[22]And he cometh to Bethsaida; and they bring a blind man unto him, and besought him to touch him. [23]And he took the blind man by the hand, and led him out of the town; and when he had spit on his eyes, and put his hands upon him, he asked him if he saw ought. [24]And he looked up, and said, I see men as trees, walking. [25]After that he put his hands again upon his eyes, and made him look up: and he was restored, and saw every man clearly. [26]And he sent him away to his house, saying, Neither go into the town, nor tell it to any in the town.

Introduction to 8:22–26 The Pharisees wanted to see a sign, but none was given them (8:11–12). The disciples could remember the baskets of broken bread, but had trouble seeing Jesus as the true Bread and the all-providing God (8:14–21). Finally, dark blindness is overcome as this man is healed. The progressive healing parallels the slow enlightening of the disciples as to Jesus' identity.

8:22 *Bethsaida.* This was the end of their voyage (8:13), landing at this village on the northeast shore of the Sea of Galilee. *begged him.* This is the last time this verb, *parakaleo*, is used in Mark. It has often been the appeal for Jesus to heal, especially by His touch (1:40; 5:23; 6:56; 7:32).

8:23 *out of the village.* Jesus heals the man away from the crowds. See 5:40; 7:33 for other moments when Jesus' healing was done in private. Given the often intrusive crowds, it is remarkable that Jesus can get away with this man when they clearly expect to see a miraculous healing. *spit on his eyes.* Jesus used His saliva as a means of healing on other occasions. See Jn 9:6 when he puts mud upon the eyes of a blind man, sending him to wash in the pool. *laid His hands on him.* While the touch of Jesus will bring healing, His first touch is a gentle reassurance which begins a trusting relationship even within the blindness. See notes on 7:33 where Jesus heals the deaf and mute man through a touch on ears and tongue.

8:24 *like trees, walking.* The man sees unclearly at first. It may indicate that the man was not born blind but lost his sight. He therefore knows something is still wrong in what he now sees. This is the only instance in which Jesus' healing isn't complete at once. Only Mark records this sequential miracle, which stands out all the more for Mark's emphasis on Jesus' instantaneous miracles and the immediate results from His healings.

8:25 *again.* The blind man receives his sight in this second step. Calvin writes, "The grace of Christ, which had formerly been poured out suddenly on others, flowed by drops, as it were, on this man" (*Harmony* 2:285). In the same way, the disciples do not understand what they are seeing; Jesus must teach them who He is again and again (v. 31; 9:31; 10:32–33). With the blind man, Jesus expresses no surprise or disappointment over the initial, imperfect sight. He has seen this coming and patiently repeats the treatment. In the same way, He will repeat His teachings on His approaching death (8:31; 9:31; 10:33). *opened his eyes . . . restored . . . saw everything clearly.* In contrast to the partial sight, now the perfect vision is stressed through this repetition of verbs. The word for "clearly," *telaugos,* used only here in the NT, means clearly, brightly, brilliantly. His vision wasn't just better, or good enough, but fully restored.

8:26 *do not even enter the village.* The removal of the man from the crowd was just the beginning of distancing. Jesus seeks again to limit the news of His miracles. He might also have wanted to spare the man some of the interrogation that came to the man born blind once he was healed (Jn 9:13–17, 24–34). Jesus frequently commanded those healed to say nothing of His miracles and this instance prepares for the great revelation and secrecy of 8:29–30 and the Transfiguration (9:9). However this is the last time in Mark that Jesus tells someone who is healed to say nothing. From this point on, Jesus' identity is the focus.

8:22–26 in Devotion and Prayer Jesus heals a blind man as His disciples continue to struggle with the issue of who Jesus is and what He has come to do. Sin blinds all of us. Yet, Jesus' gracious touch opens our eyes so that, despite our weaknesses, we recognize Him as the Christ and believe in Him unto life everlasting. • Lord, open our eyes to see You and Your ways. Help us to recognize and confess You clearly as our great physician. Amen.

Peter confesses that Jesus is the Christ in Caesarea Philippi (8:27–30)

ESV	KJV
[27]And Jesus went on with his disciples to the villages of Caesarea Philippi. And on the way he asked his disciples, "Who do people say that I am?" [28]And they told him, "John the Baptist; and others say, Elijah; and others, one of the prophets." [29]And he asked them, "But who do you say that I am?" Peter answered him, "You are the Christ." [30]And he strictly charged them to tell no one about him.	[27]And Jesus went out, and his disciples, into the towns of Caesarea Philippi: and by the way he asked his disciples, saying unto them, Whom do men say that I am? [28]And they answered, John the Baptist; but some say, Elias; and others, One of the prophets. [29]And he saith unto them, But whom say ye that I am? And Peter answereth and saith unto him, Thou art the Christ. [30]And he charged them that they should tell no man of him.

Introduction to 8:27–30 The disciples have an initial clear view of Jesus' identity as the Christ. However, how He will be the anointed Savior still remains hidden from them as the next verses will show. Peter's declaration of Jesus as the Christ confirms what has been said from 1:1 on and has been demonstrated through Jesus' miracles, teaching, and conflicts with His enemies.

8:27 *Caesarea Philippi.* This is the northernmost Galilean city Jesus visited, 25 miles north of Bethsaida, in the largely Gentile region north of the Sea of Galilee. This remote region will give Jesus time for the disciples' teaching without contentious Pharisees or demanding crowds. *on the way.* Jesus leads the discussion as they travel. "Way" (Gk *hodos*), recalls the same word in 1:2–3 where Isaiah prophesies of preparing a straight way. The long path of these first chapters is here quickly retraced by the many opinions on Jesus' identity, ending at the one correct answer. *who do people say.* Jesus knows that, like the initial sight of man just healed (8:24), many will imperfectly see Him.

8:28 *they told him.* Likely several disciples competed to answer this so that the possibilities poured out. Here they had easy answers, unlike the difficult questions of 8:17–18. *John the Baptist.* See the notes on 6:14 concerning John's courageous stand against Herod who feared that John had come back from the dead in the person of Jesus. *Elijah.* Some saw Jesus as Elijah (6:15), likely due to His miracles and the expectation that one would come in the spirit of Elijah (Mal 4:5–6). Elijah will appear with Jesus at the Transfiguration (9:4), and Jesus identifies John the Baptist as the one who fulfills Mal 4:5–6 (cf. Mt 17:12–13). *prophets.* Jesus, though indeed a prophet, is much more.

8:29 *but who do you say I am?* Jesus' point in pressing this question of His identity is to get the disciples to recognize and acclaim Him as the Messiah. They can do this by His instruction, His miracles, and also faith before the revelation of the Transfiguration. *You are the Christ.* Although Mark begins by identifying Jesus as the Christ (1:1, 11), this is the first time the disciples correctly identify Jesus as the Messiah. In Mark, however, Peter does not confess at this time that Jesus is the Son of God. That declaration will come through the centurion after Jesus' death (15:39). "Christ" means "anointed one." Priests and kings were anointed into their offices as were some prophets. Jesus, is the greatest anointed one who encompasses all of these roles, but as the Son of God, he is greater than any one role and any other man sent from God.

8:30 *tell no one.* As noted in 8:26, the silence over His miracles has ended. Yet now and in 9:9, the disciples need to delay declaring who Jesus is. Since they will struggle with what His mission will be, the less-informed crowds would have no chance of understanding.

8:27–30 in Devotion and Prayer For the first time in Mark, one of the Twelve recognizes Jesus as the Christ, God's Anointed One. How slow we are and how dull is our understanding of Jesus' divinity! We see and yet do not see. And so it is that Jesus graciously continues revealing Himself to us through Word and Sacrament. His Spirit works in us the faith that claims, "Jesus is the Christ." • Lord Jesus, help us to see You as the true Son of the Father, the Christ anointed as our prophet, priest, and king. Rule us graciously for all eternity. Amen.

Part 3

Jesus Prepares His Disciples for His Passion, Death, and Resurrection (8:31–16:8)

Jesus Reveals His Passion, Death, and Resurrection and Teaches on Discipleship (8:31–10:52)

The first Passion prediction, subsequent teaching, and events (8:31–9:29)

Jesus predicts His suffering, death, and resurrection,and rebukes Peter (8:31–33)

ESV	KJV
31 And he began to teach them that the Son of Man must suffer many things and be rejected by the elders and the chief priests and the scribes and be killed, and after three days rise again. 32 And he said this plainly. And Peter took him aside and began to rebuke him. 33 But turning and seeing his disciples, he rebuked Peter and said, "Get behind me, Satan! For you are not setting your mind on the things of God, but on the things of man."	31 And he began to teach them, that the Son of man must suffer many things, and be rejected of the elders, and of the chief priests, and scribes, and be killed, and after three days rise again. 32 And he spake that saying openly. And Peter took him, and began to rebuke him. 33 But when he had turned about and looked on his disciples, he rebuked Peter, saying, Get thee behind me, Satan: for thou savourest not the things that be of God, but the things that be of men.

Introduction to 8:31–9:1 Here is a mystery that is beyond any question Jesus might ask. He must tell the disciples for the first time that He will suffer, die, and rise again. Jesus then applies the implications of His Messiahship to the lives of His followers. Just as He willingly submits to God's will, even when that is painful, so they must also submit. Augustine writes, "The first destruction of man, was the love of himself. . . . Prefer to this God's will; learn to love yourself by not loving yourself" (*NPNF*1 6:408).

8:31 *Son of Man.* Jesus will use this title extensively in the next chapters when speaking of His suffering and death (8:31; 9:9, 31; 10:33; 14:21, 41) and also in prophecies of His resurrection (9:12), and final return (8:38; 13:26; 14:62. See further notes on 2:10, when He first used it speaking of His power to forgive, and therefore was shown to be God. *suffer . . . rejected.* Though Is 52:13–53:12 predicted that God's Servant would suffer and die for the benefit of His people, the disciples would prove unable to accept such suffering. Jesus stresses the prophetic nature of His death by saying, "It is necessary . . ." His death is not accidental, nor even a vicious injustice. It is the eternal plan of God (Eph 1:4–5). Jesus repeats this prediction twice in Mark (9:31; 10:33–34), so that there end up being three Passion predictions, one for each of Peter's denials in 14:66–72. After each Passion prediction, Jesus continues by teaching about discipleship. *elders . . . chief priests . . . scribes.* Jesus' rejection was by the breadth of Israel's leadership rather than one misguided segment. *three days rise again.* This will be the ultimate sign, pre-figured by Jonah (Mt 16:4), which will demonstrate His power as the Christ. His merciful, sacrificial love places Him on the cross. From that death, Jesus rises as the saving Christ, bestowing the benefit of His death on all.

8:32 *he said this plainly.* This was not a time for parables needing interpretation, or questions for which they could see no answer. *Peter . . . began to rebuke Him.* Peter will not accept a suffering Christ until after the resurrection. Like most Jews of his day, Peter expects a powerful warrior and conquering Messiah. Ironically, Jesus has been the one to take some aside before their healing (7:33; 8:23), and has tried to silence others (cf. 1:25–26). Now, however, Peter takes Jesus privately aside and tries to silence Jesus.

8:33 *He rebuked Peter.* Jesus is, in fact, correcting all of the Twelve, since none can accept the necessity of His sacrificial death. Peter represents them all and Jesus speaks clearly for all the disciples to hear. *Satan!* The refusal to accept God's plan of having Jesus die for all is devilish, for it threatens to undo the divine plan of salvation. Satan here tempts Jesus with a life-saving course of action, similar to daring the angels to preserve Him from a fall (Mt 4:5–7). When Jesus' course cannot be changed, Satan will be instrumental in the betrayal by Judas (Lk 22:3; Jn 13:2, 27). *setting your mind on the things of God.* To accept Jesus' suffering and believe in the resurrection is a divine gift. See Php 2:5–11 for a summary of His humiliation through the cross and His exaltation by the resurrection.

Jesus teaches His disciples and the crowd on discipleship (8:34–9:1)

ESV	KJV
[34]And calling the crowd to him with his disciples, he said to them, "If anyone would come after me, let him deny himself and take up his cross and follow me. [35]For whoever would save his life will lose it, but whoever loses his life for my sake and the gospel's will save it. [36]For what does it profit a man to gain the whole world and forfeit his soul? [37]For what can a man give in return for his soul? [38]For whoever is ashamed of me and of my words in this adulterous and sinful generation, of him will the Son of Man also be ashamed when he comes in the glory of his Father with the holy angels." 9 [1]And he said to them, "Truly, I say to you, there are some standing here who will not taste death until they see the kingdom of God after it has come with power."	[34]And when he had called the people unto him with his disciples also, he said unto them, Whosoever will come after me, let him deny himself, and take up his cross, and follow me. [35]For whosoever will save his life shall lose it; but whosoever shall lose his life for my sake and the gospel's, the same shall save it. [36]For what shall it profit a man, if he shall gain the whole world, and lose his own soul? [37]Or what shall a man give in exchange for his soul? [38]Whosoever therefore shall be ashamed of me and of my words in this adulterous and sinful generation; of him also shall the Son of man be ashamed, when he cometh in the glory of his Father with the holy angels. 9 [1]And he said unto them, Verily I say unto you, That there be some of them that stand here, which shall not taste of death, till they have seen the kingdom of God come with power.

8:34 *calling the crowd.* Jesus welcomes the crowd, increasing the number of hearers in contrast to the private conversation begun by Peter. The words of the cross are for all, and will prepare for the disciples eventually to hear and see that He is the Christ crucified (8:29–31). *take up his cross.* Accept the burdens of being an imitator of Christ. Augustine says,

> Let him bear whatever trouble he has; so let him follow Me. For when he shall begin to follow Me in conformity to My life and precepts, he will have many to contradict him . . . and that from among those who are even as it were Christ's companions. (*NPNF*1 6:409)

The cross is a denial of one's own easy, self-preserving life. *follow Me.* This echoes the first words spoken to Simon and Andrew (1:17). He has just told Peter to get behind Him, but here He renews the invitation to follow closely. Christians follow Jesus through suffering and death and into resurrection.

8:35 *whoever would save his life.* The mystery of Jesus' suffering for the life of the world turns upside down everything the disciples know and imagine. In order to save their lives, they must be willing to give them up. The chief priests and scribes will mock Him on the cross saying, "He saved others; he cannot save himself" (15:31). The sacrifice of His life saves all who have entrusted their lives to His death and resurrection. *gospel's.* Jesus' message is in parallel with Jesus Himself (v. 38). To know His word is to know Him.

8:36 *what does it profit a man.* Jesus underlines the foolishness of chasing after a fading world while being robbed of eternal life. The fool gathers in the whole world with both hands but loses hold of his soul. No wealth but Christ's blood can be exchanged for one's soul (1Pt 1:18–19). Augustine reflects on Christ's matchless worth, saying,

> Great is the world; but greater is He by whom the world was made. Fair is the world; but fairer is He by whom the world was made. Sweet is the world; but sweeter is He by whom the world was made. Evil is the world; and good is He by whom the world was made. (*NPNF*1 6:410)

8:37 *what can a man give in return for his soul?* The verse before this compares the gain of the world to the loss of the soul. This verse highlights the required payment for a soul which is greater than anything a man might have. It recalls Jesus' earlier lesson concerning what is vital, the inner or outer life of a man (7:15–23). The inner life of the soul could be bought only with another life, the act of One who would give up His life in payment and then take up His life in victory.

8:38 *ashamed.* It is unthinkable that someone would be ashamed of the mighty, loving God who would give Himself for the world. And yet, the disciples cannot accept Jesus as the suffering Messiah or confess Him truly. They wish to take Him from the cross and to remove the cross from their own shoulders. Jesus graciously promises a reward for those who accept the necessity of His death and confess Him as Savior before the world (Mt 10:32). In contrast to this warning, Paul says that he is not ashamed of the Gospel for it is the power of God unto salvation (Rm 1:16). Bengel writes, "One may confess Christ in general, and yet be ashamed of this or that word, this or that saying of His. . . . This kind of shame must also be overcome" (Bengel 534). *My words.* Jesus emphasizes His Word ("gospel's," v. 35) as the basis of faith, life, and salvation and as a parallel to Himself. This continues the emphasis on preaching begun in 1:14–15. *adulterous.* The adulterous generation seeks a new relationship when trouble and death come into the marriage between themselves and God. Faced with the cross, this generation wants promises of a pain–free life. *He comes . . . with the holy angels.* St Ambrose writes concerning the angels:

> The angels come in obedience, He comes in glory: they are His retainers, He sits upon His throne: they stand, He is seated—to borrow terms of the daily dealings of human life, He is the Judge: they are the officers of the court. (*NPNF*2 10:257)

9:1 After warning the crowd and disciples of His cross and theirs, Jesus' closing words promise that the end is near. That end will come with the power of the resurrection promised in 8:31. Eleven of the disciples, and many more, including five hundred witnesses (1Co 15:6), saw Him after the resurrection. Only Judas failed to witness the resurrection. *see the kingdom of God after it has come with power.* Though Jesus could mean the transfiguration as a fulfillment of this promise (vv. 2–13), this ultimately points to His death and resurrection as the beginning of the Kingdom in power. Jesus announced the arrival of the Kingdom in His initial preaching (1:14–15). While we wait for a new heaven and new earth (Rv 21:1), the power of the Kingdom is centered in Jesus' willingness to lay down His life and His authoritative resurrection (Jn 10:18).

8:31–9:1 in Devotion and Prayer Jesus warns that He has come to suffer, die, and rise and that everyone who follows Him must carry the cross. We are easily tempted to avoid the cross. Our reason says that God would want us to be safe. Yet, Jesus suffered for our salvation and promised to overcome Satan and all our foes. Jesus is the only one sufficient to exchange His life for ours. He invites us to carry the cross in union with Him who has already paid the price for us. • Lord, thank You for accepting the disgrace and pain of the cross. Strengthen us to follow You from Your cross to Your glory. Amen.

Jesus is transfigured before three of His disciples (9:2–13)

ESV	KJV
2And after six days Jesus took with him Peter and James and John, and led them up a high mountain by themselves. And he was transfigured before them, 3and his clothes became radiant, intensely white, as no one on earth could bleach them. 4And there appeared to them Elijah with Moses, and they were talking with Jesus. 5And Peter said to Jesus, "Rabbi, it is good that we are here. Let us make three tents, one for you and one for Moses and one for Elijah." 6For he did not know what to say, for they were terrified. 7And a cloud overshadowed them, and a voice came out of the cloud, "This is my beloved Son; listen to him." 8And suddenly, looking around, they no longer saw anyone with them but Jesus only. 9And as they were coming down the mountain, he charged them to tell no one what they had seen, until the Son of Man had risen from the dead. 10So they kept the matter to themselves, questioning what this rising from the dead might mean. 11And they asked him, "Why do the scribes say that first	2And after six days Jesus taketh with him Peter, and James, and John, and leadeth them up into an high mountain apart by themselves: and he was transfigured before them. 3And his raiment became shining, exceeding white as snow; so as no fuller on earth can white them. 4And there appeared unto them Elias with Moses: and they were talking with Jesus. 5And Peter answered and said to Jesus, Master, it is good for us to be here: and let us make three tabernacles; one for thee, and one for Moses, and one for Elias. 6For he wist not what to say; for they were sore afraid. 7And there was a cloud that overshadowed them: and a voice came out of the cloud, saying, This is my beloved Son: hear him. 8And suddenly, when they had looked round about, they saw no man any more, save Jesus only with themselves. 9And as they came down from the mountain, he charged them that they

Elijah must come?" [12]And he said to them, "Elijah does come first to restore all things. And how is it written of the Son of Man that he should suffer many things and be treated with contempt? [13]But I tell you that Elijah has come, and they did to him whatever they pleased, as it is written of him."

should tell no man what things they had seen, till the Son of man were risen from the dead.

[10]And they kept that saying with themselves, questioning one with another what the rising from the dead should mean.

[11]And they asked him, saying, Why say the scribes that Elias must first come?

[12]And he answered and told them, Elias verily cometh first, and restoreth all things; and how it is written of the Son of man, that he must suffer many things, and be set at nought.

[13]But I say unto you, That Elias is indeed come, and they have done unto him whatsoever they listed, as it is written of him.

Introduction to 9:2–13 After warning of the approaching cross, Jesus has just promised that the Kingdom will come with power. If miraculous healings aren't enough, a greater sign is about to be given. But the audience for this sign will be only three disciples (Peter, James, and John), who are witnesses along with the Father, Moses, and Elijah. In the middle of all, as God and Man, Jesus shines as the sun.

9:2 *and after six days.* Mark shows the nearness of the Transfiguration to the first declaration of Jesus' suffering and death (8:31). The disciples, reeling from the specter of the cross, need the reassurance of Jesus' power shown in the Transfiguration. *Peter and James and John.* Jesus has already set these three apart as three of the four first called (1:16–20), and as those who saw the little girl's resurrection (5:37). They will remain with Him in the Garden (14:33), these three representing all Twelve. *transfigured.* Jesus shone with the glory of His divine nature, which otherwise had been veiled (cf. Php 2:7–8). This is the glory that the disciples might have envisioned in 9:1, the sort of sign that could have been given to overwhelm the sneering Pharisees (8:11). However, there is a transfiguration that transforms the world from death to life. It is when the glorious God takes the form of a servant, ascends a dark mountain, places death upon Himself, and then rises from the grave (Php 2:7–8).

9:3 *radiant.* A word used only here in the NT. Jesus' divinity shone with the brilliance expected of God's presence on earth (cf. Ex 34:29; Rv 1:16). The overall experience of transfiguration (9:2) is focused here on His brilliant clothing, though other aspects of Jesus' appearance might also have changed. *bleach.* Only Mark speaks of the bleach which was a paste made from clean clay (fuller's earth) in which white cloth was soaked and then stretched out to dry in the sun. Once dry, the clay paste was washed away. By this, Mark stresses that Jesus' glory was beyond any king. Jesus' clothes reflected His divinity as one would expect of the only Son of God. However, His cross surprised the disciples as a sign of His humility and sacrifice.

9:4 *appeared to them.* The disciples' ability to see these two saints was a gift in itself. Their perception of Elijah and Moses recalls Elisha's assurance to his servant that those who are with us are more than those who are with them. The servant's eyes were opened to see the horses and chariots of fire (2Ki 6:16–17). *Elijah with Moses.* The great law-giver, Moses, and Elijah, the prophet who called down fire from heaven, epitomize the Law and the Prophets. See Mt 5:17; 11:13 for Jesus' use of this phrase to summarize the OT, along with the phrase "Moses and all the prophets" (Lk 24:27). Moses' forty days of meeting with God on Mt. Sinai and his return with his face shining because of his talking with God (Ex 34:29–30) is an OT prelude to this divine meeting. Moses and Elijah confronted the wicked leadership of Pharaoh and King Ahab, respectively. They were threatened with death and yet lived long by the rescue of God. Their conflicts parallel Jesus' upcoming battles against Herod and Pilate. However, while Moses and Elijah were miraculously rescued, and Elijah never tasted death, the Son of God will face the cross and suffer being forsaken by the Father.

9:5 *Rabbi.* This title is from Hbr *rabban*, "chief" or "great one." This is the first time in Mark that Jesus is called Rabbi; the last time will be Judas' greeting Jesus at his betrayal (14:45). This title "Rabbi" bridges Jesus' transfigured glory and the dark glory of the cross. *three tents.* Peter hoped to prolong their stay by providing shelter or places of worship. By staying they could bask in this glorious sight, hear more of this heavenly conversation, and delay the journey towards the cross. The tents, or tabernacles as translated in KJV, might refer to the tabernacles made during the Feast of Booths (Lv 23:42). Or, Peter might be speaking of the tent of meeting in which "the LORD used to speak to Moses face to face, as a man speaks to his friend" (Ex 33:11). In either case, Peter desired to remain with these OT saints.

9:6 *he did not know what to say.* Peter did not rightly understand what he was witnessing. The confusion of the disciples continues here from earlier instances (4:13; 7:17, 21), and is emphasized in 9:32. Moses and Elijah were preparing Jesus for going to His death (Lk 9:30–31). *for they were terrified.* The word for "terrified" (or "sore afraid" in the KJV) is *ekphobos,* which occurs only here and in Heb 12:21 where it is used in an OT quote concerning Moses' fear at being on Mt. Sinai alone with God. Facing God, especially in His unveiled glory, would terrify anyone, as Elijah himself showed when God spoke to him in a still, small voice on the mountain (1Ki 19:12–13).

9:7 *cloud.* The presence of divine glory was associated with clouds in the wilderness, overshadowing mountains, the tabernacle, and the temple (cf. Ex 13:21; 19:9; 33:9; 40:34–38; 1Ki 8:10–11). The cloud demonstrates God's over-arching power and His messages of Law and Gospel. The clouds of the Flood and the darkness covering Mt. Sinai with Moses conveyed His judgment. However, the cloud with its rainbow was also His promise of mercy (Gn 9:12–17). *This is My beloved Son.* The Father repeated the announcement from Jesus' Baptism for the disciples. The centurion will affirm this truth at Jesus' crucifixion. This announcement completes Peter's declaration that Jesus is the Christ (8:29). More than an anointed prophet, Jesus is the true Son who, as the image of the invisible God (Col 1:15), has all the fullness of God in bodily form (Col 2:9). *listen to Him.* Jesus is the ultimate expression of the Father, surpassing the prophets (Heb 1:1–2). Moses prophesied that a new prophet would come to whom the people would listen (Dt 18:15). Jesus alone knows all things from the Father (Mt 11:27) and reveals the Father whom no one has seen (Jn 1:18).

9:8 *suddenly looking around they no longer saw anyone.* Mark stresses the immediacy of this moment by using a word for "suddenly" (*eksapina*) which is used only here in the NT. The Father's command is reinforced by the instant removal of Moses and Elijah, though Peter would have enjoyed hearing more from them. But their moment and purpose has passed. Only Jesus' words matter and remain. *but Jesus only.* Jesus remaining with them is the wonder. How easily He could have left the world, escaping death just as Elijah did. But if He remains, he will die. He will save others by not saving Himself.

9:9 *tell no one*. Jesus continues the warning of silence. He cautions those healed to say nothing lest adoring crowds overwhelm His freedom, teaching, and travel (e.g. 1:44–45). Now, however, the disciples cannot tell the crowds lest they insist on seeing the miracle again. Worse, if the crowd were convinced that He is the Son of God, they would never call for His crucifixion. Secrecy is the only path to the cross. Like a treasure whose value was yet unknown, this event was tightly held by the disciples. *Son of Man had risen*. The heart of Jesus' prophecy was His death and resurrection. His glory did not dismiss the cross. The three disciples are supposed to remember this moment in the darkness of His death. The light of His transfiguration should have led them confidently to Easter.

9:10 *questioning what this rising from the dead might mean*. The disciples struggled over the necessity of Jesus' suffering. Since they could not grasp the possibility or purpose of Jesus' death, His resurrection was inconceivable. This continues their struggle with His predictions (8:32), which will only grow (9:32, 10:32). While we might envy the disciples for all that they see, merely seeing more of God's power doesn't guarantee understanding. Grasping the necessity and value of the cross unlocks the central actions of God.

9:11 *scribes*. The scribes were the teachers of the Law, aligned with the Pharisees (Mk 2:16; 7:1, 5). While they were responsible for the copying of the OT, they also interpreted the Law for the largely illiterate population of Israel and multiplied the demands of the Law (Mt 23:13, 15, 23). *Elijah must come?* The scribes taught that Elijah must return to fulfill Mal 4:5–6. The disciples naturally wonder about this prophecy since they have just seen Elijah. They might wonder if this brief appearance on the mountain was the fulfillment of Malachi's prophecy. Will Elijah come again, or had he come already, unseen, at least by them?

9:12 *Elijah . . . restore all*. John the Baptist prepared for Jesus' arrival (cf. 1:2–8). However, the road that John prepared was to lead Him to the cross. This is the mystery of which Jesus asks, "And how is it written . . ." These predictions of the cross are the mile markers signaling the planned end of John's work. *Son of Man . . . suffer . . . contempt?* This question referred to Jesus' betrayal, trial, beatings, and crucifixion. Jesus asks them to search the Scriptures which speak of Him, especially His death and resurrection. This is the question for which He supplies the answer in Lk 24:26–27 when speaking with the Emmaus disciples. They should know the necessity of His suffering and death as recorded in Moses and the prophets. These three disciples are expected to have at least a beginning knowledge of these predictions, especially after overhearing Moses and Elijah speaking of these things with Jesus.

9:13 *Elijah has come.* Matthew 17:13 explains that the disciples understood John the Baptist to be the return of Elijah. *as it is written of him.* Like Elijah, who suffered the wickedness of King Ahab and Queen Jezebel, John had to suffer under Herod and Herodias (cf. 1Ki 17–21). John's suffering continued the pattern of Elijah and also prefigured Jesus' own suffering and death.

9:2–13 in Devotion and Prayer Jesus is transfigured to display His divine glory and to prepare His disciples for His death and resurrection. We cannot imagine the glory of God, especially in Christ, who is fully human. Jesus loses none of His divine majesty in the incarnation, but His glory shines through His human nature. His glory reminds us that He freely chose death and resurrection for our sake. • Lord, bring us to that mountain where we can see Your glory shine. Let us follow You to the glory of Your cross to celebrate Your power and to marvel at Your life given for us. Amen.

Jesus casts out an unclean spirit from a boy after His disciples' failure (9:14–29)

ESV	KJV
14And when they came to the disciples, they saw a great crowd around them, and scribes arguing with them. 15And immediately all the crowd, when they saw him, were greatly amazed and ran up to him and greeted him. 16And he asked them, "What are you arguing about with them?" 17And someone from the crowd answered him, "Teacher, I brought my son to you, for he has	14And when he came to his disciples, he saw a great multitude about them, and the scribes questioning with them. 15And straightway all the people, when they beheld him, were greatly amazed, and running to him saluted him. 16And he asked the scribes, What question ye with them?

a spirit that makes him mute. 18 And whenever it seizes him, it throws him down, and he foams and grinds his teeth and becomes rigid. So I asked your disciples to cast it out, and they were not able." 19 And he answered them, "O faithless generation, how long am I to be with you? How long am I to bear with you? Bring him to me." 20 And they brought the boy to him. And when the spirit saw him, immediately it convulsed the boy, and he fell on the ground and rolled about, foaming at the mouth. 21 And Jesus asked his father, "How long has this been happening to him?" And he said, "From childhood. 22 And it has often cast him into fire and into water, to destroy him. But if you can do anything, have compassion on us and help us." 23 And Jesus said to him, "'If you can'! All things are possible for one who believes." 24 Immediately the father of the child cried out and said, "I believe; help my unbelief!" 25 And when Jesus saw that a crowd came running together, he rebuked the unclean spirit, saying to it, "You mute and deaf spirit, I command you, come out of him and never enter him again." 26 And after crying out and convulsing him terribly, it came out, and the boy was like a corpse, so that most of them said, "He is dead." 27 But Jesus took him by the hand and lifted him up, and he arose. 28 And when he had entered the house, his disciples asked him privately, "Why could we not cast it out?" 29 And he said to them, "This kind cannot be driven out by anything but prayer."

17 And one of the multitude answered and said, Master, I have brought unto thee my son, which hath a dumb spirit;

18 And wheresoever he taketh him, he teareth him: and he foameth, and gnasheth with his teeth, and pineth away: and I spake to thy disciples that they should cast him out; and they could not.

19 He answereth him, and saith, O faithless generation, how long shall I be with you? how long shall I suffer you? bring him unto me.

20 And they brought him unto him: and when he saw him, straightway the spirit tare him; and he fell on the ground, and wallowed foaming.

21 And he asked his father, How long is it ago since this came unto him? And he said, Of a child.

22 And ofttimes it hath cast him into the fire, and into the waters, to destroy him: but if thou canst do any thing, have compassion on us, and help us.

23 Jesus said unto him, If thou canst believe, all things are possible to him that believeth.

24 And straightway the father of the child cried out, and said with tears, Lord, I believe; help thou mine unbelief.

25 When Jesus saw that the people came running together, he rebuked the foul spirit, saying unto him, Thou dumb and deaf spirit, I charge thee, come out of him, and enter no more into him.

26 And the spirit cried, and rent him sore, and came out of him: and he was as one dead; insomuch that many said, He is dead.

27 But Jesus took him by the hand, and lifted him up; and he arose.
28 And when he was come into the house, his disciples asked him privately, Why could not we cast him out?
29 And he said unto them, This kind can come forth by nothing, but by prayer and fasting.

Introduction to 9:14–9:29 Jesus goes from the company of Moses and Elijah and His Father to the shriek of a demon and a father's anguished cry. Jesus steps down from the Mount of Transfiguration's glory to the tension of failed disciples and an expectant crowd. He reassures those of little faith that even the smallest trust can receive the extraordinary gifts of God.

9:14 *scribes arguing.* The disciples had just asked about the scribes' expectation that Elijah would precede the coming of Christ (9:11). Now the scribes arrive as one of the three groups present: there are disciples arguing with the scribes, all surrounded by a great crowd. How distant this wrangling scene is from the harmony and peace of Moses and Elijah speaking with Jesus on the mountain!

9:15 *immediately.* Jesus' presence is noticed instantly, likely since the disciples have been speaking of Him and longing for His return. They were left with a challenge that exceeded their experience and strength, and so they likely wondered when He would return. They likely promised that He could perform the exorcism needed. *greatly amazed.* Though Moses still shone when he returned from Mt. Sinai, it is unlikely that Jesus still carried some of the heavenly brightness of 9:2–3. Rather, the crowd was surprised that He was there, perhaps at a critical moment in the argument. The word for "greatly amazed," *ekthambeo*, is used only by Mark in the NT. It is found only here, in 14:33 speaking of Jesus' distress in Gethsemane, and in 16:5 for the women's fear at the tomb.

9:16 *and He asked them.* Though Jesus is fully aware of what they are saying, He gives them an opportunity to express their frustration. Though He asked the disciples, the answer will come from the father of the demon-possessed boy. This likely cut short a long renewal of the argument between the scribes and the disciples over how to cast out the demon.

9:17 *Teacher.* See notes on 4:38 for this word, *didaskalos*, a word used often by those requesting something of Jesus. *a spirit that makes him mute.* Other spirits had been vocal (cf. 1:24; 5:7) with an increase in the physical control and rage shown against the one possessed. This final demon to be cast out in Mark proves to be especially violent.

9:18 His condition resembles an epileptic seizure, causing recurring convulsions and loss of consciousness, but it is caused by demon possession. *Your disciples . . . were not able.* Though the father had intended for Jesus Himself to cure his son, only the disciples were available. They had cast out many demons on their mission journey (6:13), and likely felt that they could do this exorcism also. However, this demon is especially stubborn. Having afflicted the boy from his childhood (v. 21), the demon has already defeated every attempted cure. The boy's hopeless condition recalls the many others who were brought to Jesus with incurable diseases such as the paralyzed man (2:1–12), the woman with the bleeding (5:25), and the girl who died (5:41).

9:19 *them.* The father, disciples, and the gathering crowd. *faithless generation.* The father and crowd had likely despaired while Jesus was absent on the mount. Note the amazement in v. 15 (cf. 6:6; Lk 24:32, 41). The disciples' fear recalls their hopelessness when they were in the storm (6:49–50). *how long . . . How long.* His time left with them was coming to an end. How long it had been already, and how short was the time for them to gain courage, understanding and faith! If the screeching demon is too much now, how will they deal with His death on a dark cross? Also, how long will Jesus have to deal with evil in this piecemeal fashion, one demon at a time? He yearns for the time, soon to come, when He will judge the prince of this world and crush the serpent's head (Jn 12:31–32; Gn 3:15).

9:20 *immediately it convulsed the boy.* The demon showed instant rebellion. The demon in the synagogue (1:23–24) declared that Jesus was the Holy One of God and the demon of 5:7 called Him the Son of the Most High. This mute demon makes no declaration, asks no question, begs for no mercy. This demon is doomed but will leave in a defiant fury of suffering.

9:21 *How long has this been happening to him?* Jesus showed interest in the boy, who is more than a subject on which to demonstrate His power. The length of suffering is a key factor in several healing miracles such as the woman with bleeding for twelve years (5:25), the woman disabled for eighteen years (Lk 13:11), the man paralyzed for thirty-eight years (Jn 5:5), and the man born blind (Jn 9:2). The length of time shows that these are not diseases that would have run their course without Jesus' healing. The permanence of the illness and the accumulated suffering show Jesus' power and compassion.

9:22 *to destroy him.* The demon has a use and abuse relationship with the boy. He intends to occupy him for years and so he brings him to the brink of death but sustains the boy to prolong the torment. *if you can do anything.* The father conditions his request for mercy by asking, first, if Jesus can do something. Many had likely expressed compassionate concern for the life of the boy, but they could do nothing. More sympathetic sorrow is not needed. But, Jesus, if you have power, then let power and love have their day. *compassion.* See the notes on 1:41 for this important word, *splangchnidzomai,* which is usually given as the reason for Jesus' miraculous action (1:41; 6:34; 8:2). This is the only time when it is asked of Jesus. Jesus' compassion is not a futile desire but is the natural partner of His power. See Ps 62:11–12 "Once God has spoken; twice have I heard this: that power belongs to God, and that to you, O Lord, belongs steadfast love."

9:23 *if you can!* The power and love of God are constant. Jesus, by this statement, is asking, "Can you believe in the power and love of God?" Faith receives the gifts God has prepared (cf. 11:22–24; Jas 1:5–8). Faith is itself the gift of God which comes by the hearing of His promises (Rm 10:17).

9:24 *immediately the father of the child cried out.* Just as the demon had reacted instantly to Jesus (v. 20), so the father also responds at once. The father cries out with faith but struggles with his son's burden and the failure of the disciples (cf. Rm 7). The tiny seed of faith appears to be hopelessly buried beneath the years of suffering and the uselessness of every attempted cure. Yet that small faith is about to break out into remarkable growth. The Lutheran confessors write,

> Worthiness does not depend on the greatness or smallness, the weakness or strength of faith. Instead, it depends on Christ's merit,

> which the distressed father of little faith [Mark 9:24] enjoyed as well as Abraham, Paul, and others who have a joyful and strong faith. (FC SD VII 71)

Chemnitz writes, "We are justified by faith, not because it is so firm, robust, and perfect a virtue, but because of the object on which it lays hold, namely Christ, who is the Mediator in the promise of grace" (Chemnitz 8:932).

9:25 *a crowd came running together.* Though Jesus has not taken the boy far from the crowd as with some healings (7:33; 8:23), yet He does not want to escalate the public nature of this demon possession. The demon would have wanted the larger audience to show his power one last time. *I command you.* Jesus' command is personal. While this demon has not acknowledged Jesus' divinity, as did the two demons seen earlier (1:23; 5:7), it is Jesus as true God who alone can demand this instant obedience. *never enter him again.* Jesus reassures the boy and father that this is not a temporary cure, perhaps such as they might have seen, which only made the return of the demon all the more cruel.

9:26 *after crying out.* Jesus' command upends and reverses the power and nature of the demon so that the mute spirit cries out and leaves the healed boy. *boy was like a corpse.* However, in leaving the boy, the demon's departure appears to completely exhaust the boy's life. Its departure attempts to mimic the loss of one's true spirit which results in death. However, this demon, especially in the presence of Jesus, has no such power of life and death. This demonic spirit's leaving is life, not death.

9:27 *Jesus took him by the hand.* What a blessed touch from Jesus. Just as Jesus, by a touch and word, revived the girl who had died (5:41), so Jesus renews the boy's life with a touch. This touch is love, power, and life itself to a boy who has been cruelly crushed by the demon. In contrast to the departing shriek of the demon, Jesus brings life with a quiet word and gentle touch. The strong Carpenter's hands restore the broken child with a silent grace. Though it is unmentioned, we can imagine the astonishment and joy of the family, the amazed first words of the boy, and the celebration of the crowd.

9:28 *the house.* Jesus often gathered the disciples by themselves after a significant event (1:29; 4:10, 34; 9:33). As often the case, Jesus needed to take them away from the crowd even when the celebration was greatest (1:45; 6:1, 45; 8:10). *Why could we not.* The disciples had cast out demons in their mission work (6:13), but this demon defied their combined efforts. This was a leveling defeat that prevented the familiar competition between them as to which was the greatest. Failure to cast out the demon adds to their list of failures as they struggle to understand Jesus' mission leading to the cross. See the notes on 8:21; 8:32; and 9:32.

9:29 *this kind.* There are different types of demons with different powers. The disciples' earlier success in exorcism (6:13) had either not prepared them for this case or made them overconfident in their own work. *by anything but prayer.* We might have expected Jesus to say that only He, as the glorious Son of God, could do this work. However, He highlights their lack of prayer. Matthew 17:20 records Jesus answering by saying, "Because of your little faith." The two reasons work together. Lacking faith, they did not pray. They likely depended on their past experience and success, especially since they were all together. One demon versus nine experienced exorcists—this should be no problem. However, when they failed, they did not cry, as the father did, in faith for the help of God (vv. 22, 24). Some early manuscripts and the KJV add the words, "and fasting" to the end of the sentence. However, the shorter text found in ESV is also found in early manuscripts and fits better with their failure of faith and prayer. The disciples' breakdown was not due to their outward preparation or procedure, but came because of their inner self-confidence.

9:14–29 in Devotion and Prayer Jesus descends from the transfiguration and meets a defiant demon, an anxious father, an astonished crowd, and despairing disciples. The demon has arrogantly ruled the family's life, shrinking the father's faith. Despair threatens to overwhelm our faith, too, by pointing out how we fail to change or improve, suggesting that God neither cares for us nor has power to help. However, Jesus does not linger in the glory of the transfiguration, but graciously descends to a world of despair and doubt so that He might deliver us. • Lord, thank You for Your compassion, which brings You to our world of pain and dismay. Give us faith to overcome our doubts, and help us believe that all things are possible with You. Amen.

The second Passion prediction and subsequent teaching (9:30–10:31)

Jesus predicts His suffering, death, and resurrection (9:30–32)

ESV	KJV
30They went on from there and passed through Galilee. And he did not want anyone to know, 31for he was teaching his disciples, saying to them, "The Son of Man is going to be delivered into the hands of men, and they will kill him. And when he is killed, after three days he will rise." 32But they did not understand the saying, and were afraid to ask him.	30And they departed thence, and passed through Galilee; and he would not that any man should know it. 31For he taught his disciples, and said unto them, The Son of man is delivered into the hands of men, and they shall kill him; and after that he is killed, he shall rise the third day. 32But they understood not that saying, and were afraid to ask him.

Introduction to 9:30–32 This is the second of Jesus' three predictions of His death and resurrection (8:31; 10:33–34). The disciples' confusion continues, even though Jesus has taught them repeatedly. See the note on 8:31. Luther writes concerning Jesus and the cross:

> [The cross] attacks Him and kills Him. By this deed the whole world is purged and expiated from all sins, and thus it is set free from death and from every evil. But when sin and death have been abolished by this one man, God does not want to see anything else in the whole world, especially if it were to believe, except sheer cleansing and righteousness. And if any remnants of sin were to remain, still for the sake of Christ, the shining Sun, God would not notice them. (LW 26:280)

9:30 *He did not want anyone to know.* There is a wonderful tension between the crowd who knows too much and the elusive knowledge sought by the disciples. Too easily does the crowd know His location and follow Him. How much harder it is for the disciples to know what Jesus means and the reason for where He is going.

9:31 *for He was teaching His disciples.* Jesus' patience carries Him through another lesson, even while He knows that the disciples won't understand. *Son of Man.* See the notes on 8:31. *Will be delivered.* While this phrase sounds as though Jesus is taken by force, He delivers Himself to the cross. John 10:18: "No one takes [my life] from me, but I lay it down of my own accord." He will allow His enemies to imagine that they have control through their plot and power, but He brings Himself to the cross. *after three days He will rise.* This phrase is essentially identical to that in 8:31. While the details of His death will vary in the three predictions, the simple promise of His resurrection concludes each one. If the disciples cannot take in or understand His death, let them hold onto the simple promise that He will live.

9:30–32 in Devotion and Prayer Jesus repeats the prophecy of His passion and resurrection while the disciples listen in frightened silence. Death is terrifying and confusing when we cannot see the promised resurrection. Yet, Jesus bears our fears as well as our sins on the cross in order to deliver us. • Lord, break our fear of death by reminding us that You have died, never to die again. Today, open our frightened hearts with the resurrection's promise; one day, open our closed eyes with the resurrection's power. Amen.

Jesus teaches His disciples on greatness in the kingdom of God (9:33–50)

ESV	KJV
[33]And they came to Capernaum. And when he was in the house he asked them, "What were you discussing on the way?" [34]But they kept silent, for on the way they had argued with one another about who was the greatest. [35]And he sat down and called the twelve. And he said to them, "If anyone would be first, he must be last of all and servant of all." [36]And he took a child and put him in the midst of them, and taking him in his arms, he said to them, [37]"Whoever receives one such child in my name receives me, and whoever receives me, receives not me but him who sent me."	[33]And he came to Capernaum: and being in the house he asked them, What was it that ye disputed among yourselves by the way? [34]But they held their peace: for by the way they had disputed among themselves, who should be the greatest. [35]And he sat down, and called the twelve, and saith unto them, If any man desire to be first, the same shall be last of all, and servant of all. [36]And he took a child, and set him in the midst of them: and when he had taken him in his arms, he said unto them, [37]Whosoever shall receive one of such children in my name, receiveth

38 John said to him, "Teacher, we
saw someone casting out demons in
your name, and we tried to stop him,
because he was not following us."
39 But Jesus said, "Do not stop him,
for no one who does a mighty work in
my name will be able soon afterward
to speak evil of me. 40 For the one who
is not against us is for us. 41 For truly,
I say to you, whoever gives you a cup
of water to drink because you belong
to Christ will by no means lose his
reward.

42 "Whoever causes one of these
little ones who believe in me to sin,
it would be better for him if a great
millstone were hung around his neck
and he were thrown into the sea.
43 And if your hand causes you to sin,
cut it off. It is better for you to enter
life crippled than with two hands to
go to hell, to the unquenchable fire.
45 And if your foot causes you to sin,
cut it off. It is better for you to enter
life lame than with two feet to be
thrown into hell. 47 And if your eye
causes you to sin, tear it out. It is better for you to enter the kingdom of
God with one eye than with two eyes
to be thrown into hell, 48 'where their
worm does not die and the fire is not
quenched.' 49 For everyone will be
salted with fire. 50 Salt is good, but if
the salt has lost its saltiness, how will
you make it salty again? Have salt in
yourselves, and be at peace with one
another."

me: and whosoever shall receive me, receiveth not me, but him that sent me.

38 And John answered him, saying, Master, we saw one casting out devils in thy name, and he followeth not us: and we forbad him, because he followeth not us.

39 But Jesus said, Forbid him not: for there is no man which shall do a miracle in my name, that can lightly speak evil of me.

40 For he that is not against us is on our part.

41 For whosoever shall give you a cup of water to drink in my name, because ye belong to Christ, verily I say unto you, he shall not lose his reward.

42 And whosoever shall offend one of these little ones that believe in me, it is better for him that a millstone were hanged about his neck, and he were cast into the sea.

43 And if thy hand offend thee, cut it off: it is better for thee to enter into life maimed, than having two hands to go into hell, into the fire that never shall be quenched:

44 Where their worm dieth not, and the fire is not quenched.

45 And if thy foot offend thee, cut it off: it is better for thee to enter halt into life, than having two feet to be cast into hell, into the fire that never shall be quenched:

46 Where their worm dieth not, and the fire is not quenched.

47 And if thine eye offend thee, pluck it out: it is better for thee to enter into the kingdom of God with one eye, than having two eyes to be cast into hell fire:

48Where their worm dieth not, and the fire is not quenched.

49For every one shall be salted with fire, and every sacrifice shall be salted with salt.

50Salt is good: but if the salt have lost his saltness, wherewith will ye season it? Have salt in yourselves, and have peace one with another.

Introduction to 9:33–50 Following Jesus' second teaching on His death and resurrection, the disciples amazingly argue over which one of them is greatest. Instead of pointing to Himself, Jesus takes up a child as a picture of service. The disciples then receive two more lessons. Do not stop someone who is doing the work of Christ, even if he is not part of your particular group. But do stop that which causes sin for yourself or for one of those who believe in Christ. No loss here is too great compared to the gain of eternal life.

9:33 *He asked them.* After Jesus tells the disciples of His coming death and resurrection, they don't understand, but they don't ask (vv. 31–32). They fill the confused vacuum with a topic that they know well: a debate on which one of them is the greatest. So, while they could have asked Jesus to tell them more, to fill the emptiness of their understanding, but they fill the air with their own foolish competitiveness. Jesus could have ignored them, or He could have bluntly corrected them. But with His omniscient question, He invites them to confess.

9:34 *But they kept silent.* This is the fourth instance of silence in ch. 9. Jesus commands the three disciples to say nothing (v. 9), He confronts the mute spirit (v. 17ff.), and His prediction of death and resurrection leaves the disciples confused and silent (v. 32). As the cross comes near, a strained silence settles over much of His ministry. The KJV translates somewhat paradoxically, "they held their peace." Peace they withheld, but competition they turned loose. *who was the greatest.* Ironically, after the transfiguration and Jesus' Passion prediction, the disciples debated which of them was greatest. This debate will also come on Maundy Thursday after the Last Supper (Lk 22:24). It seems that the high moments of Jesus' glory and His sacrificial love paradoxically bring out the competitiveness of the disciples.

9:35 *He sat down and called the twelve.* Jesus must make this a formal moment of teaching. Stopping the journey, calling them as an exclusive circle and using the child elevates the importance of this lesson. *first . . . last . . . servant of all.* Jesus describes His own life, but leaves the disciples to make the connection. He invites them to ask, in their spirit of competition, "Who has made Himself the least of all and has served more than any?" Perhaps they will ask Jesus Himself that question and then realize that the answer was in the One of whom they are asking the question.

9:36 *and He took a child.* While the ultimate example of service is Jesus, in true humility, He focuses on an anonymous child instead. Taking the child shows His gentle nature and is a reminder of His own willingness to become a child. It is one measure of service to welcome a child; it is far more when God chooses to become a baby in a manger.

9:37 *whoever receives one such child.* Jesus emphasizes service and humility. Though the child appears insignificant, he is treasured by the Lord, who focuses on serving others. In the kingdom of God, every disciple represents the Lord. Each child recalls His youth; every cup of water given to the thirsty reminds us of Jesus' dusty journey to the cross (Mt 10:42). *Him who sent Me.* Every parent feels the kindness or the hurt given to their child. Our heavenly Father is not far away, but is found in the treatment of His children. The path to His heart is kindness to the smallest of His own people. The Father feels the need of His children. In order to save the least of them, He will give up the life of His only Son.

9:33–37 in Devotion and Prayer Confused by Jesus' prediction of His death, the disciples return to a subject they know well, their own greatness. Jesus shows them that true status is found in serving those whom God values. When we are tempted to debate who is the greatest, we should instead look to the Master who sacrificed Himself on the cross. He represents us before the Father in order to redeem us, and He leads us by the cross into a new life. • Lord, forgive us for our battles over greatness. Remind us that You alone are great, for You have served the least among us. Amen.

9:38 *someone casting out demons in your name.* This had been a signature part of the disciples' ministry (6:13), and a demonstration of Jesus' own power (1:25; 5:8; 9:25). *we tried to stop him . . . not following us.* The disciples' argument was not that this man did not know Jesus. Rather, he was not one of their particular group. Perhaps John brings this up now since the twelve were in this close circle (v. 35), and recalling this attempt was an effort to do something right after the argument on the road (v. 34).

9:39 *a mighty work in My name.* Exorcism would certainly be a divine work that should not be stopped. *speak evil of Me.* One who worked good in God's name would not curse His name. Jesus is pointing out the key qualities by which to judge the man. It is not a matter of his belonging to the circle of the disciples. Rather, the mighty work of casting out a demon places him firmly on the side of Jesus. If he sharply orders demons now, he won't soon be commanded by them against Jesus. Furthermore, his power and courage to cast out demons are more than enough reason to ignore the complaints of the disciples.

9:40 *not against us is for us.* Here Jesus gives the positive turn, centering on the man's exorcism of their mutual enemy, the demons. In Mt 12:30; Lk 11:23, Jesus says, "Whoever is not with Me is against Me." This, however, was said when Jesus was accused of casting out demons by being in league with the prince of demons. Those who accuse Him of being demonic Himself can only be enemies of His work. The Pharisees, despite their outward holiness, were dead trees with bare branches. Meanwhile, the man of Mk 9:38, known for his good work of exorcism, has shown his good nature and allegiance to Jesus. Wesley writes,

> Our Lord had formerly said He that is not with me, is against me: thereby admonishing this hearers, that the war between him and Satan admitted of no neutrality, and that those who were indifferent to him now, would finally be treated as enemies. But here in another view, he uses a very different proverb; and charitably to hope that those who did not oppose his cause wished well to it. Upon the whole, we are to be rigorous in judging ourselves, and candid in judging each other. (Wesley 119)

9:41 *whoever gives a cup of water.* After hearing of the man casting out demons, it might appear that the bar is set too high for us. We'll never do mighty works like that, and will never be counted as being for Him. However, Jesus focuses on the smallest kindness, giving a cup of water. This matches His use of a child in v. 36 to illustrate greatness. *you belong to Christ.* Even a small, generous act gives glory to Christ (v. 37). The disciples are made the receivers of the kindness here. It is a reminder of their mission journey in which they took very little along and depended on the kindness of strangers (6:8–10). *reward.* This is the only time Mk records Jesus speaking of a reward, *misthos*, though that word and the idea of reward are often found in Matthew (Mt 5:12, 46; 6:1, 2, 4–6, 16, 17; 10:41–42). The gift is not in proportion to the effort and time of the service, as the parable of the vineyard shows (Mt 20:1–16). While called a reward, it is God's grace at work. The reward of eternal blessings far exceeds any reasonable pay for small acts of kindness here.

9:38–41 in Devotion and Prayer Jesus opens the disciples' eyes to see those who do God's work in dramatic or simple ways. The work of God goes far beyond us and His mercy for the little we do surpasses anything we deserve. He shows His power and kindness through great life-changing miracles and simple cups of water. • Lord, thank You for Your work through the lives of others. Lead me to welcome those miracles and mercies that You show through every one of Your people. Amen.

9:42 *little ones.* This is from the Gk adjective *mikros*, meaning small, here used for the "smallest child." (See it more often used in Mt 18:6, 10, 14.) The use of *mikros* here stresses the value God places on even the smallest. Also, even the smallest is able to believe despite his youth and size. See Mk 9:36–37 and 10:13–16 where Jesus speaks of *paidion,* a more common word for a small child. *to sin.* This is especially that sin which would result in the loss of faith. Such a lost child would be eagerly sought by God. Just as the woman sought for the lost coin (Lk 15:8–10), God seeks for what was lost by someone else's carelessness. *great millstone.* This is the stone turned in a mill, often by a donkey, to grind seed into flour. The English adjective "great" translates the Gr adjective *onikos* which refers to a donkey. This was a stone so large that only a donkey could move it. See also Jb 41:24.

9:43–48 *if your hand causes you to sin.* While v. 42 focuses on the sin against the littlest one, Jesus now speaks of sins against ourselves. Don't let eternal salvation slip from your own careless hands. Nothing is more important than faith unto eternal life. *hell.* This is the Gk word *geenna*; from the Hbr name for the Hinnom Valley southwest of Jerusalem, where humans once were sacrificed (2Ch 28:3; 33:6) and garbage was dumped (2Ki 23:10). Fire was constantly present in the Hinnom Valley due to sacrifices and burning trash; this became a figure for the everlasting fire of hell, as the ESV translation suggests. This word is used in Mark only here (vv. 43, 45, 47). *foot . . . eye.* With the hand, foot, and eye, Jesus shows the extreme value of preserving eternal life. While no one wants to go through life without one of these vital organs, life here is short and eternity is endless. The loss of much more than hand, foot, or eye might be needed to preserve faith. Many things might need to be cut out of life. It could be a relationship which would lead to doubt and denial. It could be a lucrative business which contradicts a life of faith. It could be revenge, cutting out the pursuit of satisfying payback. Any of these things might seem our natural right, something anyone else might have. But in light of eternity, it is better to preserve the faith than to enter eternal death with our hands full of our personal privileges.

9:44 and 9:46 *where their worm dieth not* (KJV). These verses are not found in the earliest manuscripts. They are identical to v. 48 and give an expected completeness to the commands about removing hand, foot and eye. Just as Jesus gives essentially the same command three times, so there is this warning three times. However, that warning is sufficiently announced in v. 48 alone.

9:48 *worm does not die.* This is a particularly frightening image of an inner torment. Opposite of this is the outer anguish of fire. *the fire is not quenched.* This describes the essence of the physical torments of hell. This verse is a part of Is 66:24, the last verse of Isaiah. The context of Is 66 is the celebration of new life for the saved in contrast to the eternal torment of the lost. The worm and fire are insatiable, recalling Pr 30:16 and the list of four things which never say "enough." First and last on that list are Sheol and fire.

9:49 *salted with fire.* Fire purifies and salt preserves. Christians may be kept in the true faith through the trials they endure. The KJV has an additional ending to the verse: "and every sacrifice shall be salted with salt." This is found in later manuscripts, lectionaries and translations. It likely reflects Lv 2:13 which commands that every grain offering be salted. Leviticus 2:14 notes that offerings of grain should be roasted with fire. The combined image of salt and fire comes in v. 49 which only Mark records. The eternal fire of 9:48 is destructive while the roasting fire of a sacrifice makes it a pleasing aroma. The three images of losing hand, foot, and eye, vv. 43–47, describe what might be lost to preserve faith and eternal life. Verse 49 now speaks of fire and salt as what must be added to sustain faith.

Calvin wrote, "To be *salted with fire* is an incorrect phrase; but as *salt* and *fire* possess the same quality of purifying and refining, Christ applied the same term to both" (*Harmony* 1:272). The many difficulties faced by Christians are the cross which brings them nearer to Jesus' experience (cf. 8:34–37). Being salted and then cured by the fire of difficulty is not the Christian's own heroic act but is the careful work of God. He measures the heat and seasoning that each can bear. Bengel writes,

> This salt implies the Divine discipline, gently training us to the denial of self, and to the cultivation of peace and harmony with others. They who are thus salted become thereby *a sacrifice* pleasing to God, the type of which [spiritual sacrifice] existed in the Levitical sacrifices; Lev. ii. 13. (Bengel 542)

9:50 *salt is good.* The first of three parts in this verse connects with the need for salt in v. 49. See Mt 5:13 where Jesus speaks of believers as the salt of the earth. *lost its saltiness.* Salt, as a chemical compound, doesn't lose its qualities, but salt as commonly found in the first century was a mixture of sodium chloride and other minerals. If the sodium chloride leached out of the mixture, what was ostensibly salt was actually salt no longer. If disciples who are the salt of the earth lose the essential faith, how can they be salted again with any substitute? Only faith in Christ preserves them and makes them valuable. *peace.* Faith brings peace, which is especially needed among contentious disciples.

9:42–50 in Devotion and Prayer Nothing is more important than retaining the faith unto eternal life. Let nothing come between you and the Savior. Though He tests us with fire, He does not consume His own people. Rejoice, for God graciously gives us the faith by which He preserves us to eternity. This faith not only saves His disciples but makes them priceless seasoning for the world. • Lord, give us the lasting faith that can persevere through every trial. Empty our hands of anything that competes with You, and let us hold firmly to You eternally. Amen.

Jesus teaches in the region of Judea and across the Jordan (10:1–31)

ESV

10 [1]And he left there and went to the region of Judea and beyond the Jordan, and crowds gathered to him again. And again, as was his custom, he taught them.

[2]And Pharisees came up and in order to test him asked, "Is it lawful for a man to divorce his wife?" [3]He answered them, "What did Moses command you?" [4]They said, "Moses allowed a man to write a certificate of divorce and to send her away." [5]And Jesus said to them, "Because of your hardness of heart he wrote you this commandment. [6]But from the beginning of creation, 'God made them male and female.' [7]'Therefore a man shall leave his father and mother and hold fast to his wife, [8]and the two shall become one flesh.' So they are no longer two but one flesh. [9]What therefore God has joined together, let not man separate."

[10]And in the house the disciples asked him again about this matter. [11]And he said to them, "Whoever divorces his wife and marries another commits adultery against her, [12]and if she divorces her husband and marries another, she commits adultery."

[13]And they were bringing children to him that he might touch them, and the disciples rebuked them. [14]But when Jesus saw it, he was indignant and said to them, "Let the children come to me; do not hinder them, for to such belongs the kingdom of God. [15]Truly, I say to you, whoever does not receive the kingdom of God like

KJV

10 [1]And he arose from thence, and cometh into the coasts of Judaea by the farther side of Jordan: and the people resort unto him again; and, as he was wont, he taught them again.

[2]And the Pharisees came to him, and asked him, Is it lawful for a man to put away his wife? tempting him.

[3]And he answered and said unto them, What did Moses command you?

[4]And they said, Moses suffered to write a bill of divorcement, and to put her away.

[5]And Jesus answered and said unto them, For the hardness of your heart he wrote you this precept.

[6]But from the beginning of the creation God made them male and female.

[7]For this cause shall a man leave his father and mother, and cleave to his wife;

[8]And they twain shall be one flesh: so then they are no more twain, but one flesh.

[9]What therefore God hath joined together, let not man put asunder.

[10]And in the house his disciples asked him again of the same matter.

[11]And he saith unto them, Whosoever shall put away his wife, and marry another, committeth adultery against her.

[12]And if a woman shall put away her husband, and be married to another, she committeth adultery.

[13]And they brought young children to him, that he should touch them:

a child shall not enter it." 16 And he
took them in his arms and blessed
them, laying his hands on them.
17 And as he was setting out on his
journey, a man ran up and knelt
before him and asked him, "Good
Teacher, what must I do to inherit
eternal life?" 18 And Jesus said to
him, "Why do you call me good? No
one is good except God alone. 19 You
know the commandments: 'Do not
murder, Do not commit adultery,
Do not steal, Do not bear false witness, Do not defraud, Honor your
father and mother.' " 20 And he said
to him, "Teacher, all these I have kept
from my youth." 21 And Jesus, looking
at him, loved him, and said to him,
"You lack one thing: go, sell all that
you have and give to the poor, and
you will have treasure in heaven; and
come, follow me." 22 Disheartened by
the saying, he went away sorrowful,
for he had great possessions.
23 And Jesus looked around and said
to his disciples, "How difficult it will
be for those who have wealth to enter
the kingdom of God!" 24 And the disciples were amazed at his words.
But Jesus said to them again, "Children, how difficult it is to enter the
kingdom of God! 25 It is easier for
a camel to go through the eye of
a needle than for a rich person to
enter the kingdom of God." 26 And
they were exceedingly astonished,
and said to him, "Then who can be
saved?" 27 Jesus looked at them and
said, "With man it is impossible, but
not with God. For all things are possible with God." 28 Peter began to
say to him, "See, we have left everything and followed you." 29 Jesus said,
"Truly, I say to you, there is no one

and his disciples rebuked those that
brought them.
14 But when Jesus saw it, he was
much displeased, and said unto them,
Suffer the little children to come unto
me, and forbid them not: for of such
is the kingdom of God.
15 Verily I say unto you, Whosoever
shall not receive the kingdom of God
as a little child, he shall not enter
therein.
16 And he took them up in his arms,
put his hands upon them, and blessed
them.
17 And when he was gone forth into
the way, there came one running,
and kneeled to him, and asked him,
Good Master, what shall I do that I
may inherit eternal life?
18 And Jesus said unto him, Why call-
est thou me good? there is none good
but one, that is, God.
19 Thou knowest the commandments, Do not commit adultery, Do
not kill, Do not steal, Do not bear
false witness, Defraud not, Honour
thy father and mother.
20 And he answered and said unto
him, Master, all these have I observed
from my youth.
21 Then Jesus beholding him loved
him, and said unto him, One thing
thou lackest: go thy way, sell whatsoever thou hast, and give to the
poor, and thou shalt have treasure in
heaven: and come, take up the cross,
and follow me.
22 And he was sad at that saying, and
went away grieved: for he had great
possessions.
23 And Jesus looked round about,
and saith unto his disciples, How
hardly shall they that have riches
enter into the kingdom of God!

who has left house or brothers or
sisters or mother or father or children or lands, for my sake and for
the gospel, 30who will not receive a
hundredfold now in this time, houses
and brothers and sisters and mothers
and children and lands, with persecutions, and in the age to come eternal
life. 31But many who are first will be
last, and the last first."

24And the disciples were astonished at his words. But Jesus answereth again, and saith unto them, Children, how hard is it for them that trust in riches to enter into the kingdom of God!

25It is easier for a camel to go through the eye of a needle, than for a rich man to enter into the kingdom of God.

26And they were astonished out of measure, saying among themselves, Who then can be saved?

27And Jesus looking upon them saith, With men it is impossible, but not with God: for with God all things are possible.

28Then Peter began to say unto him, Lo, we have left all, and have followed thee.

29And Jesus answered and said, Verily I say unto you, There is no man that hath left house, or brethren, or sisters, or father, or mother, or wife, or children, or lands, for my sake, and the gospel's,

30But he shall receive an hundredfold now in this time, houses, and brethren, and sisters, and mothers, and children, and lands, with persecutions; and in the world to come eternal life.

31But many that are first shall be last; and the last first.

Introduction to 10:1–12 Jesus concluded ch. 9 with words of peace, but divorce is the start of ch. 10. Jesus had spoken extensively in 9:43–47 about what might need to be removed to preserve eternal life. However, the Pharisees, in asking about divorce, are actually seeking Jesus' death. Jesus redirects them beyond the commands of Moses to the original intention of God to show the lasting bond of marriage.

10:1 *region of Judea and beyond the Jordan.* This was the area east of the Jordan River south toward the Dead Sea. *as was His custom.* This is the only time that Mark uses this phrase. It is found only two other times in the Gospels: Lk 4:16 describes Jesus' custom of synagogue worship at Nazareth, even though the people of Nazareth would attempt to kill Him that day, and Mt 27:15 reports Pilate's custom of letting a prisoner go free. Jesus' preaching ministry is summarized here with a single verse, as Mark often does, with a focus on the conflict that often follows and the correction or miracle that it requires. See notes on 1:21 and 2:2 for this pattern.

10:2 *in order to test Him.* The Pharisees sought either to justify themselves or to trap Jesus. Jesus' continued popularity with the crowds and His miracles, increasingly done in full public view (e.g. 9:25), drove them to curb His influence. Translated as "tempting" in KJV, the verb "to test" *peiradzo* occurs only twice in Mark, here and 1:13 when Jesus is tempted by Satan in the wilderness. The Pharisees have joined dangerous company when they seek to tempt Jesus. Jesus' success against both temptations emphasizes His free choice of the cross. No demonic power or conniving scheme drives Him.

10:3 *what did Moses command you?* Just as Jesus defeated the temptation of Satan in the desert by quoting the Old Testament (Mt 4:4–10), so He counters the Pharisees with Moses' words. It is also a reminder that they ought already know this answer and should be subordinate to Moses' command. Moses' words are not suggestions, nor a mere foundation for their attempts to manipulate Jesus. They are the words of God, the words of the One whom they are tempting.

10:4 *certificate of divorce.* See Dt 24:1 for the OT allowance for a certificate of divorce. There was a controversy in the first century concerning the acceptable grounds for divorce. It is likely that the Pharisees favored an easy approach by which a man could divorce his wife, virtually for mere disagreement. While they appear confident in their answer, indicating no interest in Jesus' wisdom, they hope to draw Jesus into the debate. They likely hope that Jesus can be condemned as hard-hearted to either husband or wife. See Jn 8:1–11, the woman caught in adultery, for a similar trap involving hard hearts and sharp words.

10:5 *hardness of heart.* Jesus often refers to the hardness of heart, both of His disciples (6:52; 8:17; 16:14), and of His enemies (3:5; 10:5). The Pharisees were like stones, without feeling for the divorced wife, with faces of flint set against the word and intentions of God. *he wrote you this commandment.* This commandment is a painful allowance for the fallen nature. It is not a license for easy separation and the causing of more pain. This permission for divorce does not cause separation but recognizes a desertion and severance by the spouse that has already fractured the marriage.

10:6 *from the beginning of creation.* While the Pharisees might claim Dt 24:1 as their authority, Jesus goes further back in the biblical record. Moses' allowance for divorce deals with the needs of a sinful world, but Jesus' answer rests on God's plan and His Gn 1 original perfection of creation. It is a clash between "Moses allowed" and "God made." Their distortion of Moses' allowance is made clear in light of God's original plan.

10:7 *leave his father and mother.* Marriage goes beyond the closeness of parents with children. This quote of Gn 2:24 is the closing summary of God's creation of Adam and Eve, noting especially that woman was taken out of man. The return of man and woman into one flesh in marriage echoes this shared beginning. *hold fast to his wife.* "Holding onto" is an unusual word, *proskallao*, used in the NT only here and Eph 5:31. It reflects the pure attachment of Adam and Eve in Gn 2 and their union of becoming one.

10:8 *no longer two but one flesh.* God intended marriage to be lifelong. Ephesians 5:21–33 discusses marriage as a reflection of the union of Christ, the Groom, with His Bride, the Church. The creation of men and women leading to marriage was God's intentional reflection of a greater truth, His relationship with His people. Marriage is more than a convenient image of God's life with us, since this union from God is foundational to God's created order.

10:9 *what God has joined together.* The stakes have been raised. What began as an interpretation of Moses has expanded to God's plan in creation. The Pharisees' eagerness for divorce is a sad break within the perfectly united body created by God. *let not man separate.* Moses' allowance for divorce recognizes a separation that has already happened by the leaving of one marriage partner. But let no one think that this is the intention of God. For the word "separate," *choridzo,* see its use in Rm 8:35, 39 where nothing is able to separate us from the love of God. This perfect union of God and His people, inseparable despite all enemies, is like the enduring connection within marriage.

10:10 *and in the house.* The questioning Pharisees are seen no more. Likely Jesus' quoting of Gn 2 and His forceful reminder of God's purpose in creation left them without a reply again. Jesus didn't merely escape their trap. He dismantled it and handed them the broken pieces. *the disciples asked Him.* Over this point, the disciples ask for clarity, as they did with the parables (4:10, 34; 7:17). However, when Jesus proclaims other truths, especially the difficult prophecies of His death and resurrection, the disciples fail to ask and retreat to contentious silence (8:16; 9:32–34; 10:32).

10:11–12 *whoever divorces his wife and marries another.* Jesus likely shocked His disciples (cf. Mt 19:10), since other teachers were more permissive and even the Law seemed to grant divorce as a right. Jesus is describing the one who initiates the separation and obtains the divorce wanting to be joined to someone else. It is the destruction of one union while pursuing another. Even if there is some social custom or thin legality to this, God sees through the act to its selfish motivation. It is adultery in the heart which God sees, as He does with other sins, even before they become public acts (cf. Mt 5:21–28). With this explanation, Jesus concludes the question asked by the now-absent Pharisees in v. 2. Even more crucial than knowing what Moses allowed is knowing what those who seek divorce really want in their hearts.

10:1–12 in Devotion and Prayer Jesus teaches that God wants a man and a woman in marriage to be exclusively committed to each other for life. Attempts to avoid God's good intentions bring condemnation, not greater liberty. God has inseparably joined Himself to us in His love and this is a model of inseparable love for every marriage. Thoughtfully and prayerfully embrace God's ways. What He establishes is for our good and stems from His love and grace. • "O Spirit of the Father, Breathe on them from above, So searching in Your pureness, So tender in Your love That, guarded by Your presence

And kept from strife and sin, Their hearts may heed Your guidance And know You dwell within." Amen. (*LSB* 858:3)

Introduction to 10:13–16 In a natural progression, marriage leads to children. The temptation-filled question of the Pharisees is contrasted with the simple request of loving mothers who want Jesus' blessing on their children. The disciples become the obstacle as they once again, 9:38, protect their small circle around Jesus. As before, Jesus enlarges the circle and also their understanding of who belongs in the kingdom of God.

10:13 *touch.* The mothers bring their children for Jesus' touch to bless them. In the OT, blessings were given by laying on of hands (Gn 27:23; 48:14–18). Also, throughout Mark, the touch of Jesus has brought dramatic healing (1:31, 41; 3:10; 5:28, 41; 6:56; 7:33; 8:25). This is the last time in Mark when His touch of blessing is sought. Appropriately, it is not for a distinct disease which we might not have, but for a blessing which we all desire. *disciples rebuked them.* They thought children were not important and thus limited their access to Jesus. See 9:36–37 where Jesus instructs them about true greatness through the service given to a child. This could have been a moment for the disciples to demonstrate their understanding of His lesson, but they reverted back to their former prejudices.

10:14 *indignant.* Jesus' righteous anger came against the disciples for their failure to understand the nature of His kingdom. Once again, they have shown a competitive spirit (9:34, 38), which puts them in the favored place while excluding others. This will reach a climax in 10:35–45 with the request of James and John for exclusive places beside Jesus in His kingdom. In 10:41, upon hearing this, the disciples are indignant. That anger is the same word used here, *aganakteo,* to describe Jesus' disapproval towards the disciples. When our privileged place is threatened, we are indignant. When we push aside children to keep our place, Jesus is indignant. *do not hinder them.* The prepared way, begun by John (1:2–3), should be open even for children to come to Jesus and follow Him. *to such belongs the kingdom of God.* Children accept gifts as a matter of course. They make no impossible promises to be better tomorrow in order to earn today's gifts. So they are models for the kingdom of God since it comes without our effort or deserving (Eph 2:8–9). It comes without our complete understanding and works through power that the world doesn't value (1Co 1:20–29). As David did not wrestle with matters too great for him but rested himself as a child with his mother (Ps 131:1–2), so the believer entrusts himself to the care of an all-knowing, all-powerful Father.

10:15 *whoever doesn't receive the kingdom.* The kingdom of God is His gracious reign, equivalent to salvation. Jesus is clarifying (v. 14), lest we think that the Kingdom includes children as an exception. The disciples must not only allow the children to come to Jesus, but must consider how they are to be like these children. *like a child.* Children are not the marginal members of the Kingdom but are the center. Luther describes this childlike attitude of the disciples, "I act as a child who is being taught the catechism. . . . But I must remain a child and pupil of the catechism, and am glad to remain so" (LC, Longer Preface 7–8). The child's faith in a parent's love and gifts are a model for the trust shown to God.

10:16 *took them in His arms.* Jesus does more than put His hands upon the children. He gathers them up in His arms, *enagkolidzomai*, a rare verb that occurs only here and Mk 9:36 in the NT. Jesus takes the time to hold each child to stress their importance to Him. *blessed them.* This is the only occurrence of this verb (*kateulogeo*), in the NT. Jesus brings the blessing down upon these children with His gentle touch and words.

10:13–16 in Devotion and Prayer This story is the key to the chapter, showing us that salvation is a gift of grace through faith in Jesus Christ. We trust the Lord as a child trusts a parent. We do not earn God's love and favor by keeping the Law, especially when we look for loopholes to excuse our sinful behavior (cf. 10:1–12). All people, like helpless children, receive Jesus' blessing and enter the Kingdom through faith in Him. • "You have promised to receive us, Poor and sinful though we be; You have mercy to relieve us, Grace to cleanse, and pow'r to free. Blessed Jesus, blessed Jesus, Early let us turn to You. Blessed Jesus, blessed Jesus, Early let us turn to You." Amen. (*LSB* 711:3; *TPH* 387:2; *TMUH* 381:3)

Introduction to 10:17–31 The children leave blessed and a rich man dashes in to take their place before Jesus. However, despite Jesus' love for him, he will leave without the blessing given to the children. His riches become a barrier to the blessings Jesus offers. It is not money, kept or given away, that matters, but the power of God which brings the most unlikely persons into eternal life.

10:17 *a man ran up and knelt before Him.* After the children's trouble coming near to Jesus, this man has immediate access. *Good Teacher.* See the notes on 4:38 for the use of "teacher" *didaskalos*, in Mark. It is used by the disciples and others who earnestly come for instruction, as here, but is also used extensively by His enemies, likely in a mocking, challenging way (12:14, 19). *inherit.* There is a contradiction in his request. An inheritance is not given based on merit. There is nothing that can be done to earn birth into a family which provides the inheritance.

10:18 *Why do you call Me good?* Jesus is not denying His divinity but wants the man to examine his own speech and motives. If this is empty flattery, it is worthless. If the man wishes to call Jesus truly good, then he will be speaking of His divinity. Melanchthon teaches,

> Uncreated good . . . is God Himself, who is an essence wise, eternal, almighty, willing such things as He commands in His Law, the creator and preserver of the world, and the cause of good—that is, wisdom, justice, joy, and order—in creatures. (Definitions 525)

God alone. Jesus changes the focus from the man's works to who God is. The challenge for the man is to stop counting his own good works and to see the enormous demands a perfect God can make. Then his hope for eternal life will go from Law to Gospel, from his deeds to the saving action of God.

10:19 *you know the commandments.* Jesus is saving the young man from having to explain his early address of "Good Teacher" by assuring him of what he knows. The commandments are a natural complement to the perfect goodness of God (v. 18). God's perfection is reflected in His commandments. *defraud.* This phrase, unique to Mark's account, refers to coveting (Ex 20:17). See Jas 5:4 for a picture of this dishonest dealing. Jesus summarizes the second table of commandments by referring specifically to the actions of people to one another. This daunting list should be enough to give the young man pause as to his own goodness.

10:20 *all these I have kept.* The verb "kept," *phulasso*, occurs only here in Mark. It is the careful watching of a shepherd over his sheep (Lk 2:8), the guarding of a strong man over his goods (Lk 11:21), and the fierce preserving of His own by Jesus (Jn 17:12). The young man has not merely observed the commandments but claims that he has zealously protected them. While he has, in his own estimation, such a perfect record, yet he is driven to find greater security by asking what he still has to do to earn his salvation. Salvation by works drives one either to empty vanity or desperate searching. The young man embodies both at once.

10:21 *loved him.* Only Mark tells of Jesus' love for this man. Furthermore, this is the only time in Mark where it is said that Jesus loves a single individual. Jesus did not speak harshly or out of anger, but compassionately. He seeks to strip away the man's self-deception about having kept the Law while He also opens the door to a true relationship with Himself and eternal life. Though Jesus knows the young man's coming rejection, He truly loves him. *you lack one thing.* Instead of showing the many occasions when he has broken the commandments, Jesus offers him a new path. Just as a new path has been prepared for Jesus (1:2–3), so Jesus offers this man a new way through one step. *sell all that you have.* Charity doesn't earn eternal life, but Jesus is speaking to the man's heart. Does he guard the commandments or his fortune? Giving it away will be a true test of faith, faith which alone saves. Bengel writes that the man lacked "a heart freed from the [idolatry of] creatures: the selling of his goods was intended to be proof of his freedom" (Bengel 547). Calvin writes,

> Profane historians applaud Crates, a Theban, because he threw into the sea his money and all that he reckoned valuable; for he did not think that he could save himself unless his wealth were lost; as if it would not have been better to bestow on others what he imagined to be more than he needed. (*Harmony* 2:397)

Follow me. Jesus invites the young man with the same direct summons as the first disciples (1:16–20). See the blind beggar in 10:52 for a successful following which contrasts to this rich man.

10:22 *disheartened . . . sorrowful, for he had great possessions.* Certainly this is one of the most ironic verses in the Bible. The young man has riches and, in his estimation, a faultless moral life. And yet, since he cannot part with his wealth or admit his failings, he leaves sorrowful. The word "disheartened" *stugnadzo*, occurs only here and Mt 16:3 where it describes the stormy sky. The man's hopeful beginning darkened severely. See Mt 26:37 for Jesus' own sorrowful countenance as he prayed in Gethsemane. How unnecessary was this man's sorrow! For the love of him and the whole world, the Son of God was about to give up all things, even his life, and bear the sorrow that now crosses this man's face.

10:23 *and Jesus looked around.* Despite His love for the man, Jesus does not pursue him. He turns His attention to the disciples who had heard and faithfully followed His command to follow. *How difficult . . . for those who have wealth.* Wealth becomes the attachment of the heart, and so the heart is trapped with riches that last only briefly here. See 1Tm 6:9–10, 17–19 for clear direction to the wealthy who are to become rich in generosity and faith.

10:24 *amazed.* The Jews regarded wealth as a mark of God's favor. The disciples thought rich people had the best chance to enter the kingdom of God because of all the good things they could afford to do. This is a rare word, *thambeo,* used only by Mark in the NT. It is here and 1:27 where it describes the astonishment over Jesus' first exorcism and teaching. The disciples are confused by Jesus' willingness to lose his own life (9:32; 10:32–3), and now are distraught over His command concerning the loss of wealth. *Children.* This is a term of affection which recalls His teaching concerning children as examples of faith (10:14–15). *how difficult it is to enter.* This is a dramatic understatement which Jesus will demonstrate in v. 25. No one will ever enter the Kingdom based on his own reason or strength. The KJV includes the words from several later manuscripts "for them that trust in riches." This phrase, while not in the earliest manuscripts, gives a more specific reason for the difficulty in entering the Kingdom. This description also ties in well with the rich man who refused Jesus' offer (v. 22), and left sorrowful with his riches.

10:25 *camel to go through the eye of a needle.* Even the rich fail to enter the kingdom of God by their own efforts. A camel, proverbially the largest animal common seen in that era, had a better chance of slipping through the eye of a needle, typically viewed as the smallest opening, than the most favored human being had of entering the kingdom of God through works. Attempts have been made to understand this in a manner which is more possible. The opening has been explained as a small passageway which required a man to leave behind his belongings and stoop in order to enter. Or, the camel is found in a few late manuscripts to be a rope or ship's cable. These and other understandings attempt to make the contrast less extreme. But it is not necessary to find an easier understanding of this impossible challenge. The point is that no one whose only qualification is wealth can come into the Kingdom.

10:26 *exceedingly astonished.* While there have been many occasions of surprise over Jesus' teaching, only here and in 7:37 is there this superlative amazement. Here, however, the disciples are amazed at what they have misunderstood. *who can be saved?* The disciples thought that Jesus had just told them that no person could enter the kingdom of God. The rich man came asking what he had to do to inherit eternal life (10:17). If he, a model of financial blessings and moral living, was not saved, then it appears that no one's efforts will be enough. On that count, the disciples are correct. Yet, that message of the Law is only the beginning and v. 27 will bring the Gospel.

10:27 *with man it is impossible.* People cannot enter the kingdom of God on their own merit. Jesus has the disciples at the necessary point of despair over their own actions. *all things are possible with God.* Yet, God calls and gathers people into His kingdom by grace (cf. Rm 3:21–26). What the Law could not do because of our weakness, God did by sending His Son, Rm 8:3–4. God's gracious work is recognized only when all other hopes are gone.

10:28 *we have left everything and followed you.* Peter is recalling the differences between them and the rich man who refused to leave his goods and follow. Peter is pointing out that they are anything but rich men. Surely, such poverty and faithful following should have a reward. Jesus' kind response recognizes their sacrifice, but it is not the loss of family and riches that earns eternal life. What men can do is not enough for salvation, for what can a man give in exchange for his soul (Mt 16:26)? It is only the work of God who does the impossible that brings salvation. Only He who gave up His soul for the world gave enough for eternal life for the world.

10:29 *no one who has left . . . for My sake and for the gospel.* Following Jesus entailed the loss of possessions, even life itself. Melanchthon writes, "He is speaking not of those who injure wife and children, but who bear injury because of the confession of the Gospel. For the Gospel's sake we should even leave our body" (Ap XXVII 41–42). Jesus acknowledges the loss of all the things forsaken by the disciples. Unsaid is the greater loss by Jesus who has left, not earthly comforts and home, but heaven's glory and ease for a carpenter's life and the cross. The list here of what was left begins and ends with the material items of house and land. Yet, the heart of the loss is the change in family relationships. We recall Jesus' distance from His family (3:21, 31–34; Jn 7:3–5), and the ultimate loss of relationship as He was forsaken by His Father while on the cross (Mk 15:34).

10:30 *hundredfold.* This multiplication will more than replace what we lost to follow Him. The increased homes are the shared life of the believers as they become one body with Christ. Melanchthon writes,

> [Rewards] would be uncertain matters if they depended on the condition of our merits. But in those who have been reconciled, after conversion, their good works, since they are pleasing by faith for the sake of the Mediator . . . do merit spiritual and physical rewards in this life and after this life. (Topics 187)

persecutions. Only Mark includes this phrase which recalls Jesus warning that Satan will always stir up opposition against God's people (Mk 4:17; Jn 15:18–19). Yet, believers say with Paul, "For the sake of Christ, then I am content with weaknesses, insults, hardships, persecutions, and calamities" (2Co 12:10). *age to come.* After the resurrection of the dead (cf. Mt 19:28).

10:31 *first will be last and the last first.* The poor, sinners, and Gentiles with their confidence in God alone enter the Kingdom ahead of those with spiritual confidence in their power and wealth. Those who serve and accept even children (9:37; 10:13–16), and who have the faith of a child are considered the last now but they will be in the front rank of heaven. The proud and rich had best enjoy their state now, if they can (10:22), for it will be reversed. The night in which their soul is required will come soon and what can they give then (Lk 12:20–21)?

10:17–31 in Devotion and Prayer Jesus teaches His disciples that not even people with the greatest worldly means can enter the kingdom of God on their own merit. We cannot justify ourselves; we receive salvation ("inherit eternal life") solely by grace through faith in Jesus, just like a little child (10:13–16). • "My heart's delight, My crown most bright, O Christ, my joy forever. Not wealth nor pride Nor fortune's tide Our bonds of love shall sever." Amen. (*LSB* 557:4)

The third Passion prediction and subsequent teaching and events (10:32–52)

Jesus predicts His suffering, death, and resurrection (10:32–34)

ESV	KJV
32 And they were on the road, going up to Jerusalem, and Jesus was walking ahead of them. And they were amazed, and those who followed were afraid. And taking the twelve again, he began to tell them what was to happen to him, 33 saying, "See, we are going up to Jerusalem, and the Son of Man will be delivered over to the chief priests and the scribes, and they will condemn him to death and deliver him over to the Gentiles. 34 And they will mock him and spit on him, and flog him and kill him. And after three days he will rise."	32 And they were in the way going up to Jerusalem; and Jesus went before them: and they were amazed; and as they followed, they were afraid. And he took again the twelve, and began to tell them what things should happen unto him, 33 Saying, Behold, we go up to Jerusalem; and the Son of man shall be delivered unto the chief priests, and unto the scribes; and they shall condemn him to death, and shall deliver him to the Gentiles: 34 And they shall mock him, and shall scourge him, and shall spit upon him, and shall kill him: and the third day he shall rise again.

10:32 *on the road going up to Jerusalem.* This is the metaphorical road seen since 1:2–3, the straight path prepared by John which leads to the cross. *Jesus was walking ahead of them.* Jesus knew exactly where this would lead, to His death and resurrection. He walks ahead of the disciples, a shepherd leading the sheep, into the valley of the shadow of His death. *amazed . . . afraid.* The disciples feel and fear the darkness of His enemies and His prediction of death. They're surprised that He is walking openly into the stronghold of His enemies (cf. Jn 7:1–5); they expected a deadly confrontation in which they would die along with Jesus (cf. Jn 11:16). But this Shepherd will sacrifice Himself, protect the sheep, and astonish the world with His resurrection. *began to tell them what was to happen to Him.* This is the third time that Jesus predicts His death and resurrection (8:31; 9:31). The three predictions parallel our knowledge of the coming three days of His death. In addition, the three-fold repetition is needed for the message to work slowly into the disciples.

10:33 *Son of Man.* See the notes on 8:31 for this important term which Jesus uses in all three predictions of His death. *chief priests . . . scribes.* Jesus, as He did in 8:31, identifies these specific leaders and thereby the governing body, the Sanhedrin. These are the leaders among the Jews who are seeking His death, responsible far more than the crowd that will demand His crucifixion. The first plot against Jesus (Mk 3:6) began with the Pharisees and Herodians but grows now to include the highest echelon of the religious leadership. The high priest unknowingly speaks of Jesus' death as a single sacrifice which will save the whole people (Jn 11:49–51). *Gentiles.* This is the only reference to the Romans' role in His crucifixion (Jn 18:31) in the three predictions. Jesus' death is a joint project of the Jews and Gentiles. The new-found friendship of Herod and Pilate symbolizes this, fittingly since Jesus comes to save the entire world.

10:34 *mock . . . spit . . . flog.* Only in this third prediction does Jesus prophesy the details of His Passion (cf. 15:1–16:8). The disciples likely could not bear the details any sooner, but they need to know the depth of His suffering as it draws near. Jesus had noted (v. 33) that He would be handed over by the Jewish leaders and killed by the Gentiles. In keeping with this balance, He will be mocked by the soldiers (15:20), and by the chief priests (15:31). *and after three days He will rise.* While the mystery of His death is described in some detail, the greater wonder of His resurrection is simply announced. No specifics are given concerning how this could be or in what manner it will happen. Betrayal, mocking, and cruel death we know. However, the resurrection of the dead is so beyond us, no details given here will answer our questions. So He gives the simple promise on which they could hope. Nothing is said of the disciples' reaction. But we might hope that they will hold onto these closing words as the last notes of a dear song, repeating them over and over.

10:32–34 in Devotion and Prayer Jesus predicts His trial, execution, and resurrection for the third time in Mark (cf. 8:31–32; 9:30–32) while walking boldly to His death. Jesus goes to die the sinner's death, accepting the Law's penalty in our place. Faith looks to Christ crucified and risen and says "for me." Luther writes: "Who is this 'me'? It is I, an accursed and damned sinner, who was so beloved by the Son of God that He gave Himself for me" (LW 26:176). • "Your grace alone, dear Lord, I plead, Your death is now my life indeed, For You have paid my ransom." Amen. (*LSB* 555:6)

Jesus responds to the request of James and John and teaches on greatness in the kingdom of God (10:35–45)

ESV

35 And James and John, the sons of Zebedee, came up to him and said to him, "Teacher, we want you to do for us whatever we ask of you." 36 And he said to them, "What do you want me to do for you?" 37 And they said to him, "Grant us to sit, one at your right hand and one at your left, in your glory." 38 Jesus said to them, "You do not know what you are asking. Are you able to drink the cup that I drink, or to be baptized with the baptism with which I am baptized?" 39 And they said to him, "We are able." And Jesus said to them, "The cup that I drink you will drink, and with the baptism with which I am baptized, you will be baptized, 40 but to sit at my right hand or at my left is not mine to grant, but it is for those for whom it has been prepared." 41 And when the ten heard it, they began to be indignant at James and John. 42 And Jesus called them to him and said to them, "You know that those who are considered rulers of the Gentiles lord it over them, and their great ones exercise authority over them. 43 But it shall not be so among you. But whoever would be great among you must be your servant, 44 and whoever would be first among you must be slave of all. 45 For even the Son of Man came not to be served but to serve, and to give his life as a ransom for many."

KJV

35 And James and John, the sons of Zebedee, come unto him, saying, Master, we would that thou shouldest do for us whatsoever we shall desire.

36 And he said unto them, What would ye that I should do for you?

37 They said unto him, Grant unto us that we may sit, one on thy right hand, and the other on thy left hand, in thy glory.

38 But Jesus said unto them, Ye know not what ye ask: can ye drink of the cup that I drink of? and be baptized with the baptism that I am baptized with?

39 And they said unto him, We can. And Jesus said unto them, Ye shall indeed drink of the cup that I drink of; and with the baptism that I am baptized withal shall ye be baptized:

40 But to sit on my right hand and on my left hand is not mine to give; but it shall be given to them for whom it is prepared.

41 And when the ten heard it, they began to be much displeased with James and John.

42 But Jesus called them to him, and saith unto them, Ye know that they which are accounted to rule over the Gentiles exercise lordship over them; and their great ones exercise authority upon them.

43 But so shall it not be among you: but whosoever will be great among you, shall be your minister:

44 And whosoever of you will be the chiefest, shall be servant of all.

45 For even the Son of man came not to be ministered unto, but to minister, and to give his life a ransom for many.

Introduction to 10:35–45 Three times Jesus predicts His death, and now for a third time He also has to correct the disciples as to true greatness and status in His kingdom (9:34–37; 10:13–16). In the face of Jesus' incomparable sacrifice (10:33–34), the disciples can still argue over their place and share of glory in His kingdom. Jesus does not destroy their pretensions or lord over them. Instead He invites them to consider His coming sacrifice and to define greatness as a life given away.

10:35 *do for us whatever we ask.* Jesus has just predicted again His willingness to do that for which we would never ask, His death and resurrection. Yet, discounting that, the brothers hope to steal the march on the others and secure a favored place within the Kingdom. They look for a decision before they ask the question. They were either sure of Jesus' agreement, or they wanted to lock Him into agreement before revealing their plan.

10:36 *what do you want Me to do for you?* Jesus' patience in asking about things He already knows is always remarkable. He asks them what they want as a final chance to re-think this request, or to judge it for themselves as they announce it. If only they could hear its impatient selfishness, they might take it back. However, they boldly move ahead with their asking.

10:37 *right hand . . . left, in Your glory.* They are seeking the first and second positions of power. In an earthly kingdom these reflect outward glory. Their request defines His glory, as they understand it, as a visible throne surrounded by a clear hierarchy. Their competitive spirit recalls the earlier debate over the disciples' greatness (9:33–37).

10:38 *you do not know what you are asking.* The confusion of the disciples continues. While they had previously not understood what they were hearing (4:10–13; 9:32), now they are wrong in their asking. Jesus asks them the following questions, knowing they will not understand that He is speaking of His death which He alone will bear. *the cup . . . baptism.* These are figures of speech for intense experiences associated with His suffering and death. See Is 51:17 for an image of God's cup of wrath and Mk 14:36 for Jesus' coming death as a bitter cup. Jesus' death is tied to baptism especially in Rm 6:3 where all who have been baptized have been baptized into His death. Early Christians referred to martyrdom as baptism with blood.

10:39 *we are able.* Likely the disciples said this eagerly, with little understanding, hoping that they could guarantee their spots in glory this way. *you will drink . . . be baptized.* Jesus predicted a life of suffering for the sake of the Gospel. This recalls 8:34–35, where anyone following Him must take up the cross and even lose his life. Yet, while the disciples, except for John, lose their lives as martyrs, their deaths are not the same cup and baptism as Jesus'. Our suffering is not in exchange even for our own souls (8:37), while Jesus' death is in exchange for the souls of the whole world (10:45). The bitterness which He took involved even the abandonment from His Father by which He could be made sin on our behalf (2Co 5:21).

10:40 *not mine to grant.* The heavenly Father makes the decision over who sits in places of glory. The disciples can have little grasp over the true glory of heaven and those who are properly seated before them. In seeking these places, the disciples are acting out the worst behavior from the parable of the wedding feast (Lk 14:7–11). They race to the front seats only to be sent to the bottom in view of those greater than themselves. When the seventy-two disciples went out, they came back rejoicing over their success against the demons. But Jesus cautioned them to rejoice instead that their names are written in heaven (Lk 10:20). So here also rejoice that you will have a place in the Kingdom without regard to who is seated above or below.

10:41 *when the ten heard.* How the ten heard of this is unclear. Their competitive nature likely was suspicious of any private time spent with Jesus and they also likely saw the disappointment on the brothers' faces. *They began to be indignant.* The other disciples also hoped to sit in the seats of highest honor. They are indignant! This is the same word, *aganakteo*, used of Jesus' anger in 10:14 when children were prevented from reaching Him. Ironically the disciples are angry that someone might have reached a privileged place with Jesus but they would prevent children from a blessed moment with Jesus.

10:42 *those who are considered rulers of the Gentiles lord it over them.* Saying that they are considered rulers points out the deception that this might be. These "rulers" might be such in name only. The glory given them is misguided. Their domination over others is the exact opposite of what leaders within the Church should seek (see 1Pt 5:3). *Exercise authority over them.* This is not the necessary order of the civil government, but the scornful oppression by those who place themselves over others. This harsh verb is found only here and in the parallel verse (Mt 20:25).

10:43 *it shall not be so among you.* Jesus gives the positive view of the Church, even in the face of the place-seeking and competitive wrangling of the disciples. This recalls His earlier words that those who enter as children will come into the Kingdom (10:14–15). Those who insist on their glory and possessions will find no way to enter (10:25). *whoever would be great.* If the disciples still seek the title of "great" then Jesus will speak in their terms. However, this greatness is a reflection of Himself. He came in the form of a servant and was obedient to even the death of the cross (Php 2:7–8). His greatness was not only in the coming exaltation (Php 2:9–11), but also in the bearing of the sins of the world.

10:44 *whoever would be first.* Again, Jesus speaks in the language of competitive advantage, catching the interest of the disciples. In Christ's kingdom, positions of authority carried a servant's job. The best role is to be a servant who speaks of the true Lord: "For what we proclaim is not ourselves, but Jesus Christ as Lord, with ourselves as your servants for Jesus' sake" (2Co 4:5). *slave of all.* This slave serves all, but his master is not any man, but the Son of Man. He is a servant with a single Lord, and he is sent to care for the Master's own children. See 9:35–37 where Jesus teaches that whoever receives a child in His name, receives Him.

10:45 *Son of Man.* See 8:31 for the use of Son of Man in Jesus' predictions of His death. It is fitting that He uses it also here with a view to His sacrificial death. *to serve.* Jesus set aside His own welfare for the sake of sinners. As the mighty Son of God, He could have demanded service, especially if He had presented Himself with the glory just seen in the Transfiguration (9:2–7). Peter's eagerness to serve there could have been the treatment given to Jesus every day. *give His life as a ransom for many.* This expression explains Jesus' mission and describes the purpose of the cross that He will soon bear. Jesus' sacrifice is a wonder in that He will be able to exchange His solitary life for the lives of all. But such is the value of the Son of God that God makes this exchange. Also He is willing to be accounted as though He were the one guilty of all sins in order that all others might be accounted as just. Jesus is echoing Is 52:13–53:12 where the servant of the Lord is described as the One who is wounded for our transgressions (Is 53:4). He gives not only His life but also gives up His standing as the Beloved when He is forsaken and thereby pays the penalty of our sins (Mk 15:34).

10:35–45 in Devotion and Prayer Jesus puts our welfare and needs ahead of His own as He conducts His ministry, showing us what real leadership is. Jesus shows that those who lead in the kingdom of God serve others in humility. He leads by laying down His life as the sacrifice for our sins and calls us to similar sacrifice. • Dear Father, You have sent Christ to serve us, although He had the right to demand our service. Forgive us, Father. Lead us to give ourselves for the sake of others, that we, being last, might truly be first with Jesus in His kingdom. Amen.

Jesus heals blind Bartimaeus (10:46–52)

ESV	KJV
46 And they came to Jericho. And as he was leaving Jericho with his disciples and a great crowd, Bartimaeus, a blind beggar, the son of Timaeus, was sitting by the roadside. 47 And when he heard that it was Jesus of Nazareth, he began to cry out and say, "Jesus, Son of David, have mercy on me!" 48 And many rebuked him, telling him to be silent. But he cried out all the more, "Son of David, have mercy on me!" 49 And Jesus stopped and said, "Call him." And they called the blind man, saying to him, "Take heart. Get up; he is calling you." 50 And throwing off his cloak, he sprang up and came to Jesus. 51 And Jesus said to him, "What do you want me to do for you?" And the blind man said to him, "Rabbi, let me recover my sight." 52 And Jesus said to him, "Go your way; your faith has made you well." And immediately he recovered his sight and followed him on the way.	**46 And they came to Jericho: and as he went out of Jericho with his disciples and a great number of people, blind Bartimaeus, the son of Timaeus, sat by the highway side begging. 47 And when he heard that it was Jesus of Nazareth, he began to cry out, and say, Jesus, thou son of David, have mercy on me. 48 And many charged him that he should hold his peace: but he cried the more a great deal, Thou son of David, have mercy on me. 49 And Jesus stood still, and commanded him to be called. And they call the blind man, saying unto him, Be of good comfort, rise; he calleth thee. 50 And he, casting away his garment, rose, and came to Jesus. 51 And Jesus answered and said unto him, What wilt thou that I should do unto thee? The blind man said unto him, Lord, that I might receive my sight. 52 And Jesus said unto him, Go thy way; thy faith hath made thee whole. And immediately he received his sight, and followed Jesus in the way.**

Introduction to 10:46–52 Jesus is drawing near to Jerusalem as He promised to face His death. But, despite rejection by the rich man (10:22), and tensions with the disciples (10:13–15, 35–41), Jesus reaches out to a desperate man who welcomes the chance to follow Him. Giving sight to this man is one of Jesus' last healing miracles. The man's eager following of Jesus is a model for the disciples and all others who would join Jesus on the way to the cross.

10:46 *Jericho.* This ancient city's center had moved to various locations, causing writers to describe it more like a region (cf. Lk 18:35). *Bartimaeus . . . son of Timaeus.* In Aramaic, *bar* means "son of." Only Mark gives his name and he includes the translation to benefit Gentile readers. Of all the people healed by Jesus, Bartimaeus is the only one specifically named. *blind beggar.* This is the second blind man Jesus meets. He healed the first man in two steps (8:22–26), and since then He has predicted His death and resurrection three times (8:31; 9:31; 10:33–34). The disciples have struggled to understand this prediction, walking in darkness and fear towards Jerusalem. In contrast, formerly blind Bartimaeus will see and go forward with joy.

10:47 *Son of David.* Jesus comes from the genealogical line of David and fulfills the promise of God that He would raise up a Son of David to build an everlasting house and throne. See Mt 1:1, 6, 17 and 2Sm 7:12–16. Jesus overcomes the futile end of David's family and the corruption of the kingly line. Jesus' birth is the shoot that comes from the dead stump of David's family (Is 11:1). *have mercy.* This cry for help from God is frequently found in the Psalms. See Ps 26:11 "redeem me and be gracious to me," which recalls Jesus' description of Himself as the redeeming ransom, v. 45. See also Ps 27:7; 30:10; and 41:4 "be gracious to me; heal me."

10:48 *rebuked.* The rebuke here matches the disciples' reproach of the mothers bringing their children to Jesus (10:13). The crowd cannot hear Jesus' words over the annoying shouting of Bartimaeus. They had come to hear Jesus' teaching, not to listen to this beggar. On ordinary days, they ignored his pleas and so all the more today. *telling him to be silent.* Often Jesus commanded people to be silent concerning their healing or His identity (1:44; 3:12; 5:43; 7:36; 8:30; and 9:9). But this crowd is interfering with a miracle, not restrict its overly-eager announcement. *but he cried out all the more.* Just as Jesus' command for people to be silent was often ignored (1:45;

7:36), so the man here ignores this rebuke. He shows the same persistence and faith as the woman with the bleeding (5:27–28), and the Syrophoenician woman (7:28–29). Jesus was more than a passing chance of improvement. Bartimaeus believed that Jesus could heal and he wasn't going to lose this one chance.

10:49 *Jesus stopped.* Jesus stopped here as He did for the woman who was healed of her bleeding (5:30). *call him.* Jesus allows the crowd, which had tried to silence the man, now to announce His invitation. *take heart.* Jesus had used this same phrase with the disciples when He walked on the water to save them (6:50). Jesus' call for the man to come recalls the beginning of the Gospel with the call of the first disciples (1:16–20), and the call and commission of the Twelve (6:7). This blind man shows the extent of Jesus' reach. Jesus gathers not only fishermen and the able bodied but He invites many who are different from each other, such as the rich man (10:21), the children (10:14–16), and blind Bartimaeus.

10:50 *cloak.* This was likely folded on the lap to receive alms. He tossed away the cloak in order to get up, not knowing if later he will be able to find the alms and his source of warmth. What a contrast to the rich man who clung to his riches rather than follow Jesus (10:22). *sprang.* He sprang up to his feet, showing his urgent excitement. This is the only use of this verb in the NT. In manner of action, he is the opposite of the woman with the bleeding (5:27), who came stealthily towards Jesus, though they share the same faith.

10:51 *What do you want Me to do for you?* Just as Jesus let the crowd call the man, so He lets the man ask. In v. 37, the brothers want to see their place in glory; this man simply wants to see. When he sees Jesus, he will be content. *Rabbi.* See the notes on 9:5, the first time that Jesus is called Rabbi. Bartimaeus is likely repeating the title that he had heard given to Jesus. Though Bartimaeus has not heard Jesus teach, he is already demonstrating the lessons of faith and obedient following. *let me recover my sight.* He had seen at one time and wants to regain this sense. This simple gift will open the world to him again, just as seeing, knowing, and following Jesus open the Kingdom and eternal life.

10:52 *your faith has made you well.* Physical healing is only part of Christ's work. Jesus rescued Bartimaeus from sinfulness as well as its collateral damage: blindness. The healing here and throughout the Gospel demonstrates Jesus' divine power to forgive and to dismiss people in true peace. Calvin writes,

> By the word *faith* is meant not only a confident hope of recovering sight, but a loftier conviction, which was, that this *blind man* had acknowledged Jesus to be the Messiah whom God had promised. (*Harmony* 2:432)

See Jn 9:2 for the assumption that blindness was the result of serious sin. Jesus shows that blindness was not the mark of God's vengeance, but an opportunity to show God's gracious power. *immediately he recovered his sight.* It is fitting that this last healing miracle of Jesus is marked with the familiar "immediately." His miracles have often been accomplished instantly (1:42; 2:12; 5:29, 42; and 7:35), as a demonstration of His might over demons, disease, and nature. *followed Him on the way.* The man has bonded with the Savior he has just seen. It is not fear of blindness returning but the joy of being with Jesus that carries him along. By following on the way, Bartimaeus recalls the first step of the Gospel (1:2–3), the preparing of a way that will lead to Jerusalem and the cross. While the disciples are reluctant to go up toward the predicted cross, Bartimaeus follows with the simple joy of being with the One who healed him. This faith sees past the cross to the promised resurrection.

10:46–52 in Devotion and Prayer Though Jesus is intent on going to the cross, He pauses to have mercy on Bartimaeus, who can do nothing to solve his problem except cry out to the Lord, "Have mercy!" Like Bartimaeus, learn to call on the Lord and trust in His power to deliver you. Jesus will hear and respond compassionately. • "Lord, Your mercy will not leave me; Ever will Your truth abide. Then in You I will confide." Amen. (*LSB* 559:4)

Jesus Enters Jerusalem and Confronts the Religious Authorities (chs. 11–13)

Jesus enters Jerusalem to the praise of the crowds (11:1–11)

ESV	KJV
11 1Now when they drew near to Jerusalem, to Bethphage and Bethany, at the Mount of Olives, Jesus sent two of his disciples 2and said to them, "Go into the village in front of you, and immediately as you enter it you will find a colt tied, on which no one has ever sat. Untie it and bring it. 3If anyone says to you, 'Why are you doing this?' say, 'The Lord has need of it and will send it back here immediately.' " 4And they went away and found a colt tied at a door outside in the street, and they untied it. 5And some of those standing there said to them, "What are you doing, untying the colt?" 6And they told them what Jesus had said, and they let them go. 7And they brought the colt to Jesus and threw their cloaks on it, and he sat on it. 8And many spread their cloaks on the road, and others spread leafy branches that they had cut from the fields. 9And those who went before and those who followed were shouting, "Hosanna! Blessed is he who comes in the name of the Lord! 10Blessed is the coming kingdom of our father David! Hosanna in the highest!" 11And he entered Jerusalem and went into the temple. And when he had looked around at everything, as it was already late, he went out to Bethany with the twelve.	11 1And when they came nigh to Jerusalem, unto Bethphage and Bethany, at the mount of Olives, he sendeth forth two of his disciples, 2And saith unto them, Go your way into the village over against you: and as soon as ye be entered into it, ye shall find a colt tied, whereon never man sat; loose him, and bring him. 3And if any man say unto you, Why do ye this? say ye that the Lord hath need of him; and straightway he will send him hither. 4And they went their way, and found the colt tied by the door without in a place where two ways met; and they loose him. 5And certain of them that stood there said unto them, What do ye, loosing the colt? 6And they said unto them even as Jesus had commanded: and they let them go. 7And they brought the colt to Jesus, and cast their garments on him; and he sat upon him. 8And many spread their garments in the way: and others cut down branches off the trees, and strawed them in the way. 9And they that went before, and they that followed, cried, saying, Hosanna; Blessed is he that cometh in the name of the Lord: 10Blessed be the kingdom of our father David, that cometh in the name of the Lord: Hosanna in the highest.

[11]And Jesus entered into Jerusalem, and into the temple: and when he had looked round about upon all things, and now the eventide was come, he went out unto Bethany with the twelve.

Introduction to 11:1–11 Jesus' long journey reaches the crucial milestone of Jerusalem at the start of the Passion Week. Jesus sends disciples ahead, much as John was sent to prepare the overall way. He then comes into the joyous celebration we expect Him to receive. These are like the celebrating crowds that have pursued Him throughout His ministry. If we didn't have His three-fold prediction of crucifixion, we would never expect the crowds would go from blessing Him to calling for His crucifixion. However, Jesus knows the dark day to come and steps towards it. This crowd praises Him to the heavens. By Friday another crowd will condemn Him to the grave. This crowd says, "Hosanna!" (Save us now!). By being within these crowds, Sunday and Friday, Jesus does just that.

11:1 *Bethphage and Bethany.* These villages are one to two miles east of Jerusalem in the region of the Mount of Olives. *two of His disciples.* These two disciples are not named but their going recalls the sending of the disciples in their preaching/healing journey (6:7–13). They are sent to prepare one final mile of the long journey begun in 1:2–3. Just as John the Baptist came to clear Jesus' path, so the disciples continue that work.

11:2 *village.* This is likely Bethphage, the village closest to Jerusalem. *immediately as you enter it.* This means immediately both in time and distance. The disciples won't have to wonder which colt. *no one . . . sat.* This would be an unbroken colt which was normally difficult to ride. Jesus began His ministry in the wilderness temptation with the wild beasts (1:13). He ends the journey demonstrating His control and harmony over nature. One might note that it was a heifer which had never been yoked which was sacrificed for a sin offering (Nu 19:2; Dt 21:3), and two cows which had never been yoked which were hitched to pull the cart with the ark (1Sm 6:7). *untie it and bring it.* Jesus demonstrates His ownership of all creation. He tells the disciples to bring out the colt, without any other permission and without hiding their actions. He who can command wind and wave and expel the legion of demons can call a colt to His service. This should reassure the disciples of His greater predictions of death and resurrection. He who is faithful in this little matter of the colt will be faithful and true in much more, even the resurrection of Himself.

11:3 *if anyone says to you.* The disciples likely expect this objection and so Jesus arms them with the needed response. *The Lord has need of it.* The owner may have known Jesus from previous trips to Jerusalem or this bold claim will be enough to release the colt. Jesus needs the colt to fulfill the prophecy of Zec 9:9. *will send it back.* The sentence as translated here suggests that Jesus will send the colt back immediately after His use. It could also be understood to say that the owner will send it back with the disciples immediately upon hearing their explanation. That second meaning gives greater force to Jesus' words. See the KJV for this possibility, "and straightway He will send him hither." *immediately.* This is the 37th use of "immediately" (*euthus*) in Mark. It has appeared in every chapter, esp. ch. 1. It serves to begin narratives, to show the instant effect of Jesus' words, and to record the reaction of people to His work. These first thirty-seven instances bring Jesus along the straight road of 1:2–3 to this entry of Jerusalem, the last city to be reached. However, from 11:4–14:42, almost one-fourth of the verses of the book, "immediately" doesn't appear. Then when it seems that it is permanently gone, it will return four times (14:43, 45, 72; 15:1). See the notes on 1:10.

11:4 *a colt tied at a door outside in the street.* The details suggest that Peter was one of the two sent. The word for "street," *amphodos,* occurs only here in the NT and means two roads or a crooked street.

11:5 *some of those standing there.* More than just a single owner, here several people raise the question. The two disciples are bold to do what Jesus commanded despite this objection. We remember this bold move when later they will flee from following Jesus and will deny knowing Him.

11:6 *they told them what Jesus had said.* The explanation given by Jesus (v. 3) worked as He had promised. The repetition of what Jesus had said summarizes much of the Gospel. From His first miracle (1:21–28), crowds and individuals repeated His words and especially His deeds (1:45; 2:1, 12; 3:8; 5:20; 6:56; 7:36). Jesus often commands that those healed be silent since it will be these reports that are unnerving to the Jewish leaders, forcing them to plot His death. Jesus has walked a narrow balance beam. He heals and does no harm and yet He must, in the end, be so hated that He is crucified. Anyone can do evil, be hated, and be killed. Many strive to do good and be loved. Only the Son of God comes to heal and never harm and still be cruelly killed for what He has done.

11:7 *threw their cloaks on it.* The outer garments make a saddle for Jesus. By this the disciples can match the generosity of those putting cloaks on the road. Jesus is accepting of these steps as their gifts of service. He came to serve, not be served (10:45), but He knew that the disciples and crowds also needed this opportunity to show their love for Him.

11:8 *many spread their cloaks on it.* The word for "spread" (*stronnumi*), a relatively rare word, is used also in 14:15 for "furnished" describing the furnished room that would be used for the Last Supper. These two significant steps on the journey, the road of Palm Sunday and the room of the Last Supper, are prepared for Jesus as part of the work begun in 1:2–3. *branches.* Fresh branches, especially of palm trees, were used in celebrations and religious processions. See 1Macc 13:51 and 2Macc 10:6–7 for use of palm branches upon the entry by the Jews into Jerusalem and also the purification of the temple.

11:9 *those who went before and those who followed.* Jesus is thoroughly in the embrace of the crowd this day. After feeding the 5,000 and 4,000, Jesus avoided the adoring crowds (6:45; 8:10). Here Jesus deliberately puts Himself in the crowd's grasp, allowing them to express their approval. Their joy echoes the private celebration of the Transfiguration mountain with the presence of the saints and the approval of the Father. *Hosanna! Blessed is He who comes in the name of the Lord.* The people welcomed Jesus with praise drawn from Ps 118:25–26. "Hosanna" means "(Lord) save us" based on the Hbr word *yasha*, "to save." This word is the basis for Jesus' own name (Mt 1:21). The last phrase in 11:9 is exactly as found in the LXX translation of the OT in Ps 118:26. Psalm 118 is especially appropriate here as it likely is a psalm for national celebration connected with the temple. Jesus, the true dwelling of God with His people, is entering into Jerusalem, content to live with His people.

11:10 *blessed is the coming kingdom of our father David.* This is not a direct quote from a psalm but echoes the expectation that a descendant of David will be their king and shepherd (Ezk 37:24–25). This is the message of the angel Gabriel to Mary in Lk 1:32 "the Lord God will give to Him the throne of His father David." *Hosanna in* *the highest.* The joyous cry of hosanna, save us, is repeated with this added ending. It is not a desperate cry for help, but a celebration of the salvation that has come with Jesus. The joy should reach the highest pitch and also go from earth to heaven. This is the earthly echo of the celebration of the angels at Jesus' birth (Lk 2:13–14), and a prelude to the unending celebration around Him on His heavenly throne (Rv 7:9–12). There the saints, angels and all creatures sing, "Salvation belongs to our God who sits on the throne, and to the Lamb!" Jesus comes to create this salvation and to answer the cry for salvation. He will do it, not by being the untouchable King, but by being the willing, sacrificed Lamb.

11:11 *into the temple.* This is the first specific mention of the temple in Mark. The other Gospels bring Jesus to the pinnacle of the temple in His temptation (Mt 4:5), begin the Gospel with Zechariah in the temple (Lk 1:5ff.), and have Jesus cleanse the temple (Jn 2:14ff.). However, the journey to Jerusalem has foreseen the temple as His destination. The carpenter has come to the house of God that He Himself might be torn down and rebuilt. *looked around . . . late.* Malachi 3:1 foresaw the ministry of John the Baptist preparing for this entry and Jesus' coming. "I send My messenger, and he will prepare the way before Me. And the Lord whom you seek will suddenly come to His temple."

11:1–11 in Devotion and Prayer Jesus enters Jerusalem triumphantly as King, openly accepting messianic titles and fulfilling several OT prophecies. The disciples and the crowds expect Jesus to establish an earthly kingdom. They celebrate His arrival at Jerusalem without a clear view of His express purpose: to die for the sins of the world. Jesus enters Jerusalem in humility to fulfill the plan of salvation by laying down His life for sinners. • "All glory, laud, and honor To You, Redeemer, King, To whom the lips of children Made sweet hosannas ring. The multitude of pilgrims With palms before You went; Our praise and prayer and anthems Before You we present." Amen. (*LSB* 442:3; *H82* 154, 155:3; *TPH* 88:2; *TUMH* 280:3)

Jesus curses the fig tree, cleanses the temple, and teaches the disciples on faith (11:12–26)

ESV	KJV
12 On the following day, when they came from Bethany, he was hungry. 13 And seeing in the distance a fig tree in leaf, he went to see if he could find anything on it. When he came to it, he found nothing but leaves, for it was not the season for figs. 14 And he said to it, "May no one ever eat fruit from you again." And his disciples heard it. 15 And they came to Jerusalem. And he entered the temple and began to drive out those who sold and those who bought in the temple, and he overturned the tables of the money-changers and the seats of those who sold pigeons. 16 And he would not allow anyone to carry anything through the temple. 17 And he was teaching them and saying to them, "Is it not written, 'My house shall be called a house of prayer for all the nations'? But you have made it a den of robbers." 18 And the chief priests and the scribes heard it and were seeking a way to destroy him, for they feared him, because all the crowd was astonished at his teaching. 19 And when evening came they went out of the city. 20 As they passed by in the morning, they saw the fig tree withered away to its roots. 21 And Peter remembered and said to him, "Rabbi, look! The fig tree that you cursed has withered." 22 And Jesus answered them, "Have faith in God. 23 Truly, I say to you, whoever says to this mountain, 'Be taken up and thrown into the sea,'	12 And on the morrow, when they were come from Bethany, he was hungry: 13 And seeing a fig tree afar off having leaves, he came, if haply he might find any thing thereon: and when he came to it, he found nothing but leaves; for the time of figs was not yet. 14 And Jesus answered and said unto it, No man eat fruit of thee hereafter for ever. And his disciples heard it. 15 And they come to Jerusalem: and Jesus went into the temple, and began to cast out them that sold and bought in the temple, and overthrew the tables of the moneychangers, and the seats of them that sold doves; 16 And would not suffer that any man should carry any vessel through the temple. 17 And he taught, saying unto them, Is it not written, My house shall be called of all nations the house of prayer? but ye have made it a den of thieves. 18 And the scribes and chief priests heard it, and sought how they might destroy him: for they feared him, because all the people was astonished at his doctrine. 19 And when even was come, he went out of the city. 20 And in the morning, as they passed by, they saw the fig tree dried up from the roots. 21 And Peter calling to remembrance saith unto him, Master, behold, the fig tree which thou cursedst is withered away.

**and does not doubt in his heart,
but believes that what he says will
come to pass, it will be done for him.
24 Therefore I tell you, whatever you
ask in prayer, believe that you have
received it, and it will be yours. 25 And
whenever you stand praying, forgive,
if you have anything against anyone, so that your Father also who is
in heaven may forgive you your trespasses."**

**22 And Jesus answering saith unto
them, Have faith in God.
23 For verily I say unto you, That
whosoever shall say unto this mountain, Be thou removed, and be thou
cast into the sea; and shall not doubt
in his heart, but shall believe that
those things which he saith shall
come to pass; he shall have whatsoever he saith.
24 Therefore I say unto you, What
things soever ye desire, when ye pray,
believe that ye receive them, and ye
shall have them.
25 And when ye stand praying, forgive, if ye have ought against any: that
your Father also which is in heaven
may forgive you your trespasses.
26 But if ye do not forgive, neither
will your Father which is in heaven
forgive your trespasses.**

Introduction to 11:12–26 Jesus begins His time in Jerusalem with a striking miracle, the cursing of the fig tree. As noted before, Mark often reports Jesus' actions in an A-B-A or sandwich fashion, beginning an account, telling another episode entirely, and then returning to the original story. (See the notes on 3:21 for more details on this pattern.) He does so here as he records the cursing of the tree, records the cleansing of the temple, and concludes with the outcome of Jesus' curse and the lesson He teaches. In combining these two events, the curse of the tree is really Jesus' condemnation of the futility of the temple practice. However, Jesus' teaching ends with the Gospel message of forgiveness and answered prayers.

11:12 *He was hungry.* Matthew 21:18 notes that this was early in the morning. This was Monday following the triumph of Palm Sunday. Jesus might have been praying early in the morning, separated from the disciples and whatever breakfast they might have had. And so He was hungry now as they walked into the city.

11:13 *He went to see if He could find anything on it.* At first this seems to contradicts Jesus' knowledge of all things. He who knows the secret thoughts of His enemies (2:8) surely knows if there is fruit on a tree. However, this is how Jesus appears to the disciples as they follow along. He is truly hungry and they see Him going towards the tree as they would, to discover any possible fruit. According to His human nature, Jesus would look for the fruit for His hunger, while, according to His divine nature, He knows all things and the fig tree is sought for the lesson it will provide. *not the season for figs.* Early unripe figs should have been present (in March/April), even though the main harvest season had not yet arrived (August/September). The leaves should have served as a reliable indicator for these early figs. If the early figs do not appear, neither will the later ones. The outward show of the leaves raised the expectation of fruit. In the same way, outward signs of fruitfulness within Israel—the temple, sacrifices, worship, and priesthood—should indicate fruitfulness. However, Jesus will next cleanse the temple to show that there was no fruit there.

11:14 *may no one ever eat fruit from you again.* Jesus addresses the tree as though it were a person. While He does not specifically warn of the tree's death, this is the understanding in 11:21. Jesus' command recalls the vineyard parable of Is 5:1–7 where God describes Israel as a vineyard for which He has done everything possible. However, it yielded only wild grapes. Therefore He condemned the vineyard. He says of Israel that He looked for justice "but behold bloodshed, for righteousness, but behold, an outcry!" (Is 5:7). So also Jesus finds not justice but a plot to destroy Him immediately following His cleansing of the temple (Mk 11:18).

11:12–14 in Devotion and Prayer The curse and destruction of the fig tree warns Jesus' disciples of impending judgment against the temple and the unfruitful people. Works without faith are truly fruitless. True faith, and the life that flows from it, cannot be separated. They are the good and gracious gifts of our heavenly Father. • "In your hearts enthrone Him; There let Him subdue All that is not holy, All that is not true: Crown Him as your captain In temptation's hour; Let His will enfold you In its light and pow'r." Amen. (*LSB* 512:5; *H82* 435:5; *TUMH* 168:4)

Introduction to 11:15–19 Mark places the cleansing of the temple in the midst of the two halves of the story of the unproductive fig tree. Like a fig tree with leaves but no fruit, the temple compound appeared promisingly busy. However, both tree and temple were barren of true fruit.

11:15 *He entered the temple and began to drive out those who sold.* This is the second time that Jesus has cleansed the temple (cf. Jn 2:14–22). He cleansed it at the beginning of His ministry with the prediction that they will destroy the temple of His body, and He will raise it up again in three days. That prediction is about to be completed. Cleansing the temple again stresses that He is the true temple, the place of God's dwelling with His people and the place of sacrifice for sins. Jesus repeats a physical cleansing of the temple courtyard as needed but He, the perfect High Priest, comes as the single cleansing of all sins (Heb 7:26–27). *Money-changers . . . pigeons.* Travelers needed their currency changed to the temple currency so they could pay their temple tax. Pigeons were sacrificed as an offering for cleansing (Lv 15:14, 29), and so were sold here so that travelers didn't have to bring them a great distance. The rates of exchange and prices were likely outrageous so that the temple's outer court was filled with angry voices.

11:16 *He would not allow anyone.* The temple precinct was used as a shortcut between the Mount of Olives and Jerusalem. Jesus would not let people simply wander through or use the temple as a traffic bypass.

11:17 *He was teaching them.* Even after cleansing the temple, Jesus gathers His disciples and others to listen to Him. They likely come together with renewed curiosity over what He has just done. *My house shall be called a house of prayer.* This is a quote from Is 56:7. It was a promise to the Gentiles that they will be gathered along with the people of Israel and God will hear them equally. *den of robbers.* Though this is not a direct quote from Isaiah, the continued context of Is 56 describes the leaders of Israel as "shepherds who have no understanding; they have all turned to their own way, each to his own gain" (Is 56:11). These self-serving leaders have focused on their own profit and will strike against Jesus to protect that self-interest.

11:18 *chief priests . . . scribes.* Jesus has predicted that He will be killed by the elders, chief priests, and scribes (8:31). From this point on, the chief priests and scribes will lead the opposition against Jesus in ch. 11–15. *destroy.* Their plans to murder Jesus are offset by their fear of Him. They recognize His power and the effect He has upon the crowd, but, because of that, they are convinced that He has to die. *feared.* They consider Jesus dangerous because the Romans will not tolerate a popular rebellion (cf. Jn 11:45–50). They fear both the crowd's frenzied support of Jesus and what the crowd might do to them if they openly destroy Jesus.

11:19 *they went out of the city.* Jesus retreated from the city and the crowd, as was often His practice. His leaving complicates the plans of the chief priests since they want to arrest Him at night away from the crowds. However, Jesus' leaving the city takes Him out of their immediate knowledge and grasp. Jesus could have maintained this secure pattern, but He offers Himself up on Thursday. No one takes His life from Him, but He lays it down Himself to take it up again (Jn 10:18).

11:15–19 in Devotion and Prayer As prophesied in Mal 3:1–5, Jesus purifies the temple of those who use religion to line their pockets. He does so in the temple court, where genuine worship has been disrupted. Today, Jesus challenges us to eliminate all such barriers to God's Word in our lives and in our congregations. He is the proper focus of our prayers, the reason for our service; He hallows us as the temple of His Holy Spirit. • "Your name be hallowed. Help us, Lord, In purity to keep Your Word, That to the glory of Your name We walk before You free from blame. Let no false teaching us pervert; All poor deluded souls convert." Amen. (*LSB* 766:2)

Introduction to 11:20–26 This is the third installment in the series on the fig tree and temple. The disciples discover that the fig tree has truly died, but Jesus turns this lesson of Law to a time of Gospel promise. Faith receives remarkable gifts in prayer and shares the forgiveness that God gives. This shared forgiveness brings life to the spiritually dead and is the final, lasting purpose of Christ's work.

11:20 *they saw the fig tree withered away to its roots.* Jesus takes them deliberately on the route that will pass the tree. We expect the disciples will be confident that the tree is dead, given the previous miracles of Jesus. This tree has not just wilted but has withered completely as though scorched from heat. See 4:6 for such a plant in the parable of the soils. This dead plant recalls the warning of John the Baptist that every tree that does not bear good fruit will be cut down and cast into the fire (Mt 3:10).

11:21 *Rabbi, look.* See the notes on 9:5 where, in the wonder of the Transfiguration, Peter speaks of Jesus as Rabbi. Peter should have fully expected this, but he responds with an innocent exuberance. It as though Jesus has done no previous miracles but now has done more than calm the sea and raise the dead. *cursed.* This is the only use of this word, *kataraomai,* in Mark. While there will be those cursed to eternal death (Mt 25:41), the ministry of Jesus is noted more for His command to bless those who curse (Lk 6:28). Perhaps Peter's astonishment is over this aspect of Jesus' work since His healing of the sick and other acts of kindness have become common by now.

11:22 *have faith in God.* Jesus answers in the kindest way. He doesn't reprimand Peter for any doubt or for his wonder over this small miracle. Instead He directs Peter to expect great things from an even greater God. This recalls Jesus' call of Nathanael who was astonished that Jesus saw him from a distance under a fig tree. Jesus assured him that he would see greater things than these (Jn 1:50–51). So all believers have the chance to see much greater things than the withering of a tree. Have faith in God who comes to bring life from the dead.

11:23 *truly I say to you.* While Jesus has used this phrase sparingly early in the Gospel (3:28; 8:12; 9:1, 41), it is used much more in the last days as Jesus approaches the cross. It conveys His serious teaching concerning the nature of the Kingdom (10:15, 29), and the value of generous acts (12:43; 14:9). Similar to this setting, He speaks of the lesson of the fig tree (13:30), and ends with predictions of His betrayal and death (14:18, 25, 30). *does not doubt in his heart but believes . . . it will be done for him.* The word for "doubt," *diakrino*, appears only here in Mark and indicates a conflict within one's self. Doubt is an inner struggle between the received Word of God with its promises and our own denials and resistance. See Jas 1:6 for similar commands about prayer in faith. Faith is not mighty, deserving, or creative in itself. Prayer is not answered by our determination to make it so. Faith is an open way that receives the gifts of the almighty God. Doubt divides and blocks the path of prayer's answer while faith clears the way.

11:24 *believe that you have received it and it will be yours.* Faith sees what has not yet come (Heb 11:1). Faith itself is the first work of God and is the evidence of His future work. Faithful prayer knows we need to pray according to His will, but, when we do, then we have the gifts He has planned (1Jn 5:14–15). This will not be a request simply for our own glory at the expense of others (10:36–40), but instead matches the trust of the paralyzed man's friends (2:5), and the woman with the bleeding (5:28, 34).

11:25 *stand praying.* A typical Jewish posture for prayer. *forgive.* Jesus transitions to mention the greatest request one can make: the forgiveness of sins. Refusing to forgive loses forgiveness by destroying the relationship between God and the believer. Luther writes, "If you forgive, you have this comfort and assurance, that you are forgiven in heaven. This is not because of your forgiving. For God forgives freely and without condition, out of pure grace, because He has so promised" (LC III 95–96). *may forgive.* Our forgiveness of others does not cause God to forgive as though we had then deserved it. Forgiveness comes overwhelmingly to us and we share it as a natural overflow. Failure to forgive shows our rejection of forgiveness for both ourselves and others. See Mt 18:21–35 to see forgiveness given and then refused in the parable of the unforgiving servant.

11:26 As the KJV reflects, some later manuscripts have this verse beginning, "But if you do not forgive . . ." This gives the opposite result from 11:25 and is likely an echo from Mt 6:15.

11:20–26 in Devotion and Prayer Jesus teaches that saving faith rescues us from God's judgment and that, through faith, we have the power to do the work God gives us. Without faith in Jesus, it is impossible to please God or pray to Him. We know God hears our prayers even if we do not receive an answer immediately. Confident prayer, based on faith in Christ trusts God to answer in His own time and way (cf. Rm 8:32). • "Forgive our sins, Lord, we implore, That they may trouble us no more; We, too, will gladly those forgive Who hurt us by the way they live. Help us in our community To serve each other willingly." Amen. (*LSB* 766:6)

Jesus confronts the religious authorities (11:27–12:40)

Jesus responds to the question of His authority (11:27–33)

ESV

27 And they came again to Jerusalem.
And as he was walking in the temple, the chief priests and the scribes
and the elders came to him, 28 and
they said to him, "By what authority
are you doing these things, or who
gave you this authority to do them?"
29 Jesus said to them, "I will ask you
one question; answer me, and I will
tell you by what authority I do these
things. 30 Was the baptism of John
from heaven or from man? Answer
me." 31 And they discussed it with
one another, saying, "If we say, 'From
heaven,' he will say, 'Why then did
you not believe him?' 32 But shall we
say, 'From man'?"—they were afraid
of the people, for they all held that
John really was a prophet. 33 So they
answered Jesus, "We do not know."
And Jesus said to them, "Neither will
I tell you by what authority I do these
things."

KJV

27 And they come again to Jerusalem:
and as he was walking in the temple,
there come to him the chief priests,
and the scribes, and the elders,
28 And say unto him, By what authority doest thou these things? and who
gave thee this authority to do these
things?
29 And Jesus answered and said unto
them, I will also ask of you one question, and answer me, and I will tell
you by what authority I do these
things.
30 The baptism of John, was it from
heaven, or of men? answer me.
31 And they reasoned with themselves, saying, If we shall say, From
heaven; he will say, Why then did ye
not believe him?
32 But if we shall say, Of men; they
feared the people: for all men counted
John, that he was a prophet indeed.
33 And they answered and said unto
Jesus, We cannot tell. And Jesus
answering saith unto them, Neither
do I tell you by what authority I do
these things.

Introduction to 11:27–33 Following the cleansing of the temple, the chief priests and others naturally challenge Jesus' authority. They are also anxious about what He might do next. Jesus answers their question with a question, showing His authority over them even in this argument. Concerning the authority of John, they fear men but not God. Because they fear the crowds, they cannot answer. Jesus takes this silence as the answer to their question, demonstrating His power over them.

11:27 *as He was walking in the temple.* Jesus again presents Himself as the perfect Priest and the Lamb to be slain in the temple. He makes no effort to hide though He knows perfectly the plans to arrest Him. *chief priests . . . scribes . . . elders.* As noted in 11:18, the chief priests and scribes organize the plot against Jesus and are prominent in the Gospel through ch. 15. They regard Jesus as the troublesome carpenter from Nazareth while we see Him as the true High Priest and the One who will build a lasting temple for God's people.

11:28 *by what authority are you doing these things.* Jesus' authority was a hallmark of His teaching at the very beginning of His ministry (1:22, 27). In the first teaching in the synagogue, He was noted for authority over demons and teaching that exceeded the scribes. Now the assembled leaders question this authority after three years of His teaching and miracles. Jesus' actions in vv. 15–16 overturned decisions the temple leaders had made. Their practices were not explicitly forbidden by God's Law, so they believed they had acted appropriately. Their question scrutinizes all that He has done in His ministry.

11:29 *I will ask you one question.* Jesus answers with a question which, in itself, demonstrates His authority over them. They cannot compel Him to answer on their terms, but instead submit to His turning the exam against them. Jesus' question stresses the parallel between Himself and John, just as we have seen from the very beginning of Mark. John's authority leveled the path Jesus was fulfilling that very week in Jerusalem.

11:30 *baptism of John from heaven or from man?* The focus on John's baptism is especially personal for Jesus and the listening crowd. Many in the crowd might have been baptized by John (1:5). It is not John's teaching against the Pharisees that is questioned but the very personal washing he performed for those listening. If the chief priests call that a mere human act, it is an attack on the experience of the crowd. Also, the baptism of Jesus is the beginning of Jesus' ministry, especially as Mark records it (1:10–12). The baptism of Jesus by John is the intersection between the human and divine. Jesus comes to be baptized by His relative, John, even while the heavenly Father affirms that He is the only Son of God. *answer me.* Only Mark includes this sharp command. Jesus demonstrates His authority over them with these two words. He also hastens the answer, not allowing for debate or delay.

11:31 *they discussed it with one another.* This is the last time this word, *dialogidzomai,* "discuss" is used in Mark. Interestingly, it is used only in negative contexts to describe the hostile, selfish or confused debates of His enemies or disciples (2:6, 8; 8:16–17; 9:33). Jesus always knows the contents of these discussions and Mark invites us into the discussion through Jesus' knowledge of what was being said. *from heaven . . . why then did you not believe him?* They go first to the most obvious answer, but also the bitter question that it will bring. Jesus knows every one of their thoughts. They, at best, can forecast what He will say to them. If John was from God, then the central message of John—Jesus as the Son of God, the Lamb of God that takes away the sin of the world (Jn 1:29)—will be inescapable. They may have destroyed John, but his witness to the Son lives on. Their question becomes a central question for the whole Gospel: if all the witnesses to Jesus in the Gospel—Mark, John, those healed, the centurion at his death, demons cast out and the Father in heaven—if all these are correct and express the will of heaven, then why don't you believe? Here is the central issue of the Gospel unthinkingly expressed by His enemies.

11:32 *from man—they were afraid of the people.* Herod had feared John for his witness (6:20), and the chief priests and others feared the people more than John. John's authority is demonstrated by this power even when he has died. In fact, his death demonstrated his role as prophet who was opposed by a wicked king and therefore killed. *people . . . all held that John really was a prophet.* John's work as a prophet was established already in 1:2 with his fulfillment of Isaiah's prophecy. John's role as the spokesperson of God is especially galling for the chief priests and scribes who presume to have that role for the crowds. However, their claim for authority is cast aside as not worth discussing here. Only John, the rugged man of desert and river, is a candidate for the prophetic role.

11:33 *We do not know.* Fear of the people keep them from giving their opinion. How galling for them to have to admit to having no answer! Their silence over this question—which the crowds themselves have already answered—discredits them entirely. Jesus will exploit their silence by teaching in the next two chapters. *Neither will I tell you.* Silence begets silence. They must live and die by their questions and silence. Just as the crowds had already seen the divine authority of John, the reader has already answered this by seeing the greater divine authority of Jesus.

11:27–33 in Devotion and Prayer Opponents of Jesus confront Him and question His authority. Jesus refuses to engage them since He knows the true character of His authority (Mt 28:18). The anger of these leaders brings Jesus ever nearer to the cross, where He acts in weakness to overthrow the authority of the evil one for the sake of our salvation. • Lord God, heavenly Father, You sent Your Son to cleanse the temple of Jerusalem; so now cleanse the hearts of Your people, that they may be temples for Your Holy Spirit. Amen.

Jesus teaches the parable of the tenants (12:1–12)

ESV	KJV
12 1 And he began to speak to them in parables. "A man planted a vine- yard and put a fence around it and dug a pit for the winepress and built a tower, and leased it to tenants and went into another country. 2 When the season came, he sent a servant to the tenants to get from them some of the fruit of the vineyard. 3 And they took him and beat him and sent him away empty-handed. 4 Again he sent to them another servant, and they struck him on the head and treated him shamefully. 5 And he sent another, and him they killed. And so with many others: some they beat, and some they killed. 6 He had still one other, a beloved son. Finally he sent him to them, saying, 'They will respect my son.' 7 But those tenants said to one another, 'This is the heir. Come, let us kill him, and the inher- itance will be ours.' 8 And they took him and killed him and threw him out of the vineyard. 9 What will the owner of the vineyard do? He will come and	12 1 And he began to speak unto them by parables. A certain man planted a vineyard, and set an hedge about it, and digged a place for the winefat, and built a tower, and let it out to husbandmen, and went into a far country. 2 And at the season he sent to the husbandmen a servant, that he might receive from the husbandmen of the fruit of the vineyard. 3 And they caught him, and beat him, and sent him away empty. 4 And again he sent unto them another servant; and at him they cast stones, and wounded him in the head, and sent him away shamefully han- dled. 5 And again he sent another; and him they killed, and many others; beating some, and killing some. 6 Having yet therefore one son, his wellbeloved, he sent him also last unto them, saying, They will rever- ence my son. 7 But those husbandmen said among themselves, This is the heir; come, let

destroy the tenants and give the vineyard to others. [10]Have you not read this Scripture:

" 'The stone that the builders rejected
has become the cornerstone;
[11]this was the Lord's doing,
and it is marvelous in our eyes'?"

[12]And they were seeking to arrest him but feared the people, for they perceived that he had told the parable against them. So they left him and went away.

us kill him, and the inheritance shall be ours.'

[8]And they took him, and killed him, and cast him out of the vineyard.

[9]What shall therefore the lord of the vineyard do? he will come and destroy the husbandmen, and will give the vineyard unto others.

[10]And have ye not read this scripture; The stone which the builders rejected is become the head of the corner:

[11]This was the Lord's doing, and it is marvellous in our eyes?

[12]And they sought to lay hold on him, but feared the people: for they knew that he had spoken the parable against them: and they left him, and went their way.

Introduction to 12:1–12 The conflict and fear that concludes the previous periscope (11:27–33), continues in the parable of the tenants. When the chief priests, scribes, and elders are silenced by Jesus (11:33), He fills this silence with His teaching against them. They are represented by the tenants in the parable who selfishly hold the vineyard's fruit and even dare to kill the heir. Their judgment is announced that hardens their determination to kill Jesus. Jesus' teaching exposes their plot while also motivating them to carry it out.

12:1 *He began to speak to them in parables.* Since the acknowledged leaders and teachers of Israel were silenced by Jesus' single question (11:33), Jesus demonstrates His authority and wisdom immediately by teaching. His use of parables recalls ch. 4 with its three parables and the summary of 4:33–34 that He taught only in parables. The three parables of ch. 4 were all related to soils, seeds, and growth. This tenant parable continues that theme with the vineyard setting. The vineyard also recalls the cursed fig tree of 11:12–14 that was related to the cleansing of the temple. *man planted a vineyard . . . put a fence . . . dug a pit . . . built a tower.* Clearly the man did everything necessary for success. This recalls the parable of Is 5:1–7, the vineyard which was built perfectly but yielded only wild grapes. *tenants.* These were farm renters who paid the lease with either cash or a share of the crop. While the ch. 4 parables centered on the soil and seeds, it is the wickedness of the tenants that is the key here.

12:2 *season.* This is the harvest time, when the rent was due. The time of the year varied by crop. The harvest time was completely predictable and so the tenants have no excuse for being unprepared. *sent a servant.* The servant recalls the work of the prophets and especially John the Baptist. John's authority was the topic of the previous section (11:27–33), and John spoke of bearing fruit which was in keeping with repentance (Mt 3:8). *some of the fruit.* This was an agreed-upon portion of the harvest for payment. The tenants were not defrauded by this, especially in light of all the work that the owner had done to make the vineyard a success. Anything given to God is a small return on all that He has first provided for our lives.

12:3 *took him . . . beat him . . . sent him.* This is not an accidental insult or a passing moment of anger. These three verbs, and the others which follow, show their deliberate intention to attack the servants and hoard the fruit. Their actions toward the servant demonstrate complete disrespect for the owner. The OT prophets were often attacked in these ways, such as Jeremiah's imprisonment (Jer 37:15) and being cast into a well (Jer 38:6). Second Chronicles 36:15–16 summarizes it well: "The LORD, the God of their fathers, sent persistently to them by His messengers, because he had compassion on His people . . . But they kept mocking the messengers of God . . . until the wrath of the Lord rose against His people."

12:4 *he sent to them another servant.* The sending of one prophet after another shows the patience of God and the courage of the prophets. God didn't give up with a single episode of rebellion but provided many moments for Israel to hear the prophets' message and live in repentant faith. *struck him . . . and treated him shamefully.* This shameful treatment was their displaced anger against the Lord and their blind presumption that they could do this without penalty. This treatment continued also in the NT with the arrest of the Twelve in Ac 5:18, so that they rejoiced "that they were counted worthy to suffer dishonor for the name" (Ac 5:41).

12:5 *sent another and him they killed.* They have no bounds on their cruelty. Just as they had asked Jesus by what authority He did His teaching and work (11:28), so it would be fitting to ask by what authority they were empowered to beat and kill. They have no mandate but are driven by their own desire, born of temptation in the Garden of Eden, to act as God in their own small world.

12:6 *a beloved son.* The adjective "beloved" is used only two other times in Mark, recording the words of the Father at Jesus' baptism (1:11), and at the transfiguration (9:7). In these moments of glory, Jesus is acclaimed the Father's Son. The Father's love of the world is shown by His sending His only Son as a final attempt to win them to Himself. *respect my son.* This is a perfectly reasonable hope. However, the selfish blindness of the tenants knows no respect. The Father and the Son recognize this and still Jesus goes towards His death at their hands.

12:7 *come, let us kill him and the inheritance will be ours.* According to Jewish law, the tenants stood a good chance of inheriting the land when the owner died, if there was no heir. However, this was more than a business decision. Their previous attacks on the servants show their hard-heartedness. They kill the son out of hateful jealousy along with their covetousness of the vineyard. The chief priests and other leaders envy Jesus' authority, teaching, and beloved standing with the crowds.

12:8 *they took him and killed him.* The parable shows the son walking alone into the vineyard stronghold of the tenants, outnumbered and seemingly hopeless. We are in awe of the Son of God who goes into the Garden of Gethsemane to meet His enemies, surrounded by legions of angels who could defend Him in a moment (Mt 26:53). But He sets aside the use of these protective guardian angels. *threw him out of the vineyard.* So Jesus is crucified outside of the city on Calvary. His death outside the city recalls the scapegoat that was driven out of the camp, bearing the sins of the people (Lv 16:20–22).

12:9 *What will the owner . . . do?* Jesus once again asks a question of His enemies, as in 11:29. They know the answer but cannot bear to say it. Justice demands repayment for the brutal treatment of the servants and especially the son. *destroy the tenants.* The tenants receive the treatment they've given to others. This balance of justice should be expected. *give the vineyard to others.* The owner does not hoard the vineyard or destroy it in bitterness over his son's death. So God does not destroy the world over His Son's death, but through

His death reconciles the world to Himself and announces peace by His blood (2Co 5:18–19).

12:10 *have you not read the Scripture.* Jesus' question is especially harsh given the chief priests and scribes' vaunted authority as scriptural teachers. They should have known this parable as an echo of Is 5. They should also know the quote which follows. *the stone that the builders rejected . . . cornerstone.* This quote from Ps 118:22–23 describes Jesus as the essential piece in God's building, the stone on which all others rest. Though He was rejected by the leadership, He is the beloved and perfect Son of God. This image of Jesus as the once rejected, but now valued cornerstone is repeated often in the NT (Ac 4:11; Eph 2:20; 1Pt 2:7–8). See also Is 28:16 and Rm 9:33 for a similar description of Christ as the perfect foundation stone.

12:11 *the Lord's doing.* The intentional plan of God foresees the violence of His enemies, the death of His Son, and His resurrection as the cornerstone. While God does not cause the rebellion of the leaders, He harnesses it to fulfill His plan. Jesus' ministry is entirely by the authority of God, which answers the question of 11:28. *it is marvelous in our eyes.* The joy of the crowds in Palm Sunday is expressed here.

12:12 *seeking to arrest Him but feared the people.* The chief priests and other leaders exemplify the foolishness of fearing only those who can harm the body, but not fearing God who can destroy both body and soul (Mt 10:28). While the chief priests had feared Jesus in 11:18 because of His popular teaching, they have twice been noted for fear of the crowds: 11:32, and here. *They perceived that He had told the parable against them.* Mt 21:43–44 gives the words Jesus says here which make it absolutely clear that Jesus was speaking against them. He warns that they will have the kingdom of God taken from them and that those who fall onto this stone will be broken.

12:1–12 in Devotion and Prayer Jesus tells how God deals patiently with people. But eventually, God's patience runs out, and every person must face judgment. God planned the death of His Son for the sins of all people. Unlike the parable here, His beloved Son rose from the dead on the third day, taking up again the life He had laid down for us and giving us the Kingdom as a gift. • "I trust in Him with all my heart; Now all my sorrow ceases. His words abiding peace impart; His blood from guilt releases." Amen. (*LSB* 568:3)

Jesus responds to the question about paying taxes to Caesar (12:13–17)

ESV	KJV
[13]And they sent to him some of the Pharisees and some of the Herodians, to trap him in his talk. [14]And they came and said to him, "Teacher, we know that you are true and do not care about anyone's opinion. For you are not swayed by appearances, but truly teach the way of God. Is it lawful to pay taxes to Caesar, or not? Should we pay them, or should we not?" [15]But, knowing their hypocrisy, he said to them, "Why put me to the test? Bring me a denarius and let me look at it." [16]And they brought one. And he said to them, "Whose likeness and inscription is this?" They said to him, "Caesar's." [17]Jesus said to them, "Render to Caesar the things that are Caesar's, and to God the things that are God's." And they marveled at him.	[13]And they send unto him certain of the Pharisees and of the Herodians, to catch him in his words. [14]And when they were come, they say unto him, Master, we know that thou art true, and carest for no man: for thou regardest not the person of men, but teachest the way of God in truth: Is it lawful to give tribute to Caesar, or not? [15]Shall we give, or shall we not give? But he, knowing their hypocrisy, said unto them, Why tempt ye me? bring me a penny, that I may see it. [16]And they brought it. And he saith unto them, Whose is this image and superscription? And they said unto him, Caesar's. [17]And Jesus answering said unto them, Render to Caesar the things that are Caesar's, and to God the things that are God's. And they marvelled at him.

Introduction to 12:13–17 Jesus has defeated His enemies by the cleansing of the temple (11:15), asking a question they will not answer (11:30), and telling the sharp parable against them (12:1–10). They respond with a dangerous trap covered with flattery. They hope to pin Him between the Romans and the crowd, but Jesus steps through the snare to the delight of His hearers and readers still today.

12:13 *Pharisees and . . . Herodians.* These are the two groups noted in 3:6 as those who first plotted to kill Jesus. *to trap Him in His talk.* The verb "trap," *agreuo*, occurs only here in the NT and means to hunt and trap animals, fish, or birds. They hope to use their words to catch Him in His words. What a hopeless plot given that He has made all things by the strength and wisdom of His words.

12:14 *Teacher.* This is a formal but insincere address. See 4:38 for the first use of the word, *didaskalos,* which is generally used by His enemies in settings of conflict. *we know that you are true.* This flattery gives them credit as though they had the wisdom and authority to judge truth and falsehood. However, they have no respect for Jesus' teaching. *not swayed by appearances.* Though they don't believe in Jesus' teaching, this summarized Jesus' perfect justice and truthful teaching, free from the very false flattery that they were using. See Jn 2:25, Jesus "needed no one to bear witness about man, for He Himself knew what was in man." *taxes to Caesar.* The hated, Roman-instituted tax demonstrated Rome's power over Israel. To refuse the tax would be popular in many circles but also dangerous.

12:15 *knowing their hypocrisy.* Jesus has known His opponents' thoughts from the beginning of His ministry (2:8). He has already challenged the hypocrisy of the Pharisees in 7:1–8, esp. v. 5 when they asked why He didn't make His disciples ceremonially wash. Jesus noted that they taught the commandments of men, not God. Jesus here will make the same distinction between the obligations of men versus those of God. *why put Me to the test?* Why bother with this? Jesus has already bested the tempter himself (1:12–13) and defeated their previous attempts to trap Him. Besides, if He is the true teacher of God's ways (12:14), why tempt Him? *bring Me a denarius.* Jesus makes this a parable-like moment of teaching through the coin. His demonstration is clear to everyone and easily repeated throughout the crowd.

12:16 *whose likeness and inscription is this?* The denarius had an image of Tiberius Caesar who was described as the son of the divine Augustus. The true Son of God, the authentic image of the invisible God (Col 1:15), now judges the value of this token and image. By asking this question, Jesus allows the crowd to answer the question for themselves. Just as they can see the coin, they can now repeat His teaching. By this analogy, the question was easily answered without apparent danger.

12:17 *render to Caesar . . . and to God the things that are God's.* Jesus makes a clear distinction between the realm of the emperor and the realm of God. That which bears Caesar's image, let it return to him. That which bears the image of God, let that be His. Let coins go to Caesar and the body and soul to God. The obligation to Caesar can be paid externally with a simple coin. What is that compared to the call of God to a life of faith and forgiveness? The emperor's obligation is a moment; the call of God is life itself. *marveled at Him.* This is the only NT use of this word, *ekthaumadzo*, "marveled." Jesus' wise answer was both instantly clear and profound. It left them saying, "Of course" and yet also admitting that they would not have thought of it themselves.

12:13–17 in Devotion and Prayer Jesus challenges the hypocrites to examine their own hearts and repent. Human hearts naturally belong to their Maker, who stamped His image on them at creation (Gn 1:27). Though sin shattered that image in us, the Lord still wants us for His very own people and sent Jesus to make that possible (Rm 8:29; Eph 4:24; Col 3:10). • "We give Thee but Thine own, Whate'er the gift may be; All that we have is Thine alone, A trust, O Lord, from Thee." Amen. (*LSB* 781:1; *TPH* 428:1)

Jesus responds to the Saddducees on the resurrection (12:18–27)

ESV

18 And Sadducees came to him, who
say that there is no resurrection. And
they asked him a question, saying,
19 "Teacher, Moses wrote for us that
if a man's brother dies and leaves a
wife, but leaves no child, the man
must take the widow and raise up offspring for his brother. 20 There were
seven brothers; the first took a wife,
and when he died left no offspring.
21 And the second took her, and died,
leaving no offspring. And the third
likewise. 22 And the seven left no offspring. Last of all the woman also
died. 23 In the resurrection, when they
rise again, whose wife will she be?
For the seven had her as wife."
24 Jesus said to them, "Is this not the
reason you are wrong, because you
know neither the Scriptures nor the
power of God? 25 For when they rise
from the dead, they neither marry

KJV

18 Then come unto him the Sadducees, which say there is no resurrection; and they asked him, saying,
19 Master, Moses wrote unto us, If a man's brother die, and leave his wife behind him, and leave no children, that his brother should take his wife, and raise up seed unto his brother.
20 Now there were seven brethren: and the first took a wife, and dying left no seed.
21 And the second took her, and died, neither left he any seed: and the third likewise.
22 And the seven had her, and left no seed: last of all the woman died also.
23 In the resurrection therefore, when they shall rise, whose wife shall she be of them? for the seven had her to wife.
24 And Jesus answering said unto them, Do ye not therefore err, because ye know not the scriptures,

nor are given in marriage, but are
like angels in heaven. [26]And as for
the dead being raised, have you not
read in the book of Moses, in the pas-
sage about the bush, how God spoke
to him, saying, 'I am the God of Abra-
ham, and the God of Isaac, and the
God of Jacob'? [27]He is not God of the
dead, but of the living. You are quite
wrong."

neither the power of God?
[25]For when they shall rise from
the dead, they neither marry, nor
are given in marriage; but are as the
angels which are in heaven.
[26]And as touching the dead, that
they rise: have ye not read in the
book of Moses, how in the bush God
spake unto him, saying, I am the God
of Abraham, and the God of Isaac,
and the God of Jacob?
[27]He is not the God of the dead, but
the God of the living: ye therefore do
greatly err.

Introduction to 12:18–27 Another deceptive question is presented to trap Jesus. Instead of catching Jesus between Roman power and Jewish patriotism, this question uses the apparent conflict between scriptural requirements and the resurrection. Once again Jesus steps beyond the question by showing that heaven is for the living, not those bound by the earth and its past.

12:18 *Sadducees.* The Sadducees were a smaller group than the Pharisees, politically powerful, with close ties to the Romans. They denied the resurrection and were frequent opponents of the Pharisees. When the Pharisees failed to trap Jesus, they naturally stepped forward to outdo their enemies.

12:19 *Moses wrote for us.* The Sadducees believed that only the first five biblical books, written by Moses, were authoritative. They quote Dt 25:5ff which provided a home for the widow and continued the line of the deceased brother. The Sadducees twist this benevolent safety net into a snare.

12:20–22 *there were seven brothers.* This fiction goes to the barely imaginable length of seven. The failure of all seven brothers might be intended to show the futility of such rules. Jesus allows them to spin their tale, knowing that His answer will not be in the details but in the overall assumption of how heaven carries on present relationships.

12:23 *in the resurrection, when they rise again.* Smug in their certainty that there is no resurrection, they announce the resurrection twice. The Sadducees wrongly imagined that marriage would continue after death. Since their theoretical situation seems an unanswerable problem, they use it to prove there cannot be a resurrection. Their limited view of heaven and God contradict the promise of eternal life.

12:24 *you are wrong.* The word for "wrong" is the verb *plana*, meaning to wander. From this we have the name "planet" for those meandering bodies in the heavens. These men erroneously wander in their speculation. Earth-bound, they try to understand the life of heaven. *you know neither the Scriptures.* They have read the Scriptures through the narrow view of their earthly experience. The blinders of their past ignore the power of God and the newness of eternity. The bond of marriage ends when a man dies, allowing his wife to remarry (cf. the commands of Dt 25:5–10 with the prohibition of Lv 18:16; cf. also Rm 7:1–3; 1Co 7:39). *nor the power of God?* They deny the resurrection by seeing only the weakness of human flesh. However, in Jb 19:25–26, Job still was confident of the resurrection, wracked with the weakness of his flesh. He knew his Redeemer, coming to earth, would raise him so that he could see God with his own flesh and eyes. The certainty of Ps 23:4–6 knows that after the valley of the shadow of death we will be with the Lord forever. See also Ps 17:15 for further images of resurrection.

12:25 *neither marry nor are given.* A man married; a woman was given in marriage by her father. These familiar customs are on earth only. The Sadducees' question worried over the continuation of past earthly marriages while Jesus cuts off even the beginning of the marriage relationship in heaven. *like angels in heaven.* Angels and resurrected believers do not marry. Procreation was designed for earthly existence. This doesn't mean that believers are transformed into angels in heaven, but only that they share this unmarried state with the angels.

12:26 *as for the dead being raised.* Jesus takes up the real issue, the possibility of the resurrection. *have you not read.* Just as in 12:10, Jesus accuses these leaders of their fundamental failing—they do not know the Scripture. Jesus takes them to Ex 3:1–6 where God meets Moses at the burning bush. Since the Sadducees value only the five books of Moses, let Moses correct them. *I am the God of Abraham . . . Isaac . . . Jacob.* God is the God of the living. If He were only the God of these men in the past, then He was the God of Abraham. But

His preferred name is "I AM," Ex 3:14, always present and living. Just as God is eternally alive, His relationship with these saints is always living. God's rule encompasses all beings, and He defines Himself in that living relationship. Jesus speaks of this when He says that He is the resurrection and the life, so that those who die in Him live, and "everyone who lives and believes in Me shall never die" (Jn 11:26).

12:27 *not the God of the dead but of the living.* This phraseology appears in passages about salvation or protection (cf. Ex 3:15–16; 4:5). "God of the dead" would be a contradiction. God does not set time limits on His saving relationship with His people. The patriarchs, though dead physically, dwell with Him (cf. Mt 8:11). Luther writes:

> When I behold a corpse carried out and buried, it is hard to go my way and believe and think that we will someday rise together. How so, or by what power? Not by myself or by virtue of any merit on earth, but by this one Christ. And that is indeed certain, far more certain than the fact that I will be buried and see someone else buried, which I know with certainty and behold with my eyes. (LW 28:117)

Wesley writes, "[God] cannot be said to be at present their God at all, if they are utterly dead. . . . There must needs be a future state of blessedness, and a resurrection of the body to share with the soul in it" (Wesley 126). *you are quite wrong.* See v. 24 for notes on this same word for "wrong." Their question on the seven brothers was not a small misunderstanding but a fundamental rebellion against the clear teaching of Scripture and the nature of the almighty, living God.

12:18–27 in Devotion and Prayer The Sadducees try to trap Jesus, but Jesus turns their hypothetical question upside down. He shows how they deny God's power and reject His Word. Like the Sadducees, people today want to limit God to what makes sense to them. Despite our limited understanding, God keeps His promises to us. He rescues His people even from death and raises all believers in Christ to eternal life. • "There shall we see in glory Our dear Redeemer's face; The long-awaited story Of heav'nly joy takes place: The patriarchs shall meet us, The prophets' holy band; Apostles, martyrs greet us In that celestial land." Amen. (*LSB* 514:2)

Jesus responds to the question on the greatest commandment (12:28–34)

ESV	KJV
28 And one of the scribes came up and heard them disputing with one another, and seeing that he answered them well, asked him, "Which commandment is the most important of all?" 29 Jesus answered, "The most important is, 'Hear, O Israel: The Lord our God, the Lord is one. 30 And you shall love the Lord your God with all your heart and with all your soul and with all your mind and with all your strength.' 31 The second is this: 'You shall love your neighbor as yourself.' There is no other commandment greater than these." 32 And the scribe said to him, "You are right, Teacher. You have truly said that he is one, and there is no other besides him. 33 And to love him with all the heart and with all the understanding and with all the strength, and to love one's neighbor as oneself, is much more than all whole burnt offerings and sacrifices." 34 And when Jesus saw that he answered wisely, he said to him, "You are not far from the kingdom of God." And after that no one dared to ask him any more questions.	28 And one of the scribes came, and having heard them reasoning together, and perceiving that he had answered them well, asked him, Which is the first commandment of all? 29 And Jesus answered him, The first of all the commandments is, Hear, O Israel; The Lord our God is one Lord: 30 And thou shalt love the Lord thy God with all thy heart, and with all thy soul, and with all thy mind, and with all thy strength: this is the first commandment. 31 And the second is like, namely this, Thou shalt love thy neighbour as thyself. There is none other commandment greater than these. 32 And the scribe said unto him, Well, Master, thou hast said the truth: for there is one God; and there is none other but he: 33 And to love him with all the heart, and with all the understanding, and with all the soul, and with all the strength, and to love his neighbour as himself, is more than all whole burnt offerings and sacrifices. 34 And when Jesus saw that he answered discreetly, he said unto him, Thou art not far from the kingdom of God. And no man after that durst ask him any question.

Introduction to 12:28–34 This is the fourth interrogation since 11:27 and we expect nothing but short-sighted arrogance which is rebuked by Jesus. But this encounter begins through a scribe's appreciation for Jesus' previous answer. Jesus defines the essence of the Law so that the scribe demonstrates his agreement with Jesus' answer. So this round of questions ends with Jesus commending the scribe for his insights.

12:28 *seeing that He answered them well.* There have been three previous questioners just before this man (11:27; 12:13, 18). The scribe would have especially enjoyed Jesus' defeat of the Sadducees, the opponents of the scribes and Pharisees. *which commandment is the most important.* The scribe has his own answer ready and wants to see if Jesus agrees with him. The scribe is asking about far more than the Ten Commandments since scribes had catalogued hundreds of both positive and negative commandments throughout the OT. Great debate could ensue over which commandment should be counted first.

12:29 *Hear, O Israel: The Lord our God, the Lord is one.* Jesus begins with the quote from Dt 6:4, a point which only Mark records. The essence of the Law begins not with our duties but God's essence. This section of Dt 6 is known as the *Shema* from the first word, "Hear." The emphasis begins with God's distinctive Oneness, one divine Being as opposed to the polytheistic beliefs of the Canaanites of Moses' time and the continuing polytheistic beliefs of the first century. Jesus' identity as the only Son of God (Mk 1:1, 11; 9:7) doesn't deny the single Godhead, for He and the Father are one (Jn 10:30) and in Him all the fullness of the Godhead dwells bodily (Col 2:9). Belief in the One God, revealed in Father, Son, and Spirit, is the foundation of our understanding of the Law.

12:30 *you shall love the Lord your God.* Jesus continues with Dt 6:5 and the response of God's people to His unity and the revelation of Himself. Knowing that He is the One God begins our relationship and love. However, we truly love because He first revealed Himself through His Son, and thereby He first loved us (1Jn 4:9–10, 19). *all your heart . . . soul . . . mind . . . strength.* Jesus adds to the Dt 6:5 text the phrase "with all your mind" and includes it also in a similar summary of the Law in Lk 10:27. The inclusion of the mind is perfectly in keeping with the whole of one's self and is fitting especially for the appreciation of the revealed Lord who is One God. Good King Josiah was noted to have loved God with his whole heart, soul, and might, as no other king ever did (2Ki 23:25). The demands of such love are beyond our ability but they reflect Jesus' perfect devotion to the Father. He withheld nothing in keeping His Father's will. Because of His perfect completion of the Law (Rm 10:4), our failing lives and love are declared perfect by God.

12:31 *the second is this: you shall love your neighbor as yourself.* Jesus quotes Lv 19:18 as the summary of the second Table of the Law. See this love of others as the Law's summary also in Rm 13:9; Gal 5:14; Jas 2:8. From a myriad of possible duties towards God and others, here is one, clear, and inclusive task. God loved us by becoming one with us in His Son, and so we love our neighbor by treating him as ourselves.

12:32 *you are right, Teacher.* Since Jesus has correctly answered the question, the scribe can only agree and elaborate. By this, he takes Jesus' wisdom to himself. The KJV captures the commendation of the scribe: "Well, Master, thou hast said the truth." *there is no other besides Him.* The scribe condenses Dt 6:4, the truth of God's unity, and continues with the assertion that there is no other like Him. This echoes Dt 4:35; Is 40:18, 25; 45:6 and many other passages. He is set apart from idols by many characteristics: His unity, His creation of all things by a word, His redeeming relationship with His people, His revelation of Himself and His word through the prophets, and His acceptance of sacrifices for the forgiveness of sins.

12:33 *more than all whole burnt offerings and sacrifices.* These are valid expressions of love for the one true God. Offerings and sacrifices were commanded as expressions of thanks and were signs of the all-encompassing sacrifice of Christ. Colossians 2:16–17 notes that all such observances, festivals, and sacrifices are shadows but Christ is the actual substance. Faith in God is far more important than external worship. The scribe expresses the ideas of Samuel. "Has the LORD as great delight in burnt offerings and sacrifices, as in obeying the voice of the LORD?" (1Sm 15:22). See also Ps 40:6–8; Pr 21:3; Is 1:11–13, 16–17.

12:34 *Jesus saw that he answered wisely.* The word for "wisely" (*nounechos*) is used only here in the NT. It means to act discreetly, wisely, sensibly. The scribe came to evaluate Jesus but remained long enough to find himself in alignment with Jesus. *not far.* The scribe understood God's OT revelation, though he did not yet confess Jesus as the Messiah. The heart of the kingdom of God is the very Son of God who was indeed very near the scribe. If he had remained, he might have joined the crowd that recognized Jesus as the Father's

Son. *no one dared to ask*. As noted in 12:28, this was the fourth in a recent series of interrogations of Jesus. All had failed and Jesus' reputation was only growing through their attacks upon Him.

12:28–34 in Devotion and Prayer Jesus challenges an expert in the Scriptures to consider the entire Law and to turn to the Lord in faith. Only Jesus has kept the entire Law perfectly for our salvation, due to His surpassing love for us. • "Thy love to me, O God, Not mine, O Lord, to Thee, Can rid me of this dark unrest And set my spirit free." Amen. (*LSB* 567:4)

Jesus questions them about the relationship of David and the Christ (12:35–37)

ESV	KJV
35 And as Jesus taught in the temple, he said, "How can the scribes say that the Christ is the son of David? 36 David himself, in the Holy Spirit, declared, 'The Lord said to my Lord, Sit at my right hand, until I put your enemies under your feet.' 37 "David himself calls him Lord. So how is he his son?" And the great throng heard him gladly.	35 And Jesus answered and said, while he taught in the temple, How say the scribes that Christ is the son of David? 36 For David himself said by the Holy Ghost, The LORD said to my Lord, Sit thou on my right hand, till I make thine enemies thy footstool. 37 David therefore himself calleth him Lord; and whence is he then his son? And the common people heard him gladly.

Introduction to 12:35–37 Now that His opponents have stopped their questions, Jesus asks them what they can't answer. His question goes to the mystery of the incarnation, the eternal God who is Himself born the child of David. The previous question by the Sadducees, 12:18–23, tried to bring earth's limits into heaven but failed. Jesus shows the greater mystery of His incarnation as David's Son and David's Lord.

12:35 *scribes*. The scribes were the interpreters of the Scripture, especially important in a largely illiterate society. They repeatedly were Jesus' opponents, especially in this Passion week (11:18, 27; 12:28; 14:1). By bringing them into the conversation, Jesus will contrast His authoritative teaching versus the teaching which they cannot fully explain. *Christ is the son of David?* The Messiah was to be a descendant of King David (cf. 2Sm 7:13–14; Rm 1:3). The scribes were correct in teaching that the Messiah would come from David, but they could not explain the incarnation of the eternal God in the line of David.

12:36 *The Lord said to my Lord.* Jesus quotes Ps 110:1 which begins with this verse. This Psalm is quoted seventeen times in the NT, and points to the divine and human nature of Christ who overcomes His enemies. The key point of Jesus' quote is the relationship of these two Persons of the Trinity, the Father and the Son, both of whom are Lord to David. *Sit at My right hand.* Jesus is raised in power through the resurrection and ascension to the Father's right hand. That position of power and glory demonstrates His authority over His enemies, including those who presumed to kill Him on the cross. Jesus' quote of this verse is a warning of His coming glory over those opponents planning His death at that moment. See Eph 2:20–22; Php 2:9–11 for more complete pictures of His rule.

12:37 *David himself calls Him Lord.* A highly respected ancestor would never have called a descendant "my lord." When David called his descendant "lord," he showed that the Messiah is more than merely human. David knows perfectly well that the Lord our God is one (Dt 6:4; Mk 12:29). However, he expresses the truth of the distinct Persons of the Father and the Son, both his Lord. The Messiah is the son of David, which was also announced by the crowd on Palm Sunday (Mt 21:9), and by others (Jn 7:42). The failure of the scribes to realize how He could be both David's son and David's Lord showed how much of the Scriptures remained hidden to them. *the great throng heard Him gladly.* Only Mark includes this note. The word "gladly," *hedeos,* is used only twice in any of the Gospels, here and Mk 6:20 where Herod heard John the Baptist gladly. As John is the forerunner of Jesus, so it is fitting that he was also heard gladly shortly before his death. Neither Herod nor the Jerusalem crowd's approval save John or Jesus from the hateful plots of their enemies.

12:35–37 in Devotion and Prayer Jesus challenges His audience to think about the Messiah and realize that He is more than a man. He is God as well. Unbelief blinds people so they do not see Christ in the OT (cf. 2Co 3:12–18). God became man, born of Mary, born under the Law, to redeem sinners such as we (cf. Gal 4:4–5).

• "O come, Thou Key of David, come, And open wide our heav'nly home; Make safe the way that leads on high, And close the path to misery." Amen. (*LSB* 357:5; *H82* 56:5; *TUMH* 211:5)

Jesus warns against the scribes (12:38–40)

ESV	KJV
38 And in his teaching he said, "Beware of the scribes, who like to walk around in long robes and like greetings in the marketplaces 39 and have the best seats in the synagogues and the places of honor at feasts, 40 who devour widows' houses and for a pretense make long prayers. They will receive the greater condemnation."	**38 And he said unto them in his doctrine, Beware of the scribes, which love to go in long clothing, and love salutations in the marketplaces, 39 And the chief seats in the synagogues, and the uppermost rooms at feasts: 40 Which devour widows' houses, and for a pretence make long prayers: these shall receive greater damnation.**

Introduction to 12:38–44 Jesus continues on the theme of the scribes by warning against their vanity and greed. In contrast, the poverty of widows appears twice. Scribes devour the little that widows have. But a widow with nearly nothing gives it all at the temple. She is a contrast to the scribes and a foreshadowing of Jesus' coming sacrifice.

12:38 *beware of the scribes.* Jesus has battled with the scribes repeatedly in chs. 11 and 12 and has just silenced them with His question (vv. 35–37). He turns from them to the crowd with His warning about their conceit. He has destroyed their intellectual claims and now unmasks their moral failings. *long robes.* Their long robes were a mark of distinction, perhaps associated with holiness. The robes, however, couldn't hide their empty pretension. In contrast, people eagerly reached for Jesus' robes to be healed genuinely (5:28; 6:56). *greetings.* These were the titles of honor and respect (e.g., "Rabbi," "Teacher"). When the scribes and other opponents used these titles for Jesus, they did so with obvious sarcasm (12:14, 19). Since Jesus has beaten them through their own questions and their silence (12:15–17, 24–27, 35–37) Jesus is clearly the true teacher.

12:39 *best seats . . . places of honor.* These were the places at the front of the synagogue or nearest the host at a banquet. Jesus' parable of the Wedding Feast (Lk 14:7–11), speaks against this anxious snatching of the best seats. In contrast, Jesus, the true Son of God, came to take the lowest place, a servant's role, and the cross (Php 2:6–8).

12:40 *devour widows' houses.* With no other source of income, scribes often lived off the generosity of benefactors. Abuses followed through the trust of widows and the greed of the scribes. *long prayers.* These prayers, offered to impress listeners, were long in duration and short on faith. *greater condemnation.* With greater knowledge comes greater responsibility (cf. Lk 12:47–48; 1Co 3:10–15; Jas 3:1). Luther writes:

> In spiritual gifts we far surpass others; but because we acknowledge these as gifts of God, not our own, granted to us for building up the body of Christ (Eph. 4:12), we do not become proud on their account. For we know that more is required of him to whom much is given than of him to whom little is given (Luke 12:48). In addition, we know that "God shows no partiality" (Rom. 2:11). Therefore a faithful sexton is no less pleasing to God with his gift than is a preacher of the Word, for he serves God in the same faith and spirit. And so we should not honor the lowest Christians any less than they honor us. In this way we remain free of the poison of vainglory and walk by the Spirit. (LW 27:103)

12:38–40 in Devotion and Prayer Jesus warns against using self-serving religion to elevate ourselves above others. Clergy especially need to listen to Jesus at this point. Jesus shows all religious leaders and scholars the model for their leadership: humility, service, and sacrifice, for His sacrifice has atoned for us all. • Lord, grant us humble hearts and willing spirits to fulfill our callings faithfully. Amen.

Jesus teaches His disciples through the widow's offering (12:41–44)

ESV	KJV
41 And he sat down opposite the treasury and watched the people putting money into the offering box. Many rich people put in large sums. 42 And a poor widow came and put in two small copper coins, which make a penny. 43 And he called his disciples to him and said to them, "Truly, I say to you, this poor widow has put in more than all those who are contributing to the offering box. 44 For they all contributed out of their abundance, but she out of her poverty has put in everything she had, all she had to live on."	41 And Jesus sat over against the treasury, and beheld how the people cast money into the treasury: and many that were rich cast in much. 42 And there came a certain poor widow, and she threw in two mites, which make a farthing. 43 And he called unto him his disciples, and saith unto them, Verily I say unto you, That this poor widow hath cast more in, than all they which have cast into the treasury: 44 For all they did cast in of their abundance; but she of her want did cast in all that she had, even all her living.

12:41 *offering box.* Thirteen offering boxes were in the court of the women for such offerings. *Many rich people put in large sums.* This pericope begins with the grandeur of the temple and the rich people putting in lavish amounts. Jesus was recently questioned about giving tax to Caesar (12:14), and has also just cleansed the temple of dishonest dealing and trafficking in the sacrificial animals (11:15–19). Given His warnings against the hypocrisy of the scribes (12:38–40), we expect that He might show the emptiness of the offerings of the rich.

12:42 *a poor widow came.* Instead of focusing on the rich, Jesus points out the unnoticed widow. In the context of the rich, she slipped in quietly and her offering made no sound and certainly no impression on those who saw her. *copper coins.* These were the smallest coins in use. This would add up to 1/64th of a denarius, the denarius being the average wage for one day's work. It was a very small amount, unless it was all you had.

12:43 H*e called His disciples.* While there was a crowd there, Jesus taught quietly to the small circle, perhaps to safeguard the widow's privacy. She had come with the sincere desire to give to God and was the complete opposite of the empty show of the scribes (12:38–39), and the rich. *more.* She gave proportionately more than all the others. Jesus shows that this is the true estimation by which God views our gifts. See 2Co 8 for more whereby the Macedonians were commended for giving generously out of their poverty and affliction (v. 2), and that one's gift is viewed according to what one has, not what one lacks (v. 12). Bengel wrote, "He thus gives us a specimen of the judgment which He will hereafter exercise, according to the state of hearts" (Bengel 559).

12:44 *they contributed out of their abundance.* The gifts of the rich were from the easy overflow of their abundance. Nothing was seriously missing in their lives because of their gift. We suspect also that they gave so that they would receive back recognition for the large amount. *put in everything she had.* The widow kept nothing for herself (cf. 10:21; Rm 12:1–2). In her quiet, unnoticed way, with this small gift, she expected nothing in return from those who saw her. However, her gift recalls the generosity and faith of the widow of Zarephath who, in the deadly famine, shared her very last meal with Elijah. Thereafter, her flour and oil never failed (1Ki 17:8–16). The widow in Mark showed similar faith in God's providing. Calvin writes, "Our Lord applauds this sincerity, because, forgetting herself, she wished to testify that she and all that she possessed belonged to God" (*Harmony* 3:114). Her astonishing gift also foreshadows the offering of Jesus' whole life as the perfect sacrifice, the Lamb of God. He laid down His life and entrusted Himself into the care of the Father's hands (Lk 23:46).

12:41–44 in Devotion and Prayer Jesus uses the sacrifice of a widow to illustrate for His disciples the character of absolute dependence on God. Wealth and possession can pose a spiritual threat—wealth has a way of owning its possessor. Jesus' love and sacrifice motivate us to offer our whole lives to Him as our daily offering of gratitude. He gave up everything, including His life, on the cross for us. • "Take my life and let it be Consecrated, Lord, to Thee; Take my moments and my days, Let them flow in ceaseless praise." Amen. (*LSB* 783:1; *H82* 707:1; *TPH* 391:1; *TUMH* 399:1)

Jesus teaches His disciples in light of His rejection by the religious authorities ("The Eschatological Discourse"; ch. 13)

Jesus predicts the temple's destruction (13:1–2)

ESV	KJV
13 [1]And as he came out of the temple, one of his disciples said to him, "Look, Teacher, what wonderful stones and what wonderful buildings!" [2]And Jesus said to him, "Do you see these great buildings? There will not be left here one stone upon another that will not be thrown down."	13 [1]And as he went out of the temple, one of his disciples saith unto him, Master, see what manner of stones and what buildings are here! [2]And Jesus answering said unto him, Seest thou these great buildings? there shall not be left one stone upon another, that shall not be thrown down.

Introduction to 13:1–2 Jesus goes from discussing the two copper coins of the widow (12:41–44) to the enormous stones of the temple. However, the faith of the widow is what will be needed when the stones of the temple come falling down. Jesus answers His disciples' question (v. 4) about the destruction of the temple, including descriptions of what the end of the world will be like. The events of AD 70, when the Romans will destroy Jerusalem (vv. 1–23, 28–31), foreshadow the end of the world (vv. 24–27). The close comparison of these events has confused some interpreters, especially those intent on determining when Christ will return. In reading ch. 13, remember Jesus' most important point: judgment comes unexpectedly; therefore, remain faithful.

13:1 *wonderful stones . . . buildings!* Huge stone blocks, some measuring thirty-seven feet long, eighteen feet wide, and twelve feet high, and some decorated with gold, were used to build Herod's temple complex, one of the most impressive man-made structures of the ancient world. In contrast to these mammoth stones, the two copper coins of the frail widow (12:42) seem as nothing.

13:2 *do you see these great buildings?* Jesus accepts the diversion to look at the temple. He invites the disciples to take in the whole view. They likely expected Him to point out some example of beauty and grandeur. *There will not be left here one stone.* Every one of the stones would be torn down in AD 70 by the Romans and never rebuilt. The destruction of the temple will introduce the following discussion on the end of the world. How could God allow such impressive beauty, the meeting place of God and man, to be destroyed? That, of course, is the question we ponder as the Passion Week unfolds and the perfect temple—God's Son—goes forward to His destruction.

13:1–2 in Devotion and Prayer Jesus begins to talk about the fall of Jerusalem and the end of the world with a prediction of the temple's destruction. What makes a house of worship worthy is not its outward appearance but the Word of God in it. The temple in Jerusalem had been the "embassy" of heaven on earth. With the coming of Jesus, this temple would no longer serve that purpose. Now, in Jesus Christ, the fullness of the Godhead dwells bodily among us (Col 2:9). • "To this temple, where we call You, Come, O Lord of hosts, and stay; Come with all Your loving-kindness, Hear Your people as they pray." Amen. (*LSB* 909:2; *H82* 518:3; *TPH* 416, 417:2; *TUMH* 559:2)

The signs and warnings (13:3–37)

ESV	KJV
[3]And as he sat on the Mount of Olives opposite the temple, Peter and James and John and Andrew asked him privately, [4]"Tell us, when will these things be, and what will be the sign when all these things are about to be accomplished?" [5]And Jesus began to say to them, "See that no one leads you astray. [6]Many will come in my name, saying, 'I am he!' and they will lead many astray. [7]And when you hear of wars and rumors of wars, do not be alarmed. This must take place, but the end is not yet. [8]For nation will rise against nation, and kingdom against kingdom. There will be earthquakes in various places; there will be famines. These are but the beginning of the birth pains. [9]"But be on your guard. For they will deliver you over to councils, and you will be beaten in synagogues, and you will stand before governors and	[3]And as he sat upon the mount of Olives over against the temple, Peter and James and John and Andrew asked him privately, [4]Tell us, when shall these things be? and what shall be the sign when all these things shall be fulfilled? [5]And Jesus answering them began to say, Take heed lest any man deceive you: [6]For many shall come in my name, saying, I am Christ; and shall deceive many. [7]And when ye shall hear of wars and rumours of wars, be ye not troubled: for such things must needs be; but the end shall not be yet. [8]For nation shall rise against nation, and kingdom against kingdom: and there shall be earthquakes in divers places, and there shall be famines and troubles: these are the beginnings of sorrows.

kings for my sake, to bear witness
before them. [10]And the gospel must
first be proclaimed to all nations.
[11]And when they bring you to trial
and deliver you over, do not be anxious beforehand what you are to say,
but say whatever is given you in that
hour, for it is not you who speak, but
the Holy Spirit. [12]And brother will
deliver brother over to death, and the
father his child, and children will rise
against parents and have them put to
death. [13]And you will be hated by all
for my name's sake. But the one who
endures to the end will be saved.

[14]"But when you see the abomination of desolation standing where
he ought not to be (let the reader
understand), then let those who are
in Judea flee to the mountains. [15]Let
the one who is on the housetop not
go down, nor enter his house, to take
anything out, [16]and let the one who
is in the field not turn back to take
his cloak. [17]And alas for women who
are pregnant and for those who are
nursing infants in those days! [18]Pray
that it may not happen in winter.
[19]For in those days there will be such
tribulation as has not been from the
beginning of the creation that God
created until now, and never will be.
[20]And if the Lord had not cut short
the days, no human being would be
saved. But for the sake of the elect,
whom he chose, he shortened the
days. [21]And then if anyone says to
you, 'Look, here is the Christ!' or
'Look, there he is!' do not believe it.
[22]For false christs and false prophets
will arise and perform signs and wonders, to lead astray, if possible, the
elect. [23]But be on guard; I have told
you all things beforehand.

[9]But take heed to yourselves: for they shall deliver you up to councils; and in the synagogues ye shall be beaten: and ye shall be brought before rulers and kings for my sake, for a testimony against them.

[10]And the gospel must first be published among all nations.

[11]But when they shall lead you, and deliver you up, take no thought beforehand what ye shall speak, neither do ye premeditate: but whatsoever shall be given you in that hour, that speak ye: for it is not ye that speak, but the Holy Ghost.

[12]Now the brother shall betray the brother to death, and the father the son; and children shall rise up against their parents, and shall cause them to be put to death.

[13]And ye shall be hated of all men for my name's sake: but he that shall endure unto the end, the same shall be saved.

[14]But when ye shall see the abomination of desolation, spoken of by Daniel the prophet, standing where it ought not, (let him that readeth understand,) then let them that be in Judaea flee to the mountains:

[15]And let him that is on the housetop not go down into the house, neither enter therein, to take any thing out of his house:

[16]And let him that is in the field not turn back again for to take up his garment.

[17]But woe to them that are with child, and to them that give suck in those days!

[18]And pray ye that your flight be not in the winter.

[19]For in those days shall be affliction, such as was not from the

24"But in those days, after that tribulation, the sun will be darkened, and
the moon will not give its light, 25and
the stars will be falling from heaven,
and the powers in the heavens will be
shaken. 26And then they will see the
Son of Man coming in clouds with
great power and glory. 27And then he
will send out the angels and gather
his elect from the four winds, from
the ends of the earth to the ends of
heaven.

28"From the fig tree learn its lesson:
as soon as its branch becomes tender and puts out its leaves, you know
that summer is near. 29So also, when
you see these things taking place,
you know that he is near, at the very
gates. 30Truly, I say to you, this generation will not pass away until all these
things take place. 31 Heaven and
earth will pass away, but my words
will not pass away.

32"But concerning that day or
that hour, no one knows, not even
the angels in heaven, nor the Son,
but only the Father. 33Be on guard,
keep awake. For you do not know
when the time will come. 34It is like
a man going on a journey, when he
leaves home and puts his servants
in charge, each with his work, and
commands the doorkeeper to stay
awake. 35Therefore stay awake—for
you do not know when the master of
the house will come, in the evening,
or at midnight, or when the rooster
crows, or in the morning—36lest he
come suddenly and find you asleep.
37And what I say to you I say to all:
Stay awake."

beginning of the creation which God
created unto this time, neither shall
be.

20And except that the Lord had
shortened those days, no flesh should
be saved: but for the elect's sake,
whom he hath chosen, he hath shortened the days.

21And then if any man shall say to
you, Lo, here is Christ; or, lo, he is
there; believe him not:

22For false Christs and false prophets shall rise, and shall shew signs and
wonders, to seduce, if it were possible, even the elect.

23But take ye heed: behold, I have
foretold you all things.

24But in those days, after that tribulation, the sun shall be darkened, and
the moon shall not give her light,

25And the stars of heaven shall fall,
and the powers that are in heaven
shall be shaken.

26And then shall they see the Son of
man coming in the clouds with great
power and glory.

27And then shall he send his angels,
and shall gather together his elect
from the four winds, from the
uttermost part of the earth to the
uttermost part of heaven.

28Now learn a parable of the fig
tree; When her branch is yet tender,
and putteth forth leaves, ye know that
summer is near:

29So ye in like manner, when ye shall
see these things come to pass, know
that it is nigh, even at the doors.

30Verily I say unto you, that this generation shall not pass, till all these
things be done.

31Heaven and earth shall pass away:
but my words shall not pass away.

32But of that day and that hour

knoweth no man, no, not the angels which are in heaven, neither the Son, but the Father.

33 Take ye heed, watch and pray: for ye know not when the time is.

34 For the Son of Man is as a man taking a far journey, who left his house, and gave authority to his servants, and to every man his work, and commanded the porter to watch.

35 Watch ye therefore: for ye know not when the master of the house cometh, at even, or at midnight, or at the cockcrowing, or in the morning:

36 Lest coming suddenly he find you sleeping.

37 And what I say unto you I say unto all, Watch.

Introduction to 13:3–13 Jesus has much to warn the disciples about the end times: the temple will be destroyed, war, earthquake and famine will come, and they will be hated, persecuted and killed. But it is not a hopeless time. Despite all this, the Gospel will be preached throughout the world with the power of the Holy Spirit. As believers persevere in faith, they will be saved.

This section begins the longest unit of uninterrupted teaching by Jesus in Mark (13:5–37). It unites the destruction of the temple, the death of Jesus, the end of the world, and the return of Jesus all into one narrative. While many details are challenging, the overall theme is clear: Jesus' death, resurrection, return, and judgment are the center of God's kingdom which will come despite the destruction of the end times.

13:3 *Peter and James and John and Andrew.* These are the first four disciples called (1:16–20) and they are once again the exclusive circle for these words on the end times. This is fitting also given the prominent role they will play in speaking the Gospel, suffering for their faith, and remaining faithful to the end. These actions are all key parts of vv. 9–13.

13:4 *tell us.* Formerly John and James had asked for a privileged place in the heavenly kingdom (10:35–37) and had been corrected and refused. But now these four ask for clarity and Jesus agrees to the extent they are able. Their asking is a change from the fear they had shown over His prediction of His own death and resurrection (9:32). *these things*. They are focused on the destruction of the temple (v. 2) and perhaps other events Jesus might have predicted. *sign*. The disciples expected that a sign (*semeion*), would come first. They hope for something distinctive and understandable. Yet, they need to be warned as to what that sign will be and its meaning. Jesus has already been asked for a sign but refused to give anything to the Pharisees (8:11–12).

13:5 *see that no one leads you astray.* The first sign will be the continuing presence of false Christs and would-be messiahs. Before any disaster of war or earthquake, this is the most serious marker. This sign is sadly constant in all times, but shows the world's hunger for a savior. The verb "leads you astray" (*planao*), has been used in 12:24, 27 to describe the errors of the Sadducees. See the notes there for the image of a wandering planet which imitates a fixed star. These false Christs will wander in and out of sight, each one briefly promising clear directions before he fades out of sight.

13:6 *in My name.* They will claim His titles of Christ, the anointed Messiah, and Jesus, the one who saves. They will play on His role as the intermediary between God and man, the true High Priest. But none will fulfill His work of being the Lamb of God who takes away the sin of the world, who chooses to die and then to rise again. None will be shown to be Son of God by baptism, transfiguration, death, and resurrection. Use His name—yes, they'll try. But do His deeds, never. *I am he!* They will take His title, using the phrase "I am" which recalls the very name of God in Ex 3:14, "I AM WHO I AM" and also recalls the seven I Am statements of Jesus in John. *lead many astray.* The bravado of these false claims, the hunger to be led, and the hardness of hearts to the true Shepherd will undo many.

13:7 *wars and rumors of wars, do not be alarmed.* Between this moment in AD 30 and the destruction of Jerusalem in AD 70, there would be many conflicts for the Jews throughout the Roman Empire. Furthermore, the sound of battle, real or imagined, will be heard throughout history. *This must take place.* God does not cause the bloodshed of war, but these conflicts will be necessary mile markers along the road to the end. War between nations, while terrible and costly, is not the end itself, nor is it the final conflict between God and His true enemy, the devil.

13:8 *earthquakes in various places . . . famines.* Besides the destruction of war between nations, there will be destruction within nature itself. Nations rise and collide against one another as the earth crashes within itself. Famines come as nature seems to fall out of tune with itself. Natural disasters often incite conflict between nations and so these signs march together across the globe. Put together, such natural disasters also turn men away from God as they blame Him for their trouble (Is 8:21–22). *the beginning of the birth pains.* Instead of seeing these events as disaster, Jesus compares them to the birth pains which ultimately bring joyous life. Certainly, war, earthquake, and famine are bitter and dangerous. However, Jesus' analogy of birth pains shows that these disasters last for a limited time and have a much greater purpose than painful destruction.

13:9 *be on your guard.* Watch, Jesus says, despite the reassurance of the previous verses. While wars, earthquake, and famine stretch across the globe, much closer will be the persecution against Christians. Persecution of Christians was common in the early centuries and is still widespread today in parts of the world. Being on guard does not prevent these persecutions but means there is no surprise when the oppression comes. *Councils . . . synagogues . . . governors and kings.* There is a progression from the immediate context of the councils in Jerusalem, even those secret meetings plotting Jesus' death (3:6; 12:12; 14:1–2, 10–11). However, the persecutions against Christians will spread throughout the empire as Christians disperse. Not only the leaders in Jewish synagogues, but also the Roman officials and kings of the empire will oppose them. The lives of Peter and Paul are a good example of this persecution and imprisonment by both Jews and Romans (Ac 4:3, 5ff.; 5:17–18ff.; 9:23ff., 12:1–5; 14:5; 16:22ff.; 23:26ff.; 26:1ff.).

13:10 *the gospel must first be proclaimed.* Before the end of the world and Judgment Day, the Gospel must be spread. God wants no one to be surprised or lost at the end. The message that has to go out is not merely warning of the coming end, but a call to repentance and faith in the mercy of God. Jonah's preaching to Nineveh is a small example of God's desire for the whole world. Before the promised destruction happened, Nineveh heard the preaching of Jonah and repented so that God's mercy came to the city. While not all will turn by hearing the Gospel, God earnestly desires it to be preached, heard and believed. *to all nations.* Jesus announces God's plan to include the Gentiles.

13:11 *do not be anxious beforehand . . . say whatever is given you.* While they were to foresee the coming persecution, they did not need to prepare their defense. Stepping forward into their trials, they were to have the courage of Daniel facing the lions' den. *not you who speak but the Holy Spirit.* The Holy Spirit will help them bear witness to the Gospel. This is not an excuse for poor preaching by those who know they will face their congregation each Sunday. This is the reassurance for those who cannot predict where, when, and how they will be challenged. Do not fear, for He who sees all things sends the Spirit to remind believers of all He has said and to lead them into truth (Jn 14:26; 15:7–11, 26). Calvin writes,

> Our Lord's design in these words is, to relieve the disciples from that anxiety which interferes with the cheerful discharge of our duty, when we doubt our inability to sustain the burden. Not that he wishes us to fall asleep in indolent security, for nothing is more advantageous than to have such a consciousness of our weakness as produces humility and excites to prayer. (*Harmony* 3:125)

13:12 *brother will deliver brother over to death.* Anti-Christian sentiment will divide families, even to the point of close relatives handing over loved ones for execution. Jesus came to bring a sword of division to the world (Mt 10:34–36). He places Himself and His followers into the center of the world's debate over Himself and His words. Jesus' coming trial and death carries this to the extreme. The Prince of Peace is abandoned, betrayed, and denied by His disciples and walks through a hateful crowd to His death.

13:13 *hated by all.* This universal hatred comes because God's Law offends and because Jesus claimed to be the only way to salvation (Jn 14:6). The disciples will be hated because of a greater hatred against Christ (Jn 15:18–21). The world, even while rejecting Him, hates Him for making the offer of salvation. *will be saved.* Endurance through trial is not itself a meritorious work that saves. Salvation is by faith which receives the gift of grace and the strength of endurance. Jesus' promise is clear: "Be faithful unto death and I will give you the crown of life" (Rv 2:10). While John and James had asked for a privileged place in the Kingdom (10:35–37), Jesus here offers every believer the privilege of sharing in His sufferings to become like Him in His death and resurrection (Php 3:10–11).

13:3–13 in Devotion and Prayer Jesus warns His disciples about the coming troubles they will face as they bring the Gospel into the world. He encourages them to trust God and rely on the Holy Spirit, especially when they face opposition and persecution. As Christians proclaim Law and Gospel, they need to be ready to endure the loss of everything, including their lives. Because God wants all people to hear the Gospel, He prolongs the NT age so that the Church may witness to all the earth. To Him alone we owe the survival of our personal faith as well. • "Lord of harvest, great and kind, Rouse to action heart and mind; Let the gath'ring nations all See Your light and heed Your call." Amen. (*LSB* 830:6)

Introduction to 13:14–23 Jesus' prophecy turns even darker as the abomination of desolation enters the Temple. He warns believers to flee, but assures them that God has limited the time of this persecution. As hopeless as this scene appears, there will still be faith and those saved by God's election and choice. Watch out against false Christs and wait for the true Christ who will come to rescue His people.

13:14 *abomination of desolation.* This key title repeats a prophecy recorded in Dn 9:27 about the desecration of the temple under the Seleucids (1Macc 1:54–59). Jesus announces a new desolation and destruction of the Jerusalem temple, which will be carried out by the Romans in AD 70. This event will end all temple worship and sacrifice. But these desolations are only a taste of what lies in the future. Second Thessalonians 2:3–4 describes the man of lawlessness, the son of destruction, who will embody the rebellion against God. *let the reader understand.* The reader is challenged to think about these things, especially in light of Dn 9:27. A similar need for wisdom is in Rv 13:18 with the number of the beast, 666. When confronted by the confusing images of such evil, it is good to remember the clear promise of God to provide wisdom through the Holy Spirit (13:11). Jesus is the victor over all enemies, holding the keys of death and Hades (Rv 1:17–18). *flee to the mountains.* When the revolution of AD 70 began, Christians fled to the Judean hills to escape being trapped within Jerusalem.

13:15 *housetop.* Ancient homes had flat roofs used as a second level for the family, an elevated deck or balcony. When the man on the roof sees this approaching destruction, he is to act immediately. *not go down.* Houses were often adjoined or close to one another, so one could run from roof to roof. Stairs were often outside the house. Eusebius reflects this when he wrote of these events, saying, "The people of the church in Jerusalem had been commanded by a revelation, vouchsafed to approved men there before the war, to leave the city and to dwell in a certain town of Perea called Pella" (*NPNF* 2 1:138).

13:16 *the one who is in the field.* As with the one on the roof, this man is simply working, not looking for this trouble. When he sees the approaching enemies, there is no time to waste. He should not even take something as essential as a cloak. With these images of the roof and field, Jesus emphasizes the sudden and inescapable nature of destruction. Flight is their only hope. *cloak.* The outer garment workers left at home or laid on the ground when working.

13:17 *alas.* This word (Gk *ouai*), is an interjection expressing horror. Also translated as "woe" (14:21). *Women who are pregnant . . . nursing.* It is more difficult for pregnant women and new mothers to flee. Their care for their children will become a burden for them, slowing their escape and making them worry about their children's welfare.

13:18 *Pray.* Even though destruction is looming, God's power and His willingness to shape the world for His people make us pray. God promises to limit the difficulty (v. 20) just as He promises to let no temptation come that is too great for us, but with every temptation to provide a way of escape (1Co 10:13). *winter.* The winter around Jerusalem is cool, wet, sometimes even bringing snow. Food would be scarce too. Other seasons would let them flee more quickly to safety.

13:19 *for in those days.* This suffering, highlighted by the Roman destruction of the temple in AD 70, will eclipse any previous suffering the Israelites experienced. It will be worse than the destruction of the temple and Jerusalem by the Babylonians in 586 BC, or the years of exile that followed. However, there is hope in that this will be a single event that will never be repeated. *tribulation.* This will be persecution due to faith in Jesus' word and promises. Such tribulation was the reason for some to fall from the faith as described in the parable of the sower (4:17). Many expect that faith in God will deliver them from experiencing difficulty. When such trouble comes, especially troubles such as the world has never seen, they might abandon the faith, fearing that God has abandoned them. Therefore Jesus tells of this trouble beforehand so that the disciples are not surprised.

13:20 *for the sake of the elect, whom He chose.* God has His hand over the persecutions and destruction to come, to limit it for the sake of His own. He is not the source of this destruction, but He puts a limit upon it and turns it to serve Him. This powerful oversight matches the doctrine of election by which God has known His own from the foundation of the world and has adopted them through the work of His Son (Eph 1:3–6). All the power and work of election and this protection is through His hand. *He shortened the days.* God limited the severity and the length of the persecution upon Jerusalem and the difficulties that will pursue even those who flee.

13:21 *here is Christ.* Jesus returns to the opening warning of vv. 5–6. The central danger of the end time is not the falling of kingdoms but the deception of the false Christs. Fear not those who kill only the body but fear those who by their lies destroy true faith and eternal life.

13:22 *false christs and false prophets.* This pairing recalls Jesus' asking who people thought He was (8:27–28). He was imagined to be one of the prophets or John the Baptist. There was the hope that prophets would return, especially one like Elijah (Mal 4:5; Mt 17:10–12), a hope fulfilled with John the Baptist. *signs and wonders.* Genuine signs and wonders do come, as in Ac 4:30, as a witness to the Gospel and the power of Jesus' resurrection. However, counterfeit miracles can mislead people and draw them away from Jesus, the only Savior. Jesus had already been asked for a confirming sign (8:11–12), but He refused because they would not believe. The sign of Jonah has already been given and He will fulfill that sign by His death and resurrection.

13:23 *be on your guard.* Jesus repeats the same warning of v. 9 to conclude this section. He is faithful in His promise to protect and return and we are to be faithful in trustful watching. Luther writes:

> For this much is sure: So long as a Christian preacher holds on and sticks to his business, despising the world's abuse and persecution, the ministry will abide and the Gospel cannot fail; for some will always stand firm and abide, as indeed there must always be some that abide, until Judgment Day. (LW 21:64–65)

13:14–23 in Devotion and Prayer Jesus warns His followers of the imminent destruction of Jerusalem, which was fulfilled during the Jewish revolt against the Romans (AD 66–70). These events foreshadow the end of the world. Jesus tells us these things so that we may be prepared to resist evil and proclaim the Gospel more fervently while we have time to do so. When Jesus returns on the Last Day, He will judge all people. Prior to that glorious and victorious day, evil will erupt and bring destruction. Yet, God holds on to His people throughout these events, anchoring believers in Jesus Christ by His Holy Spirit. • "Jerusalem the golden, With milk and honey blest—The promise of salvation, The place of peace and rest—We know not, oh, we know not What joys await us there: The radiancy of glory, The bliss beyond compare!" Amen. (*LSB* 672:1; *H82* 624:1)

Introduction to 13:24–31 Jesus turns our attention to the large and small events of creation as signs of the end. The great things of the cosmos—sun, moon, and stars—will be shaken and fall. But He will come in the midst of this to gather His own. Then Jesus gives a lesson from the simple fig tree leaves with the message: Be alert for He is near.

13:24 *tribulation*. See the notes on 13:19 for this key word. *sun will be darkened . . . moon will not give its light*. This darkness will undo the fourth day of creation (Gn 1:14) on the Last Day. A prelude to this final darkness will come during the last three hours of Jesus' time on the cross (15:33). Sin's weight and penalty settled upon Him with all its darkness. But with Jesus' death, God instituted peace between Himself and the world, restoring the light (Col 1:20). The loss of these lights of the sky, however, will be the prelude of a new heaven and new earth (Rv 21:1). The new heaven will have no need for sun or moon, for God is its light (Rv 21:23).

13:25 *stars will be falling . . . powers in the heavens will be shaken*. These are the final heavenly elements that will be lost. When sun, moon, and stars fail, then the world has truly lost its way and the end has come. Jesus is the one who holds all things together as the head of all (Eph 1:22). The failure of these powers turns our attention to Him alone.

13:26 *Son of Man coming*. The title "Son of Man" is first used by Jesus in 2:10. See notes there for the range of its uses in Mark and background in Daniel. This is the final image of glory with the Son of Man before the betrayal of Him in 14:21, 41. *Clouds with great power* *and glory.* He is the magnificent king of heaven, but also the one willing to be betrayed in a setting of darkness and fear. While the great lights of sun, moon, and stars have failed, Jesus fills the darkness of heaven with His own presence as He comes with the clouds. His glory owes nothing to the creation, but He is the light and power Himself. The darkness of that final sky and the darkness of Calvary both show the true glory of the Son of Man.

13:27 *send His angels.* The angels here are the glorious servants seen also in 8:38 as part of His return. The first use of the word *angelos*, translated here "angels," was in 1:2. There it is translated "messenger," referring to John the Baptist. The Gospel begins with a messenger who prepares the Son of Man's way so that, when He returns with His angels, His people will be ready and gathered. *His elect.* See notes on 13:20 for the first use of this term to describe believers. See also Eph 1:4–5 for His election of believers before the foundation of the world. Before creation's start, He has known His own, created their faith, preserved them, and gathered them as creation comes to an end. *four winds . . . ends of the earth.* The elect come from every tribe and nation, without limit as to their background (Rv 7:9). He will gather them from the very ends of the earth to the edge of heaven.

13:24–27 in Devotion and Prayer Jesus will return on the Last Day to judge all humanity, fulfilling OT prophecy and His own predictions. No one will enter the kingdom of God by works, nor will any mere religion save anyone. Because Jesus died and rose for us and because the Holy Spirit created and sustained saving faith in His people, we can be sure of our salvation, no matter how fearsome the Last Day may be. • Set my heart, O Savior, on the life and hope above, so that shadows of this world may not darken my sight. Amen.

13:28 *from the fig tree learn its lesson.* Jesus goes from the sublime to the simple, from the barely imagined heavens to the familiar fig tree. His use of the fig tree parallels His love of parables (ch. 4) and His incarnation joining the human and divine. Because fig trees produce two crops each year, they became proverbial for the passing of the seasons. Unlike many trees in Israel, the fig sheds its leaves each fall. New leaves appear relatively late in spring and indicate that warm weather is about to arrive.

13:29 *these things.* Jesus is referring to the fall of Jerusalem and the destruction of the temple (v. 2), and also the rise of false christs

(vv. 5, 21–22) and the abomination approaching the temple (v. 14). *He is near.* Or, "It is nigh" (KJV). The text can be translated either way, but regardless, it is the fulfillment of the prophecy of v. 2. Jesus began His ministry with the joyous news that the time had been fulfilled and the kingdom of God had drawn near (1:15). Though the false christs, the enemy armies, and the falling stars all vie for attention, look instead for the true Christ who is approaching. The fig leaves are nothing in themselves; it is the summer's coming that matters. So these events matter only as arrows pointing to His nearness.

13:30 *generation will not pass.* Within one generation (c. 40 years) the temple will lie in ruins. The term "generation" (*genea*) generally means the time itself or the people within that time, either the whole body of people or the people of a certain characteristic. Jesus might have been speaking of the sort of people of that time, the sharply inquisitive Pharisees and Sadducees who refused to see Him as the Son of God. That type of denial will not cease, not only through AD 70 but even through the end of time.

13:31 *heaven and earth.* Up to this point, destruction has been piecemeal—the temple (v. 2), wars (v. 7), earthquakes (v. 8), even the heavenly lights darkening (vv. 24–25). But now the end of all things has come. Heaven and earth, all that has been made, will reach the end of its life so that a new creation can come (Rv 21:1). *My words will not pass away.* However, do not speculate on the new heaven and earth but set your hearts on the Word which you already have and which will not change. The Word of God, by which God spoke creation into being, will last longer than creation. Interestingly, the word *parerchomai,* "pass away," will next appear in 14:35 when Jesus asks if the bitter cup of His suffering and death could pass away. However, He was obedient to the Father's plan, and so even the harsh end of the cross was fulfilled.

13:28–31 in Devotion and Prayer Jesus answers the original question when the disciples asked when the temple would be destroyed (v. 4). The events of vv. 14–23 will take place within a generation. The fall of Jerusalem foreshadows the end of the world, which will come later (vv. 24–27). Today, we need to focus on the calling we have as Christ's Church: Gospel proclamation and outreach (cf. Mt 28:18–20). God has created this time before the second appearing of Jesus so that we may come to faith and call others to faith and salvation. • "My Savior paid the debt I owe And for my sin was smitten; Within the Book of Life I know My name has now been written. I will not doubt, for I am free, And Satan cannot threaten me; There is no condemnation!" Amen. (*LSB* 508:5)

Introduction to 13:32–37 Just as He did with the lesson of the fig tree (vv. 28–29), so here Jesus summarizes His message of the end times with an analogy of familiar domestic life. The master is out of sight but will soon return. Wise servants will be watching and ready.

13:32 *concerning that day or hour.* Jesus knows that our natural curiosity remains fixed on the final day. Given the information of the previous verses, many might hope to be able to discern the exact time of His return. However, He ends this speculation by declaring it a mystery known only to the Father. *no one knows.* Bengel notes that Jesus spoke according to His human nature and His state of humility (Bengel 562). Jesus did not always speak from His divine power of foreknowledge. According to His divine nature, He is one with the Father (Jn 10:30), and He is in very nature God (Php 2:6; Col 2:9). By this divine nature He knows the end time. But we might also speak of His human nature which shares our own limitations of knowledge. It is of His human nature, for example, that Lk 2:52 speaks when it says that He increased in wisdom and stature. *only the Father.* God knows His plans and reveals what He chooses to whom He chooses. We can rest secure that this time is known and the Father will unfold it according to His plan.

13:33 *be on guard.* This is the last time that Jesus uses this word, *blepo,* translated "be on guard." He has frequently warned His disciples to keep themselves from Pharisaical teaching (8:15), and that of the scribes (12:38). He has used it in this section to warn against the coming deception and persecution (13:5, 9, 23). Though the elect are His own to be gathered by the angels (v. 27), they are to remain alert in faith for His coming. *you do not know.* No one knows when the events Jesus prophesied will take place; therefore, Christians are to focus on the work He has given them (Mt 9:38). Augustine reminds us, "Let no one then search out for the last Day, when it is to be; but let us watch all by our good lives, lest the last day of any one of us find us unprepared" (*NPNF*1 6:411).

13:34 *it is like a man going.* Jesus returns to a parable as a summary of His teaching. This parable of a man returning to his own property recalls the parable of the tenants (12:1–12), in which a man sent his servants and son to gather his goods from the tenants. However, they killed the son in the parable, which matches the Pharisees' and leaders' plans to kill Jesus (12:12). So Jesus' parable here will also further their plans against Him (14:1–2). *puts his servants in charge.* The servants have genuine work and authority here. In contrast to James and John seeking authority and glory in heaven (10:37), Christians have important roles to fulfill here as watchful servants.

13:37 *Stay awake.* Jesus repeats the same word, *gragoreo,* that He used in v. 35. (He will use the same word in 14:34, 37–38, commanding the disciples to stay awake during His Gethsemane prayer.) As the end of time draws near, remain alert to proclaim the Gospel and practice the faith. St. Augustine writes,

> When it tells us to watch for the last day, every one should think of [this] as concerning his own last day; lest haply when you judge or think the last day of the world to be far distant, you slumber with respect to your own last day. (*NPNF*1 6:411)

evening . . . midnight . . . rooster crows . . . morning. These are the four watches of the night, each segment lasting three hours, beginning at 6:00 p.m. and going to 6:00 a.m. Jesus' return is pictured at night to stress the need for extraordinary watchfulness.

13:36 *lest he come suddenly.* Heaven bursts suddenly upon earth. It reminds us of the heavenly chorus coming to the shepherds (Lk 2:13), or Jesus' blinding light and voice upon Saul (Ac 9:3). His coming can be either Gospel or Law, the light of salvation or the piercing light which exposes every dark act. *find you asleep.* This sleep would be the laziness or arrogance that says the Master cannot and will not return. Do not be that servant doomed to condemnation. Be the servant who gladly hears His approach from a distance.

13:37 *what I say to you . . . all.* Jesus speaks beyond the circle of Peter, Andrew, James, and John (13:3), which began this section. The destruction of Jerusalem, the new creation, and the gathering of the world's faithful concern all people. Not only are the church's leaders to watch; all believers need to watch daily for His return. As each has his work, so each has to watch.

13:32–37 in Devotion and Prayer In contrast to the fall of Jerusalem (vv. 5–23), which will happen within a generation, no one knows the day when Jesus will return to judge the world (vv. 24–27). Jesus exhorts us to vigilance and encourages us to use the available time wisely, proclaiming the Gospel for the salvation of others. Jesus promises to be with us always and has poured out His Holy Spirit for the work of evangelizing the nations. • "The world is very evil, The times are waxing late; Be sober and keep vigil, The Judge is at the gate; The Judge that comes in mercy, The Judge that comes with might, To terminate the evil, To diadem the right." Amen. (*TLH* 605:1)

Jesus' Passion, Death, and Resurrection (14:1–16:8)

Jesus is anointed at Bethany amid a plot to have Him arrested and killed (14:1–11)

ESV	KJV
14 1 It was now two days before the Passover and the Feast of Unleavened Bread. And the chief priests and the scribes were seeking how to arrest him by stealth and kill him, 2 for they said, "Not during the feast, lest there be an uproar from the people." **3 And while he was at Bethany in the house of Simon the leper, as he was reclining at table, a woman came with an alabaster flask of ointment of pure nard, very costly, and she broke the flask and poured it over his head. 4 There were some who said to themselves indignantly, "Why was the ointment wasted like that? 5 For this ointment could have been sold for more than three hundred denarii and given to the poor." And they scolded her. 6 But Jesus said, "Leave her alone. Why do you trouble her? She has done a beautiful thing to me. 7 For you always have the poor with you, and whenever you want, you can do good for them. But you will not always have me. 8 She has done what she could; she has anointed my body beforehand for burial. 9 And truly, I say to you, wherever the gospel is proclaimed in the whole world, what she has done will be told in memory of her."**	**14 1 After two days was the feast of the passover, and of unleavened bread: and the chief priests and the scribes sought how they might take him by craft, and put him to death.** **2 But they said, Not on the feast day, lest there be an uproar of the people.** **3 And being in Bethany in the house of Simon the leper, as he sat at meat, there came a woman having an alabaster box of ointment of spikenard very precious; and she brake the box, and poured it on his head.** **4 And there were some that had indignation within themselves, and said, Why was this waste of the ointment made?** **5 For it might have been sold for more than three hundred pence, and have been given to the poor. And they murmured against her.** **6 And Jesus said, Let her alone; why trouble ye her? she hath wrought a good work on me.** **7 For ye have the poor with you always, and whensoever ye will ye may do them good: but me ye have not always.** **8 She hath done what she could: she is come aforehand to anoint my body to the burying.**

[10]Then Judas Iscariot, who was one of the twelve, went to the chief priests in order to betray him to them. [11]And when they heard it, they were glad and promised to give him money. And he sought an opportunity to betray him.

[9]Verily I say unto you, Wheresoever this gospel shall be preached throughout the whole world, this also that she hath done shall be spoken of for a memorial of her.

[10]And Judas Iscariot, one of the twelve, went unto the chief priests, to betray him unto them.

[11]And when they heard it, they were glad, and promised to give him money. And he sought how he might conveniently betray him.

Introduction to 14:1–11 Jesus' teaching has provoked the chief priests and scribes once again to plot His death. (See a similar pattern in 3:1–6; 12:1–12.) However, they do so in fear of the crowd which still supports Him. But our attention is not on the priests or crowd. The silent generosity of the woman is the witness of love and faith that lasts. Despite her act of love, His enemies will continue to scheme and recruit Judas for the betrayal. This section is another example of Mark's A-B-A structure, which begins a story, inserts another, and then concludes the first story. See notes on 3:21 for the other locations.

14:1 *two days before.* This was Wednesday of Holy Week. *Passover.* This is the important feast commemorating God's deliverance of His people from Egypt (cf. Ex 12:1–14). Central to the Passover was the sacrifice of the lamb whose blood protected the people from death that night. Jesus comes as the perfect Lamb of God slain to carry the sins of the people (Jn 1:29; Is 53:7, 10). *Feast of Unleavened Bread.* The Feast was the seven days that followed Passover (cf. Ex 12:15–20). The whole festival could be called by either name. *kill Him.* They had gone far from merely sending messengers to question Him (11:27; 12:13, 18). This was not a simple assassination but a plan to entrap Him legally. Then they could appear justified and He be declared guilty. Unknown to them, this was the plan of God by which the world would be justified (2Co 5:19–21).

14:2 *not during the feast.* How ironic that they safeguard the feast and themselves even while destroying the Lord of Life. They likely fear that Jesus will publicly declare Himself the Messiah in the temple during Passover and start a revolt against the Romans. *lest* *there be an uproar.* The word for "uproar," *thorubos,* is used only twice in Mk, here and in 5:38 to describe the uproar and despair over the death of the little girl. If they were to arrest Jesus and kill Him, there should be a despair and rage far beyond the grief around the girl. The crowd clamoring for His death was the astonishing opposite of this fear.

14:1–2 in Devotion and Prayer The Jerusalem leaders desperately try to find a way to execute Jesus quickly and quietly before He gains full support for His mission. Yet, God is at work in this, using even the opposition of His enemies for His gracious purposes. The Lord is likewise at work in the events of our lives today, bringing about good even amidst suffering. Pray for His aid and comfort while trusting He has a plan for you. How joyful to know His plan of salvation in Jesus, who has taken away all our sins. • Sustain us, dearest Jesus, for You are the bread of life we celebrate, our life and hope to come. Amen.

14:3 *Simon the leper.* Simon was a man who had been afflicted with a skin disease but was cured, possibly by Jesus. *a woman came.* John 12:1–8 tells us that this was Mary, sister of Martha and Lazarus. *alabaster.* This is a semitransparent stone that could be made into a vessel for liquids. The neck had to be broken in order to empty it fully. *pure nard.* This was the fragrant oil made from crushed rhizomes of the spikenard plant. Described as pure nard, it was likely of the finest grade. As seen in v. 5, it was essentially worth a year's wages, an extraordinary amount for perfume. When she pours it over His head, she acts upon Jesus' true title of the Christ, the anointed One. However, this anointing is not for life as prophet, priest, or king, but for His death as the One sacrificed for all.

14:4 *some who said to themselves indignantly.* Beginning with 2:8, Jesus has shown that He knows the thoughts of all. Here again, He uncovers their complaint and responds. *Why was the ointment wasted.* How short-sighted to complain of the loss of perfume. The Son of God is about to be poured out in offering for the sin of the world, but their concern is the small vial of perfume and the value of one year's work. They see neither the generous beauty of the woman's gift nor the majesty of the Savior's sacrifice.

14:5 *given to the poor.* Jesus' ministry likely included charity for the poor. It is doubtful that these men actually care about the poor. They use this as a cover for their own greed. She has upstaged them, done an extraordinary thing which they never imagined, and so they have to attack her to defend themselves.

14:6 *leave her alone.* Jesus has to defend someone seeking Him here, just as He did when the mothers wanted to bring their children to Him (10:14). *why do you trouble her?* Jesus' question is a sweeping accusation to be asked whenever those who do generous deeds are attacked. Why accuse the kind-hearted? Does their generosity stand as a stinging contrast to our own nature? When they do what we never imagine doing, why question their motives or actions? Rather than learn, we lash out. *beautiful thing.* Her gift was as lovely in itself as the fragrance that filled the room. Its goodness (Gk *kalos*), was beautiful for its own sake, not merely useful, but intrinsically noble. Her generosity was more beautiful since she, like the widow of 12:42, poured out all that she had within the bottle. She was a picture of whole-hearted generosity. Beyond that, she did this looking ahead to His death and burial. Her fragrant gift, poured out without reserve, is a reminder of His sacrificial death, "a fragrant offering and sacrifice to God" (Eph 5:2).

14:7 *you always have the poor with you.* Deuteronomy 15:11 says that the poor will never cease and therefore be generous to their need. Jesus doesn't contradict this command as His ministry was largely among the poor and He repeatedly met their needs, such as feeding the 5,000 and 4,000. *but you will not always have Me.* Mary understood that His time with them was short and this was her last chance to show her love in this way. Mary grasped what the disciples had misunderstood or avoided—He was going to suffer and die very soon. She faced this sad truth with generous action. In this she was the complete opposite of the fearful, plotting leaders, vv. 1–2, and greedy Judas, vv.10–11.

14:8 *she has done what she could.* Mary is the latest in a line of those who brought all they had. The poor widow gave her two coins, mothers brought their children, the desperate woman brought herself through the crowd to touch Him. It is not the amount itself but the fact that it is all that one has and all that one can do. Jesus had summarized the Law as loving God with all one's heart, soul, mind and strength (12:30). Mary demonstrated that with her generosity. *anointed . . . for burial.* Rather than embalming, Israelites used ointments and spices to prepare a body for burial. Mary understood that His death was coming and this was her chance to anoint Him. She beautified His death by her generosity. Correspondingly, His death perfects all believers so He can "present the church himself in splendor, without spot or wrinkle or any such thing" (Eph 5:27).

14:9 *what she has done will be in memory of her.* This is a prophecy fulfilled even now as Christians read of this woman's deep love for Jesus. Luther writes: "To love Christ, to confess Christ, and to take pleasure in Him—this does not happen without the Holy Spirit. To confess the faith, to bear the hatred of the world, to undergo exile and death—all this is proof of the Spirit" (LW 30:298). Her beautiful generosity is the warm light that shines between the dark plot, vv. 1–2, and the selfish grasping of Judas, vv. 10–11.

14:3–9 in Devotion and Prayer A woman anoints Jesus for His burial, sacrificing expensive ointment out of love for Him. The woman's clear focus on Jesus testifies to her devotion toward Him. Her sacrifice reveals her deep love for Him and sets a wonderful example for later Christians. Today, devote yourself to Jesus by prayer and service. He now stands at the Father's throne, praying for you, serving as your Savior. • "I'll think upon Thy mercy without ceasing, That earth's vain joys to me no more be pleasing; To do Thy will shall be my sole endeavor Henceforth forever." Amen. (*LSB* 439:12)

14:10 *Judas Iscariot.* In startling contrast to the woman whose deed is unforgettable, Judas steps forward. What he does will also be etched on our minds for his faithless betrayal. The plot against Jesus reaches the chief priests themselves and one of His select Twelve. *went . . . in order to betray.* Judas is needed to lead the authorities to Jesus at a time and place where they can arrest Him quietly. Judas is not caught or bewitched by the priests but goes of his own will. John 13:2 explains that Satan had put it into Judas' heart to betray Him. Satan had failed in His direct confrontations with Jesus, either in temptation (1:12–13), or in the three demons cast out in chs. 1, 5, 9. Now he directs Judas as he once tempted Adam and Eve. However, God has harnessed the evil of the tempter and turned it for His own purpose.

14:11 *they were glad and promised to give him money.* What a contrast to the disciples' furious protests over Mary's extravagant anointing (vv. 4–5). Here the priests gladly spend money for the one who will betray the Master. Greed, no doubt, played a part in Judas' decision to betray Jesus (cf. Jn 12:6). *he sought an opportunity.* The word for opportunity, *eukairos*, is the adverbial form of the same word which is used to describe Herodias, Herod's wife, as she sought a time to kill John the Baptist (6:21). Of the Gospel writers, only

Mark uses these two words and only here and at 6:21. What a pair these two are, Judas and Herodias! Both are seeking the right time to destroy the forerunner, John, and the greater One to come, Jesus.

14:10–11 in Devotion and Prayer Judas, one of the Twelve whom Jesus appointed, decides to betray Jesus to the authorities. Even Judas's betrayal plays an important role in the plan of salvation, culminating in the cross and empty tomb. Judas does this, thinking to grasp a few coins. But Jesus allows this in order to save the world. • My sinful heart would betray You, dear Lord, and arrest my faith. Deliver me from evil by Your grace. Amen.

Jesus celebrates the Passover with His disciples, predicts His betrayal, and institutes the Lord's Supper (14:12–25)

ESV	KJV
12 And on the first day of Unleavened Bread, when they sacrificed the Passover lamb, his disciples said to him, "Where will you have us go and prepare for you to eat the Passover?" 13 And he sent two of his disciples and said to them, "Go into the city, and a man carrying a jar of water will meet you. Follow him, 14 and wherever he enters, say to the master of the house, 'The Teacher says, Where is my guest room, where I may eat the Passover with my disciples?' 15 And he will show you a large upper room furnished and ready; there prepare for us." 16 And the disciples set out and went to the city and found it just as he had told them, and they prepared the Passover. 17 And when it was evening, he came with the twelve. 18 And as they were reclining at table and eating, Jesus said, "Truly, I say to you, one of you will betray me, one who is eating	12 And the first day of unleavened bread, when they killed the passover, his disciples said unto him, Where wilt thou that we go and prepare that thou mayest eat the passover? 13 And he sendeth forth two of his disciples, and saith unto them, Go ye into the city, and there shall meet you a man bearing a pitcher of water: follow him. 14 And wheresoever he shall go in, say ye to the goodman of the house, The Master saith, Where is the guestchamber, where I shall eat the passover with my disciples? 15 And he will shew you a large upper room furnished and prepared: there make ready for us. 16 And his disciples went forth, and came into the city, and found as he had said unto them: and they made ready the passover. 17 And in the evening he cometh with the twelve.

**with me." [19]They began to be sor-
rowful and to say to him one after
another, "Is it I?" [20]He said to them,
"It is one of the twelve, one who is
dipping bread into the dish with me.
[21]For the Son of Man goes as it is written of him, but woe to that man by
whom the Son of Man is betrayed! It
would have been better for that man
if he had not been born."**

**[22]And as they were eating, he took
bread, and after blessing it broke it
and gave it to them, and said, "Take;
this is my body." [23]And he took a
cup, and when he had given thanks
he gave it to them, and they all drank
of it. [24]And he said to them, "This is
my blood of the covenant, which is
poured out for many. [25]Truly, I say to
you, I will not drink again of the fruit
of the vine until that day when I drink
it new in the kingdom of God."**

**[18]And as they sat and did eat, Jesus
said, Verily I say unto you, One of you
which eateth with me shall betray me.**

**[19]And they began to be sorrowful,
and to say unto him one by one, Is it
I? and another said, Is it I?**

**[20]And he answered and said unto
them, It is one of the twelve, that dip-
peth with me in the dish.**

**[21]The Son of man indeed goeth, as it
is written of him: but woe to that man
by whom the Son of man is betrayed!
good were it for that man if he had
never been born.**

**[22]And as they did eat, Jesus took
bread, and blessed, and brake it, and
gave to them, and said, Take, eat: this
is my body.**

**[23]And he took the cup, and when he
had given thanks, he gave it to them:
and they all drank of it.**

**[24]And he said unto them, This is my
blood of the new testament, which is
shed for many.**

**[25]Verily I say unto you, I will drink
no more of the fruit of the vine, until
that day that I drink it new in the
kingdom of God.**

Introduction to 14:12–25 Following the dinner at Bethany (vv. 3–9), and the final step in the plot against Him, Jesus inaugurates the Lord's Supper. This brings together the two elements of vv. 1–11 (the warmth of a private, final dinner with the certainty of His death). However, this dinner is not limited to this circle of followers or to this evening but extends to all believers.

14:12 *first day of Unleavened Bread.* The Feast of Unleavened Bread began the day after the Passover, but since leaven had to be removed from the house before the Passover, this term could be used for the entire time including Passover (see Lv 23:5–6; Ex 12:18). *sacrificed the Passover lamb.* The Passover festival required the slaughter of a one-year-old male lamb or goat in the temple forecourt in the afternoon. It was eaten as the main course of the evening meal (cf. Dt 16:1–8). *eat the Passover?* The disciples rightly assume that Jesus will celebrate the Passover with them and take the initiative to prepare.

14:13 *two.* Luke 22:8 identifies these two as Peter and John. *man carrying . . . water.* Since this was normally a woman's job, the man would stand out. These directions are similar to the sending of the disciples to find the colt used for Palm Sunday (11:2–3). The secrecy of the house reflects the plot of Judas (vv. 10–11) and the priests' desire to find Jesus at night apart from the crowds. Jesus does not want this meal to be interrupted and so He employs this secretive step. It also demonstrates His prophetic power. The disciples could remember this simple prophecy and then recall the prophecy of His death and His resurrection.

14:14 *master of the house.* This is a typical title for the owner of the house. *Teacher.* This is the last use of this title, *didaskalos*, for Jesus. See the notes at 4:38 for its wide use through the Gospel. The homeowner was expected to recognize Jesus through this title. We can only speculate what previous connection he might have had with Jesus. *where is My guest room.* Jesus' question is for the sake of the disciples so that they can be led to the room and prepare the meal.

14:15 *upper room.* A meal for thirteen people would require a large room, a table, and dining couches, all set up before dinner could begin. The room was a level above the street, removed from the noise and interruptions of others entering. This meal was for the disciples to be fed in body and soul, strengthened for the challenging days ahead. *furnished and ready.* The room's furnishings would be the couches and tables needed for the meal. The disciples would need to prepare the meal but the room itself was ready for Jesus. This spacious, prepared room is the least we expect for the King, a sharp contrast from the stable and manger at His birth and the three years of traveling without a home.

14:16 *found it just as He had told them.* Peter and John find this room prepared as He had said. On Easter morning, these same two will race to another room, the tomb. They will find it not furnished but empty just as He had said it would be (Jn 20:2–9). Jesus gives them this meal, His body and blood, so that they can face the empty tomb and believe His resurrection even if they do not fully understand.

14:17 *evening*. The Passover celebration began at sundown. *twelve*. Only the Twelve are mentioned as partaking of the Lord's Supper with Jesus. Judas comes with the disciples and is with Jesus even while He speaks of His betrayal (Lk 22:21), and marks Judas as the betrayer (Jn 13:26–27). This meal is the last time that the Twelve will be alone with Jesus. The Passover meal originally gathered families on the night when the angel of death came upon Egypt. So this meal, the fulfillment of Passover, gathers this family of faith on the night when betrayal and death will come. On this night, the first born of all creation, the only Son of God, will offer Himself for the death deserved by others and be the perfect, saving Lamb.

14:18 *one of you will betray Me, one who is eating with Me*. Despite the secluded setting of the meal, the plot against Jesus has come into this small circle. Judas is still with the Twelve (Lk 22:21). He should have remembered that Jesus knows the thoughts of his heart and the plans he has made against Him. Jesus enters the evening clearly seeing the betrayal and death to come and will even tell Judas to do quickly what he intends to do (Jn 13:27).

14:19 *they began to be sorrowful*. Each disciple can recall that he had disappointed Jesus in some way. While none plotted as Judas did, each was fearful that he was the one who would fail in some way. What a contrast to their frequent competition to be the greatest (9:34; Lk 22:24). When the topic is which of them is the greatest, they eagerly argue, "It is I!"When betrayal is the topic, they sorrowfully and sincerely ask, "Is it I?" Thankfully, they ask this of the One who saves all, even the greatest of sinners (1Tm 1:15).

14:20 *dipping bread*. Pieces of bread were commonly torn off the loaf, dipped into a bowl of fruit sauce or stew, and then eaten. John 13:25–26 tells us that John asked who it was and Jesus dipped the bread into the bowl and gave the bread to Judas. It was clear to John, but not all, that Judas was the betrayer.

14:21 *Son of Man*. Jesus has used this phrase especially in regard to His death and resurrection. See the notes on 8:31. *goes as it is written of Him*. Jesus is following the divine plan and is not driven by the plots of His enemies. He makes this clear especially to the Emmaus road disciples, frustrated that they did not realize that the OT required that the Christ suffer and die (Lk 24:26–27). *better . . . not been born*. Jesus foresaw the sad end for the betrayer. He knew of Judas' role early in His ministry (Jn 6:70). Jesus must die at His enemies' hands, but that does not excuse their action. As in the parable of the tenants (12:1–9), Judas and the priests are the vicious, greedy servants who kill the Son for their own gain. By so doing, Judas prepared his own despairing, violent end (Mt 27:3–5).

14:12–21 in Devotion and Prayer Jesus arranges for the Passover to be eaten at a secret location in Jerusalem. Opposition to the Gospel comes from Satan, the world, and even from within the ranks of Jesus' followers. God cures through the illness itself, and so He uses these enemies to accomplish His plan of salvation at the cross. The sacrifice of the Passover lamb foreshadows the sacrifice of our beloved Redeemer for us. • "A Lamb goes uncomplaining forth, The guilt of sinners bearing And, laden with the sins of earth, None else the burden sharing; Goes patient on, grows weak and faint, To slaughter led without complaint, That spotless life to offer." Amen. (*LSB* 438:1)

14:22–25 The Last Supper is in many respects a climax in the Gospel story, which helps the reader interpret and apply the meaning of Jesus' death and resurrection. For this reason, what one believes about the Supper has climactic significance. The reformers understood this and as a consequence of differing views, the Lord's Supper became one of the most hotly contested topics of the Reformation. In the following commentary, different reformers are cited and considered.

14:22 *blessing*. What a contrast from the dark warning of v. 21. Jesus turns the disciples from their individual fear and their suspicions of each other to the blessings He alone can give. Jesus followed a traditional Jewish pattern but used these elements in a new way. The bread was the unleavened bread commanded for the first Passover (Ex 12:8). The blessing and breaking of bread recalls the same action in feeding the 5,000 (6:41), and the 4,000 (8:6). Jesus' blessing reminds the disciples of His tie with the Father. His blessings have stretched from the first Passover and will continue through every celebration of the Supper. *this is My body*. Luther confessed that by His word, Christ effects a communion between the bread and His body for all who eat of it. On this union, see 1Co 10:16. Luther writes:

> For as soon as Christ says: "This is my body," his body is present through the Word and the power of the Holy Spirit. If the Word

is not there, it is mere bread; but as soon as the words are added they bring with them that of which they speak. (LW 36:341)

14:23 *a cup.* This was the wine for the Passover meal. *given thanks.* Jesus' thanks recalls the breaking and blessing done with the bread. Thankfulness recognizes the gift of the wine itself but, even more, the salvation that comes through the blood of the Lamb. On Passover night, this blood marked God's people and separated them from the angel of death. Now in the Supper, the blood comes to them, not as death but as life. Jesus consecrated the wine before it was distributed. The later Lutheran reformers write, "Christ's body and blood are received with the bread and wine, not only spiritually through faith, but also orally. Yet not in a 'Capernaitic' way, but in a supernatural, heavenly way, because of the sacramental union" (FC Ep VII 15). Bengel writes, "All drank, even Judas" (Bengel 566).

14:24 *This is My blood.* First Corinthians 10:16 describes the Presence of Christ in the Supper this way, "The cup of blessing that we bless, is it not a participation in the blood of Christ?" In, with, and under the wine is the blood of Christ in the Supper. The blood of Christ conveys the forgiveness of sins, as 1Jn 1:7 notes, "the blood of Jesus His Son cleanses us from all sin." The blood covers our sins, speaks for God's mercy, and washes us clean. *covenant.* Covenant is *diatheke*, "testament." Jesus sealed His last will and testament with His own precious blood to establish the Lord's Supper (1Co 11:23–26). He was the sacrificial Lamb of God, who takes away the sin of the world (cf. Jn 1:29). By this blood, He creates a new covenant on the basis of His death and His fulfillment of the conditions of the covenant. The Supper is a gift of mercy, not an obligation of our making. The covenant rests on Jesus' accomplished sacrifice and the perfection that He bestows (Heb 9:26; 10:10). *many.* This is a Hebrew idiom for "all people." Jesus' sacrifice reconciles the entire world to God (2Co 5:18–19).

Luther reacted sharply to the view of the Swiss reformer, Ulrich Zwingli, who maintained that the bread and wine of the Supper were only symbols of Christ's body and blood. Calvin explained the passage by emphasizing the Lord's Supper as "remembrance," affirming that Christ shed His blood for "the whole human race," and that "it is only by a spiritual drinking of *blood* that this *covenant* is ratified" (*Harmony* 3:214). He writes,

> It may easily be inferred from [testament/covenant], how foolishly superstitious the Papists and others of the same stamp [i.e., the Lutherans] are in rigidly adhering to the words. . . . The cup is called *blood,* because *it is the new testament* IN BLOOD. . . . They have no right now to contend that we ought to rely on the simple words of Christ. (3:214)

Calvin's words about "spiritual" eating and drinking are different than Zwingli's, but they do not represent a mediating position between Zwingli's description of the Lord's Supper as symbolism and the emphasis of Lutherans and Roman Catholics on eating and drinking the true body and blood of Christ. For example, the 1560 Geneva Bible prepared by Calvin's contemporaries freely mixes talk of symbolism and spiritual nourishment (see its note on Mt 26:26). Calvin's wording may be an attempt to soften the blow for those accustomed to long standing Christian views about the nature of the Sacrament—one might commend his gentleness—but like Zwingli's view, it denies the bodily presence of Christ in, with, and under the bread and wine. Although the churches of the sixteenth century—both Protestant and Roman—could agree on the central importance of the Supper, they did not agree on its meaning and benefits.

14:25 *I will not drink again.* Christ will not observe the Passover again with His disciples. The disciples should have realized this was their last Passover with Jesus, but He reminds them of this without going into the details of His coming death. This evening has the warmth of their precious time together while the darkness of His death lingers at the door. *fruit of the vine.* The wine of the Supper. Since grapes or their juice could not be preserved from their harvest in the fall until the Passover in the springtime; this could only be wine and not mere juice. *until that day when I drink it new in the kingdom of God.* The Kingdom is often pictured as a banquet and celebration (Mt 8:11; Lk 13:29). See the parable of the bridegroom (Mt 25:1–11), and the parable of the banquet (Lk 14:15–24). The coming kingdom celebration will be without ending, without the darkness of death, and with a circle of saints beyond number from every tribe and nation (Rv 7:9).

14:22–25 in Devotion and Prayer Jesus establishes the Lord's Supper, giving communicants His true body and blood for the forgiveness of sins under the bread and wine. Because of our sin, we cannot have fellowship with God. When He approaches us, especially in view of His body and blood, given and shed because of our sins, we should fear His nearness. However, Jesus creates a new relationship between God and sinners through His suffering and death on the cross. By His blood, He seals His testament of peace and forgiveness, which we receive in this Sacrament. The Passover is fulfilled not by a greater distance from Him, but by His gracious coming within us through His body and blood.• "O Lord, we praise Thee, bless Thee, and adore Thee, In thanksgiving bow before Thee. Thou with Thy body and Thy blood didst nourish Our weak souls that they may flourish: O Lord, have mercy! May Thy body, Lord, born of Mary, That our sins and sorrows did carry, And Thy blood for us plead In all trial, fear, and need: O Lord, have mercy!" Amen. (*LSB* 617:1)

The Reformers on the Lord's Supper

In the comments on Mk 14:22–25 are cited some passages from Luther and Calvin about the nature of the Lord's Supper. In the following article, we briefly summarize how other reformers taught on this issue.

Ancient and Medieval Teaching

The earliest Fathers consistently taught that participants at the Lord's Supper partook of the body and blood of Christ by eating and drinking the Sacrament, without questioning or defining the simple statements of Jesus and the apostle Paul. Tertullian wrote of the bread and wine as "signs" (Lat. *signum*) for the body and blood of Christ, though it must be understood that his term did not mean the bread and wine were mere symbols but were elements that conveyed what they signified so that those communing received the promised body and blood. Nevertheless, even with this clarification of Tertullian's wording, one can see how Christians would later struggle and agonize over how to speak about the nature of the Supper.

Paschasius Radbertus (c. 790–865) was the first theologian to write a treatise especially on the Lord's Supper. He emphasized that the flesh of Christ—born of Mary, crucified, and risen—was multiplied in the consecration of the Sacrament so that participants could receive the very body of Christ. His treatise was attacked by some other medieval theologians, such as the monk Ratramnus (d. 868), who wrote his own treatise. The work of Ratramnus was ultimately condemned; the medieval church sided with Radbertus and medieval theologians went on to develop the later doctrine of transubstantiation, teaching that the consecration turned the bread and wine into the body and blood of Christ so that bread and wine were no longer present. This view was largely defined as official teaching through the 1215 Lateran Council. However, the English theologian John Wycliffe (c. 1330–84) attacked transubstantiation as superstition and argued for a symbolic understanding.

The Reformers in Germany and Switzerland

As noted on pp. 258–59, Luther concluded from Scripture that both bread and wine and the very body and blood of Christ were eaten in the Sacrament. Zwingli viewed the Sacrament as symbolic. Calvin, like Luther, believed there is a real partaking of Christ's body and blood. But unlike Luther, he did not regard body and blood as present in the bread and wine. To Calvin, Christ's body is in heaven and only the communicant's soul spiritually partakes of it through the work of the Holy Spirit. As a result, three different views persisted among the reformers although all of them rejected the late medieval teaching of transubstantiation, which Roman theologians affirmed at the Council of Trent (1551).

To make matters more confusing for Protestants, after Luther died in 1546, his colleague Philip Melanchthon changed the wording of some of the principal Lutheran confessional writings. Calvin was convinced that Melanchthon had sided with him on the doctrine of the Lord's Supper but Melanchthon never repudiated Luther's teaching or endorsed Calvin's. Other Lutheran theologians of the time insisted that Melanchthon say more and write more clearly to settle the unrest but Melanchthon died in 1560 without doing so. With the leadership of Martin Chemnitz and others, Lutheran theologians settled the matter among Lutherans by reaffirming Luther's views in the 1580 Formula of Concord, which became the Lutheran standard for doctrine.

The Reformers in England and Scotland

As Luther's tracts crossed the English Channel, many Christians there embraced Luther's views about the Gospel and the Sacrament. However, the influence of Ratramnus and John Wycliffe ensured that English theologians would likewise welcome the views of Zwingli and Calvin. From The Ten Articles (1536) by Henry VIII and following, Anglican confessions and catechisms ranged from the Roman view to Zwingli's view.

There has been much debate about the development of Thomas Cranmer's view, the archbishop of Canterbury who compiled the Book of Common Prayer and authored doctrinal articles that would become the basis of the Anglican Church's Thirty-Nine Articles. When Cranmer was put on trial for false teaching (1555), here is what he said about the Sacrament:

> Now as concerning the sacrament, I have taught no false doctrine of the sacrament of the altar: for if it can be proved by any doctor above a thousand years after Christ, that Christ's body is there really, I will give over. My book was made seven years ago, and no man hath brought any authors against it. I believe, that whoso eateth and drinketh that sacrament, Christ is within them, whole Christ, his nativity, passion, resurrection, and ascension; but not that corporally that sitteth in heaven. (Cranmer 4:85)

His wording might be claimed by disciples of Zwingli or Calvin but Lutherans and Roman Catholics would not accept it and, indeed, it did not satisfy everyone in England. There remained a desire to reconnect with earlier Christian teaching. For example, when Bishop of Norwich John Overall (1560–1619) was asked to prepare questions and answers on the Sacraments for the Anglican Catechism in the Book of Common Prayer (1662), he provided the following:

> Ques. What is the outward part or sign of the Lord's Supper?
>
> Ans. Bread and wine, which the Lord hath commanded to be received.

Ques. What is the inward part, or thing signified?

Ans. The body and blood of Christ, which are verily and indeed taken and received by the faithful in the Lord's Supper. (*The Book of Common Prayer from the Original Manuscript Attached to the Act of Uniformity of 1662, and Now Preserved in the House of Lords*. London: Eyre & Spottiswoode, 1892.)

Although this wording is more sympathetic toward the Calvinist view, it allowed conservative Anglicans to commune in the faith that they were eating and drinking the very body and blood of Christ in the Sacrament.

In Scotland, John Knox labored to ensure that Calvin's view would be taught. Knox worked with others to prepare The Scottish Confession (1560). When this confession was superseded by the Westminster Confession (1647), Calvin's view of the Sacrament was retained.

Dialogues Today

Efforts to reconcile Protestant views of the Sacrament of the Altar have continued to the present day, spurred especially by the twentieth century ecumenical movement. When discussions take place, invariably the differing views reemerge and compromise language is commonly sought. Nevertheless, any future discussions must always begin with the simple words of Jesus, cited here as Mark recorded them, "Take; this is My body. . . . This is My blood of the covenant, which is poured out for many" (14:22, 24). ❧

Jesus predicts Peter's denial (14:26–31)

ESV	KJV
26 And when they had sung a hymn, they went out to the Mount of Olives. 27 And Jesus said to them, "You will all fall away, for it is written, 'I will strike the shepherd, and the sheep will be scattered.' 28 But after I am raised up, I will go before you to Galilee." 29 Peter said to him, "Even though they all fall away, I will not." 30 And Jesus said to him, "Truly, I tell you, this very night, before the rooster crows twice, you will deny me three times." 31 But he said emphatically, "If I must die with you, I will not deny you." And they all said the same.	26 And when they had sung an hymn, they went out into the mount of Olives. 27 And Jesus saith unto them, All ye shall be offended because of me this night: for it is written, I will smite the shepherd, and the sheep shall be scattered. 28 But after that I am risen, I will go before you into Galilee. 29 But Peter said unto him, Although all shall be offended, yet will not I. 30 And Jesus saith unto him, Verily I say unto thee, That this day, even in this night, before the cock crow twice, thou shalt deny me thrice. 31 But he spake the more vehemently, If I should die with thee, I will not deny thee in any wise. Likewise also said they all.

Introduction to 14:26–31 Mark now turns from the beauty of the Supper to Peter's abandonment. Mark produces another of his A-B-A structures here. First Jesus discusses the betrayal of Judas (14:17–21), then comes the intervening union and blessing of the Supper (14:22–25), and concluding is the betrayal of Peter's denial (14:26–31). Jesus sees the scattering of all the disciples as frightened sheep, but He will stay the course set by the Father.

14:26 *sung a hymn.* Pss 113–118 were the Psalms commonly sung before and after the Passover. At the end of the meal, they would have likely sung Ps 115–118. If so, especially meaningful in light of His coming death would be Ps 116:3–6: "the snares of death encompassed me . . . I suffered distress and anguish. Then I called on the name of the LORD . . . When I was brought low, he saved me." *They went out to the Mount of Olives.* They return to the mount where they had heard Jesus' teaching (13:3). This played into Judas' plans so that he could guide the troops to Jesus.

14:27 *you will all fall away.* When Jesus warned that one would betray Him, each one asked if it was he (14:19). Their concern for their future failure was justified. While only Judas would betray, all would flee. *I will strike the shepherd.* This is a quote from Zec 13:7 where the good shepherd is destroyed, even though he is the true shepherd who faithfully united and guarded the sheep (Zec 11:7). Yet, despite this sacrifice and the scattered flock, it is this death which will finally bring the whole flock together (Jn 10:15–16; 11:51–52). God accomplished forgiveness of sins when the Good Shepherd was struck for the sheep. Luther writes:

> [Christ] Himself also submitted to smitings without any guilt of His own, and He did this also so that men might not regard the kingdom of Christ as something worldly. For to the world it is to be a very offensive kingdom, as St. Paul says, 1 Cor. 1:23. (LW 20:335)

14:28 *but after I am raised up.* Jesus returns to the resurrection promise He has made three times (8:31; 9:31; 10:34). His death by betrayal needs no repetition, but the resurrection can always be restated. Jesus' simple declaration of His resurrection has the ring of an already accomplished act. *I will go before you to Galilee.* Jesus gives new steps beyond His resurrection. By this He assures the disciples that both He and they will live past the dangerous days ahead. He acts as the true shepherd, going before His flock and gathering them by His leadership.

14:29 *I will not.* Peter focuses neither on the resurrection nor the gathering of the disciples but on separating himself from the other disciples. His attention is not on the resurrected Christ, nor on the gathered flock, but on showing himself to be different from all others. Rather than asking in humility if he would fail, as they asked in 14:19, he turns to the competitive boasting that often plagued the disciples. This was a boast that was eventually fulfilled by his martyrdom (cf. Jn 21:18–19).

14:30 *truly I tell . . . twice . . . three times.* There is an ascending numerical order to Jesus' prophecy. He gives this single, solemn warning marked by the key phrase, "Truly I tell you." He also notes that it will happen that very night. Moving from the single warning, next there is the repeated warning of two crows of the rooster. But all these will not be enough to prevent the three-fold denial. Whether the warnings are solemnly immediate or loudly repeated, they cannot break through Peter's confidence and competitive certainty.

14:31 *he said emphatically.* Only Mark includes "emphatically," the Gk word *ekperissos,* which occurs only here in the NT. (Peter's preaching in Rome is likely echoed here as he remembered his response.) Peter wishes to stand out from the prophecy and from the other disciples. The vehemence of his answer matches the intensity of his upcoming denial. In contrast, Judas makes no protest when identified as the one who will betray (14:20; Jn 13:26–27). *if I must die with you.* Peter might be facing the truth of Jesus' predicted death. However, he does not see that Jesus will die a solitary death that carries the sins of the world, a death from which men will hide their faces (Is 53:3, 6).

14:26–31 in Devotion and Prayer Jesus fulfills the Scripture that promises the forgiveness of sins through the sacrifice of the Shepherd, even though all His sheep desert Him. Good intentions do not substitute for faith. Only through God's strength can any Christian face trial. Even though Jesus' sheep will run away, He will lay down His life for them. • Faithful Shepherd, keep me close this day and always. Amen.

Jesus prays in Gethsemane and is arrested (14:32–52)

ESV	KJV
[32]And they went to a place called Gethsemane. And he said to his dis- ciples, "Sit here while I pray." [33]And he took with him Peter and James and John, and began to be greatly distressed and troubled. [34]And he said to them, "My soul is very sor- rowful, even to death. Remain here and watch." [35]And going a little far- ther, he fell on the ground and prayed that, if it were possible, the hour might pass from him. [36]And he said, "Abba, Father, all things are possible for you. Remove this cup from me. Yet not what I will, but what you will." [37]And he came and found them sleep-	[32]And they came to a place which was named Gethsemane: and he saith to his disciples, Sit ye here, while I shall pray. [33]And he taketh with him Peter and James and John, and began to be sore amazed, and to be very heavy; [34]And saith unto them, My soul is exceeding sorrowful unto death: tarry ye here, and watch. [35]And he went forward a little, and fell on the ground, and prayed that, if it were possible, the hour might pass from him. [36]And he said, Abba, Father, all things are possible unto thee; take

ing, and he said to Peter, "Simon, are
you asleep? Could you not watch
one hour? 38 Watch and pray that you
may not enter into temptation. The
spirit indeed is willing, but the flesh
is weak." 39 And again he went away
and prayed, saying the same words.
40 And again he came and found them
sleeping, for their eyes were very
heavy, and they did not know what to
answer him. 41 And he came the third
time and said to them, "Are you still
sleeping and taking your rest? It is
enough; the hour has come. The Son
of Man is betrayed into the hands of
sinners. 42 Rise, let us be going; see,
my betrayer is at hand."

43 And immediately, while he was
still speaking, Judas came, one of
the twelve, and with him a crowd
with swords and clubs, from the
chief priests and the scribes and the
elders. 44 Now the betrayer had given
them a sign, saying, "The one I will
kiss is the man. Seize him and lead
him away under guard." 45 And when
he came, he went up to him at once
and said, "Rabbi!" And he kissed him.
46 And they laid hands on him and
seized him. 47 But one of those who
stood by drew his sword and struck
the servant of the high priest and cut
off his ear. 48 And Jesus said to them,
"Have you come out as against a robber, with swords and clubs to capture
me? 49 Day after day I was with you
in the temple teaching, and you did
not seize me. But let the Scriptures
be fulfilled." 50 And they all left him
and fled.

51 And a young man followed him,
with nothing but a linen cloth about
his body. And they seized him, 52 but
he left the linen cloth and ran away
naked.

away this cup from me: nevertheless
not what I will, but what thou wilt.

37 And he cometh, and findeth them
sleeping, and saith unto Peter, Simon,
sleepest thou? couldest not thou
watch one hour?

38 Watch ye and pray, lest ye enter
into temptation. The spirit truly is
ready, but the flesh is weak.

39 And again he went away, and
prayed, and spake the same words.

40 And when he returned, he found
them asleep again, (for their eyes
were heavy,) neither wist they what
to answer him.

41 And he cometh the third time, and
saith unto them, Sleep on now, and
take your rest: it is enough, the hour
is come; behold, the Son of man is
betrayed into the hands of sinners.

42 Rise up, let us go; lo, he that
betrayeth me is at hand.

43 And immediately, while he yet
spake, cometh Judas, one of the
twelve, and with him a great multitude with swords and staves, from the
chief priests and the scribes and the
elders.

44 And he that betrayed him had
given them a token, saying, Whomsoever I shall kiss, that same is he;
take him, and lead him away safely.

45 And as soon as he was come, he
goeth straightway to him, and saith,
Master, master; and kissed him.

46 And they laid their hands on him,
and took him.

47 And one of them that stood by
drew a sword, and smote a servant
of the high priest, and cut off his ear.

48 And Jesus answered and said unto
them, Are ye come out, as against a
thief, with swords and with staves to
take me?

49 I was daily with you in the temple teaching, and ye took me not: but the scriptures must be fulfilled.
50 And they all forsook him, and fled.
51 And there followed him a certain young man, having a linen cloth cast about his naked body; and the young men laid hold on him:
52 And he left the linen cloth, and fled from them naked.

Introduction to 14:32–52 The precious final evening continues in the Garden. Peter, James and John are called to pray, but are overwhelmed by sleep. Jesus wrestles with the sorrow of death but perseveres in prayer. He asks if the Father might remove the fatal cup, but He steels Himself to the coming betrayal and death. Judas comes and the Twelve are together for one last moment. When He is arrested, this small flock scatters while He is led away silently.

14:32 *Gethsemane.* Gethsemane was a garden on the lower edge of the Mount of Olives across the Kidron Valley from Jerusalem. How fitting that in a garden the Son of Man is tested and faces the burden of the first sins committed in the Garden of Eden. *sit here while I pray.* Jesus commands all the disciples to join Him in His prayer. They should know by now that this night will fulfill His often-predicted death.

14:33 *Peter and James and John.* Along with Peter's brother Andrew, these are the first disciples called by Jesus (1:16–20). These three went to the Mount of Olives and saw Him in His brilliant glory; now they will watch Him in troubled darkness. They heard the Father's voice of love on the mountain; now they hear Jesus ask about the Father's plan and will. They are to pray both for Jesus and themselves. *greatly distressed and troubled.* Jesus anticipated the great suffering that will soon come. The word "greatly distressed," *ekthambeo*, is used only by Mark, here and at 9:15 and 16:5. In 9:15 the people are astonished at Jesus' appearance after the mount of transfiguration, while 16:5 records the women's alarm at the empty tomb. This one word spans transfiguration, Gethsemane, and Easter. Jesus' distress came as He drew near to the weight and agony of bearing the sins of the world.

14:34 *My soul.* This Hbr expression signifies one's whole being, such as Ps 103:1, "Bless the LORD, O my soul." *is very sorrowful, even to death.* Jesus' sorrow was all encompassing, an inescapable sadness that pointed only to death. This unusual word, "very sorrowful," *perilupos,* is used only here and 6:26 where Herod is sorrowful at the girl's demand for the head of John the Baptist. *watch.* The Gk word is *gregoreo,* "be alert." (The Latin translation *vigilate* gives us the English word "vigil," teaching one to stay awake and pray against the temptations of Satan.) Jesus used this word three times in 13:34, 37, 38, to urge all to be alert for the Second Coming. The disciples have the opportunity to be alert now for the few hours before the definite coming of His death.

14:35 *a little farther.* Luke 22:41 tells us that it was a stone's throw distance, perhaps thirty yards. Jesus' time of prayer was private but near His disciples. This recalls other times of His prayer separate from the disciples (1:35; 6:46; Lk 6:12). This time with the three disciples present is most like the Mount of Transfiguration prayer (Lk 9:28). *fell on the ground.* His posture reflected deep grief. *hour.* This is not simply 60 minutes, but the whole ordeal He must face. Jesus has waited for this time of final conflict, but its burden is now crushingly present. *pass from Him.* Jesus fully experienced the agony of soul caused by the burden of sin He bears even unto death. Ambrose says, "He has taken upon Him the substance of man, and therewith its affections. . . . Not as God, then, but as man, speaks He, for could God be ignorant of the possibility or impossibility of aught?" (*NPNF*2 10:228).

14:36 *Abba.* This is the Aramaic name for "father." It is a familiar, warm name that captures the parent/child relationship. *All things are possible for you.* That very freedom and power make this sacrifice all the deeper. God had no command from another, no necessity outside or beyond Himself. No one takes Jesus' life from Him, but He is free to lay it down and to take it up again (Jn 10:18). Only His love for the world compels God to sacrifice His Son and to demand this death as the payment for sins and an expression of His love. *cup.* Jesus earlier spoke of His death as the cup (10:38). Death and the penalty of sin are often pictured as a bitter cup (Ps 75:8; Is 29:9; 51:17; 63:6; Lm 4:21). *Yet not what I will, but what You will.* While Jesus according to His human nature recoils from the bitter cup of His suffering, He gains strength from the will of the Father. His trust of the Father brings the power to accept this death. The will of the Father is not a cruel rod but an empowering staff upon which Jesus is leaning.

14:37 *he found them sleeping*. Jesus comes to wake and watch over the disciples. While He prepares to carry the weight of the world, He must also watch over these men. He is a shepherd for the few and for the whole world. *Peter.* Jesus focuses on Peter since he is the leader of the three and the Twelve and had made the strongest boasts of fidelity (14:31). *Simon, are you asleep?* Jesus asks that which He fully knows. But He does so as an invitation for Peter to answer for himself. Here is a chance for Peter to admit his weakness and find forgiveness and strength from Jesus. Though Jesus knows that Peter will fail soon, He gives him these hours to fulfill some measure of his promise to remain with Jesus. He need not die with Jesus as he boasted but he might remain awake, pray for Jesus and comfort Him in this darkness.

14:38 *Watch and pray*. As noted in v. 34, this is the third time (vv. 34, 37, and here) that Jesus speaks of being alert. They were to watch not only for the very end of time (13:9, 22, 37), but also during that evening. The quiet darkness of Gethsemane masked the ending of something more dramatic than even the destruction of Jerusalem. The end of God's dwelling among them through the incarnate Word was at hand. *not enter into temptation*. Jesus' command is similar to the sixth petition of the Lord's Prayer (Lk 11:4). They were to pray that they would be spared the harshest test and be given the strength to stand up under the trials that were about to come (cf. 1Co 10:13). *the flesh is weak*. The weakness of the flesh is the complete depravity of the whole person. Paul calls out that in him, that is in his flesh, dwells no good thing (Rm 7:18). He can wish to do the right but lacks the power in himself to do it. Luther writes: "When our hearts are troubled with sorrow, then truly God Himself sorrows, who died that we might be justified, holy, and full of joy" (LW 13:138).

14:39 *and again he went . . . saying the same words*. Jesus' trust and patience with the Father changes how He prays. He prays not only for the answer, but for the relationship which is strengthened through the repetition and the time together. Jesus knows the cup will not pass away, but being with the Father, pouring out His thoughts and feelings, prepares Him for the cross. These repeated prayers are the peak of the many mountaintop times of prayer Jesus has had already. See the notes on v. 35 for His practice of private prayer.

14:40 *for their eyes were very heavy.* This is the only NT use of the word *katabaruno,* to make very heavy, burdened. Everyone has experienced this: the resolve to stay awake, the extreme fatigue, the slipping of consciousness, the sweetness of sleep, and the guilt upon waking. Heavy was the burden on their eyes, but what was this compared to the burden being placed on the shoulders of Jesus, carrying the sins of the world? And yet, He comes to watch over them. *what to answer.* The disciples had no excuse for their failure to watch and pray. There was no boasting or comparing with each other. They had simply failed and admitted it by their silence.

14:41 *and He came the third time.* Jesus continued to gain strength with the Father through prayer while the disciples slept through another precious chance to stand with Him. *it is enough.* Only Mark has this phrase here. The word *apecho* can refer to a bill or debt paid in full (Mt 6:2, 5, 16). Jesus likely means that there has been enough sleeping, waking, and promising to do better. The time of preparation for Him is done and so is the time of sleeping. *Son of Man.* Jesus has repeatedly spoken of Himself as the Son of Man, especially when speaking of His coming death. It is both a picture of His humanity but also His glory, using the imagery of Dn 7:13–14. See the notes on 2:10 and 8:31. *betrayed.* In contrast to this OT image of a glorious Son of Man, He is about to place Himself in the hands of sinners so that He might save all. Little do the soldiers and Judas know their part in this work of reconciling the world through the death of God's Son.

14:32–42 in Devotion and Prayer On the eve of His Passion, Jesus prays in agony, yet He concludes by praying that the Father's will be done. The disciples fall asleep while praying, slipping in the critical hour. Spiritual sleepiness steals over us too when we need to watch and pray, but our Savior always intercedes on our behalf. • Faithful High Priest, intercede for us at Your Father's throne, that He may pardon and bless us for Your sake. Amen.

14:43 *and immediately.* Mark's signature word, "immediately" returns for the first of its four last occurrences (14:43, 45, 72; 15:1). It was last seen at 11:3, the preparations for Palm Sunday. Almost one-fourth of the Gospel appears from 11:3 to 14:43, recounting the whole of Passion week for which Mark did not use his favored term.

Now Mark uses "immediately" again these last four times. The first four uses of the term (1:10, 12, 18, 20). For example, in 1:20 Jesus speaks without hesitation, and in 14:43 while He is still speaking, Judas appears. In 1:20 Jesus immediately finishes calling the first four disciples. In 14:43 the Twelve are together for the last time. *with him a crowd.* More than just soldiers, this included officials and police from the chief priests and Pharisees (Jn 18:3). *chief priests . . . scribes . . . elders.* This is the familiar trio of opposition that Jesus has predicted and faced in various combinations (8:31; 10:33; 11:18, 27; 14:1). Jesus has bested them in their intellectual and moral arguments. Now, hidden by the dark, their hatred comes out with blunt force.

14:44 *sign.* This is the only use of this word, *syssemon,* in the NT. It is a signal or token between associates. In the dark, with so many involved, something obvious was needed. *kiss.* Jesus had been asked for signs of His authority (8:11) and refused to give it. He was asked for signs of the end of time (13:4) and spoke of the many false christs who would come (13:5, 21–22). But the final sign needed was the empty kiss of betrayal, accepted by Jesus who knew its lie completely. He needed to be marked as the man to be arrested, so that He would also be marked as the Son of God on the cross (15:39).

14:45 *he went up to him at once.* This is another use of the word *euthus,* "immediately" or "at once." Judas comes without hesitation, just as the first disciples came immediately to follow Jesus (1:18). Jesus called the first two, Peter and Andrew, and knew they would come instantly. He knows also that Judas will come instantly also in this final approach. Yet, He called all the disciples to bring about this hour. *Rabbi!* This is the title for one's teacher and has been used with respect and even awe at the Mount of Transfiguration (9:5), by others in need (10:51), and by those seeing Jesus' miracles (11:21). Judas uses it as a verbal signal, along with the kiss, that this was the one to be captured. See notes on 9:5.

14:46 *laid hands on Him.* John tells of the crowd falling back when Jesus identifies Himself (Jn 18:6). Many have sought to touch Jesus throughout the Gospel for the healing He brings (3:10; 5:28; 6:56). Here, without their knowing, is the touch which will bring healing of the world's sin. As Jesus allowed the woman to touch Him (5:28) and knew the healing it would bring her, so He allows Himself to fall into the guards' hands for the curing of the world.

14:47 *one of those.* John 18:10 tells us that it was Peter who struck the servant. Here Peter acts decisively in keeping with his promise of faithfulness (14:31). He dares to die, as he promised, but Jesus was not to die in this darkness, but in a far greater darkness the next day. By then Peter will have slipped into the safety of his denial. Peter's action is the natural resistance the disciples have expressed towards Jesus' predictions of death. They have not understood (9:32), and have dragged their feet as it has come near (10:32). Now Peter expresses this defiance with this one blow. This moment recalls the question about the two greatest commandments (12:28–31). Peter tries to show his love for Jesus with his strength and might, but fails to use fully his mind to understand that Jesus must die.

14:48 *Jesus said to them.* Mark doesn't record Jesus' rebuke to Peter (Mt 26:52–54). Jesus makes it clear that if He wished, He could call on twelve legions of angels, far more than Peter's single sword. But He came not to be saved but to save through His life given as a ransom. *Have you come out as against a robber.* Jesus addresses the crowd who came armed and in great number, as though He were a violent man surrounded by His own furious crowd. But He is the Lamb of God willing to be taken.

14:49 *day after day I was with you in the temple teaching.* Jesus' teaching, begun in the synagogue (1:21), has caused controversy throughout the Gospel (see notes on 1:21). During Passion week His opponents came repeatedly to challenge His authoritative teaching (11:15–18, 28; 12:12–13, 18, 28, 35). His opponents were determined that His teaching, done in the temple, had to be torn down, just as He predicted that they would destroy the temple of His body (Jn 2:19). *let the Scriptures be fulfilled.* The OT promised salvation through the death of the Messiah (cf. Lk 24:25, 44–47). Luther writes:

> Such courage must be the work of none other than the Holy Spirit. . . . The world is not able to have or give this courage; for it places its reliance only in the things it sees, in goods, reputation, and high honor. When what it boasts of comes to an end—as it all must come to an end—its courage also vanishes, and sheer despair remains. (LW 24:118–19)

Jesus is speaking through the strength received from His hours of prayer and His determination to follow through the Father's will.

14:50 *and they all left Him and fled.* The disciples' flight fulfilled Is 53:3, 6. The sheep run when the Shepherd is taken, and He remains in their place so that they can get away. As Joseph was taken alone into slavery and his brothers went safely home (Gn 37:25–36), so Jesus is taken, innocent of any wrong, while the disciples slip into the dark.

14:51 *young man followed Him.* Only Mark records this small episode. Many suggest that this was Mark himself, whose home was in Jerusalem (Ac 12:12). When Mark says that the young man followed, the verb is *sunakoloutheo,* rarely used in the NT. It likely means someone who followed Jesus outside the circle of the Twelve (see Lk 23:49). *linen cloth.* A linen robe was worn under a woolen outer garment. *they seized him.* While the other disciples safely escaped, the young man might have lingered too long or might not have realized the danger of the moment. Regardless, he is the only one recorded whose arrest was attempted along with Jesus.

14:52 *ran away naked.* He was in such a desperate hurry that he left behind the garment (cf. v. 51). He fled for his life regardless of the cost or appearance. The linen cloth he left was usually a square or oblong sheet, wrapped around himself. This type of cloth, *sidon*, was also the sheet of linen used to wrap a dead body (Mt 27:59; Mk 15:46; Lk 23:53).

14:43–52 in Devotion and Prayer Representatives of the Jewish ruling Council arrest Jesus, apprehending Him at night outside the city to avoid causing a riot among His supporters. God's plan of salvation moves forward, using the "success" of these enemies to move closer to the cross for the sake of our salvation. • "O wondrous Love, what have You done! The Father offers up His Son, Desiring our salvation. O Love, how strong You are to save! You lay the One into the grave Who built the earth's foundation." Amen. (*LSB* 438:3)

Jesus is tried before the high priest and is denied by Peter (14:53–72)

ESV

53 And they led Jesus to the high priest. And all the chief priests and the elders and the scribes came together. 54 And Peter had followed him at a distance, right into the courtyard of the high priest. And he was sitting with the guards and warming himself at the fire. 55 Now the chief priests and the whole Council were seeking testimony against Jesus to put him to death, but they found none. 56 For many bore false witness against him, but their testimony did not agree. 57 And some stood up and bore false witness against him, saying, 58 "We heard him say, 'I will destroy this temple that is made with hands, and in three days I will build another, not made with hands.' " 59 Yet even about this their testimony did not agree. 60 And the high priest stood up in the midst and asked Jesus, "Have you no answer to make? What is it that these men testify against you?" 61 But he remained silent and made no answer. Again the high priest asked him, "Are you the Christ, the Son of the Blessed?" 62 And Jesus said, "I am, and you will see the Son of Man seated at the right hand of Power, and coming with the clouds of heaven." 63 And the high priest tore his garments and said, "What further witnesses do we need? 64 You have heard his blasphemy. What is your decision?" And they all condemned him as deserving death. 65 And some began to spit on him and to cover his face and to strike him, saying to him,

KJV

53 And they led Jesus away to the high priest: and with him were assembled all the chief priests and the elders and the scribes.

54 And Peter followed him afar off, even into the palace of the high priest: and he sat with the servants, and warmed himself at the fire.

55 And the chief priests and all the council sought for witness against Jesus to put him to death; and found none.

56 For many bare false witness against him, but their witness agreed not together.

57 And there arose certain, and bare false witness against him, saying,

58 We heard him say, I will destroy this temple that is made with hands, and within three days I will build another made without hands.

59 But neither so did their witness agree together.

60 And the high priest stood up in the midst, and asked Jesus, saying, Answerest thou nothing? what is it which these witness against thee?

61 But he held his peace, and answered nothing. Again the high priest asked him, and said unto him, Art thou the Christ, the Son of the Blessed?

62 And Jesus said, I am: and ye shall see the Son of man sitting on the right hand of power, and coming in the clouds of heaven.

63 Then the high priest rent his clothes, and saith, What need we any further witnesses?

"Prophesy!" And the guards received
him with blows.
66And as Peter was below in the
courtyard, one of the servant girls
of the high priest came, 67and seeing
Peter warming himself, she looked
at him and said, "You also were
with the Nazarene, Jesus." 68But he
denied it, saying, "I neither know nor
understand what you mean." And he
went out into the gateway and the
rooster crowed. 69And the servant
girl saw him and began again to say
to the bystanders, "This man is one
of them." 70But again he denied it.
And after a little while the bystanders
again said to Peter, "Certainly you are
one of them, for you are a Galilean."
71But he began to invoke a curse on
himself and to swear, "I do not know
this man of whom you speak." 72And
immediately the rooster crowed a
second time. And Peter remembered
how Jesus had said to him, "Before
the rooster crows twice, you will
deny me three times." And he broke
down and wept.

64Ye have heard the blasphemy: what think ye? And they all condemned him to be guilty of death.

65And some began to spit on him, and to cover his face, and to buffet him, and to say unto him, Prophesy: and the servants did strike him with the palms of their hands.

66And as Peter was beneath in the palace, there cometh one of the maids of the high priest:

67And when she saw Peter warming himself, she looked upon him, and said, And thou also wast with Jesus of Nazareth.

68But he denied, saying, I know not, neither understand I what thou sayest. And he went out into the porch; and the cock crew.

69And a maid saw him again, and began to say to them that stood by, This is one of them.

70And he denied it again. And a little after, they that stood by said again to Peter, Surely thou art one of them: for thou art a Galilaean, and thy speech agreeth thereto.

71But he began to curse and to swear, saying, I know not this man of whom ye speak.

72And the second time the cock crew. And Peter called to mind the word that Jesus said unto him, Before the cock crow twice, thou shalt deny me thrice. And when he thought thereon, he wept.

Introduction to 15:53–72 Silence settles over the next two scenes. Jesus is repeatedly accused but He makes no answer until He makes a final declaration that He is indeed the divine and powerful Son of Man. That brief truth delivers Him to death. Peter then has the chance to fulfill his promise to stand by Jesus, but he cannot say the simple truth that he is a follower. Instead he rushes forward through the three denials. As the rooster's final crow fades away, Peter faces the sad realization of what he has done.

14:53 *chief priests . . . elders . . . scribes came together.* See the notes on 14:1, 43 for the previous appearances of the chief priests, elders and scribes as leaders of the opposition to Jesus. Their long-planned arrest of Jesus finally happened in secrecy without an opposing crowd. Now they can condemn Jesus on their terms without a crowd supporting Jesus. Instead, they can bring their witnesses to condemn Him.

14:54 *Peter had followed Him at a distance.* To Peter's credit, he and John follow Jesus (Jn 18:15). John proceeds farther into the courtyard, leaving Peter with the guards. This became Peter's vulnerable isolation. Here another Marcan A-B-A structure begins. Peter's placement in the courtyard is the first setting. Mark then tells the account of Jesus' trial, the B segment, and finally returns to Peter's denial (14:66–72). *courtyard of the high priest.* This was in his residence on the south side of Jerusalem. This group may have met here for privacy. *he was sitting with the guards.* Peter showed courage to come this far and to remain in this exposed place alone. He must have yearned for any bit of news of the trial going on inside. Little did he imagine that his own trial was about to begin also.

14:55 *the chief priests and the whole Council were seeking testimony.* To gain a death sentence, the accusers needed proof that Jesus threatened Roman rule. Although there was no evidence that Jesus was an insurrectionist, they would charge Him as such (15:3). Eagerly they gathered in the dark of night to hear these lies. When the Son of God taught in the daylight of the temple, they were silent and defeated (12:34). But now the whole court comes urgently to pass judgment. *but they found none.* Jesus had accomplished the impossible: He harmed no one and taught no falsehood, and yet He was hated by the whole Council. Anyone can do evil and be hated. Only the perfect Son of God, the Lamb to be sacrificed, can be completely good so that even lies cannot stand against Him. And yet, they are determined to destroy Him who is only good.

14:56 *many bore false witness . . . but their testimony did not agree.* OT Law required testimony to be established by two or three witnesses. Each man spun his own lie, but they couldn't agree. It recalls the failure of the many who came against Jesus in His teaching

(2:7–12; 2:15–3:6; 3:22–27; 7:1–8; 10:2–12; 11:28–33; 12:13–27). They came in a long line, each attempting to best Jesus' understanding of the Scripture and His life of teaching and healing. But each failed, confirming the authority of His word.

14:57 *some . . . bore false witness against him.* When no honest recollection of His teaching could condemn, outright lies are all that are left. There should be no wonder at this. Evil came into the world through the first question, "Did God actually say . . . ?" (Gn 3:1). It is no surprise that the culmination of evil should again question the clear words of God. But it is by this distortion that God will finally crush the power of the tempter. God uses the illness itself to work the cure. Their lies will deliver Him to the cross and there He will do the undeniable work of reconciling the world to God.

14:58 *we heard Him say, "I will destroy this temple."* They were close but still incorrect with this remembrance. In Jn 2:19, after cleansing the temple at the beginning of His ministry, Jesus said, "Destroy this temple and in three days I will raise it up." The witnesses have changed the statement from Jesus' predictive command of their destruction of Himself. Jesus, as Jn 2:21 makes clear, was speaking of His body as the temple to be destroyed and rebuilt. They will destroy and He will rebuild. The witnesses have reversed this, charging Jesus with the temple's destruction and imagining that they are the ones now preserving it. *not made with human hands.* Jesus' resurrection is the divine work which shows Him to be the Son of God (Rm 1:4). Paul uses the image of a resurrection body not made with human hands in 2Co 5:1.

14:59 *yet even about this their testimony did not agree.* As noted in v. 57, the lies begun in Gn 3 continued to increase through the temptation of Eve. So here, the trial of Jesus is bound to increase in deceptions. Truth won't be found once the lies begin.

14:60 *the high priest stood up and asked.* Increasing contradictions threaten to undo the trial and erode the authority of the chief priests in arresting and charging Jesus. The chief priests, scribes and elders had challenged Jesus' authority to teach (11:27–33) but Jesus undid them by asking by whose authority John baptized. Now the right of these same men to judge Jesus must be questioned when they cannot gather even two or three witnesses to agree. *Have you no answer?* The witnesses cannot be heard any longer since they disagree. So the chief priest hopes that Jesus will condemn Himself by answering. Jesus' silence will baffle men throughout His trial and crucifixion. He can save others, but He will not save Himself. He could end the lies of these men, but He came to end His own life instead. *What is it that these men testify.* Here is a chance for Jesus to correct the men's recollections and to resume His stance as teacher, but He has taught always knowing that many will "see but not perceive . . . hear but not understand" (4:12).

14:61 *but He remained silent and made no answer.* Why should He answer these men? His silence is an eloquent majesty. The King of Kings rises in silence above these small men with their petty power. *again the high priest asked Him, "Are you the Christ, the Son of the Blessed?"* Since Jesus will not respond to their contradictory charges, the priest takes on the central question, Jesus' identity. The question throughout Mark is not so much what He teaches, but who He is. Mark 1:1 has declared Him to be the Son of God. His teaching has been briefly summarized (see 1:21). But His identity is the central knowledge that must be clear. *the Blessed?* The priest avoided using the name of God as a custom of respect for the divine name.

14:62 *I am.* Jesus decisively identifies Himself as the Son of God. In Mt 26:64, it is recorded that Jesus says the synonymous phrase, "You have said so." But in Mark, it is unquestionable that Jesus says, "Yes, I am." Jesus was not deceived or baited into this statement. He has foreseen each turn of the trial and has waited for this opportunity to make this true witness. *Son of Man seated at the right hand of Power.* Jesus contrasts the small setting of this court in the dark with the coming display of power when He returns in glory. They will no longer be His presumptuous judges, but will become His witnesses, able to testify truly of His glory and power. See Dn 7:13–14 for this scene of power which underlies the title of Son of Man. See also notes on 2:10 and 8:31 for the use of this title in Mark. This is the last of its fourteen appearances.

14:63 *tore his garments.* Tearing one's robe indicated grief and dismay at what had just happened. See Gn 37:34; Jsh 7:6; 2Sm 1:11; Jb 1:20. The high priest believed that Jesus committed blasphemy by claiming to be God. The tearing of his cloak was the snapping of the trap. By this, the high priest signaled the end of the trial. While their own witnesses failed, Jesus had surrendered Himself to them with these words. *what further witnesses do we need?* They had enough in Jesus' words while also slightly acknowledging the uselessness of the early witnesses. Jesus' admission that He is the Son of Man and the Son of God was impossible for them to believe. They did not deny the existence of God or the coming of the Son of Man from Daniel, but they were certain that He would never come as the Nazareth carpenter, the one who ate with sinners and broke their own holiness traditions (2:15–3:6).

14:64 *blasphemy.* To claim to be divine was a capital crime in Judaism. Jesus' first confrontation with the Pharisees centered on their charge of blasphemy (2:7), because He had forgiven sins. Only God can do that, and only the Son of God has done it through the coming sacrifice of Himself. It is interesting that Jesus is charged with blasphemy in regard to His forgiveness of sins and His willingness to stand condemned for being the Son of Man. He concealed the glory that would have proven His divinity and is condemned in His saving humility. *all condemned Him.* All who were there passed unanimous judgment. They reasoned God would not actually let His "Chosen One" suffer such humiliation and defeat. The same reasoning is in their upcoming challenge when He is on the cross: "Let [Him] come down now from the cross that we may see and believe" (15:32). But if that had happened, they would have had only a self-saving God in which to believe. We believe in a God who saves others at His own expense.

14:65 Blindfolding and striking reflected a misunderstanding of Is 11:2, the expectation that the Messiah will come with the Spirit of wisdom and understanding. Their mocking contradicted His divine claims. The innocent One is blindfolded so that the guilty can act with impunity. When they are done, He will carry their guilt as His own and pay for it with His life.

14:53–65 in Devotion and Prayer The Jewish ruling Council convicts Jesus of blasphemy for claiming to be the messianic King. Even though all of Jesus' supporters have abandoned Him, He stands ready to bear the sins of the world. God uses the plans and plots of His enemies to accomplish our salvation. • "Jesus, I will ponder now On Your holy passion; With Your Spirit me endow For such meditation. Grant that I in love and faith May the image cherish Of Your suff'ring, pain, and death That I may not perish." Amen. (*LSB* 440:1)

14:66 *as Peter was below.* The trial of Jesus took place on an upper floor of the residence. With Jesus' trial done, Peter's temptation begins. This concludes the A-B-A structure of 14:54–72. Jesus has faithfully kept His promises of being delivered to sinful men. Now Peter must meet his challenges. *One of the servant girls . . . came.* Jesus faced the powerful fury of the Jewish leadership and their guards. In contrast, Peter meets a servant girl on the edge of the crowd.

14:67 *seeing Peter warming himself.* She might have seen Peter with Jesus during the week or especially during Palm Sunday's triumphant entrance. *You also were with the Nazarene, Jesus.* We don't know in what tone she said this. It could have been accusingly or as a question asking for information. She might have been condemning Peter, or she might have invited him to speak the truth about Jesus. Peter obviously hears it as a dangerous accusation. Her title for Jesus, the Nazarene, reflects His growing up in Nazareth and echoes Mt 2:23.

14:68 *he denied it.* Peter was frightened by her recognition and the possibility of being identified. While he might have done well on a grand stage such as the trial court—just as he did when walking at first on the raging sea (Mt 14:29)—he fails in the small space of the dark courtyard. Perhaps also he reasoned that this small denial didn't count, but as temptations always do, this small step begins a terrible journey. *I neither know nor understand what you mean.* Peter already denies more forcefully than is needed. He hopes that bluster will end his trial, but it only makes it worse. *He went out into the gateway and the rooster crowed.* Peter moves to escape the immediate confrontation. However, the rooster has kept pace with him. It is doubtful that Peter takes notice of this first warning.

14:69 *the servant girl saw him and began again to say.* When you know you are right, someone's denial only makes you more determined. So the girl is spurred on by Peter's disowning of Jesus. She brings others into the conversation, which might have stopped with her if Peter had acknowledged his tie with Jesus. But now she is determined to be proven right. *This man is one of them.* The girl has taken a new direction. Rather than identifying Peter with Jesus alone, she ties him in with the other disciples. This might have played upon the charge that Jesus was a revolutionary with followers ready to proclaim Him king (Lk 23:2; Jn 19:12).

14:70 *but again he denied it.* Peter heard the girl's accusations even from a distance and denied them. Likely he increased his anger and raised his voice (Mt 26:72). *One of the bystanders.* Others have agreed with the servant girl by now so that the accusing circle has grown around Peter. *you are a Galilean.* This may have been obvious from Peter's accent (cf. Mt 26:73). Now Peter is accused of something undeniable, his background and speech. If he will not acknowledge his tie with Jesus, he must admit to his home.

14:71 *invoke a curse.* This is the dramatic word *anathematidzo,* in English "anathematize." This was Peter's desperate means to make the people around him believe his lie, but he protests too much. Notice that Peter does not deny being a Galilean or being with the followers of Jesus (vv. 69–70), but returned to the central issue, his relationship with Jesus. He denies this bond, but no one believes him.

14:72 *and immediately the rooster crowed a second time.* Now the rooster announces Peter's lie. This is the second-to-last time in the Gospel where Mark uses the word "immediately." The second time it was used (1:12), it signaled the beginning of Jesus' temptation in the desert. Now it heralds the end of Peter's temptation in the courtyard. *And Peter remembered how Jesus had said.* Now the prediction comes back clearly and Peter can see each step which fulfilled it. The small, dark, and hidden lies are now laid out before him, but they cannot be changed. *he broke down and wept.* Peter was deeply sorry for his denial. Luther writes:

> The church of God has great need of these examples. For what would become of us? What hope would be left for us if Peter had not denied Christ and all the apostles had not taken offense at Him, and if Moses, Aaron, and David had not fallen? Therefore God wanted to console sinners with these examples and to say: "If you have fallen, return; for the door of mercy is open to you. You, who are conscious of no sin, do not be presumptuous; but both of you should trust in My grace and mercy." (LW 7:11)

14:66–72 in Devotion and Prayer While Jesus stands firm before Caiaphas, on trial for His life, Peter three times denies knowing Jesus. Fear leads us to do things we later regret. Only God can give us the courage to face difficult situations, especially persecution. Not only did Jesus later forgive Peter, but He also even reinstated this apostle to his office (cf. Jn 21:15–19). Therefore, be comforted because your Lord will likewise be merciful toward you. • "What punishment so strange is suffered yonder! The Shepherd dies for sheep that loved to wander; The Master pays the debt His servants owe Him, Who would not know Him." Amen. (*LSB* 439:4)

Jesus is tried before Pilate (15:1–15)

ESV

15 1 And as soon as it was morning, the chief priests held a consultation with the elders and scribes and the whole Council. And they bound Jesus and led him away and delivered him over to Pilate. 2 And Pilate asked him, "Are you the King of the Jews?" And he answered him, "You have said so." 3 And the chief priests accused him of many things. 4 And Pilate again asked him, "Have you no answer to make? See how many charges they bring against you." 5 But Jesus made no further answer, so that Pilate was amazed.

6 Now at the feast he used to release for them one prisoner for whom they asked. 7 And among the rebels in prison, who had committed murder in the insurrection, there was a man called Barabbas. 8 And the crowd came up and began to ask Pilate to do as he usually did for them. 9 And he answered them, saying, "Do you want me to release for you the King of the Jews?" 10 For he perceived that it was out of envy that the chief priests had delivered him up. 11 But the chief priests stirred up the crowd to have him release for them Barabbas instead. 12 And Pilate again said to them, "Then what shall I do with the man you call the King of the Jews?" 13 And they cried out again, "Crucify him." 14 And Pilate said to them, "Why, what evil has he done?" But they shouted all the more, "Crucify him." 15 So Pilate, wishing to satisfy the crowd, released for them Barabbas, and having scourged Jesus, he delivered him to be crucified.

KJV

15 1 And straightway in the morning the chief priests held a consultation with the elders and scribes and the whole council, and bound Jesus, and carried him away, and delivered him to Pilate.

2 And Pilate asked him, Art thou the King of the Jews? And he answering said unto them, Thou sayest it.

3 And the chief priests accused him of many things: but he answered nothing.

4 And Pilate asked him again, saying, Answerest thou nothing? behold how many things they witness against thee.

5 But Jesus yet answered nothing; so that Pilate marvelled.

6 Now at that feast he released unto them one prisoner, whomsoever they desired.

7 And there was one named Barabbas, which lay bound with them that had made insurrection with him, who had committed murder in the insurrection.

8 And the multitude crying aloud began to desire him to do as he had ever done unto them.

9 But Pilate answered them, saying, Will ye that I release unto you the King of the Jews?

10 For he knew that the chief priests had delivered him for envy.

11 But the chief priests moved the people, that he should rather release Barabbas unto them.

12 And Pilate answered and said again unto them, What will ye then that I shall do unto him whom ye call

the King of the Jews?
13 And they cried out again, Crucify him.
14 Then Pilate said unto them, Why, what evil hath he done? And they cried out the more exceedingly, Crucify him.
15 And so Pilate, willing to content the people, released Barabbas unto them, and delivered Jesus, when he had scourged him, to be crucified.

Introduction to 15:1–15 Having been condemned by the chief priests and council, Jesus now faces Pilate. Pilate, however, is the opposite of the Jewish leadership. He is reluctant to condemn and would offer a substitute, Barabbas, to save Jesus. Jesus acknowledges that He is the King of the Jews and then silently lets the leaders of Israel manipulate Pilate into condemning Him. Pilate, amazed at Jesus' silence, and angered at the crowd's insistence on Jesus' death, fulfills the plan of God by ordering the crucifixion.

15:1 *And as soon as it was morning.* This is the last occurrence of Mark's frequent adverb, *euthus,* usually translated "immediately." A literal translation would be, "And immediately it was dawn." We might expect that the last "immediately" would be Jesus' death or the dawn of Easter. But the last milestone on the journey begun in 1:2–3 is reached here, the dawn of Good Friday. Interestingly, the first time *euthus* appears (1:10), it is Jesus' baptism and the breaking open of heaven. Then in 1:11 the Father announces that He is the beloved Son. Here, dawn breaks open the sky (15:1), and Pilate asks if Jesus is the King of the Jews, to which Jesus agrees (15:2). *chief priests . . . elders and scribes . . . whole Council.* These are all the members of the Sanhedrin, seventy in all. They were all finally gathered for this final step, even if they had missed the earlier parts of the overnight trial. *consultation.* This is the final consultation, fulfilling the plot begun already in 3:6 and darkly finalized with Judas in 14:1–2, 10–11. *they bound Jesus and led Him away and delivered Him over to Pilate.* Luther wrote: "The Jews and Pilate, however, were our God's chisels, picks, and stone mallets, which He used to polish this Stone [Jesus] so that He might lay the foundation of His new temple" (LW 20:219). *Pilate*. Pilate was the Roman governor, AD 26–36.

15:2 *Are you the King of the Jews?* This is the charge that matters to Pilate. If Jesus is a potential king, then He is a political rival to Rome. Pilate's focus on the identity of Jesus matches the theme of Mark since 1:1. Whether announced by God the Father (1:11; 9:7) or shrieked by demons (1:24; 5:7), the knowledge of Jesus as the only Son of God is key. *You have said so*. This appears to us to be an enigmatic answer. It means, "Yes, it is as you have said." Jesus uses Pilate's question to present the truth also to Pilate. However, Jesus is not the sort of king Pilate would understand (Jn 18:36). Jesus is the king who willingly takes the worst place for the sake of all. Luther writes:

> Not one of the saints thinks or says that he is righteous but rather always prays and waits to be justified, and for this reason he is regarded by God as righteous, because He has regard for the humble. Thus Christ is King of the Jews, that is, of those who confess that they are always sinners and yet seek to be justified and hate their sins. (LW 25:246)

15:3 *the chief priests accused him*. This accusation, *katagoreo*, is found only here, at 15:4, and at 3:2. The enemies have been watching Jesus from the earliest days of His ministry to find fault with His healing and teaching. They likely recounted their many disputes with Him on matters of the Law, the keeping of the Sabbath, and the interpretation of the Scripture. Pilate would have little interest in these debates. In fact, he might have viewed Jesus as a kindred spirit, as he himself was also often in conflict with the Jewish leadership over these same matters.

15:4 *have you no answer to make?* Pilate is used to defendants denying all guilt and explaining all their deeds. But here was a man majestically silent. Why should Jesus, the King, answer the questions of the mere governor? He was on His Father's course. Jesus' years of teaching have come to an end now that His predicted crucifixion is in sight.

15:5 *no further answer*. Jesus' silence gave Pilate nothing to use for His defense, though the clear injustice of the charges left Pilate to try (vv. 10–11). *Pilate was amazed*. This word amazed (*thaumadzo*) appeared in 5:20 when the man delivered from the legion of demons told all that Jesus had done and people were astonished. Now Jesus' enemies tell all that He has done, and by Jesus' silence, Pilate is amazed. Only one step of amazement remains (15:44), when Pilate is astonished that Jesus dies so quickly. Jesus, in word and deed, silence and death, astonished all.

15:1–5 in Devotion and Prayer The Jewish leaders bring Jesus to Pilate, hoping to get a death penalty conviction from him. The world does not understand the kingdom of God, where God rules by grace through faith in Jesus Christ, nor does the world understand its King. Jesus endures His trial silently, without making a legal defense. He willingly goes to the cross for us. • "O mighty King, no time can dim Thy glory! How shall I spread abroad Thy wondrous story? How shall I find some worthy gifts to proffer? What dare I offer?" Amen. (*LSB* 439:8)

15:6 *the feast.* Passover. *release . . . one prisoner.* This was a local custom designed to reduce tensions among crowds at the feast and thus to keep a lid on anti-Roman sentiment. Pilate now sees this as a solution to a more immediate problem. He is in the vise between the pressuring Jewish leaders and the silent, innocent Jesus. Offering Barabbas would allow Pilate to put another into the murderous trap set for Jesus. Pilate could then thwart the leaders' plans, decide justly for an innocent man, and rid Jerusalem of a dangerous murderer.

15:7 *the insurrection.* This refers to a recent uprising against the ruling authorities that is otherwise unknown, as only Mark records this event. *Barabbas.* His name is Aramaic for "son of the father." Barabbas was the type of revolutionary leader who concerned Pilate, the type Jesus was accused of being.

15:8 *crowd.* The crowd is too convenient and focused on Jesus' death to be completely spontaneous. They may have been employees of the temple and therefore directed by the chief priests. *began to ask Pilate to do as he usually did for them.* They knew of the tradition of one being set free. How ironic that their request for one to be set free becomes the foundation of Jesus' crucifixion. Jesus does what He has always done, saving others at His own expense, and fulfilling the promises He has made concerning His death and resurrection.

15:9 *Do you want me to release for you the King of the Jews?* This could have been Pilate's way out of condemning an innocent man. If Jesus were chosen, His guilt or innocence would not have to be determined. Furthermore, the genuinely guilty Barabbas could then be executed. Also, by naming Jesus as the King of the Jews, Pilate showed his power over every Jew, even a so-called king.

15:10 *it was out of envy.* Pilate likely had heard of Jesus' work and His triumphant entry on Palm Sunday. The priests accused Jesus of many things (v. 3). Their chief, though unspoken, charge was that He had greater authority and power than they. Pilate could see Jesus as a tool and even an ally in his own power struggle against these leaders.

15:11 *the chief priests stirred up the crowd.* Stirring up, *anaseio,* is used only here and in Lk 23:5. It is a seismic uplifting of the crowd. Interestingly, here the priests agitate the crowd, while in Lk 23:5 they accuse Jesus of doing the same. The priests push for Barabbas' freedom, likely using the crowd's desire for independence from Rome. Barabbas, the would-be leader of a temporary freedom, is released, while the true Prince of Peace and ruler of an eternal kingdom is condemned.

15:12 *then what shall I do with the man you call the King of the Jews?* Pilate puts the title of king on Jesus and the responsibility for the title on the people of Israel. He stresses his power over their king, but wants them to accept responsibility for his decision. It would be ideal for Pilate to have power without responsibility. But he will not be able to escape. In Mark's Gospel, Pilate's one successful question (v. 2) is about whether Jesus is King of the Jews, and it is on this point that Jesus will be tried and condemned.

15:13 *they cried out again.* The first cry of the crowd had been for Barabbas' merciful release. Now they cry "Crucify." They shift quickly from asking mercy for the worst criminal to death for the innocent. *Crucify.* This was punishment so horrific that it was illegal to inflict it on Roman citizens. Death on the tree of the cross recalls the OT condemnation that a hanged man is cursed by God (Dt 21:23; Paul quotes this in Gal 3:13). Christ became the accursed to bring the blessing of God on all (Gal 3:13–14).

15:14 *what evil has He done?* Pilates' plan for the Barabbas/Jesus exchange came apart instantly. Asking the crowd for Jesus' crimes was hopeless. Even the orchestrated witnesses at His trial could not agree on any wrong (14:56). The crowd has no answer except to renew their demand for His death. This exchange between Pilate and the crowd acts out 2Co 5:21, "He made Him to be sin who knew no sin."

15:15 *wishing to satisfy the crowd.* Pilate has lost on all sides by now. He cannot compel Jesus to speak. He cannot outmaneuver the chief priests' plot. He cannot persuade the crowd to ask for Jesus. By now he is reduced to serving the crowd to protect himself. *re-*

leased for them Barabbas. Almost forgotten, Barabbas is released as a picture of the world's deliverance. A thoroughly guilty man walks free while the Son of God walks beneath the cross. *scourged.* This was a common prelude to crucifixion, adding to its physical agony. It shows Pilate's complete surrender to the crowd's demands.

15:6–15 in Devotion and Prayer Despite knowing that Jesus is innocent, Pilate condemns Him to death by crucifixion under pressure from the Jewish leadership and the crowds. Even though Pilate wants to release Jesus, he sentences Him to death to keep himself out of trouble. Often, Christians face similar temptations to act contrary to God's Word and will for their own safety. We can pray that the Lord would grant us courage to trust His will and share His will. He has promised to give us His Holy Spirit to strengthen us for every challenge. • "I'll think upon Thy mercy without ceasing, That earth's vain joys to me no more be pleasing; To do Thy will shall be my sole endeavor Henceforth forever." Amen. (*LSB* 439:12)

Jesus is mocked by the soldiers, crucified, and dies (15:16–41)

ESV	KJV
16 And the soldiers led him away inside the palace (that is, the governor's headquarters), and they called together the whole battalion. 17 And they clothed him in a purple cloak, and twisting together a crown of thorns, they put it on him. 18 And they began to salute him, "Hail, King of the Jews!" 19 And they were striking his head with a reed and spitting on him and kneeling down in homage to him. 20 And when they had mocked him, they stripped him of the purple cloak and put his own clothes on him. And they led him out to crucify him. 21 And they compelled a passerby, Simon of Cyrene, who was coming in from the country, the father of Alexander and Rufus, to carry his cross. 22 And they brought him to the	16 And the soldiers led him away into the hall, called Praetorium; and they call together the whole band. 17 And they clothed him with purple, and platted a crown of thorns, and put it about his head, 18 And began to salute him, Hail, King of the Jews! 19 And they smote him on the head with a reed, and did spit upon him, and bowing their knees worshipped him. 20 And when they had mocked him, they took off the purple from him, and put his own clothes on him, and led him out to crucify him. 21 And they compel one Simon a Cyrenian, who passed by, coming out of the country, the father of Alexander and Rufus, to bear his cross.

place called Golgotha (which means
Place of a Skull). 23And they offered
him wine mixed with myrrh, but he
did not take it. 24And they crucified
him and divided his garments among
them, casting lots for them, to decide
what each should take. 25And it was
the third hour when they crucified
him. 26And the inscription of the
charge against him read, "The King
of the Jews." 27And with him they
crucified two robbers, one on his
right and one on his left. 29And those
who passed by derided him, wagging their heads and saying, "Aha!
You who would destroy the temple
and rebuild it in three days, 30save
yourself, and come down from the
cross!" 31So also the chief priests
with the scribes mocked him to one
another, saying, "He saved others; he
cannot save himself. 32Let the Christ,
the King of Israel, come down now
from the cross that we may see and
believe." Those who were crucified
with him also reviled him.

33And when the sixth hour had
come, there was darkness over the
whole land until the ninth hour.
34And at the ninth hour Jesus cried
with a loud voice, "Eloi, Eloi, lema
sabachthani?" which means, "My
God, my God, why have you forsaken
me?" 35And some of the bystanders
hearing it said, "Behold, he is calling Elijah." 36And someone ran and
filled a sponge with sour wine, put it
on a reed and gave it to him to drink,
saying, "Wait, let us see whether Elijah will come to take him down."
37And Jesus uttered a loud cry and
breathed his last. 38And the curtain
of the temple was torn in two, from
top to bottom. 39And when the centu-

22And they bring him unto the place Golgotha, which is, being interpreted, The place of a skull.

23And they gave him to drink wine mingled with myrrh: but he received it not.

24And when they had crucified him, they parted his garments, casting lots upon them, what every man should take.

25And it was the third hour, and they crucified him.

26And the superscription of his accusation was written over, THE KING OF THE JEWS.

27And with him they crucify two thieves; the one on his right hand, and the other on his left.

28And the scripture was fulfilled, which saith, And he was numbered with the transgressors.

29And they that passed by railed on him, wagging their heads, and saying, Ah, thou that destroyest the temple, and buildest it in three days,

30Save thyself, and come down from the cross.

31Likewise also the chief priests mocking said among themselves with the scribes, He saved others; himself he cannot save.

32Let Christ the King of Israel descend now from the cross, that we may see and believe. And they that were crucified with him reviled him.

33And when the sixth hour was come, there was darkness over the whole land until the ninth hour.

34And at the ninth hour Jesus cried with a loud voice, saying, Eloi, Eloi, lama sabachthani? which is, being interpreted, My God, my God, why hast thou forsaken me?

35And some of them that stood by,

rion, who stood facing him, saw that in this way he breathed his last, he said, "Truly this man was the Son of God!"

40There were also women looking on from a distance, among whom were Mary Magdalene, and Mary the mother of James the younger and of Joses, and Salome. 41When he was in Galilee, they followed him and ministered to him, and there were also many other women who came up with him to Jerusalem.

when they heard it, said, Behold, he calleth Elias.

36And one ran and filled a spunge full of vinegar, and put it on a reed, and gave him to drink, saying, Let alone; let us see whether Elias will come to take him down.

37And Jesus cried with a loud voice, and gave up the ghost.

38And the veil of the temple was rent in twain from the top to the bottom.

39And when the centurion, which stood over against him, saw that he so cried out, and gave up the ghost, he said, Truly this man was the Son of God.

40There were also women looking on afar off: among whom was Mary Magdalene, and Mary the mother of James the less and of Joses, and Salome;

41(Who also, when he was in Galilee, followed him, and ministered unto him;) and many other women which came up with him unto Jerusalem.

Introduction to 15:16–41 The long journey comes down to these last few steps. Jesus is clothed and hailed as King, then stripped and killed as a criminal. Those around Him vary. Some mock Him for His weakness, some taunt Him with His past saving of others, while others silently serve Him as they can. Finally the centurion speaks for the entire Gospel by recognizing Him as the Son of God even in death.

15:16 *the soldiers . . . the whole battalion.* Jesus is now in the custody of Pilate's Roman guards rather than the palace guard of the Jews. All the soldiers turn out to see and handle the King of the Jews. Here was no ordinary criminal. The condemnation of Jesus is an opportunity for the soldiers to insult the Jews and demonstrate their power. They have none of Pilate's worries over His innocence.

It was time for them to express through mockery the hatred that had surrounded Jesus through this Passion week.

15:17 *clothed Him in a purple cloak.* This is used in mockery of a royal robe. It was likely a soldier's cloak, a short cape, and was purple or scarlet (cf. Mt 27:28). It would have appeared scornfully similar to the royal robes of a true king. *crown of thorns.* The thorns were a sadistic imitation of a crown. Adam's fall into sin caused the earth to be cursed with thorns and thistles (Gn 3:18). The new Adam now bears the thorns as He pays for the sins of all. Luther writes: "Now sin, as we well know, is removed by nothing but the suffering of Christ. For that is the power and the fruit of His suffering, the forgiveness of sins, as Is 53 and Peter and Paul teach in many places" (LW 20:219).

15:18 *they began to salute Him.* This greeting, *aspadzo,* is used only twice in Mk. In 9:15, as Jesus comes from the Mount of Transfiguration the crowd greets Him in amazement. Now before He goes up Mount Calvary, the soldiers salute Him with mocking. Little does either group realize that they have met the true Son of God, capable of shining majesty and the praise of the Father. *Hail, King of the Jews!* The soldiers likely are echoing the greeting they would give Caesar, but said with sneering disdain for this king.

15:19 *they were striking His head with a reed.* The reed was both His scepter and His scourge in their mocking drama. The soldiers showed their power in giving Him this token of authority and then beating Him with it. *spitting on Him.* Jesus had foretold this mocking and spitting (10:34), an unimaginable part of His prediction when He was surrounded by devoted followers. *kneeling down in homage to Him.* This last step completed their ridicule, a mockery of true worship. The word translated "in homage" is the verb *proskuneo,* usually translated "worship" as in the KJV here. It is the word describing the Wise Men's worship of Jesus (Mt 2:2, 11). In Mark it appears only here and 5:6 where the demonized man kneels before Jesus. Only at the end of time will all the world finally bend the knee and confess that He is Lord (Php 2:9–11).

15:20 *when they had mocked Him.* Here and in 15:31, mockery sums up the treatment given to Jesus. His humble majesty is completely new to them, and so mockery is their only response. *they stripped Him of the purple cloak.* When the mockery has run its course, the cloak is returned to its owner, and Jesus' own clothes, perhaps bloody from the early abuse, are returned to Him. When they lead Him into the crowd with the title "King of the Jews," they want nothing to suggest that He is truly a king.

15:16–20 in Devotion and Prayer Roman soldiers mock Jesus as the King of the Jews, inflicting terrible physical and emotional pain. Paying for the sin of the world was costly. Jesus' tremendous love for us kept Him on course to the cross. • "Whence come these sorrows, whence this mortal anguish? It is my sins for which Thou, Lord, must languish; Yea, all the wrath, the woe, Thou dost inherit, This I do merit." Amen. (*LSB* 439:3)

15:21 *Simon of Cyrene.* Simon was a man from the northeast coast of Africa who had come to Jerusalem for the festival. As an eyewitness to these events, he could share his experience with the Gospel writers. Simon, innocently bearing the cross, is an image of Jesus' own journey, except that Jesus chose the cross with every right to escape from it. *Alexander and Rufus.* These two men were known to the original readers, Rufus perhaps being the man mentioned in Paul's greeting (Rm 16:13). If so, they were early Christians in Rome who had a unique connection with Christ through their father. *carry His cross.* Just the crossbeam, which could weigh as much as 100 pounds. Often during His decades as a carpenter Jesus must have lifted such a beam and known how His life would end. What courage it took to live with that knowledge, surrounded daily by wood, hammer, and nails.

15:22 *Place of a Skull.* It is unclear whether Golgotha was so named because people were crucified there or because the hill looked like a skull. Regardless, it was a forbidding place outside the city. This setting is reminiscent of the hill outside of Nazareth where the people of Nazareth brought Jesus to throw Him off the cliff (Lk 4:28–30). At Nazareth He simply walked away, for His hour had not yet come. But now, on this other forlorn hill, far from His home, His hour has come.

15:23 *wine mixed with myrrh.* This was a narcotic offered to make the condemned prisoner easier to control. The mention of myrrh recalls the gift of the Magi (Mt 2:11) and the spices, including myrrh, used by Nicodemus when wrapping His body (Jn 19:39–40). From birth to death, this fragrant spice has bracketed His life. Matthew 27:34 notes that the wine was also mixed with gall, a bitter drug either as a narcotic or poison, while the myrrh might have been included to make the drink palatable. *He did not take it.* Jesus was nailed to the cross without any drugs, fully experiencing the Law's punishment for the sins of the world.

15:24 *they crucified Him.* This short phrase captures the whole event, especially the nailing of Jesus to the cross and his elevation upon the upright cross. *lots.* The lots were cast using dice made from bone. The casting of lots and dividing of His clothes fulfilled this prophecy of Ps 22:18. John 19:23 notes that the tunic was one piece. Better that one man get it whole than for it to be uselessly divided. Remarkably, the whole benefits of Jesus' death come to every person on earth, not by lot or merit, but by the mercy of the Father who gives up His Son.

15:25 *it was the third hour.* The third hour, according to the Jewish clock, was 9:00 a.m. The trial before Pilate was going on at 6:00 a.m. (Jn 19:14), and so a few hours have passed for His condemnation, mocking, and walk to Golgotha. The next six hours will pay the world's debt and bring this ministry of humble service to an end.

15:26 *the inscription of the charge against Him.* The criminal charge against the condemned (cf. Jn 19:19–22) was written on a board hung around His neck. Then it was placed on the cross at the execution site. *the King of the Jews.* His title, which was the hope of many, becomes His condemnation. He is a king whose kingdom is not of this world, but He claims this one place, the throne of the cross, as His alone.

15:27 *and with Him they crucified two robbers.* Isaiah 53:12 prophesied that He would be numbered with the transgressors. Luther reflects,

> And all the prophets saw this, that Christ was to become the greatest thief, murderer, adulterer, robber, desecrator, blasphemer, etc., there has ever been anywhere in the world. . . . In short, He has and bears all the sins of all men in His body—not in the sense that He has committed them but in the sense that He took these sins, committed by us, upon His own body, in order to make satisfaction for them with His own blood. (LW 26:277)

robbers. These were likely rebels who sought the violent overthrow of the Romans in Judea; they were similar in crime to Barabbas.

15:28 *the Scripture was fulfilled that says, "He was numbered with the transgressors."* While many manuscripts include this verse, the earliest manuscripts do not. The reference is to Is 53:12, a prophecy also used in Lk 22:37 in regard to Jesus' disciples having two swords at the Mount of Olives. Jesus fulfills this prophecy with both the disciples and these anonymous criminals. By His association with all of us, He is numbered with the transgressors and then delivers to all the righteousness of God.

15:29 *derided.* Literally, "blasphemed," insulted and mocked. Jesus was first blasphemed for forgiving the paralytic's sins (2:7), and now finally for His prediction that they would destroy the temple of His body and He would raise it. He is not condemned for any evil, but for the divine gifts of forgiveness and resurrection. *Aha!* This is the only time this short term of derision is used in the NT. *you who would destroy the temple.* The mockers return to the initial charge against Jesus (14:58), which is distorted here as when He was on trial. With His death, they are fulfilling His prediction (Jn 2:19) that they will destroy the temple of Himself. They revile Him since He appears powerless, but it is through this weakness that God does His work (1Co 1:23–24).

15:30 *save yourself, and come down from the cross.* Save yourself, indeed. We cannot save ourselves and He will not save Himself. They dare Him to show His power to preserve His own life. That would be a selfishness that they could understand. But His power will come with the resurrection that they can't imagine. As for saving life, He will only be satisfied when He saves the whole world.

15:31 *chief priests . . . scribes.* Just as the charge against Him returned (v. 29), so also His principal opponents reappear. They have come to see their plot victoriously through. Now they can come into the crowd fearlessly instead of hiding their hatred (14:1–2). *He saved others.* When Jesus is on the cross, the priests will grant His miracles of healing. Perhaps silently on the fringe of the crowd were some who were actually healed. They watch in wonder as He dies. *He cannot save Himself.* They have confused His choice with weakness. By their conniving, they have saved their authority for now. They cannot see the love and power in Jesus' willingness to be crucified.

15:32 *Christ, the King of Israel.* The two titles here, Christ and King of Israel, were used interchangeably. Here is the title that began it all, Christ (1:1), the Son of God. They promise to believe if He merely comes down from the nails of the cross. Our faith is founded on the greater miracle, His coming out from the stone of the grave. *reviled.* Only Luke tells of the repentant thief (Lk 23:39–43). Likely both of the thieves abused Him at first, until the repentant thief saw Him as a merciful King.

15:21–32 in Devotion and Prayer Jesus is crucified, bearing the punishment for the sins of the world. This is what it costs to atone for sins. At any time, Jesus can halt the proceedings, save Himself, and condemn His enemies. His love for us and His obedience to the Father lead Him to make this sacrifice instead. • "The sinless Son of God must die in sadness; The sinful child of man may live in gladness; Man forfeited his life and is acquitted; God is committed." Amen. (*LSB* 439:5)

15:33 *sixth hour . . . ninth hour.* From noon to 3 p.m. *darkness.* This darkness recalls the ninth and tenth plagues upon Egypt. Three days of darkness, the ninth plague (Ex 10:21–23), preceded the Passover night when the firstborn of Egypt died, but Israel was set free (Ex 12:12). Now darkness comes upon the world. It is the sign of judgment over sin, the sorrow of the Father over His Son's death, and the covering under which slaves to sin are set free.

15:34 *loud voice.* A crucified man died of asphyxiation and was quiet at the end; therefore, Jesus' cry required superhuman effort. *Eloi.* This Aramaic name sounded identical to "Elijah." Ambrose says: "Christ, in naming God as His God, does so as man. . . . He suffers as a man" and "as man, therefore, He is distressed, as man He weeps, as man He is crucified" (*NPNF*2 10:216, 230). *why have you forsaken me?* The Father forsakes the Son as He carries the curse of sin. According to His human nature, Jesus can experience this forsaken state even while He is one God with the Father. By His divine nature, His suffering has the power to atone for the sins of the world.

15:35 *Behold, He is calling Elijah.* They misunderstood His call to the Father (v. 34). Rather than appealing to the departed saint for help, He was calling to the Father with whom He is one God. Yet for our sakes, He was forsaken even within that divine relationship so that He could become sin for us (2Co 5:21).

15:36 *sour wine.* This cheap drink was used by Roman troops ,and so it was likely a soldier who offered this drink. John 19:28 notes that Jesus called out, "I thirst." His genuine suffering and His desire to call out clearly His last words left Him parched. *Wait, let us see whether Elijah will come.* While the soldier likely gave Him the wine, these words could come from the mocking crowd. They thought He had called on Elijah (vv. 34–35), and this was another small test they were sure He would fail. Elijah not coming would prove that Jesus was no king and not God. This one verse contrasts the soldiers and the crowd in a small kindness and a mocking derision.

15:37 *loud cry.* Crucifixion made this extremely difficult. Hanging on the cross with the pain of the nails limited a man's ability to fill his lungs. Jesus did not slip into death with a murmur but marked His end with this triumphant cry. *breathed His last.* Christ gave up

His life of His own accord (Jn 10:18). He gave up His spirit (Mt 27:50), trusting the Father's care (Lk 23:46).

15:38 *the curtain of the temple was torn in two.* Tearing of the curtain, which separated the Most Holy Place of the temple from the Holy Place, symbolized the opened fellowship between God and people through Christ (cf. Heb 10:19–22). The word for "torn," *schidzo,* is used twice in Mark. In 1:10, the heavens are torn open upon His baptism, and now the temple curtain is torn open upon His death. Both acts affirm that Jesus is the Father's Son who opens the Kingdom of heaven to all.

15:39 *the centurion . . . Truly this was the Son of God.* This is the climax of Mark. Jesus' identity as the Son of God has been highlighted (1:1, 11; 8:29; 9:7), by Mark himself, God the Father, and Peter. Now even the centurion, a Roman like Mark's initial readers, confessed Jesus as the Son of God. Matthew 27:51–54 notes that the centurion and others observed the earthquake at His death. The centurion may not have fully understood his confession, but Mark's readers recognized that Jesus is true God and true man. Even in death His divinity was clear. Luther writes: "For we are sinners and thieves, and therefore we are worthy of death and eternal damnation. But Christ took all our sins upon Himself, and for them He died on the cross" (LW 26:277).

15:40 *there were also women looking on.* In striking contrast to the crowd and the centurion, these women faithfully, courageously watched from the side. *Mary Magdalene.* Mary leads the list as also in Lk 8:2 and will be first to see Jesus (Jn 20:11–18). *Mary, the mother of Joses.* John 19:25 tells us this is the wife of Clopas and the sister of Jesus' mother, Mary. *Salome.* She was the mother of James and John (Mt 27:56). What a transition there is in the crowd around Jesus. We journey through the scornful chief priests and scribes (v. 31), the misunderstanding crowd (v. 33), the kind soldier (v. 36), the confessing centurion (v. 39), and end with the women and those who come to bury Jesus (vv. 42–47).

15:41 *they followed Him and ministered to Him.* They had joined His ministry travels early on (Lk 8:2–3). They likely had heard His predictions of His death and resurrection and faithfully stayed to see Him through to the end. Their faithful watching was the opposite of the sleeping by the three disciples in the Garden (14:32–41).

15:33–41 in Devotion and Prayer Jesus pays for the sins of the world on the cross, opening the way to God through faith in Him. As God and man in one person, He dies under the curse of the Law

(Gal 3:13–14). The penalty for sin is death (cf. Rm 6:23a). Jesus pays that penalty for us all (cf. Rm 6:23b). • "What language shall I borrow To thank Thee, dearest Friend, For this Thy dying sorrow, Thy pity without end? O make me Thine forever! And should I fainting be, Lord, let me never, never, Outlive my love for Thee." Amen. (*LSB* 450:5; *H82* 168, 169:4; *TPH* 98:3; *TUMH* 286:3)

Jesus is buried (15:42–47)

ESV	KJV
42 And when evening had come, since it was the day of Preparation, that is, the day before the Sabbath, 43 Joseph of Arimathea, a respected member of the Council, who was also himself looking for the kingdom of God, took courage and went to Pilate and asked for the body of Jesus. 44 Pilate was surprised to hear that he should have already died. And summoning the centurion, he asked him whether he was already dead. 45 And when he learned from the centurion that he was dead, he granted the corpse to Joseph. 46 And Joseph bought a linen shroud, and taking him down, wrapped him in the linen shroud and laid him in a tomb that had been cut out of the rock. And he rolled a stone against the entrance of the tomb. 47 Mary Magdalene and Mary the mother of Joses saw where he was laid.	**42 And now when the even was come, because it was the preparation, that is, the day before the sabbath, 43 Joseph of Arimathaea, an honourable counsellor, which also waited for the kingdom of God, came, and went in boldly unto Pilate, and craved the body of Jesus. 44 And Pilate marvelled if he were already dead: and calling unto him the centurion, he asked him whether he had been any while dead. 45 And when he knew it of the centurion, he gave the body to Joseph. 46 And he bought fine linen, and took him down, and wrapped him in the linen, and laid him in a sepulchre which was hewn out of a rock, and rolled a stone unto the door of the sepulchre. 47 And Mary Magdalene and Mary the mother of Jesus beheld where he was laid.**

Introduction to 15:42–47 Three followers of Jesus step forward at His death. Joseph of Arimathea takes courage to ask for His body, receives it and buries it while Mary Magdalene and Mary, the mother of Joses, watch. As the sun sets, they lay Him to rest in a peaceful darkness. All is now ready for His resurrection.

15:42 *evening*. Between 4 and 5 p.m. *day of Preparation*. This was Friday when all had to be prepared for the Sabbath that would begin at sundown. This left little time for Joseph to get permission for the burial and to carry it out. Jesus would be fully laid to rest by the start of the day of rest.

15:43 *Council.* Joseph was one of the seventy in the Sanhedrin, the ruling Council. *himself looking for the kingdom of God, took courage.* Joseph had found hope in the Messiah and was considered a disciple of Jesus (Mt 27:57). The verb "took courage" (*tolmao*) occurs twice in Mark. In Mk 12:34, Jesus told a perceptive scribe that he was not far from the kingdom of God, and thereafter no one dared to ask Jesus questions. Now, Joseph, looking for the kingdom of God, dares to ask for the body of Jesus. *asked for the body.* He requested permission to bury the body of Jesus. This was risky because Jesus had been executed for treason. That Pilate releases the body (v. 45) reflects his belief that Jesus was innocent.

15:44 *Pilate was surprised.* Pilate had been amazed by Jesus' silence when questioned (15:5), and is surprised now by His sudden death. *already died.* A man ordinarily lasted at least twenty-four hours on the cross. To hasten death and remove the bodies before the Sabbath, the legs of the criminals were broken (cf. Jn 19:31; see also Jos, *Life*, 420–21). *summoning the centurion.* The centurion has seen Jesus' death and the earthquake that followed. Darkness turned to light upon Jesus' death also. When asked if Jesus was dead, the centurion could answer "Yes," and might have said more about the identity of Jesus and the events around His death.

15:45 *he granted the corpse to Joseph.* It would be an elegant solution: give the body to a member of the Council whose members had campaigned for Jesus' death. However, this man would take the body to care for it, not to dishonor it.

15:46 *a linen shroud.* This was used to wrap the body for burial. *laid Him in a tomb.* Luther says,

> Christ tells us how He destroys death and how I am rescued from death. He will be death's venom. Death and Law, to be sure, will condemn Him. Therefore He will have to die and be buried. But He will rise again from the dead. And where I shall be then, the devil will have to retreat. But how do I approach this Savior and Redeemer? By means of . . . rules? No! Just cling to the Son in faith. (LW 22:355–56)

tomb . . . cut out of the rock. The tomb, cut out of the rock, was expensive, as expected of a rich man (Mt 27:57). In this way, Jesus fulfilled Is 53:9, being "with a rich man in His death."

15:47 The women watched and so knew the location of the tomb (cf. 16:1). We can imagine them making their plans for Sunday's anointing even while they were still filled with grief. Sorrow and love today will become astonishment and joy on Sunday.

15:42–47 in Devotion and Prayer Friends bury the body of Jesus quickly. The approaching Sabbath Day was holy to the Lord, and no work could be done (Ex 20:8–11). Jesus completes His mission with this last stage in His state of humiliation. He has fully paid for the sins of the entire world! • Grant me patience, dearest Jesus, to bear the reproaches of those who do not know and confess the blessings of Your death and resurrection. Give me boldness to confess You before the world. Amen.

The women find the empty tomb and hear that Jesus is risen (16:1–8)

ESV	KJV
16 [1]When the Sabbath was past, Mary Magdalene and Mary the mother of James and Salome bought spices, so that they might go and anoint him. [2]And very early on the first day of the week, when the sun had risen, they went to the tomb. [3]And they were saying to one another, "Who will roll away the stone for us from the entrance of the tomb?" [4]And looking up, they saw that the stone had been rolled back—it was very large. [5]And entering the tomb, they saw a young man sitting on the right side, dressed in a white robe, and they were alarmed. [6]And he said to them, "Do not be alarmed. You seek Jesus of Nazareth, who was crucified. He has risen; he is not here.	**16 [1]And when the sabbath was past, Mary Magdalene, and Mary the mother of James, and Salome, had bought sweet spices, that they might come and anoint him. [2]And very early in the morning the first day of the week, they came unto the sepulchre at the rising of the sun. [3]And they said among themselves, Who shall roll us away the stone from the door of the sepulchre? [4]And when they looked, they saw that the stone was rolled away: for it was very great. [5]And entering into the sepulchre, they saw a young man sitting on the right side, clothed in a long white garment; and they were affrighted.**

See the place where they laid him. [7]But go, tell his disciples and Peter that he is going before you to Galilee. There you will see him, just as he told you." [8]And they went out and fled from the tomb, for trembling and astonishment had seized them, and they said nothing to anyone, for they were afraid.

[6]And he saith unto them, Be not affrighted: Ye seek Jesus of Nazareth, which was crucified: he is risen; he is not here: behold the place where they laid him.

[7]But go your way, tell his disciples and Peter that he goeth before you into Galilee: there shall ye see him, as he said unto you.

[8]And they went out quickly, and fled from the sepulchre; for they trembled and were amazed: neither said they any thing to any man; for they were afraid.

Introduction to 16:1–8 Sorrow becomes joy as the angel announces Jesus' resurrection. The Gospel began with John as the messenger, announcing Jesus' coming and kingdom. Now the Gospel concludes with another messenger, the angel in the tomb. The world was unprepared for John's arrival and work, but the women who begin ch. 16 come fully prepared for Jesus' anointing. They are unaware, however, of their true mission. Anointing the dead becomes rejoicing with the living. They race off, the news of resurrection leaving them speechless.

16:1 *Sabbath was past.* The Sabbath concluded after sundown on Saturday. The women must have waited anxiously through that night for their first chance to go to the tomb in the dawn's first light. *Mary Magdalene.* Mary was also listed first in 15:40 among the women who followed and ministered to Jesus. See the note there and 15:47. *spices . . . anoint.* Sweet-smelling ointments were usually wrapped around corpses in strips of cloth before entombment. This was their chance to serve Jesus in a final way, matching the courageous work of Joseph and Nicodemus who buried Jesus on Friday.

16:2 *very early on the first day.* The women are free to travel and work now that the Sabbath is over. The day of rest is done but the true work that is about to be done is much greater than they could ever imagine. Jesus, the ultimate Sabbath rest, begins now a new work with His resurrection. By this all people condemned to death are given new life and He is declared the Son of God by His resurrection (Rm 1:4). *when the sun had risen.* How fitting that Jesus' resurrection comes with the joy and hope of dawn.

16:3 *who will roll away the stone for us.* The women were thorough in their preparations of spices and energetic in coming so early. These arrangements crowded out the sad question of the tomb's stone. They had always been able to meet Jesus, being some of those joyfully near Him. But now the stone stands fixed between them and their Lord. They had likely seen Nicodemus and Joseph set the stone in place with effort, but had no arrangement with them for this morning. Who then will help?

16:4 The stone is rolled away as a sign of the resurrection. It was not necessary as part of Jesus' coming to life and leaving. He passed through the stone so that when it is rolled back, the women and guards can see that the tomb is already empty (Mt 28:1–6). The symbol of death becomes the first mark of the resurrection.

16:5 *entering the tomb.* Commend the women for their courage in going into the tomb, given this strange beginning. They had planned to enter it, but not like this. *young man.* Angels typically appear in the form of young, adult males. *white robe.* Matthew notes that the robe is stunning in whiteness (Mt 28:3). Such brilliance recalls the transfiguration, a moment of heaven stepping onto the earth.

16:6 *alarmed.* People were often filled with awe and fear in the presence of angels. The word *angelos*, usually translated "angel," is first found in Mk 1:2, referring to John the Baptist as a messenger. Angels come first in Mk 1:13, aiding Jesus in His temptation. How appropriate that their final appearance is to announce His complete victory. *He has risen.* Jesus had taken up His life just as He had laid it down on Good Friday (cf. Jn 10:17–18). Romans 4:25 says that He was crucified for our sins and raised for our justification. Luther says,

> The blessed resurrection . . . is pure joy, because we hear that our greatest Treasure, over which we rejoice, is already in heaven above, and that only the most insignificant part remains behind; and that He will awaken this, too, and draw it after Him as easily as a person awakens from sleep. There will no longer be any grief or suffering, and neither world nor devil will plague and sadden us anymore. (LW 28:115)

16:7 *but go, tell.* As fascinating as the empty tomb and the angel might be, there is work to do! The angel is not an attraction unto himself but is a messenger of greater news. *His disciples and Peter.*

How Peter must have cherished this simple inclusion of himself as one of the disciples. Here is forgiveness and a new beginning in just a word. Melanchthon notes the power of cases of forgiveness for all: "Examples of mercy help . . . such as when we see Peter forgiven his denial" (Ap XXI 36). *Galilee.* This was the original home of Jesus and His disciples. This fulfills Jesus' promise in 14:28. *you will see Him.* Peter's last glance from Jesus was the look after the third denial (Lk 22:61), while John had endured watching Jesus on the cross (Jn 19:26–27). But this future sight will be the complete opposite: Jesus in resurrection power.

16:8 The women were directed to seek the disciples, but the shock of the angel and the empty tomb was the chief motivation for their flight. The word for "astonishment," *ekstasis*, is used twice in Mark. In 5:42, the parents and disciples were greatly astonished at the resurrection of the little girl. So here again, resurrection leaves them completely astounded. Matthew 28:8 tells us that they left with fear and joy, but went to tell the disciples. *they said nothing.* The women are temporarily silenced by fear. Peter, James, and John were similarly silent on the Mount of Transfiguration (9:6). Luther says:

> A Christian must accustom himself to think about Christ's victory—the victory in which everything has already been accomplished and in which we have everything we should have. Henceforth we live only to spread among other people the news of what Christ has achieved. (LW 24:421)

Their silence is a strange ending to the Gospel, if v. 8 is the intentional ending. It might be fitting if, as 1:1 says, these sixteen chapters are but the beginning of the Gospel. Then the work of telling the full story falls to all who have read and believed.

16:1–8 in Devotion and Prayer Three women come to the tomb but find it filled with the angel and his news. Jesus has risen from the dead! Jesus fulfilled His predictions of death and resurrection (8:31–32; 9:31; 10:33–34) despite His disciples' fears and doubts. Now proclaim His victory to all creation. He has provided for all believers a resurrection to eternal life on the Last Day. • "Christ Jesus lay in death's strong bands For our offenses given; But now at God's right hand He stands And brings us life from heaven. Therefore let us joyful be And sing to God right thankfully Loud songs of alleluia! Alleluia!" Amen. (*LSB* 458:1; *H82* 185,186:1; *TPH* 110:1; *TUMH* 319:1)

Part 4

The Long Ending (16:9–20)

ESV

[Some of the earliest manuscripts do
not include 16:9–20.]
9 [[Now when he rose early on the
first day of the week, he appeared
first to Mary Magdalene, from whom
he had cast out seven demons. 10 She
went and told those who had been
with him, as they mourned and wept.
11 But when they heard that he was
alive and had been seen by her, they
would not believe it.
12 After these things he appeared in
another form to two of them, as they
were walking into the country. 13 And
they went back and told the rest, but
they did not believe them.
14 Afterward he appeared to the
eleven themselves as they were
reclining at table, and he rebuked
them for their unbelief and hardness of heart, because they had not
believed those who saw him after he
had risen. 15 And he said to them, "Go
into all the world and proclaim the
gospel to the whole creation. 16 Whoever believes and is baptized will be
saved, but whoever does not believe
will be condemned. 17 And these signs
will accompany those who believe: in
my name they will cast out demons;
they will speak in new tongues;
18 they will pick up serpents with their
hands; and if they drink any deadly

KJV

9 Now when Jesus was risen early the first day of the week, he appeared first to Mary Magdalene, out of whom he had cast seven devils.

10 And she went and told them that had been with him, as they mourned and wept.

11 And they, when they had heard that he was alive, and had been seen of her, believed not.

12 After that he appeared in another form unto two of them, as they walked, and went into the country.

13 And they went and told it unto the residue: neither believed they them.

14 Afterward he appeared unto the eleven as they sat at meat, and upbraided them with their unbelief and hardness of heart, because they believed not them which had seen him after he was risen.

15 And he said unto them, Go ye into all the world, and preach the gospel to every creature.

16 He that believeth and is baptized shall be saved; but he that believeth not shall be damned.

17 And these signs shall follow them that believe; In my name shall they cast out devils; they shall speak with new tongues;

18 They shall take up serpents; and if they drink any deadly thing, it shall

poison, it will not hurt them; they will lay their hands on the sick, and they will recover."

19So then the Lord Jesus, after he had spoken to them, was taken up into heaven and sat down at the right hand of God. 20And they went out and preached everywhere, while the Lord worked with them and confirmed the message by accompanying signs.]]

not hurt them; they shall lay hands on the sick, and they shall recover.

19So then after the Lord had spoken unto them, he was received up into heaven, and sat on the right hand of God.

20And they went forth, and preached every where, the Lord working with them, and confirming the word with signs following. Amen.

Introduction to 16:9–20 These verses are not found in some of the most important early manuscripts, but are in a large number of later manuscripts. The verses tell the expected ending of the resurrection as we know it from the other Gospels. It is likely that a more complete ending original to Mark either was lost or wasn't written, and vv. 9–20 were written by a well-intentioned copyist. There are many words in vv. 9–20 which appear nowhere else in Mark, including "walking" (*poreuomai*, v. 12), "seen," (*theaomai* vv. 11 and 14), "does not believe" (*apisteo*, v. 16), "hurt" (*blapto*, v. 18), and "confirmed" (*bebaioo*, v. 20). It is likely that the copyist echoed the vocabulary of the NT, adding these words and others into Mark's last verses. However, regardless of the origin of these verses, nothing in them is doubtful. The events of the resurrection and ascension are known through the other Gospels and therefore Mk 16:9–20 are trustworthy as expressions of the truth of Jesus' victory.

16:9 *when He rose early.* While the women came with the first light, even before that Jesus rose with the first hint of dawn. *Mary Magdalene.* Mary's encounter with Jesus here summarizes Jn 20:11–18 where she meets Jesus after entering the tomb and meeting Peter and John. *seven demons.* Mary had been afflicted with the demons (Lk 8:2), and thereafter became the woman customarily named first among those who followed Jesus. See the notes on 15:40, 47; 16:1.

16:10 *she went and told.* John 20:18 gives her joyous news, "I have seen the Lord." She was the first to say those words and her announcement personalized the message of the angel at the tomb. Jesus further told her that He was about to ascend to the Father (Jn 20:17), but He would not do so without seeing the disciples again.

they mourned and wept. The disciples are still gripped by the loss of Jesus and also fear for their own lives (Jn 20:19). Their sorrow is expressed well by the two men on the Emmaus road. They hoped that Jesus' mighty deeds signaled the arrival of the kingdom of God, but they thought Jesus' death ruined their hopes (Lk 24:20–21).

16:11 *they would not believe it.* The astonishment of the women at the empty tomb (v. 8) is replaced by doubt and denial in the disciples. This disbelief is found in Lk 24:11 where their report is considered as foolish nonsense. Luther writes: "Faith is a divine work which God demands of us; but at the same time He Himself must implant it in us, for we cannot believe by ourselves" (LW 23:23).

16:12 *another form.* The unnamed disciples were kept from recognizing Jesus during the walk to Emmaus (Lk 24:13–34). Jesus' resurrection was transforming enough that both Mary (Jn 20:15), and the Emmaus road disciples saw Him as an ordinary person whom they had never met. Later, Jesus used His wounds as identifying marks for the disciples (Jn 20:20). *to two of them.* Jesus first spoke with Mary (Jn 20:16) and the women from the tomb (Mt 28:9). We might expect Jesus' next appearance would be with the Eleven disciples, but He meets the two Emmaus road disciples. (Lk 24:34 reports an appearance to Peter that is not fully described elsewhere.) The Emmaus road disciples had not appeared in any Gospel before this. Jesus' appearance to them shows His love for all and the spread of His message through a widening circle of believers.

16:13 *they did not believe them.* Even after a second eyewitness report, the disciples did not believe that Jesus was risen from the dead. Thomas famously doubted (Jn 20:24–25), and even upon Jesus' appearance to them, some doubted (Mt 28:17). Tertullian writes,

> It was well, however, that the unbelief of the disciples was so persistent, in order that to the last we might consistently maintain that Jesus revealed Himself to the disciples as none other than the Christ of the prophets. (*ANF* 3:422).

16:14 *the eleven themselves as they were reclining at table.* This is the meeting recorded in Lk 24:36–49 and Jn 20:19–23. *unbelief and hardness of heart.* As noted in v. 13, they doubted upon hearing of the resurrection and even after seeing Jesus. Mark has stressed Jesus' identity as the Son of God, radiant in transfiguration power and faithful in His promises of death and resurrection. Jesus is angry over their failure to know His true identity and to trust His promises.

16:15 *Go into all the world and proclaim the gospel.* Despite their unbelief, Jesus commissions them as His messengers. As John began the Gospel, so the Eleven will carry on the work of announcing His kingdom. This verse captures the Great Commission (Mt 28:18–20). There are also the commands to preach repentance and forgiveness of sins (Lk 24:44–49), and the forgiveness and retention of sin (Jn 20:21–23). Hus says,

> Christ preached to the people on the sea, in the desert, in the fields and houses, in synagogues, in villages and on the streets, and taught his disciples. . . . And these, going forth, preached everywhere, that is, in every place where the people were willing to listen, God working with them. (*Church*, pp. 205–6)

16:16 *whoever believes and is baptized.* Faith is a gift from God, which He bestows through the Word and through Holy Baptism. Melanchthon writes, "Concerning Baptism, our churches teach that Baptism is necessary for salvation [Mark 16:16] and that God's grace is offered through Baptism" (AC IX 1). He also notes, "Baptism is not a work that we offer to God. It is a work in which God baptizes us. In other words, a minister baptizes us on God's behalf" (Ap XXIV 18). Chemnitz writes, "For this reason the devil is so hostile to the doctrine of faith. . . . He knows that without faith there is no benefit for us" (Chemnitz 8: 906). *Whoever does not believe will be condemned.* The message of Jesus' death and resurrection is the world's only hope for salvation. He is not one way of many, and His death is not simply an example of self-sacrifice. He is the only way, truth, and life, and the only path to the Father (Jn 14:6). The Gospel is proclaimed to give life but rejection of the Gospel leads to eternal death.

16:17 *signs.* These miracles point beyond the disciples and show the power of their Gospel preaching. The disciples cast out demons and healed diseases in their preaching journey (6:13). These merciful deeds enforced the truth of their message centered on Jesus. Bengel writes, "Even in our day, faith has in every believer a hidden power of a miraculous character: every effect resulting from our prayers is really miraculous, even though that miraculous character be not apparent." However, before relating the story of a miracle that took place in his own time, he also noted that the miraculous power does not exert itself in the same way as it did in the time of the New Testament. "Signs were in the beginning the props and stays of faith: now they are also the object of faith" (Bengel 575–76). *in My name.* The disciples will do these things by Jesus' authority and in accordance with His will. *they will speak in new tongues.* This anticipates Pentecost (Ac 2), when the disciples speak in the tongues of the nations gathered in Jerusalem. For this passage, Wesley quoted Bengel and referred to him as "an eminent author." But Wesley did not bring out Bengel's emphasis on distinguishing the apostolic period from the present (Wesley 136). For more on Wesley's views, see note 3:30.

16:18 *pick up serpents . . . drink any deadly poison.* God promises to protect us, but we should not tempt or test Him. In Ac 28:3, Paul is protected from a poisonous snake, but this is not a sign guaranteed for all believers. *lay their hands on the sick.* This was a way of communicating blessing and the Holy Spirit (cf. Ac 19:6). St. Ambrose says: "There is no power of man exercised in these things, in which the grace of the divine gift operates" (*NPNF*2 10:335). James 5:14–15 describes the anointing of oil and prayer which lead to healing. These depend on the power and will of God who knows whether to grant the power to endure illness or to grant healing.

16:19 *taken up into heaven.* Acts 1:6–11 gives the most complete account of the ascension. The ascension is the expected end of the Gospel. The highway first prepared by John the Baptist (1:2–3) ends with Jesus' return to the Father's side in heaven. *sat down at the right hand of God.* This expression states that Christ rules the universe as Lord and God in the same way that a ruling son has a throne beside his father. See Eph 1:20–21. By His omnipresence, Jesus fills heaven and earth, rules above all creation and yet fulfills His promise to never leave us while we walk here. Calvin writes,

> Christ was raised on high, that he might be exalted above angels and all creatures; that by his agency the Father might govern the world. . . . Therefore, we must not imagine to ourselves any one place, since *the right hand* is a metaphor which denotes the power this is next to God. This was purposely added by Mark, in order to inform us that Christ *was taken up into heaven,* not to enjoy blessed rest at a distance from us, but to govern the world for the salvation of all believers. (*Harmony* 3:393)

16:20 *preached everywhere.* The spread of the Gospel began with Jerusalem and then was extended throughout the Roman province of Judea-Samaria and finally Rome itself. This fulfilled Jesus' promise of Ac 1:8. *worked with them.* Jesus does not leave us alone but is always with us in this outreach (cf. Mt 28:20). The disciples knew that they performed their miracles only by the power and presence of Jesus. See the healing of the cripple (Ac 3:6), where Peter says, "In the name of Jesus Christ of Nazareth, rise up and walk!" *confirmed the message*. Peter and John, when arrested following the healing of the cripple said that "by the name of Jesus Christ of Nazareth, whom you crucified, whom God raised from the dead—by him this man is standing before you well" (Ac 4:10). The miracles of the early church demonstrated the resurrection power of Jesus and His compassion for the needs of all.

16:9–20 in Devotion and Prayer Like us, the disciples are slow of heart and deaf to the good news of their reconciliation with God. Yet He still rose for them and commissioned them to proclaim the Gospel everywhere. That is still the gracious commission to the Church from Christ. The Gospel invitation is open to all. God wants all people to be saved through Jesus (1Tm 2:3–4). • "Now let the heav'ns be joyful, Let earth its song begin, Let all the world keep triumph And all that is therein. Let all things, seen and unseen, Their notes of gladness blend; For Christ the Lord has risen, Our joy that has no end!" Amen. (*LSB* 478:3; *H82* 210:3; *TPH* 118:3; *TUMH* 303:3)

Biographical Sketches

The following brief sketches introduce preachers and commentators cited or referenced in this volume. They appear in chronological order by the date of their death or era of influence. Although some of them are ancient and medieval Church Fathers respected by the reformers, they are primarily writers of the Reformation era and heirs of the Reformation approach to writing biblical commentary. This approach includes:

(1) Interpreting Scripture in view of Scripture and by faith, so that passages are understood in their literary and in their canonical contexts;

(2) Emphasis on the historic and ordinary meaning of the words and literary expressions;

(3) Careful review of manuscripts and texts in search of greater accuracy;

(4) Faith in the canonical Scripture as divinely inspired, truthful, and authoritative;

(5) Respect for the ancient, ecumenical creeds (Apostles', Nicene, and Athanasian) as touchstones of faithful interpretation and application of Scripture; and most importantly

(6) Focus on Christ and justification through Him as the chief message of Holy Scripture (e.g., the distinction of Law and Gospel or sin and grace in interpretation and application).

For more information about these figures, see Edward A. Engelbrecht, gen. ed., *The Church from Age to Age: A History from Galilee to Global Christianity* (St. Louis: Concordia, 2011).

Ancient and Medieval Fathers

Tertullian. (c. 160–c. 225) North African theologian who may have practiced law. The first substantive theological writer in Latin who wrote mostly apologetic treatises. Became a Montanist in his latter years.

Eusebius. (c. 260–c. 340) Bishop of Caesarea. Known as the father of Church history. He participated as a moderating theologian in the Council of Nicea and was trusted by Emperor Constantine.

Ambrose. (c. 339–97) Governor of Milan who was suddenly made bishop, though only a catechumen at the time. He became a great preacher and defender of orthodoxy, influencing the conversion of Augustine.

Augustine. (354–430) Bishop of Hippo Regius, near Carthage, North Africa. His extensive and profound writings, including commentary on Genesis, the Psalms, and the Gospels, made him the most influential theologian in western Christendom. The reformers drew constantly upon his insights.

Hus, John. (c. 1372–1415) Priest and martyr. Lecturer and rector at the University of Prague, an enormously popular preacher and writer, greatly influenced by Augustine's theology and John Wycliffe's writings. Hus was falsely accused of heresy and condemned at the Council of Constance when the medieval church was sorely divided. His efforts heralded the Reformation.

Reformers

Luther, Martin. (1483–1546) Augustinian friar and preeminent reformer, lecturer on the Bible at the University of Wittenberg. Luther's preaching, teaching, and writing renewed biblically based piety in western Christendom. His translation of the Bible influenced the work of Bible publication throughout Europe, notably William Tyndale and the King James translators.

Cranmer, Thomas. (1489–1556) Archbishop of Canterbury and martyr. Cranmer served as a writer and editor for the Book of Common Prayer, one of the most influential works of the Reformation.

Melanchthon, Philip. (1497–1560) Lecturer on classical literature and languages at the University of Wittenberg. Melanchthon's *Commonplaces* and the Augsburg Confession laid the foundation for all subsequent works of Protestant dogmatic theology. He wrote significant biblical commentaries.

Calvin, John. (1509–64) Preacher and lecturer on theology, founder of the Academy of Geneva. Calvin organized reformation efforts for Swiss, French, Dutch, and English Protestants. Calvin's *Institutes of the Christian Religion* and his extensive commentaries on Scripture are the most influential works of the second generation reformers.

Knox, John. (c. 1513–72) Scottish preacher and reformer. Knox edited the Book of Common Order used in Scottish churches and wrote a history of the Reformation in Scotland.

Chemnitz, Martin. (1522–86) Pastor and theologian at Brunswick, Germany. Chemnitz was largely responsible for the Formula of Concord that unified churches in Lutheran territories following the deaths of Luther and Melanchthon. His *Examination of the Council of Trent* equipped Protestant churches for responding to the Roman Catholic Counter-Reformation.

Heirs of the Reformation

Gerhard, Johann. (1582–1637) Professor of theology at Jena and devotional writer. Gerhard wrote the most extensive dogmatic of the Protestant age of orthodoxy, the *Theological Commonplaces*, and was widely regarded for his knowledge of biblical Hebrew.

Bengel, Johann Albrecht. (1687–1752) New Testament scholar and professor. Bengel wrote the first scientific study of Greek New Testament manuscripts. His *Gnomon* on the New Testament is an influential, succinct commentary of enduring value.

Wesley, John. (1703–91) Missionary preacher. Wesley preached throughout England, Scotland, Ireland, and the American colonies. His *Explanatory Notes upon the New Testament* is a classic evangelical commentary, which drew upon principles and emphases of the reformers.